Introduction to Behavioral Research on the Internet

Michael H. Birnbaum

California State University
Fullerton, California

D1537922

Prentice
Hall

Upper Saddle River, New Jersey 07458

Library of Congress Cataloging-in-Publication Data

Birnbaum, Michael H.
   Introduction to behavioral research on the Internet / Michael H. Birnbaum.
      p. cm.
   Includes bibliographical references and index.
   ISBN 0-13-085362-3
   1. Psychology—Research—Methodology.   2. Psychology, Experimental.   3. Internet
   (Computer network)   I. Title.

BF76.6.157 B57 2000
150′.285′4678—dc21
                                                      00-029673

VP, Editorial Director: Laura Pearson
Acquisitions Editor: Jayme Heffler
Assistant Editor: Allison Westlake
Managing Editor: Mary Rottino
Production Liaison: Fran Russello
Project Manager: Kelly Ricci, The PRD Group
Prepress and Manufacturing Buyer: Tricia Kenny
Art Director: Jayne Conte
Cover Designer: Bruce Kenselaar
Marketing Manager: Sharon Cosgrove

This book was set in 9.5/10.5 Baskerville by The PRD Group
and was printed and bound by R. R. Donnelley, Harrisonburg.
The cover was printed by Phoenix Color.

©2001 by Prentice-Hall, Inc.
A Division of Pearson Education
Upper Saddle River, New Jersey 07458

Printed in the United States of America

10 9 8 7 6 5 4 3 2 1

ISBN 0-13-085362-3

Prentice-Hall International (UK) Limited, *London*
Prentice-Hall of Australia Pty. Limited, *Sydney*
Prentice-Hall Canada Inc., *Toronto*
Prentice-Hall Hispanoamericana, S.A., *Mexico*
Prentice-Hall of India Private Limited, *New Delhi*
Prentice-Hall of Japan, Inc., *Tokyo*
Pearson Education Asia Pte. Ltd., *Singapore*
Editora Prentice-Hall do Brasil, Ltda., *Rio de Janeiro*

CONTENTS

PART I   BASIC COMPONENTS OF WEB EXPERIMENTS

Chapter 1   Introduction to Behavioral Research on the Internet   1

The Purposes of Research   1
Philosophical Criteria for Explanation   2
Causal Experiments   3
Generality   5
Experimental Designs   6
Within-Subjects Research   8
Web Research   9
About the Web   9
Comparisons Between Web and Lab Research   10
Summary   12
Exercises   12

Chapter 2   Your First Web Page   13

You Need to Know HTML   13
A Simple Web Page   13
Creating a Web Page Without Knowing HTML   17
Uploading and Downloading to the Web Server   18
Using Netscape to FTP   18
Downloading Software from the Web   18
Using an FTP Program with Your Local Server   19
Summary   21
Exercises   23

Chapter 3   Putting the Hyper in Hypertext   25

Email from a Web Page   25
Linking to Another Page   25
Linking to Parts of the Same Page   27
Linking to an Anchor in Another Page   28
Linking to a File in Another Folder   28
Including Images and Linking from Images   29
Discussion and Summary   30
Exercises   31
Links for Graphics   31

Chapter 4   Additional Tricks in HTML   33

Comments in HTML   33
Creating a Horizontal Rule   33
Controlling the Appearance of Text   33
Aligning and Formatting Paragraphs   36

Headings and Lists   39
Tables   39
Frames   40
Summary   43
Exercises   43

Chapter 5   **Surveys and Experiments Using Forms   45**

Example Illustrating FORM and INPUT   45
Using a Script to Process Data   49
Hidden Variables   49
Radio Buttons   50
Textareas, Passwords, and Checkboxes   51
Pull-Down Selections   53
St. Petersburg Paradox and Selection Lists   54
Between-Subjects Experiment   56
Summary   58
Exercises   58

Chapter 6   **Data Analysis with Excel and SPSS   59**

Introduction to Excel   59
Download the Data   62
Filtering with Excel   62
Filter the Probability Data   63
A Pivot Table for the Probability Problem   65
Analysis of the St. Petersburg Paradox   69
Introduction to SPSS   72
Importing CSV Data to SPSS   73
Crosstabs in SPSS   73
Summary   78
Exercises   79

Chapter 7   **Images and Logical Thinking   81**

Displaying Images with HTML   81
A Problem in Logic   81
Image Maps   82
A Pivot Table for the Logic Problem   84
Summary   84
Exercises   86

Chapter 8   **A Study of Decision Making   87**

Psychology of Decision Making   87
Expected Value and Expected Utility   88

The Principle of Dominance   89
Decision-Making Experiment   89
Rank-Dependent Expected Utility Theory   90
Comparing Rival Theories   91
Data Analysis of Decision Experiment   91
Filtering the Data   93
A Pivot Table Report for Decision Making   94
Statistical Test of Correlated Proportions   96
Summary   98
Exercises   99

PART II   MAKING SURVEYS, TESTS, AND EXPERIMENTS

Chapter 9   Making Surveys with SurveyWiz   101

How to Use SurveyWiz   101
Copy HTML to a Text Editor and Save   103
Results of Numbers Study: Between-Subjects and Within-Subjects Designs   105
Range-Frequency Theory of Contextual Effects   107
Discussion and Summary   107
Exercises   108

Chapter 10   Personality Testing   110

Constructing a Simple Personality Test   110
Causation and Correlation   111
Assessing Tests: Internal Consistency, Reliability, and Validity   113
Analysis of Personality Data in SPSS   114
Summary and Discussion   119
Exercises   119

Chapter 11   Using FactorWiz for Factorial Designs   120

How to Use FactorWiz   120
Copy the HTML to a Text Editor and Save   121
Add Instructions and Warmup Trials   121
View the File with Your Browser   124
Check the Experiment and Data File Created   125
Adding Other Random Orders   125
Summary   126
Exercises   126

PART III   APPLICATIONS WITH DATA

Chapter 12   Analysis of Impression Formation   131

Checking the Data   131
Finding Means   134

Arranging the Matrix of Cell Means   135
Making a Graph of the Data   137
Examining Individual Data   143
ANOVA with SPSS   146
Summary   148
Exercises   150

Chapter 13   Analysis of Social Balance   151

Graph of Multiplication   152
Filter the Data and Find Column Means   155
Copy the Means and *Paste Special* to Make the Matrix   155
How to Fit a Multiplicative Model   155
Graphing the Predictions and the Data   161
Summary   164
Exercises   165

Chapter 14   Presenting Psychophysical Stimuli   167

A Bit of History   167
A Table of Neutral Colors   168
An Application of Frames   170
Working with Graphics   171
Mueller-Lyer Experiment   172
Including Sounds in a Web Page   173
Summary   175
Exercises   175

Chapter 15   Psychological Scaling with "Ratios" and "Differences"   176

Subtractive Model   177
Ratio Model   177
Two-Operation Theory   178
One-Operation Theory   178
Clean and Filter "Ratios" and "Differences" of Occupational Prestige   178
Find Averages and Arrange Data Matrices   180
Make Graphs of "Ratio" and "Difference" Judgments   182
Fit of the Two-Operation Theory   184
Fit of the One-Operation Theory   187
Summary   190
Exercises   190

Chapter 16   Bayesian Inference and Human Inference   192

Bayes' Theorem   192
Bayesian Calculator   194
The Cab Problem   194
Extract the Data for the Cab Problem and Find Means   196
Graph the Data   197

Compute Bayes' Theorem   198
Graph Predictions of Bayes' Theorem   200
Subjective Bayesian Theory   201
Averaging Model of Source Credibility   201
Summary   206
Exercises   206

PART IV   PROGRAMMING TECHNIQUES

Chapter 17   Introduction to JavaScript   207

A Simple JavaScript   208
Illustration of Random Numbers   209
Random Assignment to Conditions Using JavaScript   210
Selecting a Random Number from 1 to n 212
Review of JavaScript Fundamentals   212
Exercises   213

Chapter 18   Interactive Web Pages with JavaScript   214

Alert, Prompt, and Confirm   214
Date and Time Information   216
Loops and Learning Models   217
Functions in JavaScript   219
Probability Learning   220
Summary   220
Exercises   221

Chapter 19   JavaScript and Forms   222

Calculators   222
Checking for Missing Data   225
Scoring and Timing a Test with Feedback   227
The Barnum Effect   227
Creating a New Web Page   228
Summary   229
Exercises   229

PART V   METHODS AND METHODOLOGY

Chapter 20   Advanced Techniques for Experimentation on the Web   231

Advanced JavaScript Techniques   231
Java Programming   232
Use of Authorware/Shockwave Techniques   234
Server-Side Programming to Control Experiments   235

Summary   236
Exercises   236

Chapter 21   Methodology, Ethics, and Publicizing Your Study   237

Methodological Suggestions   237
Steps in Planning Your Research   241
Ethical Review   243
Methods for Advertising a Web Study   245
Summary   247
Exercises   247

Appendix A   Creating and Using Scripts   248

Review   248
Polyform   248
How to Make a Script with Polyform   249
Variables in Polyform   254
Exercises   255

References   256

Glossary of Web Terms   260

Index   264

PREFACE

In the last few years, a new method of behavioral research has become available, thanks to the World Wide Web. Those who have explored this new medium of research are enthusiastic about its advantages over traditional methods. Virtually anything that can be done in the laboratory using paper and pencil, a slide projector, or a computer can be done via the Web. The advantages of Web research over paper and pencil research in the lab include:

- Freedom from the constraints of testing people at a particular time and place,
- Automatic coding and construction of data files,
- Opportunity to obtain large and heterogeneous samples,
- Possibility to conduct cross-cultural research without the expense of traveling,
- Opportunity to study specific populations of rare conditions,
- Reduced costs of experimental assistants, and
- Standardization of experimenter effects.

At the same time, there are new issues with this new method: experimental control and sampling of participants.

Research that compares Web and lab results shows a good convergence between the two methods (Krantz & Dalal, 2000). In fact, some comparisons show that Web data are of higher quality than lab data (Birnbaum, 1999c). Between 1998 and 1999, the number of studies online doubled. To get an idea of the kinds of studies currently on the Web, check the American Psychological Society list of Psychological Research on the Net, maintained by John Krantz (http://psych.hanover.edu/APS/exponnet.html).

Even for those investigators who plan to conduct research in the laboratory with college freshmen and sophomores, the Web is a convenient network for the collection of data and also for the publication to other scientists of the exact method by which an experiment was conducted. The advantages in convenience of data processing and for open communication among scientists will cause more and more behavioral research to be done via the Web.

This book presents an introduction to methods and techniques basic to conducting research on the Internet. It also covers problems unique to this form of research and various ways to handle these potential problems. The book also teaches content and methods of data analysis. Each main idea is illustrated by examples included on the companion CD.

PREREQUISITES AND ORGANIZATION OF THE BOOK

It is assumed that you know how to use a browser such as Netscape Navigator or Internet Explorer to "surf the net" (explore files on the Web) and use a search engine, such as Yahoo [http://www.yahoo.com/]. It is also assumed that the reader knows how to use a word processor program (such as Microsoft Word or WordPerfect) and a text editor (such as NotePad, SimpleText, or BBEdit). Everything covered in this book has been tested on both a PC and Mac. Everything covered runs under Netscape Navigator (3.0 or above) and almost everything also runs under Internet Explorer (4.5 and above).

The ideas have been presented in a sequence designed to allow a college sophomore enrolled in a course in research methods, a graduate student planning a first-year project, and a professor of psychology experienced in research (but wanting to learn these methods) to profit from the same book.

To get the most out of this book, you should have taken courses in introductory psychology, research methods, and statistics. However, the book is designed to be self-contained and it does not presume this background. Psychological content (logical reasoning in Chapter 7, decision making in Chapter 8, contextual effects in judgment in Chapter 9, personality testing in Chapter 10, impression formation in Chapter 12, social balance theory in Chapter 13, psychophysics in Chapter 14, scaling in Chapter 15, or Bayesian inference in Chapter 16) is presented without the assumption that the reader is knowledgeable in these topic areas. A glossary of terms used heavily in this area of research is also included at the end of the book.

When studying this book, let your computer and the Web be your companions. The CD that accompanies this book contains example HTML, programs, and sets of data. You can follow along with the book by doing the analyses described in the chapters and working with the examples. Many useful links to resources on the Web are also included in the list of examples on the CD. The best way to get started with the examples is to load the file *examples.htm* in your browser. This file provides links to the chapter examples.

Examples are designed to illustrate both computer techniques and principles of psychological research at the same time. Chapters 1 through 4 teach basic HTML (HyperText Markup Language), use of FTP (File Transfer Protocol) to transfer files, links in HTML, and methods of formatting text and paragraphs in HTML. A novice can study each of these chapters in about an hour each and should spend about an hour practicing the techniques of each chapter on a computer. A college instructor could present each of these chapters in a single 50-minute class or lab session and cover the first four chapters in 2 weeks, assuming that the students will work with the examples and exercises in the lab or as homework. The reader who already knows HTML and FTP can skim Chapters 2 through 4 and proceed to Chapter 5.

Chapter 5 illustrates the use of HTML forms to collect data from people via the Web. A simple experiment is developed that collects a single response from the reader of the page, who can type an answer in a box and push a button to send the datum. This first example illustrates how data can be sent to the experimenter by email. The next example shows how to use a script to append data to a file on the Web server. Three input methods are featured: the *text box* allows the participant to type a number or short answer, *radio buttons* allow the reader to click from a multiple choice set, and *pull-down selection lists* allow the user select one response from a list. An experiment on the classic St. Petersburg Paradox is presented to illustrate a simple method for assigning participants to different conditions and also to illustrate how the choices in a selection list might bias the responses. Chapter 5 requires two 50-minute lectures, and it could be covered in class in 1 week, with students working 2 hours in the lab.

Chapter 6 gives a basic introduction to both Excel and SPSS. Data from the studies in Chapter 5 are analyzed to illustrate the use of Pivot Table Reports in Excel and crosstabs in SPSS. The techniques required to import, filter, and work with data in these programs are described. Procedures for calculating a *t*-test are also described. An instructor could spend either one or two 20-minute lectures on this chapter, depending on whether the plan was to cover only one or both of these programs. Students would require 2 or 3 hours in the lab or at home to work through the examples in this chapter with their computers.

Chapter 7 explains how to incorporate images and define image maps n HTML files. These ideas are illustrated with an experiment and a debriefing page based on the classic Wason (1960) logic problem. Experimental materials and sample data are included on the CD. The data can be analyzed by either SPSS or Excel using methods described in Chapter 6. This brief chapter would require about 20 to 30 minutes of class time and about the same in the lab.

Chapter 8 presents basic ideas of decision-making research and data analysis. The chapter is intended to make this historical area of psychological research accessible. The chapter should prepare an undergraduate to read current work in the field (Birnbaum, 1999b) and design his or her own Web studies in the field. Both the experimental materials and sample data are included on the CD to facilitate this process. These chapters build on and consolidate ideas presented in Chapters 1 through 6, showing how those ideas alone are sufficient to conduct interesting research. An instructor may choose to present only one of Chapters 7 and 8, depending on the student level. Chapter 8 is the more difficult in terms of psychological content, requiring at least one 50-minute lecture. Two lectures are needed if theories beyond the Expected Utility theory will be covered.

Chapter 9 explains how to use surveyWiz (software included on the CD) to make simple surveys and questionnaires. With this software, a person with minimal background can quickly make a simple survey, questionnaire, or personality test that will run on the Web. The chapter also illustrates an example of a between-subjects study of judgments of the "size" of numbers to show how between-subjects designs can lead to the conclusion that 9 is a "bigger" number than 221 (Birnbaum, 1999a). The chapter describes contextual effects in judgment that are important to interpreting results of between-subjects designs.

Chapter 10 presents another example of the use of SurveyWiz showing how to construct and evaluate a personality test. The chapter explains how to make the HTML for the personality test (also included on CD) and how to analyze data from a personality test. Data included on the CD are analyzed by correlational analyses, including factor analysis, to examine the factor structure of the test and the internal consistency of the scales measured.

Chapter 11 explains how to use FactorWiz, additional software included on the CD, to make within-subjects, factorial experiments. The software constructs the factorial combinations, randomizes their order, and creates the HTML form. Several examples of factorial experiments are included on the CD. Chapter 11 illustrates how to use the program by constructing a factorial design of all pairs of adjectives from two sets, to test a theory of impression formation.

Chapter 12 covers the topic of impression formation, showing how to analyze the data from a factorial design to determine if the whole is equal to the sum of its parts—in other words, to test if there is an interaction between two factors. This chapter covers the additive (or constant weight averaging) model of impression formation and methods for the graphical and statistical analysis of interactions.

Chapter 13 discusses Heider's (1946) theory of balance in social relations. This chapter contains some material (the first three sections) that is designed for undergraduates; later sections of the chapter contain material for the advanced student. An instructor might plan to present the first three sections to undergraduates and the entire chapter to graduate students. This chapter illustrates a very powerful type of interaction, yet one that is compatible with a simple model. The advanced material shows how to use Excel to fit a multiplicative model to the data and to evaluate the fit of the model.

Chapter 14 explains how to include psychophysical stimuli, with an illustration of the HTML technique of frames. Methods for working with graphics and sound are presented. This chapter forms a bridge between Chapter 11, which explains how factorial designs can be created, and Chapter 15, where judgments of "ratios" and "differences" are used in scaling. These methods of scaling have been applied most often in psychophysics, but are also applicable to study of social variables such as the prestige of occupations, the stressfulness of life changes, or the badness of crimes.

Chapter 15 discusses the use of "ratio" and "difference" judgments to scale psychological stimuli (illustrating the topic with data for judgments of the prestige of occupations). This chapter contains material that is best suited for advanced students or students looking for project ideas.

Chapter 16 discusses Bayes' Theorem as a descriptive theory of human inference. Like Chapter 13, this chapter can be covered at the undergraduate level (in the first seven sections) or the entire chapter for advanced students.

Each of Chapters 10, 12, 13, 14, 15, and 16 could be the topic of one or two 50-minute lectures, depending on the depth of coverage. Each would require about 3 to 4 hours of lab work or homework by students to follow the analyses. Each of these chapters would make good starting points for a student project.

Chapters 17, 18, and 19 introduce JavaScript, the most popular scripting language in use on the Web. Chapter 17 shows how to use JavaScript to randomly assign participants to conditions. Chapter 18 covers techniques of loops, functions, and connections between HTML forms and JavaScript. Chapter 18 also introduces the reader to mathematical learning models. Chapter 19 continues the discussion of JavaScript, showing how to make calculators, check for missing data, score and time a test, and give feedback on a score to the participant. Chapter 17 could be covered in a 50-minute lecture. Chapters 18 and 19 could occupy three or four lectures. Students should allow 1 hour for Chapter 17 in the lab and 2 hours each for Chapters 18 and 19.

Chapter 20 discusses advanced techniques used in cognitive psychology experiments, including Authorware/Shockwave and Java programming language. Each of the topics reviewed in the chapter could be the basis for an entire course if handled at the advanced level. This chapter is also a good source of ideas for student projects that emphasize computer techniques. Finally, Chapter 21 discusses methodological and ethical issues in Internet experimentation. It suggests ideas of how to recruit participants on the Web. This chapter could be treated at the review level in one 50-minute lecture.

Appendix A describes the program Polyform, which creates scripts that process, organize, and place data in a file, and sends the reader to a Web page that delivers a thank-you message. Novices and students who use a canned script provided by their Internet Service Provider or instructor can skip this material. Those who plan to write their own scripts can skim the chapter, but should look at the examples and linked resources.

 ## NOTATION

This book uses the following conventions. Computer code is set in `Courier` font, in which all letters and numbers have the same size. HTML tags are set in `ALL CAPS IN COURIER`. HTML works in either upper or lower case letters, but it will help you spot tags to see them in all caps. Names and values in HTML that are optional or up to you are written in `lower case` and in *`italic courier,`* when needed for clarity. Menus in computer programs, such as the **File** and **Edit** menus, are written in **bold,** and choices that can be selected from them, like *Save As* or *Paste*, are written in *italic font.* Button names, file names, and variable names are also set in *italics.*

 ## TO THE INSTRUCTOR

Web-based research is inherently interesting to students. Students also recognize the relevance of Web skills to their future activities whether they plan to go into academics or business. Graduate students are eager to learn skills that will help them collect and analyze data in a manner that can reduce the time to complete a project by a factor of 10.

At the time of this writing (July, 1999), I am unaware of any other book in English to fill this need. This book is designed, therefore, to be useful to several different classes in which segments on this new form of research might be presented. Because it attempts to satisfy the needs of several different courses, it contains more material than could be easily covered in a semester. To help instructors decide what to pick and choose for different uses, the connections among the chapters are explained in Table P.1. Chapters that are prerequisite to each chapter are listed in parentheses. Bold indicates the aspect most emphasized.

Note that Chapters 7, 8, 10, 12, 13, 14, 15, and 16 emphasize content topics in psychology. Each of those chapters includes data (on CD) that can be analyzed to answer a question in psychology. These chapters can be selected or skipped without much interruption to the flow of the book. These chapters also provide good ideas for students to present to the class as projects.

I have found it helpful to assign students to do one replication study and one original study in a semester lab course. Students must write an APA-style report on each study and present it to the class with their ideas of what should be done next. By replicating a study, students learn more about the topic than they get by merely reading and reporting articles to a class. After replicating a study, students often think of original ideas of how to test a theory.

Students who have the assignment of designing an original project can begin by replicating one of the studies from Chapters 7 through 16. Having replicated and analyzed the study, the student will soon see ways to revise it to test new ideas. These chapters also devote attention to computer analysis of the data. There is a measure of redundancy in explanations of how to do the comptuer analyses. This additional description permits a student to skip to one chapter and still be able to follow the next. Some repetition may also help reinforce the techniques and help students see that the same techniques can be used in more than one type of experiment.

TABLE P.1. Connections Among Chapters

CHAPTER	TOPIC	NEW COMPUTER METHOD	PSYCHOLOGY	STUDIES	DATA
1	Methodology	No	**Yes**	No	No
2	HTML, FTP	**Yes**	No	No	No
3 (2)	HTML links	**Yes**	No	No	No
4 (3)	HTML tricks	**Yes**	No	No	No
5 (1, 4)	HTML forms	**Yes**	Yes	Yes	Yes
6 (1, 5)	Data analysis	Excel, SPSS	Yes	No	**Yes**
7 (1–6)	Logical thinking	Image maps	Yes	Yes	Yes
8 (1–6)	Decision making	No	**Yes**	Yes	**Yes**
9	SurveyWiz	**Yes**	Yes	Yes	No
10 (9)	Personality	No	**Yes**	Yes	**Yes**
11	FactorWiz	**Yes**	Yes	Yes	No
12 (11)	Impression formation	No	**Yes**	Yes	**Yes**
13 (11, 12)	Social balance	No	**Yes**	Yes	**Yes**
14 (4, 7, 11)	Psychophysics	Yes	Yes	Yes	Yes
15 (11, 14)	Scaling	No	**Yes**	Yes	**Yes**
16 (11)	Bayesian inference	No	**Yes**	Yes	**Yes**
17 (5)	JavaScript	**Yes**	No	No	No
18 (17)	JavaScript	**Yes**	Learning	Yes	Yes
19(18)	JavaScript	**Yes**	No	No	No
20(19)	Advanced	**Yes**	No	No	No
21 (1, 5)	Methods and tactics	Yes	**Yes**	No	No

Note: Chapter numbers in parentheses show chapter prerequisites.

In a graduate course on computer techniques in Web experimentation, the instructor might choose to assign Chapters 2 through 6, 9, 11, 14, 17, 18, 19, 20, 21, and possibly Appendix A. That would be 14 chapters that could be supplemented by reprints of current articles and online resources. If students are assigned to devise an individual project, you can suggest that students select from Chapters 7, 8, 12, 13, 15, and 16 as sources of ideas for student projects. Project ideas are also included in the exercises to the chapters. For advanced computer projects, Chapter 20 opens the door.

In an upper division undergraduate course in advanced research methods or computer methods, you can assign Chapters 1 through 6; one of 7 or 8; 9 through 11; one of 12, 13, 14, 15, or 16; 17; and 21. You can allow students to pick a project from the unselected chapters. Notice that this suggested plan includes the introduction to JavaScript in Chapter 17, but not the more advanced material on JavaScript. If you plan to cover programming, you may choose to cover Chapters 2 through 6, skip Chapters 7 through 11, and proceed to Chapters 17 through 19 to teach programming. After programming has been presented, you could then return to a selection from Chapters 9 through 16.

An instructor of an undergraduate laboratory in research methods might present a brief segment (2–3 weeks) on Internet research as part of a larger course that includes research design, statistics, and report writing. One approach would be to get students interested in the Web with a few online experiments. Then teach them Chapter 9 or 11, and follow that up with one of content chapters (Chapters 9 and 10 or Chapter 11 and one of 12, 13, 15, or 16) that explains how to analyze data from one such study. Students could be assigned to replicate the study, then to devise and conduct an original study that investigates a new issue in their chosen area of study.

The instructor who wishes to include only a brief segment (1 week in class and 1 week of homework) on Internet research might assign students to do three activities on the basis of two chapters only. (1) Make the stimuli using factorWiz (Chapter 11), which allows a student to create a Web experiment without knowing HTML. (2) Serve as a participant in the study using the appropriate materials on the CD. It is very helpful to students to experience the experiment as a participant in order to understand the theory and analysis of the study. (3) Analyze the data provided on the CD to understand how to analyze the data from such an experiment. (If APA-style writing is part of the course, the instructor could assign students the task of writing an APA style paper on one of the studies whose data are included on CD.) Each of the topics in Chapters 12, 13, 15, and 16 illustrates the analysis of an interesting interaction between two factors. The purpose of the limited treatment would be to make students aware of the possibility of Internet research, give them a basic tool for constructing a student project, and teach the concept of interaction. Having completed this segment, the student would be in a position to design and carry out an original project that extends the topic.

A 4-week plan for undergraduate research methods would present Chapters 1 through 6, which provide the foundation. This plan would be especially useful for a research methods sequence that takes a year, rather than a single semester. Chapters 1 through 6 could be covered in the first semester (or quarter); Chapters 9 and 11, with a selection from the content chapters, would then fit well in the second course in the sequence.

 ## ACKNOWLEDGMENTS

The preparation of this book was made possible by a sabbatical from California State University, Fullerton. Completion of the research reported here was also supported by the National Science Foundation under Grant No. SBR-9410572. Any opinions, findings, and conclusions or recommendations expressed in this material are those of the author, and do not necessarily reflect the views of the National Science Foundation.

I thank Rob Bailey, who stimulated my interest in this topic by suggesting that I look up my deceased friend Mance Lipscomb on the Web, by translating one of my BASIC programs to JavaScript, and by describing the incredible response to his data collection efforts on the Web. Thanks are due to Chris Cozby, who installed and maintains the psych.fullerton.edu server and showed me the use of Polyform. Jonathan Baron, Tom Buchanan, and Ulf Reips read sections of the book and provided useful suggestions. William Schmidt provided helpful advice for surveyWiz and factorWiz and wrote the Perl scripts described in Appendix A. For guidance on this project and for many of the definitions in the glossary, I thank the contributors of chapters to my edited book on advanced applications in Web research (Birnbaum, 2000b). I also thank my former students Melissa Lott, Teresa Martin, Juan Navarrete, Jamie N. Patton, and Dana Storm for their assistance in pilot testing of studies included in this book. Finally, I thank the reviewers for their helpful suggestions and comments: Alison Piper, Simmons College; Ching Fan-Sheu, DePaul University; Chris Schunn, George Mason University; and Kent Norman, University of Maryland.

Michael H. Birnbaum
California State University–Fullerton

Part I

BASIC COMPONENTS OF WEB EXPERIMENTS

Chapter 1

INTRODUCTION TO BEHAVIORAL RESEARCH ON THE INTERNET

This chapter reviews concepts that are essential to understanding research. It cannot replace a good textbook on research methods, but does give an overview of the key ideas needed to interpret research. It also reviews ways in which Web research differs from laboratory research.

 ## THE PURPOSES OF RESEARCH

The purpose of research is to answer questions. One type of research involves searching for articles and books in the library to find out what other people have discovered or theorized. The other type of research involves making a new investigation to find answers by making controlled observations and measurements. The type of knowledge that comes from gathering evidence is known as *empirical* knowledge. The term *empirical* is distinguished from knowledge based on *theory* or *authority*.

What has been published in the past is not always correct. For example, Aristotle (384–322 B.C.) theorized that men have more teeth than women. His conclusion was based on the premise that teeth are all about the same size, but men have bigger mouths, and both men and women have mouths full of teeth; therefore, men have more teeth. This theory survived by authority, unquestioned for almost 1900 years, until Vesalius (1514–1564) bothered to count. Vesalius observed that men and women have the same number of teeth. Theories that have been published should not always be accepted on faith or authority; they must be tested for their accuracy. Science progresses by testing theories and proposing new ones to replace those that have been disproved.

Psychology is the *science* of the behavior of people and other living organisms. A *science* is the study of alternative explanations. As a study of alternative explanations, it must compare rival or alternative ways to explain the same phenomena.

These ideas can be illustrated by the story of Clever Hans (Klugerhans), the horse who could answer questions by tapping with his hoof. This horse could answer mathematics problems, such as, "What is two plus one?" Clever Hans would tap out three taps, sigh, and put his hoof down, to the amazement and delight of the audience. Even more amazing was that the horse could answer questions posed in different languages and could even answer factual questions, such as, "How many days are in a week?"

1

Two alternative explanations were proposed to explain the behavior of this horse. The first explanation was that Clever Hans was *sehr klug* (very clever) indeed, that he understood the questions and knew the answers. The rival explanation was that it was a trick, and the horse was getting information from people present.

To test between these two theories, experiments were conducted. In one experiment, the faces of the people in the audience were hidden from Clever Hans, and it was found that the horse could not do his tricks unless he could see the faces of the audience. In another test, a card that showed four spots was shown to the horse, and by a slight-of-hand trick, a different card, with three spots, was shown to the audience. Clever Hans tapped out three taps, matching what was shown to the audience, not what he was shown. Apparently, the horse was getting information from the faces in the audience.

The story of Clever Hans shows the scientific method in action. Psychology is the study of alternative explanations of behavior. The behavior to be explained was the behavior of the horse: How was the horse able to answer questions? Second, the two alternative explanations were theories of how the horse got right answers. One of these theories predicted that he should continue to be right, even if the audience is hidden or if they were shown a different card, because the horse knew the right answers. The other theory was that the horse simply tapped until the audience gave a clue, by blinking and raising their eyes, that the right answer had been reached. The experiments were designed to test between these rival explanations.

 ## PHILOSOPHICAL CRITERIA FOR EXPLANATION

Explanations are theories. In psychology, they are theories of behavior. An explanation satisfies five criteria. An explanation is deductive, meaningful, predictive, causal, and general. Each of these criteria deserves some discussion.

The first criterion of a theory is that it is *deductive*. Given the explanation, one can *deduce* the event to be explained from the explanation. For example, suppose we wanted to explain the behavior of Clever Hans, and someone said, "The horse got the answers right because he was a horse." The sentence that Clever Hans was a horse is correct, but that fact does not explain the behavior.

It would be deductive to say, Clever Hans is a horse; all horses can answer questions correctly; therefore, Clever Hans can answer questions correctly. That would be deductive, but just plain false, because not all horses can do those tricks.

Theories are to data (observations) as premises are to conclusions. True premises and logic lead to true conclusions. However, a correct deduction with false premises can lead to a true conclusion. For that reason, one cannot use the truth of a conclusion to argue for the truth of the premises. For example:

> Everything made of cyanide is good to eat.
> Bread is made of cyanide.
> Therefore, bread is good to eat.

The conclusion is true, but the premises are false. A person cannot prove the theory true by eating bread, showing that it is good to eat. To *test* a theory, one makes observations that might show the theory is *not* true. However, if the conclusion is false, then something is wrong with the premises. Thus, a theory can be disproved by experiment, but never proved.

Second, an explanation is *meaningful*. The *meaning* of a sentence is equivalent to the set of testable implications of the sentence. If a sentence has no implications, then it is meaningless. For example, suppose someone suggested the following theory of behavior:

> Everything is caused by the action of invisible, undetectable, and logically unverifiable Brownies. These Brownies cause everything. If they did not exist, nothing could happen. Because things happen, we know the Brownies exist. They compete with each other to cause events in the world, and the more dominant Brownie always wins. These Brownies cannot be tested, observed, or measured in any way. But they exist, they cause everything, and they explain everything.

The problem with this so-called theory is that it is meaningless. If the Brownies are logically unverifiable, then it is a contradiction to assert that one could test their existence. There is no experiment, no test, no action we can take to find out if the theory is false. Such ideas are meaningless, and one should not waste one's time arguing about them. It is sometimes surprising how much energy can be spent arguing over matters that cannot be put, even in principle, to empirical test.

The third criterion of a theory is that it is *predictive*. If the explanation were known in advance, the behavior would have been predicted, in principle. Given a good theory of the solar system, one should be able to predict eclipses of the sun and moon and the relative positions of the planets in the sky on any date in the future. If a "theory" could not predict events (for example, eclipses) until after they happen, then it is called *post hoc*. A good theory, if known in advance, would allow one to predict what will happen next.

However, prediction is not enough. Suppose someone asked, "Why were there ten murders in a certain town last year?" Suppose another person answered, "Because that town has one thousand telephone poles, and the number of murders in a town can be predicted from the equation $Y = .01*X$, where X is the number of telephones and Y is the number of murders." This system is meaningful (we can test if it is true for all towns and we can test if $X = 1000$), it is deductive (we can deduce from X what Y should be), and it is predictive (knowing $X = 1000$, we predict $Y = 10$). However, the theory does *not* tell us what would happen if someone chopped down those telephone poles. It is not causal.

The fourth criterion of a theory is that it is *causal*. In principle, the explanation of a behavior tells one how to *control*, or change the behavior in question. The idea of *in principle* means that we may not be able to make the change in practice. For example, in astronomy, there are theories of what would happen if two stars were made to combine their masses, but no one is yet able to actually cause that to happen. The theories are still causal because they dictate what would happen if one could combine stars.

Causation must be distinguished from *correlation*. The number of telephone poles in a city is *correlated* with the number of murders in a city. One can use the number of telephone poles to predict the number of murders, or vice versa. However, correlation does not allow one to predict what would happen if the number of telephone poles or murders was made to change. Causation, in contrast, allows one to predict what would happen if we chopped down the telephone poles and buried the cables underground. Chopping down the telephone poles in some cities but not others would involve an *experiment. Experiments* allow one to predict the effect of changes; they allow one to test causal hypotheses. More is said about causation and correlation in Chapter 10.

 ## CAUSAL EXPERIMENTS

The purpose of an experiment is to test a *causal hypothesis*. A *hypothesis* is a conjecture that has not been proved or established. A causal hypothesis is to be distinguished from the *null hypothesis,* which is that there is no causal relation. The key idea of an experiment is control. The experimenter controls or causes the suspected cause to vary and examines if the suspected effect is affected.

To illustrate a causal experiment, consider the hypothesis that penicillin would cause a reduction in the probability of death among people with *Streptococcus* infections. Strep throat infections are diagnosed by high fever, sore throat, and white streaks in the throat that (when sampled and examined under the microscope) contain *Streptococcus* bacteria. This hypothesis has already been tested, so you may already be convinced. However, please imagine yourself in 1928, before the safety and effectiveness of penicillin were known.

In an example of the classic *double-blind experiment,* people with Strep throats are randomly assigned to one of two conditions. *Random assignment,* means that a coin is tossed (or some other random mechanism is used) to decide which condition each person will receive. In one condition (the *treatment group*), patients receive pills with penicillin. In the other condition, called the *control group,* patients receive pills that look identical, but contain no penicillin. The pills that contain only the inert ingredients (starch and flavors) are known as *placebos.* A *placebo* is an inert treatment used with the control group. Without the control group, we would not know how many people would have lived if the disease went untreated. There would be no way to evaluate the treatment.

The experiment is called a *double-blind* study because the patients who receive the medicine and the doctors who administer the medicine are both "blind" with respect to whether the pills contain penicillin or just placebo. The reason to keep the patients blind is that when people think they have received a powerful medicine, they often get better from the Voodoo effect. In Voodoo, one can make another person sick by suggesting that pins stuck in a doll will cause pain and injury to the person who is represented by the doll. Similarly, placebos can help a person get better; the effect can be as powerful as some medicines. Many new medicines have side effects that can make a person sick or may even kill them; therefore, a placebo is often superior to a pill because it is less dangerous. In evaluating a new medicine, it is important to show that it is more effective than a placebo.

The reason to keep doctors "blind" is to keep them from switching patients between the experimental and control groups. Often a doctor will try to help make the new medicine look good. Young, strong, and otherwise healthy people are moved to the treatment group, and old, infirm, and otherwise unhealthy people are moved to the placebo group. That might make a harmful medicine look good; however, that would also deceive the scientists and future patients, who really want to know if the medicine is beneficial. By trying to help, doctors (and even experimenters) can ruin experiments. Another reason to keep doctors "blind" is that they may reveal (by subtle cues) to the patient that they do not expect the patient to live, and such attitudes can become self-fulfilling prophesies.

In some studies, there is also a third person who should be "blind" with respect to the treatment—the judge who rates the success of the treatment. In studies of acne cream, for example, one might use judges to rate how pimply the faces of patients appear. It is important to keep the judge from knowing if the patient received the medicine or the placebo. Such studies in which the patient, the doctor, and the judge are "blind" with respect to the treatments are called *triple-blind experiments.* In order to keep these people "blind," bottles of medicine are coded with numbers that the experimenter has recorded to keep track of which bottles have medicine and which have placebo.

Suppose in the penicillin study, there were 200 patients with Strep throats. Suppose 100 were assigned to each group. Suppose 80 of the treatment group lived to the end of the year, and 20 in the control group lived to the end of the year. What can we conclude? Apparently, more people lived in the placebo condition, but this might have happened by chance.

INDEPENDENT VARIABLE	DEPENDENT VARIABLE	
RANDOM ASSIGNMENT TO	DEAD	ALIVE
Placebo ($n = 100$)	80	20
Penicillin ($n = 100$)	20	80

If one had 200 cards, of which 100 said *dead* and 100 said *alive,* there is a chance that if they were mixed randomly and dealt into two piles, one pile might have 80 alive and the other might have 20. How do we know if the treatment was effective, if the result might have happened by chance?

The answer is that statistics allows us to calculate the probability that such a difference might have happened by chance, given the null hypothesis that the treatment had no effect. In this case, the probability of getting such an extreme result, given the null hypothesis, is less than one chance in 20. When the probability is small that the result occurred by chance, one rejects the null hypothesis. Therefore, we reject the hypothesis that the data occurred by chance in favor of the hypothesis that the result was caused by the difference in treatments. In this case, the result indicates that people who received penicillin are *significantly* less likely to die than the people who received the placebo. The term *significant* is used to denote that the result is extremely unlikely by chance alone, according to the null hypothesis.

When the statistic is *not* significant, it does *not* prove that the null hypothesis is true. For example, a researcher might have done the penicillin study with 10 patients, and found that 4 of the 5 treated survived and only 1 of 5 who received placebos survived. That is the same proportion as in the larger study; however, this result is not unusual enough to warrant rejection of the null hypothesis. Failure to reject the null hypothesis does *not* show that the null hypothesis is true.

The situation is like looking for a key in a large wheat field. If one finds the key, one can reject the null hypothesis that there was no key. However, if one looks and does not find the key, it does not prove that there was no key; it just means one did not find it. Maybe the key is still there, and might be found by a more thorough search. Thus, there are really three possible conclusions of a study: The null hypothesis may be false, it may be true, and the data may yield no answer. Nonsignificance means no conclusion.

The *power* of an experiment refers to the probability of finding significant results if the null hypothesis is false. The more powerful our search, the more likely we will find the key if it is there. Power increases as measurements become more precise and as the sample size is increased. As noted later, Web research is usually more powerful than lab research, because it uses large samples.

 ## GENERALITY

The fifth criterion of a theory is that it is *general.* By *general* is meant that one can deduce from the theory not only the behavior that was to be explained, but also more implications for new experiments that give the explanation *predictive power.* The greater the number and variety of implications, the greater the generality of the theory.

People were extremely impressed when Newton (1642–1727) showed that a few simple ideas plus some mathematics could be used to derive implications not only for the motions of objects on Earth, but also for the motions of the moon and planets. The number and variety of different experimental implications were extremely large, and the few simple premises could be used to predict the results of thousands of experiments involving motions of objects. Because the theory made so many interesting predictions that could be tested by a variety of experiments, the theory was recognized as having great generality.

 ## EXPERIMENTAL DESIGNS

The classic two groups design is not the only way to do research. In fact, in psychology, certain types of between-groups studies can lead to strange conclusions, such as that the number 9 seems "bigger" as a number to people than does the number 221 (see Chapter 9).

The penicillin study is termed *between subjects* or between groups because the experimental variable is different for different people—each person gets only one level of treatment, either placebo or penicillin.

Why is random assignment to groups important? Why not let some people volunteer to take the new medicine and let the others be in the control group? The answer is that, on the one hand, the people who volunteer might be those who are younger and more optimistic. If so, then they are more likely to live anyway, even if they did not receive the drug. On the other hand, the people who volunteer might be those who are the most sick and desperate; perhaps these people would be more likely to die anyway. Therefore, we must not allow such variables to be *confounded* with the treatment. The term *confounded variables* refers to variables that might confuse or confound our attempts to learn if the medicine works.

The variable that is suspected as the cause is made *independent* of all other variables by random assignment to conditions. The *independent variable* is the variable that the experimenter manipulates. The suspected effect, or *dependent variable,* is the variable that the experimenter measures to assess the effect of the treatment. Sometimes people use the term *independent variable* for a variable that they believe is the cause, even though the variable is not independent of other variables. Such misuse of terms is called *deception.*

A classic study that disentangled confounded variables was the study by the royal commission appointed to investigate if animal magnetism was a real phenomenon. Mesmer (1734–1815) created a great sensation in France by putting people into trances by supposedly using animal magnetism. Mesmer or his assistants could mystically "magnetize" or mesmerize an object, and a person who touched the object would fall into a trance. The commission, which included the American scientist and publisher, Ben Franklin (1706–1790), realized that the knowledge that the object had been mesmerized was confounded with the actual procedure of mesmerizing it. They created a within-subjects, factorial design in which a tree either was or was not mesmerized, and each person was either told that the tree was mesmerized or not. This experiment revealed that trances only occurred when people were told that the tree had been mesmerized, and that there was no effect of actually "magnetizing" the tree. By teasing out the beliefs of the person from the actual procedures of magnetizing an object, the commission concluded that the phenomenon was psychological, and not due to any new magnetic or electric force.

It is important to emphasize that a variable is something that varies. The independent variable in the penicillin study is the *difference* between placebo and penicillin. The dependent variable in that study is the *difference* between being dead and alive. The independent variables in the study of animal magnetism were belief whether the tree was mesmerized or not, and whether the tree was mesmerized or not. The dependent variable was whether the person fell into a trance or not.

Variables must therefore have at least two levels, but they can take on more than two levels. For example, in a study of a disease that does not kill, one might measure the number of days each patient spends at home (away from work) as the dependent variable. The independent variable can also have a number of levels. For example, one might study four different doses of a new medicine, with a fifth level as the placebo. The purpose of such research would be to find an optimal dose that is both effective and safe from side effects. If the dose is too small, the medicine may not be effective; if the dose is too large, it may be toxic. Before putting the drug on the market, it is important to find the optimum level of drug to accomplish its purpose without harming the patient.

Experiments can include more than one dependent variable. For example, in a drug study of the effectiveness of a cold remedy, dependent variables might include number of days that the patient feels sick, the number of days with fever, the temperature of the highest "spike" fever, the number of days with body pains, and so on.

Experiments can also include more than one independent variable. Factorial designs are experiments that are designed to investigate how two or more independent variables combine. For example, consider an experiment on the effects of two antibiotics for patients in hospitals with "fever of unknown origin." Such fevers may be due to nosocomial infections—infections that are given to patients by nurses or doctors who do not wash their hands or change gloves between patients. Failure to follow these precautions spreads disease from one patient to another within modern hospitals. More people are killed by germs in hospitals each year this way than are killed by bullets and traffic accidents combined.

Suppose there are two antibiotics that are effective against different strains of bacteria. Suppose each antibiotic would be shown to be effective if tested against placebo in a double-blind study with two groups. However, suppose the combination of antibiotics is poisonous, causing damage to the kidneys. The only way to find this out would be in a factorial design with (at least) four treatment combinations, as shown in Table 1.1.

In the factorial design, there are four groups of patients in a double-blind study. Patients are randomly assigned to the four conditions. Every patient gets two bottles of medicine and is instructed to take one dose from each bottle. The first group receives two placebos. The second group receives placebo B (made to look like drug B) *and* drug A. The third group receives placebo A (made to resemble drug A) *and* drug B. The fourth group receives drug A *and* drug B. There are two independent variables in this study, drug A versus placebo A and drug B versus placebo B.

The first row of the factorial design is a simple test of drug A (two groups, double-blind experiment). The first column of the factorial design is a simple test of drug B. The factorial design also includes the combination of both drugs A and B. If each drug were effective against a different type of bacterium spread in the hospital, one might

Table 1.1. Results of Hypothetical Factorial Drug Experiment[a]

	PLACEBO A	DRUG A
Placebo B	50	80
Drug B	70	30

[a]Each entry is the percentage of patients who had "fever of unknown origin" in the hospital, who survive for 1 year after their stay in the hospital. Note that each drug is effective when tested against a placebo; however, in combination, they are worse than no treatment at all.

hope that the results would be additive, in which case the combination would be more effective than either drug alone. However, the hypothetical data show that the combination is worse than no medicine at all. This would be an example of an interaction between two factors. In this case, the drug interaction is harmful. In another type of interaction, two drugs might be more effective in combination than the sum of each one separately.

WITHIN-SUBJECTS RESEARCH

Some studies are done *within subjects*. In a within-subjects experiment, each subject receives all of the treatment combinations. For example, one might have a drug study to investigate the effects of two ingredients in a cold tablet—aspirin and caffeine. A factorial design would mean that there are four types of pills to be tested: pills that contain two placebos, pills that contain aspirin only, pills that contain caffeine only, or pills that contain both aspirin and caffeine. Pills might be labeled A, B, C, D. Each patient would be instructed to take pill A for one cold, pill B for the second cold, pill C for the third, and pill D for the fourth.

Within-subjects designs pose new issues that must be handled. For example, suppose the labels of the drugs has an effect. Maybe people would like a pill labeled "A" more than one labeled "B." Similarly, perhaps the first cold in a flu season is more severe than subsequent colds. To counterbalance the effects of the labels, one might use a Latin-Squares design, such as is illustrated in Table 1.2.

Notice that in the Latin-Squares design, each label is equally often applied to each treatment, and each treatment gets each of the labels. Four groups would receive the drug combinations, but each group would be in one of the rows of the Latin Square. Thus, in the first group, the placebo is labeled A, but in the second row, the placebo is labeled D, then C, then B.

The order of taking the medicines can also be counterbalanced. One group would be instructed to take pill A, followed by B, then C, then D. Another group might be instructed to take pill D, then C, then B, then A. Thus, the treatment order can be counterbalanced, either by a Latin-Square, which would be created within each row of Table 1.2, or in a complete counterbalancing of all 24 possible orders.

Counterbalancing of such factors does two things. First, it averages out and disentangles the effects of unwanted phenomena, such as the effects of the labels of the medicines. Second, it allows the investigator to study these effects, to see if they are substantial in magnitude. If the label of the pill does in fact have a large effect on how people respond to the medicine, then this information is itself of value.

Notice that when a within-subjects experiment is properly counterbalanced, one

Table 1.2.   Latin Square Design for Pill Labels[a]

GROUP	PLACEBO	INGREDIENT 1	INGREDIENT 2	BOTH INGREDIENTS
1	A	B	C	D
2	D	A	B	C
3	C	D	A	B
4	B	C	D	A

[a]In this design, the column means represent the treatment effects, and differences among the rows represent effects of labeling.

can always look at the first treatment as a between-subjects design. Therefore, a counterbalanced, within-subjects study contains a between-subjects study. Within-subjects experiments are more powerful than between-subjects experiments, and they have other advantages in behavioral research that are explained in Chapter 9. More information about within-subjects factorial experiments is presented in Chapters 11 through 16.

Not all research uses causal experiments. Some research is concerned with prediction. There can be value in being able to predict which parole candidate will commit crimes if given parole, which candidate for law school will flunk out in the first year, or which person will quit a job after receiving an expensive course of training. Prediction research is based on correlational methods. The researcher collects several dependent variables and computes correlations among them to see if some variables are related to others. This type of research is treated in Chapter 10.

 ## WEB RESEARCH

Since 1995, it has become possible to conduct research by a new method that has several advantages over traditional laboratory research. This new method uses the Internet as a medium for conducting behavioral research. The Internet allows one to collect data not only in laboratories with Internet-connected computers, but also large quantities of high-quality data from people all over the world. At the same time, there are special considerations and potential problems that require additional skills in the design and execution of Internet research.

At present, few researchers are trained in the techniques that must be mastered to conduct meaningful research on the Web. The purpose of this book is to provide the background needed to conduct this type of research. The skills that are covered in this book will be of lasting value, not only to those who plan to do graduate research in the behavioral sciences, but also to students who plan to enter the workforce, where expertise in the Internet has become a valued asset.

 ## ABOUT THE WEB

Since the late 1980s, a new protocol for the exchange of information between computers was introduced to the Internet. The *Internet* refers to the network of computers that are connected to each other and exchange information by email and other protocols. The new protocol introduced in 1990 was *http,* which stands for *HyperText Transfer Protocol.* By 1993, there were about 100 computers communicating by this new protocol, and this network of computers and the information they contained became known as the *World Wide Web* (WWW), or simply the Web.

The Web pages sent via this new protocol contained commands (*tags*) in a new language known as Hypertext Markup Language (HTML), which displayed text, graphics, and other multimedia, and allowed users to link one portion of a document to other information on the Web. These HTML files became known as Web *pages.* When Web *browsers,* programs that use a graphical interface to load and display Web pages, were introduced, the Web grew at an astonishing rate.

As computers and their software became more powerful, less expensive, and easier to operate, more and more institutions and individuals became attached to the Web. Web *servers,* computers that "serve" files in response to requests from remote browsers, were now affordable to small organizations, research laboratories, and individuals. At the same time, the new languages of Java and JavaScript were introduced. These languages allowed programs delivered with Web pages to remotely control distant browsers, even though those remote browsers might be running with different systems on different platforms (for example, PC or Mac), and they might be on the other side of the world.

In 1995, the new standard of HTML supported Web forms, which allow one to receive data from a person using a Web browser. At this time, a few behavioral researchers began to collect data via the Web. The early pioneers of Web research soon found that it was possible to collect large quantities of high-quality data in this way. A number of these investigators have shared their experiences and contributed much good advice for other professionals in a book edited by Birnbaum (2000b). Musch and Reips (2000) surveyed the pioneers of Web experimentation and found that they were quite pleased with their Web experiments and planned to conduct future research that way.

The number of Web studies listed by the American Psychological Society (APS) doubled from 1998 to 1999. It is reasonable to predict continued growth in this type of research because it has many advantages over the most common type of laboratory research done in the behavioral sciences (Schmidt, 1997; Reips, 2000). Studies that have compared Web and lab research on the same topic have found that these two research methods lead to the same conclusions (Birnbaum, 1999c; 2000a; Buchanan, 2000; Buchanan & Smith, 1999; Krantz, Ballard, & Scher, 1997; Krantz & Dalal, 2000; Pasveer & Ellard, 1998; Pettit, 1999; Stanton, 1998).

The typical study in psychology is conducted using paper-and-pencil methods. The data are collected via questionnaires from subjects, usually college students recruited from a subject pool of people who receive credit toward an assignment in lower division psychology. A research assistant in a laboratory collects the data at a prearranged time. The assistant then codes the data and enters them in the computer for statistical analysis. Additional time is required to verify that the data have been properly coded and entered and to fix any errors. In contrast, a typical Web experiment allows the participant to complete the materials on-line, the data are coded by computer, and saved to a data file for immediate analysis. The time required to conduct a study may be reduced by a factor of 10 or more (Birnbaum, 2000c).

 ## COMPARISONS BETWEEN WEB AND LAB RESEARCH

One can compare Web and laboratory research with respect to the dimensions listed in Table 1.3. Laboratory research is typically conducted with students in psychology courses. In the past, psychology enrolled a nearly even mix of males and females. At the present time, however, the subject pool in psychology is predominantly female. The Web was once considered predominantly male; however, participants in Web experiments are more nearly equal in sex ratios than the subject pool, and some studies show that more females than males participate in on-line psychology studies (Birnbaum, 1999c).

College students are very homogeneous in education: they have all graduated high school and none have graduated college. On the Web, participants are more heterogeneous. There are people who dropped out of school in the eighth grade, there are many college graduates, and there are some who have advanced degrees. The comparison of age is similar. Because samples recruited from the Web are so heterogeneous on such demographic characteristics, one can divide the sample on these variables to examine if the data support the same conclusions within each demographic group.

Web samples can also be recruited by techniques that are designed to reach specialized, rare populations. For example, identical twins are fairly rare in the general population, but could be easily recruited via the Web from on-line groups such as Moth-

TABLE 1.3.   Comparisons of Traditional Laboratory Research against Web-Based Research

ASPECT	LAB RESEARCH	WEB RESEARCH
Sample characteristics	Not random: College students	Not random: depends on recruitment
Education	Homogeneous	Better educated; more diversity
Age	Most 18–23 years	Heterogeneous; older
Occupation	Temporary jobs, minimal	Heterogeneous; careers
Gender	Mostly female	More equal sex ratio
Specialized samples	Impractical	Recruit via Internet
Large samples	Impractical or costly	Easy to accomplish
Cross-cultural research	Difficult or impossible	Fairly easy to do
Equipment, space needs	Considerable	Minimal
Data coding, entry	Expensive, time-consuming	By computer
Lab assistants	Necessary	Not required
Experimenter effects	Relevant	Avoided, uniformity
Variety of experiments	Equipment, drugs, surgery, scans, etc. possible	Many IV and DV not possible
Data quality	Good	Higher by some comparisons
Control	Highly controlled; depends on experimenter present	Less controlled conditions; depends on programming
Interface	Unfamiliar	Familiar
Drop-outs: Between subjects	A problem	Bigger problem
Motivation	Credit to class assignment, pay, or incentives	Volunteers, interests, incentives offered
Ethical review	Unit IRB	Unit IRB, some new issues
Multiple submissions	Rarely considered	A concern; handled by data checking

IV = independent variable; DV = dependent variable; IRB = institutional review board.

ers of Twins clubs. Similarly, transvestites constitute perhaps 1 or 2 percent of the general population, but can be contacted via social clubs that have Web sites.

Lab research must be conducted in a special place at a present time. An assistant must unlock the door, greet the participants, and conduct the test or experiment. Web research collects data around the clock and around the world. Participants typically come on-line at times convenient to them from computers at home, school, or work. For these reasons, it is possible to collect large samples with high power on the Web.

In many universities in which many professors and students have active research programs, there is competition for the available subject pool, so it is not possible to test large numbers of subjects. In addition to the ethics review, which ensures that the benefits of the research outweigh any risks and that participants are treated with respect, many universities also have an allocation of subject-hours from the limited subject pool. In contrast, once a Web project is approved by the ethics committee, there are currently no limits on the number of people that can be tested. In some universities, an investigator might be lucky to obtain 200 subject-hours per year from the subject pool. On the Web in 1999, it was quite reasonable to test 6000 people per year. Thus, the amount of data that might be collected in a year in the lab can be obtained in weeks on the Web.

Because the Web is worldwide, it is possible to test people in other countries from other cultures. Without the expense of travel, it is possible therefore to do cross-cultural research. To do such research in the lab, one would need to either travel, or at least to make contact with colleagues in different countries who can collaborate on the cross-cultural project.

Of course, the Web is not used by primitive people (people who do not use computers). Therefore, anthropological research still requires a person on the scene. Nevertheless, an anthropologist armed with a laptop can send data to home base instantly via the Web.

Web research cannot be used to investigate issues that require the experimenter to have "hands on" the subject. It is not possible, for example, to inject drugs, measure EEGs (electroencephalograms), take PET (positron emission tomography) scans, image X-rays, do surgery, or other such manipulations and measures that require one to have contact with the subject.

However, some Web research may benefit from there being no experimenter to introduce "experimenter bias" to the results. In some studies it has been found that experimenters seem to bias the subjects to produce certain results. They may unintentionally give subtle cues that reinforce certain behavior by participants. They may do this by obvious methods, such as giving instructions that "help" the experiment to work, or they may even alter data as they are reported by the subject. With lab research, experimenter effects can cause investigators at different universities to find contradictory results that may require a great effort in the lab to resolve.

Web studies have a situation that is familiar to users of the Internet (the browser interface), a situation that can be easily described and replicated. Thus, with Web research, it is possible to standardize the situation, allowing more exact replication. Web studies can be made public to other scientists, making the process of research more open. When everyone can do the same experiment, different investigators can produce the same results.

The benefits of doing research on the Web justify the efforts required to learn how to do this new style of research.

SUMMARY

This chapter reviews the goals and terminology of basic research. The purpose of research is to answer questions—in particular, questions about explanations of behavior. Behavioral scientists use experiments to investigate causation. The concepts of independent variable, dependent variable, and random assignment to conditions are defined and illustrated with examples. Differences between Web research and lab research are considered. It is noted that Web research can more easily achieve large samples, which allow powerful tests of the null hypothesis.

EXERCISES

1. What are the philosophical criteria for an explanation? Why is each criterion needed?
2. Why is random assignment to conditions needed in a study to investigate the effects of a new drug?
3. Why is a control group needed?
4. What is a placebo?
5. Define the following terms: independent variable, dependent variable, treatment group, control group.
6. Why do within-subjects designs require counterbalancing?
7. What are the chief differences between Web and lab research?
8. Distinguish causation from correlation.
9. In the experiment to test if Clever Hans could answer questions if the faces of the audience were covered, what were the independent and dependent variables? Was it a within-subjects or between-subjects design?

Chapter 2

YOUR FIRST WEB PAGE

Even though you can create a Web page without knowing HTML, in order to run experiments on the Internet, you need to know some HTML. HTML stands for *HyperText Markup Language*, and it refers to the *tags*, or instructions, that allow your browser to display pages that contain formatted text, hyperlinks, and multimedia files (such as, pictures, graphics, sounds, and video). This chapter reviews how to make a bare-bones Web page by typing the HTML in a text editor. It reviews how to make a Web page without knowing HTML. It also teaches how to download files from the Web and how to upload your files to a Web server, where they can be read by anyone in the world.

 ## YOU NEED TO KNOW HTML

Anyone planning to do experiments on the Internet should learn some HTML. There is more to HTML than can be reviewed in this book, but this book teaches everything that you need to do the experiments in this book.

Although programs that create HTML or convert other documents to HTML may be useful, they cannot do everything you need done to run an experiment. Therefore, you should learn enough HTML so that you would not need them—in fact, once you learn HTML, you may prefer not to use such programs. As a person doing experimentation on the Web, you must know how things work to get the result you want. If you do not know what you are doing, you will get stuck and waste time solving problems that a little knowledge of HTML would fix quickly. You must know what is covered in chapters 2–4. You can learn the material on HTML in these chapters in about 4 days.

 ## A SIMPLE WEB PAGE

Here is how to create a simple document in HTML that can be displayed by a Web browser. Start a simple text editor such as NotePad, SimpleText, or BBEdit Lite; these programs all allow you to save files as text only. To make a Web page, you should save as text (ASCII) only, and give the file an extension of *.htm* or *.html*. These extensions help browsers and other applications recognize that this text file contains HTML.

Consider the case of a student planning to do her senior thesis on the topic of visual illusions. She might advertise her interest and request help from the Internet community by means of a Web page such as in Figure 2.1. Type the contents of Figure 2.1 into your text editor exactly as displayed. To avoid confusion, you should use a text editor (such as NotePad or SimpleText) rather than a word processor (like MS Word) for this example.

This document, or *page* has HTML commands, or *tags,* that are placed in angle brackets <>. These tags instruct the browser how to display the page.

Most commands in HTML have a beginning tag and an ending tag. Ending tags contain a slash (/). For example, <HTML> says that what follows is HTML, and the tag </HTML> designates the end of the HTML document. Everything in between is the HTML page.

Each HTML page has a HEAD and a BODY. The `<HEAD>` and `</HEAD>` tags designate the head of the document, which contains the title that is displayed at the top of the window. You will learn other things that can go in the HEAD later.

`<TITLE>` *This is the title* `</TITLE>` contains the title displayed at the top of the browser's window.

`<BODY>` *text* `</BODY>` contains the body of text for the document.

The `<PRE>` tag indicates to the browser that the next text is preformatted. Preformatted text is displayed in an equal-spaced font. In an equal- or mono-spaced font, each character or number has the same size. If your document contains line returns and tabs, these are also preserved in preformatted text. `</PRE>` turns off the preformatting.

Figure 2.2 shows how the page will look when typed into NotePad, a text editor for the PC. When you save, be careful to click the *Save As Type* pull down list in the *Save* dialog box, as shown in Figure 2.3, and choose *All Files;* otherwise, NotePad adds the ex-

FIGURE 2.1.   The composition of a simple Web page.

```
<HTML>

<HEAD>

<TITLE>Visual Illusions on the WWW</TITLE>

</HEAD>

<BODY>

<PRE>


Hi. I'm a junior in psychology at Anytown College.

I'm planning to do a senior research project

next year on visual illusions, and I hope to

put my experiment on the World Wide Web.

I would be grateful for your

assistance.


If you are conducting such research, or if you know of

others doing such research, please write me:


Ms. Ann E. Student

100 College Lane, Box 100

Anytown, State 10000-100


Thank you for your help.

</PRE>

</BODY>

</HTML>
```

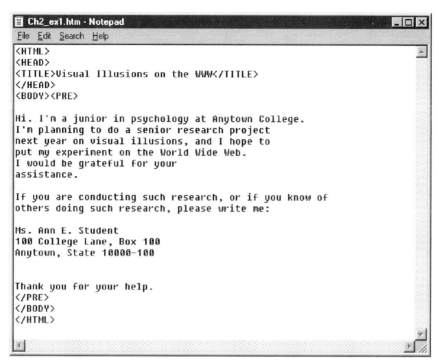

FIGURE 2.2. Appearance of Example 1 in NotePad. This file is available as *Ch2_ex1.htm* on the CD that accompanies the book. On a Macintosh computer, you could use SimpleText or BBEdit Lite as your text editor.

FIGURE 2.3. *Save As* dialog in NotePad. Be sure to select in *Save as type: All files,* and give the file an extension of *.htm* or *.html*.

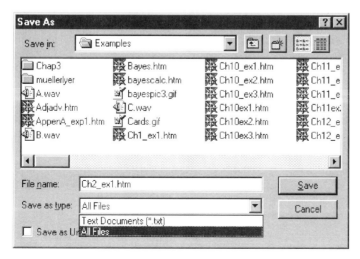

tension of *.txt*. When you try to open HTML files in NotePad, you should also select *All files*, or NotePad will only display files with the *.txt* extension.

Type a file with the above information in it (or open the example, *Ch2_ex1.htm*, from the CD that accompanies this book in your text editor), and save it on your hard drive. Save the file with the name *test.htm*. When you open the file in the browser, it should display as in Figure 2.4 (which illustrates the display in Netscape Communicator 4.05 for PC). You can also open this example from the CD that accompanies your book, which saves you the labor of typing it. Open the file *examples.htm* in your browser, and click the link to *Chapter 2 Example 1*. Now paste in some other formatted text to replace the body, such as your vita or résumé (you can change the title to *Vita Of Your Name*), which you might save with the filename *vita.htm*. To see what your file will look like on the Web, start your browser (e.g., Netscape, Internet Explorer), and choose *Open File* from the **File** menu.

If you made an error, failing to put in a closing tag, using parentheses ( ) instead of angle brackets `<brackets>`, misspelling the commands in a tag, or some other error, then your page may not display correctly. When there is an error, different browsers may display your page differently, so it is important to correct any error you catch. Even if everything looks correct on your own browser, it may not display correctly for somebody using Explorer instead of Netscape or on a PC instead of a Mac.

FIGURE 2.4.   This figure shows how the sample file *Ch2_ex1.htm* looks when displayed by Netscape.

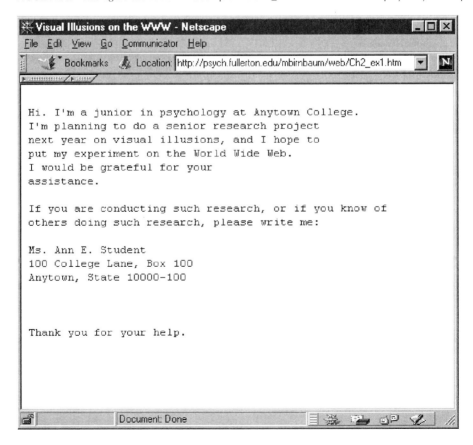

HTML is not case sensitive. That means that you can use <HTML> or <html>, and it will work the same either way. However, JavaScript *is* case sensitive, so be careful when you get to Chapter 17. In this book, HTML tags are written in all capital letters to make them easier to spot, but they do not have to be written that way.

When you are content that your file displays correctly on your browser and there are no errors, you can upload the file to your server by means of an FTP program, as described later.

CREATING A WEB PAGE WITHOUT KNOWING HTML

If you can use a modern word processor, such as Microsoft Word or WordPerfect, then you can create a document in HTML. You can create a document in Word or Word-Perfect and then save it as HTML. You can also create HTML files using programs such as Netscape Communicator (Composer), PowerPoint, and many others.

Suppose you want to place a paper you have just written on the Web. Your report might be an MSWord document that contains graphic images, equations, charts, tables, and pictures. Load it into your word processor; next, select *Save As HTML . . . or Save As a Web Page* from the **File** menu.

The *Save As HTML . . .* dialog allows you to give the file a name. When you *Save As HTML,* you should save your file under a new name to make sure that you do not erase your original file and lose information when you save as HTML. You should give it a filename with an extension of *.htm* or *.html.* This extension helps various programs recognize the file as a file that contains HTML. Depending on your program and system, the extension may be added automatically for you. You should save into an empty folder so that you can keep track of all of the separate files created. When you save, MSWord creates several files that contain the text and graphics, and it creates the HTML to link these files together. If your document contains line drawings or pictures, then these are saved as separate files along with the file of formatted text.

You can display the HTML files you create this way in your browser. You can also open the HTML file in the application that created it. For example, you can open your HTML files in MSWord. In MSWord, you can view the HTML source from the **View** menu by selecting *HTML Source* from the **View** menu.

Browsers also allow you to view the HTML code for any file that is displayed. In Netscape, for example, you select *Page Source* from the **View** menu; in Explorer, you select *Source* from the **View** menu.

This means that you can view (and save) the HTML of any page on the Web. You can save the HTML of another person's page and use it to learn. You can also save graphic images and pictures from your browser as well. To save a graphic on a PC, point to it and right-click. A menu will appear giving you the option to copy or save the image. On a Mac, click and hold down the mouse button, and the same menu will appear. When you save another person's HTML code or images, you should realize that you have copied another person's work and you should obtain permission from the author and copyright holder before you use it in any way that might violate copyright laws or ethics. More is said on this topic (ethics) in Chapter 21.

Once you have created an HTML page with a word processor, view the source file and you see each of the tags that were explained in this chapter and some others as well. You will learn about those other tags in later chapters.

To place your paper on the Web so that others can read it from anywhere in the world, you must now upload to your files to a public folder on a Web server. A Web *server* is a computer connected to the Internet that delivers (serves) files via the Web's protocol, known as HTTP for *HyperText Transfer Protocol*. The term *upload* means that you send copies of the files you created (when you saved as HTML) from your personal computer to your Web server. The next sections teach you how to use FTP (File Transfer Protocol) programs for uploading and downloading programs to and from a Web server.

UPLOADING AND DOWNLOADING TO THE WEB SERVER

To send files to a server (upload) and to retrieve files from a server (download), you need a program that can send and receive files. Programs based on FTP such as **Fetch** for the Macintosh and **WS FTP** or **CuteFTP** for Windows can do this task. Browsers can also transfer files by FTP, but they do not have all of the features of a dedicated FTP program.

USING NETSCAPE TO FTP

In your browser, type *FTP://* instead of *http://* in the address box. To connect to the psych.fullerton.edu site via Navigator or Explorer, type the following line:

ftp://guest:guest99@psych.fullerton.edu

Note three things in the above line. First, it is *ftp://* instead of *http://*. Second, the format of the line is *userid:password@server.address*. Third, this line includes an @, as is seen in email addresses but not Web addresses. The userid in this case is "guest" and the password is "guest99." This password allows you to download but not upload.

Figure 2.5 shows the appearance of an FTP session in Netscape. You see a list of files that can be downloaded. By clicking on the file, you may or may not be able to view the file—you may see only a blank screen. Regardless of whether you can view it, you should next select *Save As* from the **File** menu and save the file in a location that you will find easily later. (On a Mac, clicking a file may automatically download a copy of the file to the desktop. On a PC, people often "lose" files that they save in these situations, so if you use a PC, you should make a note of the directory folders in which you saved any file that you download. If you clicked *Save* and you do not know where it went, make a note of the file name immediately, and use your *Find File* utility, which you can reach from the **Start** button. If you forget the filename too, you can try searching by date with Find File.)

Netscape also allows you to upload files (if you have permission), by selecting *Upload file* from the **File** menu. Internet Explorer also supports file transfers by FTP in much the same way.

DOWNLOADING SOFTWARE FROM THE WEB

Although browsers can handle file transfers by FTP, it is more convenient to use dedicated programs when you have many files to manage. If you do not already have an FTP program, there are many that you can download for free. In fact, there are many programs for all kinds of purposes that you can find free on the Web. To search for programs, you can use your browser with a search engine to find vendors and free software sites maintained by clubs and users groups.

A site that supports downloading of freeware, shareware, and commercial software has the URL:

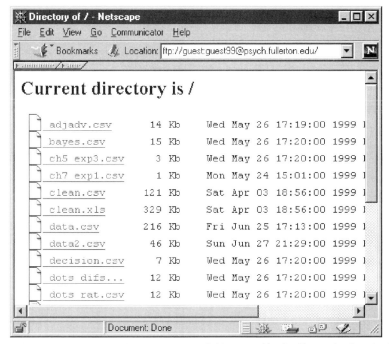

FIGURE 2.5. Using FTP in Netscape. By clicking on a file, the file can be downloaded.

http://www.download.com

Use your browser to get to the site, then check to make sure that you are in the site for PC (if you have a PC) or Mac (if you have a Mac). If you are at the wrong site, scroll down the page and click the link to send you to the appropriate site for your computer.

To search for FTP programs, type *ftp* in the search box and click the *search* button. A number of programs will be listed. You can read brief descriptions of the programs, including information on when the programs were posted and how many people have downloaded those programs. When you have selected a program, you can click the link and follow directions for downloading and installing your software.

USING AN FTP PROGRAM WITH YOUR LOCAL SERVER

Now you have FTP software. Now you need an account and password for your local server. Next, you upload your file to the appropriate location. When you have uploaded your HTML file (e.g., from Fig. 2.1) to an appropriate folder on a Website server (a computer that is connected to the Internet and has Website software running on it), anyone in the world can read your document if they know the URL.

If you are at an educational institution, you should become acquainted with the person who runs your department's or unit's server. That person can give you a password and an account name (folder name) for your space on the server. That person may also be able to help you with programs to upload and download to and from the server. The person who runs your server can also tell you the URL that takes your browser to your territory on the Web (your directory or folder). The person who runs the server will also ask you about *security*, which refers to the issues of who gets to read the files in your folder and who gets to write to them. You want to be able to write to them by password only. For the experiments in this book, you want your folder to be readable to everyone. When your folder has been established with read access to everyone and write access to you by password only, you will upload your files to that folder.

If you have a commercial Internet service provider, you should check the materials they sent you about uploading and downloading files. Your commercial provider may require you to use special programs for Web access and sending and receiving files. The price of your service may depend on how much material you plan to upload to the server.

Suppose you do not yet have an account and a password on your server. (Eventually, you will need one to carry out independent research on the Internet.) In the meantime, you can practice using your ftp software with the following download-only ftp site that is available to you.

The ftp software needs to know the name of the host computer to which you wish to connect, it needs to know your user ID (sometimes known as an *account name*), your *password*, and it may also request the *directory* to which you wish to connect. To connect to the *psych.fullerton.edu* server, enter the following information into your ftp program in the "connect" or "establish new connection" dialog box:

> **Host:** psych.fullerton.edu
> **User ID:** guest
> **Password:** guest99
> **Directory:** (if this is listed, leave it blank; if account number is requested, either leave it blank or insert your user ID).

If the host type is requested, set it to *Automatic Detect*, if possible. If you know what type of server you have, you can enter that in the appropriate space. The psych.fullerton.edu server is a Windows NT server.

When you have entered this information to your program, you click the button that says "OK" or "Connect," and the program shows you a list of files available for you to download. This step is illustrated for WS FTP LE (Limited Edition) in Figure 2.6.

Remember: For this site, you cannot upload files to *psych.fullerton.edu*, and if you try, you will get a message telling you that you cannot do that. You can download files, however, and there are several files related to this book at that site. The files available to download from this site include examples of experiments and data files containing data from various experiments.

FTP programs usually have a button to click or box to check that indicates the type of file you are transferring. Some have a button for "automatic," which is supposed to figure out what type of file it is by its extension or from information within the file itself. When you are working with HTML, you should send and receive the files as text by selecting text (or ASCII) for the type of file to be transferred. When sending files containing images, send as binary (sometimes called *raw data*). You can also use binary to send and receive ASCII. Do not upload files in compressed formats, or formats like MacBinary that do not transfer to all users. This step is illustrated in Figure 2.7.

Figures 2.6 and 2.7 illustrate the screens on the PC for WS FTP LE. In Figure 2.7, the left side shows the local computer, and the right side shows the remote (server)

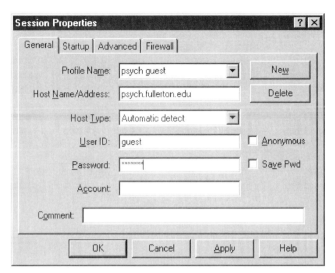

FIGURE 2.6.   Using WS FTP LE (Limited Edition). Connecting to a server by FTP requires that you enter the host name, the user ID, and password. Here the host name is *psych.fullerton.edu*, the user's ID is *guest,* and the password (hidden) is *guest99.* Clicking OK establishes the connection. WS FTP also saves the settings for future sessions.

computer. After selecting a file, pressing the arrow pointing left sends a file from the server to the local computer. If you have uploading privileges, pressing the right-pointing arrow would send the selected files from your local computer to the server. Be very careful with any FTP program to send files the right direction! You must be careful to upload the new version of the file, especially when you want to make changes to a file that already exists, or you may accidentally replace the new version on your local computer with the old version. It happens fast without an "Are you sure?" warning. Be careful not to double click on a file name, as that will send it. One idea is to keep copies of files in working folders, then *copy* them to a special folder that will be used for file transfer. That way, you have your originals in their original folders even if you accidentally download when you meant to upload. Be careful.

Once you have uploaded your file to a public folder on the Web, anyone can enter its URL in their browser and read the document. Anyone in the world can now read your file if they know the URL. In later chapters, you will learn how to publicize your site to help people find it.

 ## SUMMARY

In this chapter, you learned that you can create HTML documents either by using an application such as MSWord or by typing HTML in a text editor (such as, NotePad) and saving as text with an extension of *.htm* or *.html.* You should now understand the HTML tags in Table 2.1, which you should be able to use to create a simple page.

You should also understand how to upload and download files to and from your server. If you know the terms in Table 2.2 and you can do the exercises, then you are prepared to go on to the next chapter.

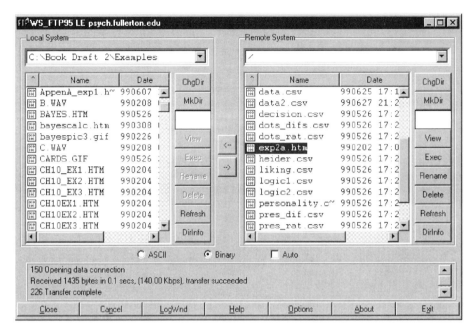

FIGURE 2.7. Downloading a file by WS FTP LE. The local system's directory can be changed with the *ChgDir* key, by double clicking a folder to open a visible folder, or by clicking the up arrow to go to the next higher level. To transfer a file, click on it (which highlights it), and click the arrow to send the file. Be very careful which arrow you click! This file, *exp2a.htm*, is being sent from the server to a folder on the local computer's C drive. The *View* key opens the selected (highlighted) file in NotePad.

TABLE 2.1.   Summary of HTML Tags in Chapter 2

HTML TAG	WHAT IT DOES
<HTML></HTML>	Signals HTML start and ending.
<HEAD></HEAD>	Signals the beginning and ending of the head of an HTML page
<TITLE></TITLE>	Place the title to be displayed between these tags.
<BODY></BODY>	The body of the HTML page is placed between these tags.
<PRE></PRE>	Preformatted text. Tabs, returns, and spaces will be preserved and displayed. Each character will have the same width.

TABLE 2.2   Terms Used in File Transfer

FILE TRANSFER TERMS	DEFINITIONS
FTP	File Transfer Protocol
Upload	Send file from local computer to server
Download	Receive file on local computer from server

 **EXERCISES**

1. After you have viewed the first example in your browser, try removing the `<PRE>` and `</PRE>` tags from the document. Save the new version, and reload it in the browser. How does the document look now? What has happened to spacing, tabs, and line returns?

2. Try changing the HTML tags from all caps to lower case. Does the file still display the same way? It should look the same (unless you made a typo).

3. Use a word processor to create a page with formatting such as bold, italics, different fonts, etc. Use *Save As HTML* to create a page. Load this page into a browser. Does the page look the same in your browser as it does in your word processor? Now load it in your text editor and examine the many interesting tags. Find the ones of Table 2.1.

4. Use a text editor such as SimpleText or NotePad to create a Web page using the tags in Figure 2.2 and Table 2.1. For example, take your résumé or vita, and convert it to a Web page by adding a title and using the Pre-formatted text tags. Load this page in your browser. How does the page look? You can edit the page and save your changes, then use "Reload" ("Refresh" in Internet Explorer) to bring your browser up to date. How does it look in the browser?

5. Use your ftp program to download the file *exp2a.htm* from the *psych.fullerton.edu* server. Open this file in your browser. Also try opening it with a text editor such as SimpleText or NotePad. You will see some HTML tags that look familiar, and you will also see some tags that you may not recognize. You will learn all of them by Chapter 5.

6. Use your browser or ftp program to upload the files you created to your local Web server. Then use your browser to display the files from the URL of your Web pages. To do this exercise, you will need a local Web server with a username and password.

Chapter 3

Putting the Hyper in Hypertext

In Chapter 2, you learned how to make a simple HTML page and how to upload, or "publish," it on the Web. However, to get responses from people in *Ch2_ex1.htm,* you have to wait for them to write you letters and send them through the mail. It would be nice if the person reading your page could respond by email, which might increase the likelihood that they will respond at all because they do not have to copy down your address and pay for postage. It is also better not to have to wait for postal mail (also called "snail mail") to arrive.

So far, the bare bones HTML document created in Chapter 2 is not interactive. In this chapter, you learn to make links to email, to other documents, and to other parts of the same page. You also learn how to incorporate images in HTML pages and how to link from images. These links put the *hyper* in *hypertext.*

EMAIL FROM A WEB PAGE

To add a "link" to an email address, you can add the following tags in the body of the page:

```
<A HREF="mailto:astudent@address.domain">Click to send me email</A>
```

Anything between the `<A HREF="">` and `</A>` tags will be displayed as a "hot" link, which when clicked instructs the browser to send email addressed to the address specified after `mailto:` (assuming that the browser supports email). This feature converts HTML from a passive display formatting system to an active system, one that supports two-way communication. In this case, it facilitates getting responses because somebody reading the page can just click on the link and type in a response without having to print out a letter, put it in an envelope, affix a stamp, and put it in the mailbox. Load *Ch3_ex1.htm* from the page of examples on your CD.

LINKING TO ANOTHER PAGE

To link to another page, you can use the following variation of the `<A HREF></A>` tags:

```
<A HREF="http://www.ulb.ac.be/psycho/brmic.html">Museum of
Perception</A>
```

To check the effects of these links, type them as additions to the simple page from Chapter 2 and use your browser to load the revised pages. Notice what is displayed and try clicking on the links to see the effects. Clicking on a link should send the browser to the address specified. If this does not work, check to see if you have made any error in typing in the tags. Check if you have left out the closing tag, `</A>`, or if you have mistyped the address. Check if you have used parentheses `()` instead of the brackets `<  >`. Try *Ch3_ex2.htm.* Examine it in a text editor and in your browser.

Within your own Web site (i.e., the same directory on your server), you can simplify links by simply specifying the filename without the entire address. This method is called a *relative* address. Thus, if the file displayed is already in the folder that contains `examples.htm`, then the link can be written as follows:

```
<A HREF="examples.htm">Return to Index of Examples</A>
```

The result is illustrated in Figure 3.1, which you can load as *Ch3_ex1.htm* from the CD that accompanies this book.

There is a good reason to use a relative address instead of a complete address. Suppose you created a set of files that refer to one another using absolute addresses (that is, complete URLs). Then suppose you move your files to another server, and suppose your files are removed from the old server. You will have to change all of the links in many pages to make them all work. However, if all of the links within your site are relative, then when you move the entire set of files to another server, everything within your pages will still work.

Anyone outside your server who had a link to your old address will still send people to the wrong address. If you have explored the Web, you have undoubtedly clicked on a link or entered a URL only to find that it takes you to a dead end of "file not found." After checking your spelling, you find that the file is no longer there. Because the Web is ever-changing, every click is an adventure.

Because students get their degrees at one university and then move to other uni-

FIGURE 3.1.   Appearance of links to email and to another page (*Ch3_ex1.htm*).

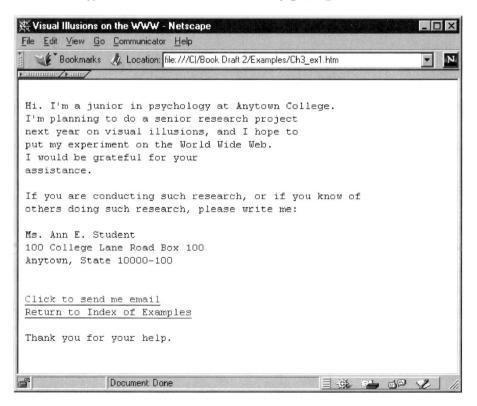

versities or to jobs in industry, students often need to move all of their Web files from one location to another. Professors also take new jobs and move from one university to another. Furthermore, your old server might become crowded, and you might be asked to move your files to another location, or you might acquire your own server. Therefore, it is a good idea to plan ahead and use relative addresses to refer to pages in your own site.

 ## LINKING TO PARTS OF THE SAME PAGE

It is also possible to use linking to send the reader to different parts of the same page. You need anchor tags to name the locations, and anchor reference tags to send them to the locations. For example:

```
<A NAME="req">Course Requirements</A>
This course requires that you will attend, do the homework, take
exams, and complete the course project before the last day of the
semester.
```

The tag `<A NAME="req">` names the anchor line of information as "req," which refers to a section of a course description. There might be separate sections for prerequisites, assigned readings, exam policy, exam dates, and so on. Each section could be identified by its own anchor name. The following link sends the viewer to the location in the file of the "req" anchor.

```
<A HREF="#req">Click here to see course requirements</A>
```

The file *examples.htm* on the CD uses this device to allow the reader to click one of the chapter numbers at the top of the page to jump to the examples for that chapter. The reader might also scroll down the list, but it is faster and more convenient to click the link. A possible disadvantage is that by clicking such a link, the reader may become psychologically "lost" (following the hyperlink), and not realize that he or she is still reading the same document. Incidentally, to keep from getting lost, read the title and URL of the pages you read and note the position of the handle in the scroll bar.

Another useful trick is to provide a link to the top of the same page, as in the following example:

```
<A HREF="#top">Top</A>
```

This example takes the reader to the top of the page, even though no anchor specifically defines the top of the page. This trick is also illustrated in the *examples.htm* file on the CD.

 LINKING TO AN ANCHOR IN ANOTHER PAGE

It is also possible to link to a particular place in another page. This is done by placing one or more anchor name tags in the second page and linking from the first page to the second by using both an address and a name. For example, suppose you are in a document called *home.htm*, a professor's home page. To link to course requirements in a particular course syllabus, the following could be used:

```
<A HREF="syllabus101.htm#req">Click here for requirements in my 101
course</A>
```

Another example is in *Ch3_ex1.htm* and *Ch3_ex2.htm*,

```
<A HREF="examples.htm#three">Return to Index of Examples</A>
```

This link and others like it in the examples take the reader from one file to the appropriate spot in another document. In this case, it takes the reader back to the list of examples for Chapter 3, which has an anchor tag <A NAME="three">, in *examples.htm*.

 LINKING TO A FILE IN ANOTHER FOLDER

One can always use the complete URL to link to any file on the Internet. However, sometimes it is useful to link to a folder inside the current directory with a relative link. The example of *Ch3_ex3.htm* illustrates how to use a relative link to go into a subdirectory, *Chap3*, to get the file *hi.htm*. Notice that the slashes are *forward* slashes(/), unlike the backslashes (\) used to define paths in DOS.

```
<HTML><HEAD><TITLE>Linking to inside another
folder</TITLE></HTML></HEAD>
<BODY><P><A HREF="Chap3/hi.htm">This links to file inside Chap3
sub-directory</A>
</BODY></HTML>
```

The following example, *hi.htm*, shows how to return back to the parent directory.

```
<HTML><HEAD><TITLE>Linking Back out of a Folder</TITLE></HEAD>
<BODY><P>
<P>HI, now you are inside the folder chap3.
<P><A HREF="../examples.htm#three">Return to the index of
examples</A>
</BODY></HTML>
```

In this example, . . / is used to go out of the current directory to the next higher level directory.

INCLUDING IMAGES AND LINKING FROM IMAGES

Example *Ch3_ex4.htm* illustrates how to include an image in a Web page:

```
<IMG SRC="email.gif" ALT="computer mail" ALIGN="left" WIDTH=75
HEIGHT=75 BORDER=0>
```

Two popular formats supported by HTML for Web images are "JPEG" and "GIF", which have extensions of *.jpg* and *.gif.* You can use a program to create or convert your images to one of these formats. For photographs, JPEG (joint photographic experts group) files seem best, and for graphics such as line drawings, GIF (graphic interchange format) are usually best. GIF images use fewer colors than JPEG, so GIF files can be smaller (taking less time to load) than JPEG.

You can create and edit artwork and photographs in commercial programs such as Adobe Illustrator and Adobe PhotoShop. For simple graphics and word art, MS Word and PowerPoint can be useful and convenient. You can use a scanner and its software to scan in photographs or artwork and edit the images. You can also download freeware and shareware programs that allow you to create pictures and convert images from one format to another. You can click the links to graphic resources from the examples for this chapter. More is said about graphics in Chapters 7 and 14.

The text in ALT=text specifies a verbal description of the image. The description is helpful for people who have set their browsers to not download images. Some people do not download images to save time in reading Web pages. The ALT description may not show if a picture loads quickly, but it will show if the load is slow, if the user has turned off images, or if the image is missing. In some browsers, ALT shows when the mouse pointer is placed on an image and left still. People who are visually impaired use the ALT description to understand what is pictured. For these reasons, you should supply a description for each picture.

The HEIGHT, WIDTH, and BORDER specify the dimensions and border around the image. Change these values in the example to see their effects. Also, try changing

ALIGN=left, ALIGN=middle, and ALIGN=right to see the effects of aligning an image in a Web page of text. Remember, you must save your changes *and* reload the file in the browser to view the changes in the browser (in IE, click the "refresh" button).

You can nest an IMG tag within the tags that specify a link, as in *Ch3_ex5.htm*. As you might expect, clicking on the picture (nested inside the <A HREF=URL> and </A> tags) has the effect of clicking on a link of text between the same tags.

```
<A HREF=mailto:user@address.edu><IMG SRC="email.gif"
ALT="computer mail" ALIGN="left" WIDTH=75 HEIGHT=75 BORDER=0></A>
```

 ## DISCUSSION AND SUMMARY

If you look at other people's Web pages, you will see many graphics that have been included to liven up the link to email. (If these appeal to your sense of taste, you can look at the page source of such pages (and the images) and learn how to emulate them. You can also search the Web for catalogs of graphic images, video clips, and animations that authors have placed on the Web for free use by anyone who agrees to acknowledge credit to the artist. There are many images and animations that may be used freely. You should be careful, however, not to use copyrighted material that is not intended for public use. As you peruse the Web, you will also find many graphics that include advertising with invitations to click them to receive commercial messages—the clutter can get pretty annoying! Some think you should keep Web pages fairly clean and simple (they load faster and are easier to read), but your taste may be different, so if you like graphics to liven up your pages, go ahead and include them.

Linking allows a dynamic, interactive component to HTML. The browser's display depends on the person's decision to click one link or another. Table 3.1 summarizes the tags used in this chapter.

Table 3.1. Tags Creating Links to email, to Other Pages, Within a Page, and to Display an Image

TAG	DESCRIPTION
<A NAME="*anyname*"></A>	Anchors a line of text by giving it a name
<A HREF="mailto:*nb@nowhere.edu*">click</A>	Creates a link that when clicked starts an email message to the address specified after mailto:
<A HREF="#*anyname*">click here</A>	Creates a link in the same document to the anchored name.The same name must be defined in an anchored name tag.
<A HREF="*address#anyname*">click</A>	Links to another page at the address given and location defined in the other page.
<A HREF="*name/file.htm*">click</A>	Links to a file in the folder, name,to a page named file.htm.
<A HREF="*../file.htm*">click</A>	Links to the file file.htm in the parent directory of the current folder.
<IMG SRC="*file.gif*" ALT="*description*" ALIGN="*left*" WIDTH=75 HEIGHT=75 BORDER=0>	Displays the image file, file.gif, left-justified, with width and height of 75 pixels and no border.

EXERCISES

1. Write a simple Web page to take a vote on some proposition; it sends email to one address if the person has one opinion and to another address if the person has the opposite opinion. Use two different email addresses. By counting the number of messages sent to the two addresses, one could count the number of people who vote each way. (One solution is in *Ch3_ex6.htm*.) In Chapter 5, you see a much better way to do this that does not require two email addresses and does not require handling of all of those emails.

2. Add an image to the link of *Ch3_ex2.htm*. Use the image included on the CD named *MuseumTiny.gif*. This image is used with permission of Marielle Lange of the Museum of Perception and Cognition at Universite Libre of Brussels, Belgium. Arrange the page so that clicking on the logo sends the reader to the museum.

3. Develop a set of Web pages containing some instructional materials with a multiple-choice problem. When students click on the correct answer, they should be sent to a page that tells them they were correct; if the answer was wrong, send them to a page that gives tailored additional instruction. Use one Web page for the test, and use links to send the student to appropriate additional instruction for each wrong answer and to the next question if they are correct. You should supply a return link from each page of corrections to the appropriate item in the test.

4. Construct two questionnaires, one for males and one for females. Then create a page that asks the person to click according to their gender, with HTML to automatically send them to the appropriate questionnaire. Use relative addresses.

5. Write two Web pages. Make one a home page for a student. Make the other a list of hobbies and interests for the same student with sections for Academic interests, Musical interests, Hobbies, Jokes, and Pictures. Put links at the beginning of the file to the sections in the same file. In the home page put a link to the Jokes in the Hobbies and Interests file.

6. Examine the page source (HTML) of the file on your CD called *examples.htm*. You can open this file in NotePad, or open it in your browser and select *Page Source* from the **View** menu. This file consists of links to examples and other addresses. You should now understand how this file (*examples.htm*) works.

7. Open your Word Processor, such as MS Word, and select *Picture* from the **Insert** menu. Look at the pictures that come with the word processor. Insert an image, and select *Save as HTML* from the **File** menu, being careful to note the folder in which you save it. Open the folder and look at the image files, which have names such as *image1.gif, image2.gif*, and so on. Open the image files from the browser. You can rename the images to more useful names. The images in *Ch3_ex5.htm* were made by this procedure.

 LINKS FOR GRAPHICS

Paint Shop Pro (for PC) and BME (for Mac) are inexpensive and can be used to do many of the same tasks as the more expensive (and powerful) program Adobe Photo-Shop. Links to programs and graphic resources on the Web are included in the examples to this chapter. These sites tell you the rules for using their images and animations.

Chapter 4

Additional Tricks in HTML

In this chapter you learn additional HTML tags that allow you to control the format of the displayed Web page. In addition, this chapter explains how to create tables and to use frames to organize how information is displayed in the window.

COMMENTS IN HTML

Anything placed between `<!.......` and `...>` will not be displayed by the browser unless you view the HTML source.

Sometimes it is helpful to put comments that are not displayed into HTML pages. When making experiments on the Web, you'll need to remember why you did what you did, or when you did it. Including comments in your pages will save you the work of trying to figure out why you did that. It is also easier to read other Web pages now that you know that anything written inside these marks is not displayed.

CREATING A HORIZONTAL RULE

The tag `<HR>` creates a horizontal line or "rule." This feature can separate sections of a document or improve the appearance of a page. This is one of the exceptions in HTML, in that it does not have a closing tag. `<HR>`

CONTROLLING THE APPEARANCE OF TEXT

As noted earlier, `<PRE>` `</PRE>` puts text into monospaced font and preserves formatting such as tabs and line breaks, as in *Ch4_ex1.htm*, the first part of which is shown in Figure 4.1. Figure 4.2 shows how preformatting is preserved in the display.

The `<TT>` and `</TT>` tags put text into monospaced font without preserving formatting, also from the file *Ch4_ex1.htm*:

```
<TT>This text will be displayed with equal spacing
    for letters
    and numbers.
However, formatting will not be preserved.</TT>
```

To put text into bold type, use `<B>` and `</B>`, as follows:

```
<B>This text will be displayed in bold type</B>.
```

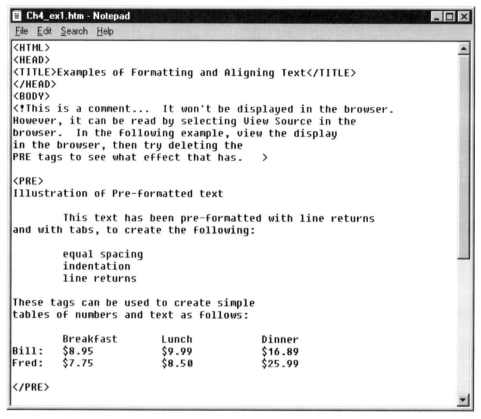

FIGURE 4.1.   Preformatted text preserves spaces, tabs, and line returns.

To put text into italics, use `<I></I>`, as in the following example:

`<I>This text will be displayed with Italics</I>.`

To underline text, use the tags `<U>` and `</U>`, as in the following example:

`<U>This text will be displayed with Underlining</U>.`

These features can be nested to create combinations, as in the following example:

```
<I><B>This will be <U>underlined</U>, and displayed in bold</B>and
italics</I>.
```

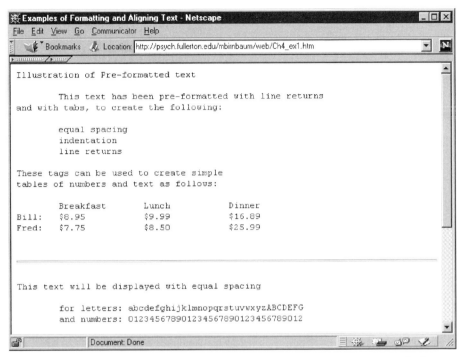

FIGURE 4.2. This figure shows how the preformatted text of Figure 4.1 appears in the browser. To experiment with the effect of the `<PRE></PRE>` tags, delete the tags, save the change, and reload the file. [Keep your text editor and browser running at the same time. After you delete the tags, save the changes in your text editor to your hard drive and remember where you put it. Then go back to the browser and reload (or refresh) the page to see the effect of the change. To see the effect, you must save the changes *and* reload the page.]

To create a subscript, use `<SUB>` and `</SUB>`; to create a superscript, use `<SUP>` and `</SUP>`. The following example illustrates the use of subscripts and superscripts:

```
<PRE>Suppose judgments of ratios satisfy the following equation,
    R<SUB>ij</SUB> = e<SUP>(s<SUB>i</SUB> - s<SUB>j</SUB>)
    </SUP></PRE>
```

The `<FONT>` tag can be used to set the font face, size, and color. For example, to set the font to *Times,* use `<FONT FACE="Times"></FONT>`. Because the viewer's browser and system must supply the font, you may wish to include a second-choice font, as in the following example: `<FONT FACE="Times,Garamond"></FONT>`. To set the font, size, and color of the font, use the method in the following example:

```
<FONT FACE="Times, Garamond" SIZE="5" COLOR="purple">
Hi! I'm Interested in Research on Twins on the Internet</FONT>
```

Try experimenting with the <FONT> command to achieve different effects. By nesting HTML tags, one can combine fonts with italics, bold, underlining, and other features. These effects are shown in Figures 4.3 and 4.4.

ALIGNING AND FORMATTING PARAGRAPHS

Notice that except for the use of the <PRE> tag, the material is displayed unformatted. Even though the lines with different styles of type were on separate lines, with line returns typed in the file, the browser displays these sentences run together, ignoring blank lines, line returns, and multiple spaces.

When you are not using preformatted text, you need ways to separate paragraphs and make line returns. To produce a line return, use <BR>. Try adding this tag at the end of each sentence illustrating styles. The <BR> tag, like the <HR> tag, does not take a closing tag.

The paragraph tag, <P>, is also a bit of an exception in HTML because the clos-

FIGURE 4.3.   Appearance of *Ch4_ex2.htm* in Navigator. This example illustrates subscripts, superscripts, bold, and italics.

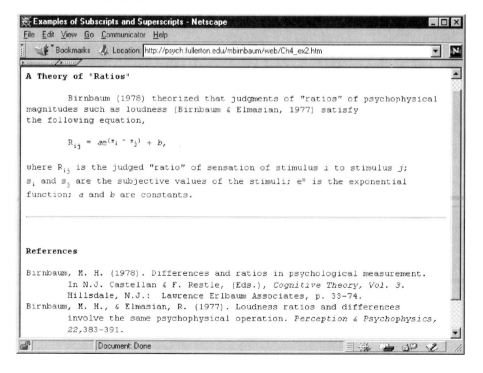

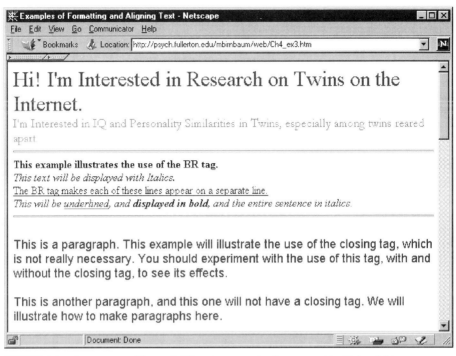

FIGURE 4.4.   Appearance of fonts of different types and colors as used in *Ch4_ex3.htm.*

ing tag, `</P>`, is optional. To format paragraphs, use the `<P>` and `</P>` tags at the beginning and end of the paragraph. If you leave out the ending tag, the next `<P>` establishes the next paragraph. This tag also creates a gap between the text of paragraphs. Example 3 *(Ch4_ex3.htm)* illustrates how to use the paragraph tag. One can also center, align left, or align right with the paragraph tag; for example, `<P ALIGN="center">` centers the text in a paragraph, as illustrated in *Ch4_ex3.htm.*

```
<P ALIGN="right">This paragraph was formatted with ALIGN="right."
```

The default is to `ALIGN="left"`, so no specification, `<P>`, produces the usual left-aligned text.

```
<P ALIGN="Center">This paragraph was formatted with ALIGN="center."
```

Try changing the shape of your browser's window to see the effects on both preformatted text and on paragraphs formatted with differently aligned paragraph tags. When you change the shape of the window, notice the effects on the paragraphs formatted with different alignment.

You will find that preformatted text is frozen under the window (you have to use the scrollbar to see everything), but paragraphs formatted with the `<P>` tag adjust their shape to fit the window.

You can also align sections of text, including multiple paragraphs and including titles and figures, by the *division* tags, `<DIV>` and `</DIV>`, as in the following example:

```
<DIV ALIGN="right">This text will also be aligned right <P>
The DIV tag will carry over from one paragraph to the next, as this
paragraph illustrates. The closing tag is needed to end the
formatting</DIV>.
```

The <BLOCKQUOTE> and </BLOCKQUOTE> tags can be used to create margins around text without having to use tables.

```
<BLOCKQUOTE>This material will be centered, indented with margins on
both the left and the right.</BLOCKQUOTE>
```

Some people find it more attractive or easier to read if there are margins, but realize that someone with a small monitor will be using the scrollbar often to get through your page. Also experiment with the effect of changing the window shape and size on how the text inside BLOCKQUOTE tags is displayed. Nesting BLOCKQUOTE tags, as illustrated in the example on the CD, can create interesting effects, as illustrated in Figure 4.5.

FIGURE 4.5.   Illustration of BLOCKQUOTE tag.

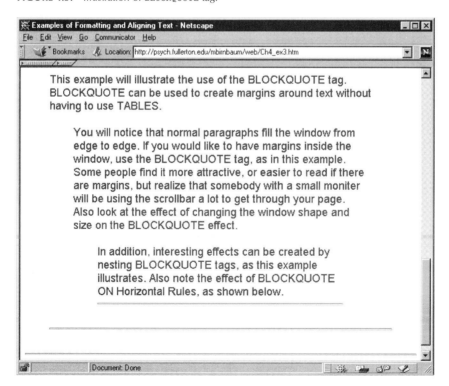

HEADINGS AND LISTS

To create bold headings of different sizes, use the <H1></H1> to <H6></H6> tags. These are illustrated in the following examples:

```
<H1>This is an H1 Heading</H1>
<H4>This is H4 Size Heading</H4>
<H6>This is H6 Size Heading</H6>
```

To center or right-align a heading, nest it inside the DIV tag, as in the following example:

```
<DIV ALIGN="Center"><H1>H1 Heading Centered</H1>
<H3> This Example Illustrates How to Use DIV to Center Headings</H3>
</DIV>
<DIV ALIGN="Right"><H1>H1 Heading Right-Aligned</H1></DIV>
```

You can load *Ch4_ex4.htm* to examine the effects of these tags, which are displayed in Figure 4.6.

Use <UL> and </UL> to create an unnumbered list of bulleted, indented paragraphs. Begin each paragraph with <LI>. The list item tag <LI> is another of those tags that does not require a closing tag. One can nest these <UL> </UL> lists inside one another. The list of examples illustrates how these lists appear. The examples for Chapter 4 illustrate a list within a list.

 ## TABLES

Load *Ch4_ex5.htm*, which illustrates the tags used to create tables. The HTML to create the table is shown in the example below.

```
<TABLE BORDER=12 CELLSPACING=12 CELLPADDING=12>
<TR><TD> </TD> <TD ALIGN=center COLSPAN=2>Column Factor Level </TD>
</TR>
<TR><TD ALIGN=center>Row</TD><TD>Column=1</TD> <TD>Column=2 </TD>
</TR>
<TR><TD>Row=1</TD>      <TD> Row 1 Col 1</TD><TD>Row 1 Col 2</TD></TR>
<TR><TD>Row=2</TD>      <TD> Row 2 Col 2</TD><TD>Row 2 Col 2</TD></TR>
</TABLE>
```

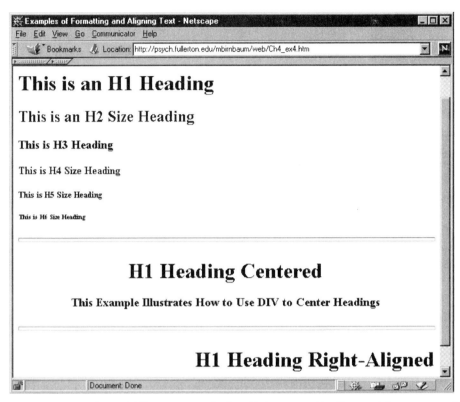

FIGURE 4.6. Headings of different sizes, as displayed in Netscape. Headings are left-, center-, or right-aligned.

The TABLE tag in the example,

```
<TABLE BORDER=12 CELLSPACING=12 CELLPADDING=12>
```

creates a table with large borders, large gaps between the cells, and large space within the cells. To examine the effects of BORDER, CELLSPACING, and CELLPADDING, change each one to zero (one at a time), save to disk, and load from disk into your browser. If you change only one attribute at a time, you will understand the effect of each of these attributes.

For each new row of the table, use the tags, <TR> and </TR>. For each table datum, use <TD> and </TD> tags. To make one cell span two rows, use <TD ROWSPAN=2>. To have one datum span two columns, use <TD COLSPAN=2>, as illustrated in the example, shown in Figure 4.7.

 FRAMES

The technique of frames allows one to subdivide the window. Frames offer some additional power over tables because it is possible to display one HTML file in one frame and another HTML file in another frame. In addition, you can have links in one frame that cause files to be displayed in another frame.

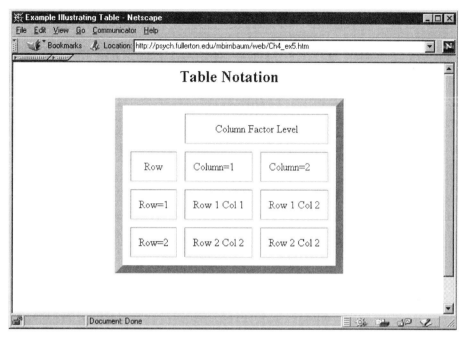

FIGURE 4.7. Illustration of table. Try changing the attributes of the table and observe their effects on the display.

Frames are created and controlled by the `<FRAMESET></FRAMESET>` and `<FRAME>` tags. The `<FRAMESET>` tag can be used to subdivide the screen into two or more pieces, as in the following example:

```
<FRAMESET ROWS="20%,80%">
```

This tag divides the screen into two rows, the first of which occupies 20% of the window. By changing `ROWS` to `COLS`, you can also split the screen into two columns. It is also possible to specify the pixel size of the row, as follows:

```
<FRAMESET ROWS="75,100,*">
```

This tag subdivides the screen into three pieces, the first of 75 pixels, the second of 100 pixels, and the third (`*`) taking up the remainder.

The FRAME tags are nested inside the `<FRAMESET></FRAMESET>` tags. Each FRAME tag defines what file is to be displayed in that frame. The FRAME tag does not require a closing tag. If there are fewer FRAME tags than frames defined in the FRAMESET tag, then the remaining frames will be blank. An example FRAME tag is as follows:

```
<FRAME SRC="filename.htm" NAME="AnyName">
```

The *filename.htm* can be any valid URL. The NAME attribute, which is optional, is used so that links can be used to specify where a document will appear.

Example 6 of Chapter 4 actually uses three files, *Ch4_ex6.htm, Ch4List.htm,* and *Ch4_ex1.htm.* The first file, *Ch4_ex6.htm,* contains the FRAMESET and FRAME tags, as shown on the next page:

```
<HTML>
<HEAD><TITLE> Frames Example</TITLE></HEAD>
<FRAMESET COLS="20%,*" FRAMEBORDER=yes BORDER=20 >
     <FRAME NAME="Lside" SRC="Ch4List.htm">
     <FRAME NAME="Rside" SRC="Ch4_ex1.htm">
</FRAMESET>
</HTML>
```

Note that there are no <BODY></BODY> tags here. Instead, the FRAMESET defines two columns, one of which is 20% of the window. The two frames have been given names that will make it easier to remember which is which.

The links are contained in *Ch4List.htm*. The links now include the attribute TAR-GET. The TARGET attribute can be associated with any link. Because the links are named, the TARGET can specify where to display the linked document. That allows links in one frame to control the appearance of the other frame.

Using TARGET="_blank" creates a new page, which leaves the previous browser window with its frames behind. The following example illustrates this type of link:

```
<A HREF="filename.htm" TARGET="_blank">Click here</A>
```

TABLE 4.1.   Tags Used for Formatting, Tables, and Frames

TAG	DESCRIPTION
`<!   Comments go here...>`	Comment. Everything in here is not displayed.
`<HR SIZE="5">`	Horizontal rule. Creates a horizontal line. Size (optional) creates different widths.
`<PRE></PRE>`	Preformatted text
`<TT></TT>`	Monospaced text
`<B></B>`	Bold text
`<U></U>`	Underlined text
`<I></I>`	Italic text
`<SUB></SUB>`	Subscript
`<SUP></SUP>`	Superscript
`<FONT FACE="font"></FONT>`	Font style. Also use SIZE= and COLOR= to affect size and color of font.
`<P></P>`	Paragraph. Closing tag is not required. Use ALIGN to right-align or to center a paragraph.
` `	Line return
`<BLOCKQUOTE></BLOCKQUOTE>`	Indents margins around text on both sides
`<DIV ALIGN="center"></DIV>`	Divides a page and specifies alignment
`<H1></H1> to <H6></H6>`	Headings of different sizes
`<TABLE BORDER=10></TABLE>`	Establishes a table with wide border. Also use CELLSPACING and CELLPADDING to change the appearance of the table.
`<TR></TR>`	Defines a Table Row
`<TD></TD>`	Table Datum. Use ALIGN=center to center text within a cell.
`<FRAMESET ROWS="100,*">`	Divides the window into two horizontal frames
`</FRAMESET>`	
`<FRAME NAME=name SRC=URL>`	Names the frame and defines the file to be loaded into that frame.

TARGET="_top" also displays the document at the top of the window, but it does not create a new browser window. One can get "stuck" in a frame. To keep a page always at the top, one can include the following little JavaScript routine to break out of FRAMES no matter what document called the file:

```
<BODY OnLoad="if(self !=top) top.location=self.location">
```

This line basically says that when the body of the page loads, if the document is not at the top of the page, then its location should be the top. You will find that any link to the page of examples breaks free of the FRAMES, even though the link did not specify TARGET="_top".

Frames can be useful in certain circumstances. However, in many applications, they can be quite annoying. They limit the effective size of the window, and your reader can get stuck in frames within frames. Use them carefully. An example is shown in Chapter 14, where it is desired to keep a stimulus on the screen in one frame while the participant makes judgments in another frame.

SUMMARY

Table 4.1 summarizes the tags used in this chapter.

EXERCISES

1. Open the file *Ch4_ex1.htm* in your browser. Now open the same file in your text editor (for example, NotePad or SimpleText). Try making changes in the text file, saving the changes, and reloading the page in your browser to see the effects of your changes.
   a. Experiment by removing the <PRE></PRE> tags at the beginning of the file.
   b. Now replace the <PRE> tag, and move the </PRE> tag to just before the </BODY> tag, to see the effect on the text.
2. Try removing the <! from the comment in *Ch4.ex1.htm*. What happens?
3. Open *Ch4_ex2.htm*. Remove the <PRE></PRE> tags, and then use other formatting to arrange the formatting of the file, so that the equation is displayed. Hint: Use <BLOCKQUOTE> to display the equation.
4. Write the following equation with subscripts and superscripts:

$$y_{ij} = a_j b^{1.5} + c_0 + e_i$$

5. Write the HTML to display the following reference:

   Smith, J. B. (1999). The meaning of everything. *Journal of the Association of Psychonomics, 23*, 1–46. Put the underlined text in underlined and italics. Now put the last name in bold type.

6. Load *Ch4_ex3.htm* and *Ch4_ex4.htm* in both the browser and the text editor. Study the examples, to make sure you know how each of the tags works. Now take any page from a book or journal and see if you can make it display properly by means of the HTML tags in Chapters 2–4.
7. Use the tags of this chapter to create two pages: one a personal Web page (for yourself) and the second a page inviting people to participate in an (imaginary) experiment. In your home page, include a link to your experiment's page. In your experiment page, include a link to return to the home page. In both pages, include a link to email. Load each in your browser to view it, and correct your errors until each file displays as you wish. Then upload them to your Web site. Illustrate the links with images, if you like.
8. Take the example of Chapters 2 and 3 (Ann E. Student). Add a centered, size 2 heading to her page. Also, make the font in Helvetica. Now, see if you can add some material that allows you to use all of the tags in Chapters 2–4.

Chapter 5

SURVEYS AND EXPERIMENTS USING FORMS

In the methods of preceding chapters, for you to get information from the person reading your Web pages, you had to wait for the reader to send you a letter, either by postal mail or by email. Chapter 3 described how to use a link to facilitate response by email. However, not everyone who reads your Web pages has email (e.g., a person in a public library); in addition, email is not anonymous.

In this chapter, the real action begins. You learn the technique of *forms,* which allows the viewer to respond directly on the page and send data by clicking a button. Even a person without email can participate if he or she is using a computer connected to the Internet. The method of forms also allows people to remain anonymous. This chapter illustrates these techniques with two classic studies, one on probability reasoning and the other on the St. Petersburg paradox.

 EXAMPLE ILLUSTRATING FORM AND INPUT

The next example illustrates FORM and INPUT tags with a study of reasoning about probability. Consider the HTML in Figure 5.1, which you can load from the CD as *Ch5_exp1.htm.*

There are two new tags used in Figure 5.1 (*Ch5_exp1.htm*): <FORM></FORM> and <INPUT>. These two tags work together to facilitate two-way communication between you and the reader of the page. The <FORM></FORM> tags indicate that the material between contains information that can be displayed in the form or entered by the reader of the page. The INPUT tags allow you to create different instruments for communication. There are two variations of INPUT tags in this example, making three lines to examine more closely.

First, consider the <FORM> tag in the example:

```
<FORM METHOD="post" ACTION="mailto:user@address.domain"
ENCTYPE="text/plain">
```

The METHOD should be set to POST for the examples in this book. The ACTION in this case indicates that when the reader of the form clicks the submit button, then the answers are sent by email to the address given. Change the email address to your own, save it, and try out the page in your browser. If your browser is configured to send email, then you will get an email message with the value that you typed into the form for the INPUT. The attribute ENCTYPE="text/plain" is used here to make the email easier to read.

Second, look at the <INPUT TYPE="text"> tag, which creates a text box for the response:

```
<INPUT TYPE="text" NAME="00answer" SIZE="2" MAXLENGTH="3">%
```

This tag creates a text box that is two characters in width, and it will accept three digits, which allows a person to type in "100." Note that there is a percent sign (%) after the

```
<HTML><HEAD><TITLE>A Problem in Probability</TITLE></HEAD>

<BODY>

<! Change the email address in the line below to your address >

<FORM METHOD="post" ACTION="mailto:user@address.domain" ENCTYPE="text/plain">

<H2>Find the Probability</H2><FONT SIZE=4>

<P>Joe tossed two fair pennies and peeked at them. He said,

<P><FONT COLOR=blue>"At least one is HEADS

 but I won't tell you which." <BR>

What is the probability that the other coin is also HEADS?

<P>Type your probability, expressed as a percentage,

in the box below:<BR>

<INPUT TYPE="text" NAME="00answer" SIZE="2" MAXLENGTH="3">%

<FONT color="black">

<P>Please check your answer. When you are done,

push the button below.

<P><INPUT TYPE="submit" VALUE="I'm done">

<H2>Thank You!</H2>

</FONT></FONT>

</FORM>

<A HREF="answer.htm">To see the answer, click here</A>

</BODY></HTML>
```

FIGURE 5.1.   Listing of *Ch5_exp1.htm.*

box, put there to remind the user that you want a percentage (not a decimal), and also to suggest to the user that he or she need not type in the percent sign (%). If some people enter "%" symbols in the response box and others do not, you must edit them out of your data before data analysis. (For that purpose, you might use the search and replace feature of NotePad to replace all % signs with a null string, i.e., nothing.)

The NAME is the name given to the variable, and this information is sent along with the value to the destination in the ACTION of the form. The message sent, either from Netscape Navigator or Internet Explorer, is the message "00answer=33." If you entered 50, you would get the message "00answer=50."

You may wonder why the variable name begins with two leading zeros. The scripts used in this book create data files in which the data are put in order according to these leading numbers in the variable names. Therefore, for this book you should get used to numbering variables in the order that you want them to appear in the data file, starting with 00, 01, 02, and so on. The order in which the variables appear in the HTML file has no effect in this scheme.

Third, examine the `INPUT` tag that creates a submit button:

```
<INPUT TYPE="submit" VALUE="I'm done">
```

When the user clicks on a form's submit button, the variables defined in the form are sent. The `TYPE="submit"` designates this button as the button that sends the data, the `VALUE` is simply what is printed on the button; the `VALUE` has no effect on the action of the button. A similar button is the `"reset"` button, which erases everything from the form when it is pushed. It has the following tag:

```
<INPUT TYPE="reset" VALUE="erase the form">
```

There are other ways to request input besides `<INPUT TYPE="text">`, and these are covered later in this chapter. The appearance of the page in Netscape is shown in Figure 5.2.

When the person using this page clicks on the link at the bottom of the page, the link brings up a page that presents the correct solution, listed in Figure 5.3. There is nothing really new in Figure 5.3 besides the correct answer, which is that the correct probability is one third, or 33%. This example is sometimes considered a "trick" ques-

FIGURE 5.2.   Appearance of the text box and submit button in Netscape for example *Ch5_exp1.htm.*

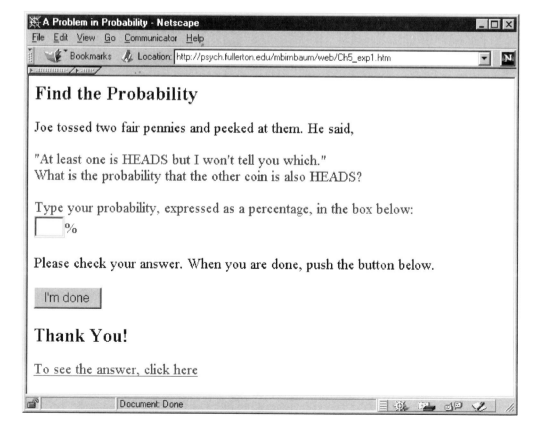

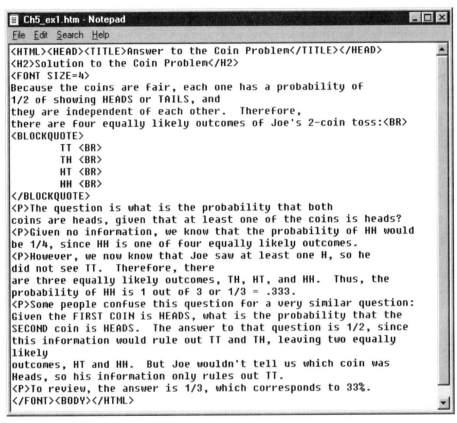

FIGURE 5.3.   HTML for a page of debriefing, which gives the correct answer.

tion in classes on reasoning and problem solving or statistics. The trick, if there is one, is a weakness among people who are unschooled in probability to jump to conclusions without working out the solution by counting the equally likely possibilities. As noted in Figure 5.3, 50% is the right answer to the wrong question.

This "test" has a number of problems, however. Note that our student could have clicked the link to the answer, then used the BACK button to return to the page, and then entered the correct answer. This procedure might be fine for a computerized tutorial, but it would not be very good procedure for a test because it allows people to "cheat." It would also not be good procedure for an experiment that was designed to find out the proportion in the population who can figure out the correct answer on their own.

Also, with any real experiment that has hundreds or even thousands of participants, it would be quite a nuisance to get the data in the form of so many separate email messages.

The solution to these problems is the CGI (Common Gateway Interface) script, which allows the server to process and save the data, which saves you the worry of dealing with all those emails.

USING A SCRIPT TO PROCESS DATA

Change the FORM tag in *Ch5_exp1.htm* as follows:

```
<FORM METHOD="POST" ACTION="http://psych.fullerton.edu/cgi-
win/polyform.exe/generic">
```

Now when the user clicks the submit button, the data are sent to a script that resides at the above address. This script processes the data, puts them in order of the numbers that precede the variable names, and puts them in a file called *data.csv*. The script then sends the user to a URL that delivers a generic "Thank you for serving in a student's experiment" message. You can test if you have correctly entered the script address by pushing the *Submit* button and seeing if you receive the *Thank you* message. This new variation of the FORM tag is used in *Ch5_exp2.htm*. The ENCTYPE attribute is not used with the scripts in this book.

The script residing at the address above sends data to a file, *data.csv*, on the *psych.fullerton.edu* server, from which you can retrieve the file by FTP, as described in Chapter 2. Therefore, you can practice running experiments with this script to put your data in a file that you can examine. Try it. Enter a "strange" number or some letters, download the file, and look for your "strange" data at the end of the file.

When you start doing serious experimentation, you will eventually want your own script(s) so that you will not be dependent on our server. With your own script, you can save data on your local server. You can get your scripts in one of several ways.

First, you can ask the person who runs your department's server for a script you can use. If you are a student in a lab, your instructor may arrange one or more scripts for students to use. If you have an account with an Internet service provider, your provider can supply a script for you and give you additional instructions on how to use it. Your provider's script will probably support adding such variables as date and time to your data file.

Second, you can write a script yourself for your server in a CGI language such as *Perl* (Practical Extraction and Reporting Language), which can be downloaded free [http://www.perl.com/CPAN/]. Schwartz (1998) has written a tutorial on Perl describing its advantages for this purpose. A script in Perl that will work with the examples of this book is included on the CD (Appendix A).

Third, you can use a program to create scripts for you, such as PolyForm [http://software.ora.com/download/], or WWW Survey Assistant (Schmidt, 1997; URL [http://survey.psy. buffalo.edu/]).

The generic protocols used in this book were made with PolyForm, which creates scripts for a Windows NT server [http://polyform.ora.com/book/]. Appendix A gives more information about scripts, including a discussion of how to use PolyForm. Until you get your own scripts, you are welcome to use the address here and download your data from *psych.fullerton.edu* by FTP.

 ## HIDDEN VARIABLES

Hidden variables can be added with the following tag:

```
<INPUT TYPE="hidden" NAME="00exp" VALUE="Ch5_exp3">
```

This variable will not be displayed to the viewer of the page (but it can be seen in the page source HTML). Hidden variables can be added to the data file to keep track of such things as the name of the experiment and the condition that the subject received. For example, a hidden variable might identify "Condition A" or "Condition B" in a between-subjects design, in which different people send their data from different Web pages (each presenting different conditions) to the same script. As with any variable, it must have a name and a value. Hidden variables can also be used to hold the date, time, and other information (Appendix A). The VALUE is returned as datum.

The scripts used in this book support insertion of date, time, and the Remote Address (IP) from which the data are sent (this is a number such as, 137.151.76.48). To insert the time and date, for example, use the following hidden variables:

```
<INPUT TYPE="hidden" NAME="02date" VALUE="pfDate">
<INPUT TYPE="hidden" NAME="03time" VALUE="pfTime">
```

The script replaces the values pfDate and pfTime with the actual date and time that the *submit* button was pressed, according to the clock on the server. For remote address, use pfRemoteAddress; both capitalization and spelling must be exactly as shown.

RADIO BUTTONS

Radio buttons are a very useful method for collecting data. They are also convenient for the participant, because they only require a point and click, without typing. In the following example, the participant is asked to indicate his or her gender (M or F). Although gender has two levels, you should use three radio buttons, as follows:

```
<P><INPUT TYPE="radio" NAME="02sex" VALUE="" CHECKED>
What is your gender?<BR>
<BLOCKQUOTE><INPUT TYPE="radio" NAME="02sex" VALUE="M">Male<BR>
            <INPUT TYPE="radio" NAME="02sex" VALUE="F">Female<BR>
</BLOCKQUOTE>
```

The reason to use three buttons instead of two is that some participants may not answer. If so, then you do not want to wrongly put down either male or female for them. Therefore, you should add an extra radio button that is initially checked, whose value will be null (i.e., "") unless the subject clicks either male or female.

In this example, the values M and F were assigned to male and female, but it would be just as clear to use 1 and 0. Think ahead to how the data will be analyzed. If you plan to compute a correlation coefficient between gender and a numerical variable, you should use numerical values such as 1 and 0 to code gender. If you plan to count frequencies of certain behaviors by males and females in a table, however, then the table may be easier to read if you use verbal labels such as *Male* and *Female*, or M and F.

The new version of the experiment, *Ch5_exp3.htm*, illustrates hidden variables and radio buttons. Data for this version are analyzed in Chapter 6.

```
<FORM METHOD="POST" ACTION="http://psych.fullerton.edu/cgi-win/
polyform.exe/generic">
<INPUT TYPE="hidden" NAME="00exp" VALUE="Ch5_exp3">
<INPUT TYPE="text" NAME="01answer" SIZE="2" MAXLENGTH="3">%
<FONT color="black">
<INPUT TYPE="hidden" NAME="02exp" VALUE="Prob Study 1">
<P><INPUT TYPE="radio" NAME="03sex" VALUE="" CHECKED>What is your
gender?<BR>
<BLOCKQUOTE><INPUT TYPE="radio" NAME="03sex" VALUE="M">Male<BR>
          <INPUT TYPE="radio" NAME="03sex" VALUE="F">Female<BR>
</BLOCKQUOTE>
<P>Please check your answer. When you are done,
push the button below.
<P><INPUT TYPE="submit" VALUE="I'm done">
<H2>Thank You!</H2>
</FONT>
</FORM>
```

Each group of radio buttons is connected by the same NAME. Only one button in a group can be CHECKED at a time; clicking one deselects the previously checked item. Radio buttons are easy for the subject to use for choices between two or more alternatives. They are the natural way to put multiple-choice tests, including True/False, on the computer. Rating scales (e.g., Likert scales) used for attitude questionnaires or personality tests can also be well implemented using radio buttons. Figure 5.4 shows the appearance of the set of three radio buttons. Note that the one in the margin next to the question has a black dot. When the reader clicks on one of the buttons, the dot moves to the selected button.

HTML also supports a data input method known as the *checkbox,* described next for the purpose of understanding only. I strongly advise you: Do not use checkboxes! Anything that you can do with a checkbox you can do better by using two or three radio buttons. With two radio buttons, one radio button can represent nonselected ("No") and the other radio button represents the "checked" alternative ("Yes"). With three radio buttons, one can represent "Yes," one "No," and the third can be "No response." That way you can distinguish three possibilities by asking the subject to click once. Another problem with checkboxes is that when they are not checked, they often send nothing. That can create havoc when you go to analyze the data with most data analysis packages because the variables are not in the same columns. Take my advice: Use radio buttons instead of checkboxes in research.

TEXTAREAS, PASSWORDS, AND CHECKBOXES

For a short answer consisting of a few words, the text box is best (SIZE=60 or 100 characters). However, sometimes you may want to invite the participant to give a lengthy answer of a paragraph or more. Textareas are ideal for this situation. Here is an example that illustrates the textarea:

```
<TEXTAREA NAME="03Comments" ROWS=5 COLS=60
WRAP=virtual>text</TEXTAREA>
```

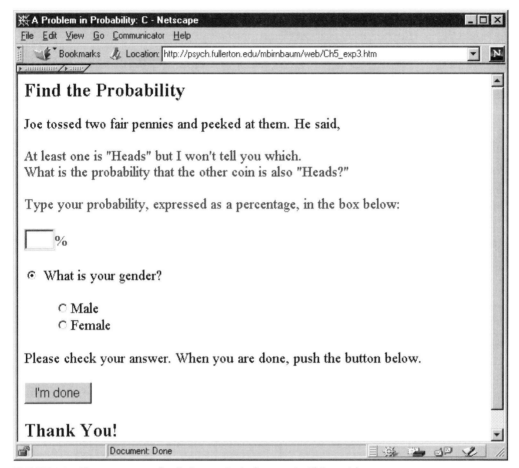

FIGURE 5.4.   The appearance of radio buttons in the browser in *Ch5_exp3.htm*.

Note that there is a closing tag, `</TEXTAREA>`, that includes text to be displayed in the box, which is usually something like, "Please type your answer in this box."

The password Input tag is useful for obtaining a response that a person would not want seen if someone were looking over his or her shoulder. A password is one example, and a sensitive or personal question might be another. The following example illustrates its use:

```
<INPUT TYPE="password" NAME="04Password" SIZE=10 MAXLENGTH=15>
```

The password input tag works just like text input, except that it displays asterisks or dots instead of characters in the box on the screen.

The checkbox can be made as follows:

```
<INPUT TYPE="checkbox" CHECKED>
```

The checkbox is either initially checked or not. With this response device, it is not possible to distinguish a failure to respond (because the person did not read the question) from a decision not to check the box. Also, this input device may send nothing (not even a null response) when it is left unchecked. Example *Ch5_exp3b.htm* illustrates this problem. Try leaving both checkboxes blank; then check both and compare the data.

PULL-DOWN SELECTIONS

A selection list works like a pull-down menu. When the participant clicks on the list, the list appears, and the participant can drag the mouse to select an answer from the list of responses. Pull-down selections are interesting because there is a lot of potential psychology in how an experimenter might bias the answers he or she gets by changing the choices on the list or the manner in which they are displayed. This response procedure is appropriate when there is a clear, finite set of all possible answers. This procedure can also be used for multiple-choice items. The HTML for a pull-down selection list is in Figure 5.5.

An illustration of the various methods for responding is in *Ch5_exp3b.htm* on the CD. Play with this example to study how these response devices work. Note that in the selection lists, a clear nonanswer is preselected.

You may also find the psychology of response procedures interesting, and you may want to join psychologists who are studying the psychophysical and judgmental processes that affect how people respond when presented with different types of response devices. Schwarz (1999) reviews literature showing that how the question is asked, including the choices of responses, strongly affects the answers found in questionnaire studies.

FIGURE 5.5. HTML for a pull-down selection list, in Condition 512.

```
<SELECT NAME="01amount">

      <OPTION VALUE="0" SELECTED>0

      <OPTION VALUE="1">1

      <OPTION VALUE="2">2

      <OPTION VALUE="4">4

      <OPTION VALUE="8">8

      <OPTION VALUE="16">16

      <OPTION VALUE="32">32

      <OPTION VALUE="64">64

      <OPTION VALUE="128">128

      <OPTION VALUE="256">256

      <OPTION VALUE="512">512

</SELECT>
```

ST. PETERSBURG PARADOX AND SELECTION LISTS

This section presents an experiment on the classic St. Petersburg Paradox to illustrate how pull-down lists work and also to investigate how they might bias the results in certain situations. The St. Petersburg Paradox was originally posed as a mathematical problem, and was answered in 1738 in a classic paper by Daniel Bernoulli.

There is a gamble that has an infinite expected value, yet people prefer gambles with much lower expected value. Here is how the gamble works: A coin is tossed, and if it is heads, you win $2; if it is tails, however, then it is tossed again. Now if it is heads, you win $4, but if tails, then it is tossed again, and heads on the next toss would win $8. Each time tails occurs, the prize for heads on the next toss doubles, and so on forever. How much would you pay to play this gamble once? Would you rather play this gamble once, or have $15 for sure?

The expected value of the St. Petersburg gamble is one-half times $2 plus one-fourth times $4 plus one-eighth times $8 plus, and so on forever. Therefore, the expected value is the sum of an infinite number of $1's. Thus, if you value the gamble at its expected value, you should prefer playing this gamble once to receiving any finite amount of money.

Bernoulli (1738) gave a solution to the St. Petersburg Paradox. He argued that although the expected value is infinite, this gamble is worth only $4, for psychological reasons. Bernoulli theorized that if the subjective value of money ("utility" of money) is logarithmically related to objective money, then the gamble has a finite worth. This idea influenced Gustav Fechner, whose work on psychophysical measurement led directly to the creation of the field of psychology. The idea of diminishing marginal "utility" of money also had considerable impact in the field of economics as well. You will learn more about Bernoulli's expected utility theory of decision making in Chapter 8, and more about Fechner in Chapter 14.

The experiment in Figure 5.5 shows the HTML for one condition (Condition 512) of an experiment to investigate both the St. Petersburg Paradox and the effect of the options in a selection list.

Another condition of the experiment is listed in Figure 5.6. In contrast with Figure 5.5's version of the experiment, this variation (*Ch5_exp4.htm*) uses a different selection list, with 11 equally spaced values from $0 to $10.

Selection lists can also appear as a box with a scroll bar, which you control with the SIZE attribute. Try changing the <SELECT> tag in the previous example as follows:

```
<SELECT NAME="01amount" SIZE=3>
```

SIZE determines the number of options showing in the scroll window. Try changing the value of SIZE in the example of Figure 5.6 to see its effect. The appearance of a pull-down selection list is shown in Figure 5.7.

Different values of SIZE might interact with the options given in a selection list to produce different responses from participants. Perhaps options that show without scrolling are more likely to be selected than options that require a considerable time to reach by scrolling. As a psychologist, you should be concerned that the results might be affected by biases produced by response formats presented to participants. One type of bias to avoid is the use of a reasonable answer as a preselected option. Always code the default option as a nonresponse so that your participant must act to make a response. Otherwise, the study will be biased to confirm the choices set as defaults in the HTML.

```
Ch5_exp4.htm - Notepad

File  Edit  Search  Help

The St. Petersburg gamble is played as follows: A fair coin
will be tossed, and if it is HEADS, you win $2 and the game
is over. If it is TAILS,
the coin is tossed again, and now if it is HEADS, you win $4.
If TAILS, it is tossed again, and this time HEADS pays $8.
The gamble doubles in value each time TAILS occurs, but once
HEADS occurs, it pays off and the game is over.
This gamble could go on forever and ever, doubling
its payoff for each TAILS. However, the probability of
ending at $2 is 1/2;the probability of ending at $4 is 1/4;
the probability of ending at $8 is 1/8;
and the probability halves each time,
just as the winning doubles.

<FORM METHOD="POST"
ACTION="http://psych.fullerton.edu/cgi-win/polyform.exe/generic">
<FONT color="black">
<INPUT TYPE="hidden" NAME="00Ch5_exp4" VALUE="Ch5_exp4_StPete1-10">
<P>What is the most you would pay (in dollars) for
the chance to play the
St. Petersburg gamble once?<BR>
$<SELECT NAME="01amount">
        <OPTION VALUE="0" SELECTED>0
        <OPTION VALUE="1">1
        <OPTION VALUE="2">2
        <OPTION VALUE="3">3
        <OPTION VALUE="4">4
        <OPTION VALUE="5">5
        <OPTION VALUE="6">6
        <OPTION VALUE="7">7
        <OPTION VALUE="8">8
        <OPTION VALUE="9">9
        <OPTION VALUE="10">10
</SELECT>
```

FIGURE 5.6.   A portion of the HTML for *Ch5_exp4.htm.*

Here is the question: Do you think that Condition 10 (equally spaced options from $0 to $10) and Condition 512 (geometrically spaced options from $1 to $512) would produce the same results? Notice that Condition 10 has a maximum of $10, but Condition 512 has a maximum of $512. It seems reasonable to predict that the mean judgment of value will be greater in Condition 512 than in Condition 10. Any participants who might have been willing to say the gamble is worth more than $10 cannot express it in *Ch5_exp4.htm*, but they can go as high as $512 in *Ch5_exp5.htm*.

If anyone wanted to say the gamble was worth, for instance, $6400, that person would not be able to express this response with *either* of the option lists of these experiments. Do you think the experiment would yield different results if, instead of pull-down selections, you used a text box to ask how much a person would pay to play the gamble? You might think it would not introduce any bias to just ask in a text box what

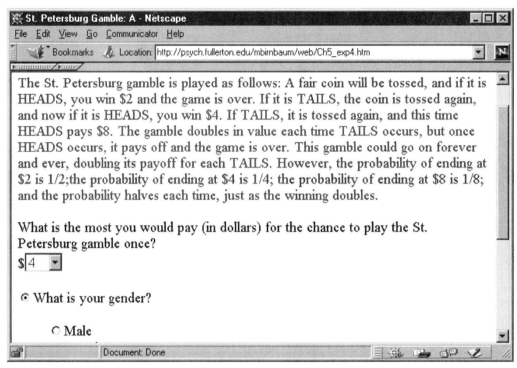

FIGURE 5.7.   Appearance of a pull-down menu in *Ch5_exp4.htm* or *Ch5_exp5.htm*. Clicking on the arrow brings up a finite list of responses. Such a list might bias the response.

the gamble is worth. However, even a text box will have a size (in columns) that gives the participant an idea of how big a number they are expected to enter.

To allow people to enter a large number, you can display 30 columns in the text box and allow 40, as follows:

```
<INPUT TYPE="text" NAME="01amount" SIZE=30 MAXLENGTH=40>
```

This INPUT tag is used instead of the pull-down lists in *Ch5_exp6.htm*. The next section describes a mechanism for assigning people to different versions of the experiment, *Ch5_exp4* through *Ch5_exp6*.

 BETWEEN-SUBJECTS EXPERIMENT

The file *Ch5_exp7.htm* contains a simple method for assignment to conditions in a between-subjects experiment. People are invited to click the month of their birth, and then are assigned to *Ch5_exp4.htm*, *Ch5_exp5.htm*, or *Ch5_exp6.htm*, depending on which month they click. To remove any effect of astrological horoscope on the data, you should counterbalance the relationship between months and experiments during the

```
<HTML><HEAD>
<TITLE>St.Petersburg Gamble</TITLE></HEAD>
<H2>Please click on the of your birth below</H2>month
<B><PRE>
</B><AHREF="Ch5_exp4.htm"><B>Jan          April       July        Oct</B></A>
<AHREF="Ch5_exp5.htm"><B>     Feb      May         Aug         Nov</B></A>
<AHREF="Ch5_exp6.htm"><B>          Mar     June     Sept      Dec</B></A>
</PRE></BODY></HTML>
```

FIGURE 5.8. Web page to assign people to conditions to investigate the effect of response procedures. The connection between birth months and conditions is counterbalanced over the run of the experiment. A method of random assignment using JavaScript is presented in Chapter 17.

experiment, so that an equal number of people from each birth month eventually end up in each condition (see Chapter 1). You can then separate the effect of horoscope from the effects of the conditions.

At one time, people believed that mechanisms such as the outcome of rolling dice or time and date of a person's birth were caused by the same forces that ruled the universe, so dice rolls or birthdates were believed useful for predicting future events. Based on considerable evidence with these mechanisms, however, scientists now treat such mechanisms as definitions of randomness. The HTML for this method of assignment is in Figure 5.8.

TABLE 5.1. Summary of Tags in Chapter 5

TAG	DESCRIPTION
`<FORM></FORM>`	Material within these tags can contain fields for two-way communication.
`ACTION=URL`	Data are sent to URL to be processed by the script residing at the address.
`ACTION="mailto:user@address.ext"`	Data from the FORM are sent by email when the participant clicks the "submit" button. `ENCTYPE="text/plain"` improves the appearance of the email.
`<INPUT TYPE=text NAME=varname SIZE=3 MAXLENGTH=5>`	Defines an instrument for communicating with a text box of size 3 with room for 5 characters.
`<INPUT TYPE=radio NAME=varname VALUE=x>`	Creates a radio button whose value is x if the button is clicked.
`<SELECT>` `<OPTION VALUE="x">Option 1 label` `<OPTION VALUE="y">Option 2 label` `</SELECT>`	Defines a selection list. Each option has a value and a description.
`<TEXTAREA NAME=varname ROWS=r COLS=c WRAP=virtual> Anytext </TEXTAREA>`	Creates a textarea that is r rows by c columns. *Anytext* appears in the textarea.
`<INPUT TYPE=reset VALUE="erase">`	Creates a button that clears the form.
`<INPUT TYPE=submit VALUE="Done">`	Creates a submit button that says *Done*.
`<INPUT TYPE=password SIZE=8 MAXLENGTH=8 NAME=varname>`	Creates a text box that does not display the response

SUMMARY

In this chapter, you learned that by placing a form within a Web page, you can collect data via the Web, either by email or by sending the data to a CGI script that can save the data to the server. With a script to organize and save the data, the Web experiment or survey eliminates the need for an experimenter to be present, or for a researcher to code and enter data.

This chapter described different methods for eliciting responses from subjects, including text boxes (which can be used for either numerical or short answers), radio buttons (which can be used for Likert scales, multiple choice, etc.), textareas, and selection lists. It was recommended that you use radio buttons instead of checkboxes, and that you use TEXT boxes when there is a large set of possible answers. The selection list is appropriate when there is a finite list of possibilities, such as choosing one's nationality from a finite list of nations. In the next chapter, you learn that the choices in a selection list do influence the results.

Table 5.1 summarizes the tags in this chapter.

 EXERCISES

1. Use your text editor to modify *Ch5_exp1.htm* in Figure 5.1. Put your own email address in the ACTION="mailto:*user@address.domain*". See if your browser will send you the data by email. If it does, then you can use this method to check your experiments before you really need a script. ENCTYPE="text/plain" is not necessary, but makes the email look neater. Repeat with *Ch5_exp3.htm* and *Ch5_exp3b.htm*.

2. Now change the ACTION to the URL of the generic script in *Ch5_exp2.htm*. Delete ENCTYPE= "text/plain". Load the HTML page into your browser and click the "I'm done" button. If you get a "Thank You" message, then everything has worked, and your data should be available for viewing, along with much other data from a mix of experiments, in the file *data.csv*, which you can download from *psych.fullerton.edu* using your FTP program. Instructions are given in Chapter 2. Your data will be added to the end of the file.

3. Write the HTML to use radio buttons to collect the poll question of Chapter 3, Exercise 1. Include a third button so that you will know if the participant failed to respond.

4. Perform the exercise in *Ch5_exp3b.htm* and study the example. Next, make your own form that has at least one example of each of the following input devices: text box, radio buttons, textarea, password, and pull-down selection list. Include hidden variables of survey's name (name it "*00exp*"), date, and time. Include submit and reset buttons. Check that your form works with the generic script and that your data are properly returned to the file. Check to see if the time and date are correct. Remember, the clock is set by Pacific time.

5. Check with your Internet service providers or your local server administrator to see if you can get help with scripts to process and save your data. In the meantime, you can use the generic script to test the examples in this book and pilot studies (see Appendix A).

Chapter 6

DATA ANALYSIS WITH EXCEL AND SPSS

This chapter introduces techniques of data analysis. You learn about Excel and SPSS, two programs widely used by psychologists and others to analyze data. You learn how to import data from a Web experiment into Excel, how to filter the data, and how to perform simple analyses. You learn how to import data to SPSS and how to carry out cross-tabs in SPSS. If you plan graduate work in psychology, then you will eventually learn both of these programs. SPSS and Excel can do many of the same tasks, but each program has advantages for certain tasks. If you are an undergraduate, your instructor may choose to focus on one of these programs and leave the other for a future course. It is well worth learning both programs if you plan to study in graduate school or to join the workforce in a job in which financial records, client records, tables, data, or charts are to be analyzed.

 ## INTRODUCTION TO EXCEL

Excel is a powerful spreadsheet program that can be used to perform many mathematical and statistical calculations. It also supports graphing of data. Start Excel and examine the window, which resembles that in Figure 6.1.

When you start the program, your toolbars may differ from those displayed in Figure 6.1. That is because there are many different toolbars that may either be displayed or hidden, and they can also be moved around the screen. Pull down the **View** menu, as shown in Figure 6.1, and be sure that the *Formula Bar, Status Bar, Standard Toolbar,* and *Formatting Toolbar* are all checked. You can experiment by selecting these different toolbars (which toggles them on and off) and examine the effects on the display. The toolbars can also be moved around the screen, which also changes the appearance of the window. To move one of the toolbars, click your arrow pointer on the handle at the left and drag the toolbar around the screen to where you want it. Now that you know how to display and move the toolbars, you can make your screen match what is shown in the book. You can also get help from the **Help** menu or by clicking on the question mark icon on the Standard Toolbar. From **Help,** you can select an "assistant" to offer advice for using the program. When you are trying new tasks in Excel, it may be of help to keep the assistant on the screen, as the assistant offers suggestions pertaining to the tasks you are doing. Clicking the assistant brings up Help screens.

Note that the spreadsheet (the grid) is labeled with letters for columns and numbers for rows. A particular cell is designated by its column letter and its row number. For example, A1 is the first cell in the upper, left-hand corner of the spreadsheet; A2 is the cell directly below A1. B1 is the cell in the next column, directly to the right of A1, and so on. A range of cells is designated by its upper-left and lower-right corner cells, separated by a colon. For example, A1:C5 refers to the 15 cells from A1 to A5, B1 to B5, and C1 to C5.

Suppose you measured the heights and weights of students in a class. You could enter the data for each case (i.e., each person) in a separate row, and use a different column for each variable (the person's name, height, and weight).

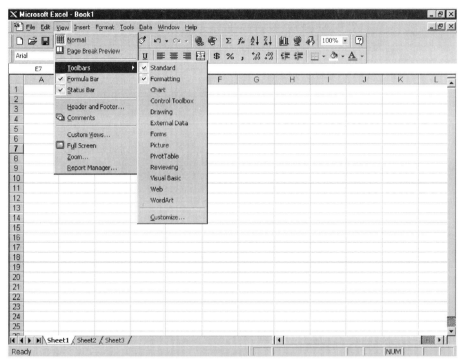

FIGURE 6.1.   The **View** menu in Excel can be used to display the Formula Bar, Status Bar, Standard Tool-bar, and Formatting Toolbar. If these are not checked, use the **View** menu to select them. You can also get help from the **Help** menu.

Figure 6.2 shows data obtained from eight students who had their heights measured (in inches) and weights measured (in pounds). Note that the first row has been used to label the variables as *name, height*, and *weight*. Type the same values into your spreadsheet. After typing each value, you can push either *Enter* or *Tab*. If you push *Tab*, the datum is entered and the selected cell moves to the right. If you push *Enter*, the datum is entered and the selected cell drops to the next row.

Saving Excel Data

To save the data, select *Save As* from the **File** menu. Excel allows you to save your data in many different formats. On the Save dialog, near the bottom, appears the *Save as type* box. Click the drop down arrow, and select *Microsoft Excel Workbook*. Give the file the name *heights.xls*. (On a PC, the *.xls* extension will be added for you; on a Mac, you should add it yourself.)

The Excel workbook contains three worksheets. You can click back and forth to view the three worksheets by clicking the tabs at the bottom of the window for *Sheet1*, *Sheet2*, and *Sheet3*. For now, only the first sheet has data, and the others are empty.

You can also save (one worksheet at a time) in Comma Separated Value (CSV) format. This format is very useful because CSV files can be imported to a text editor such as NotePad or SimpleText. Files in CSV format can also be imported easily to Excel, SPSS, and many other programs. When you save data from Excel into CSV format, you should first save your data (give it a different name) as an Excel workbook, because CSV

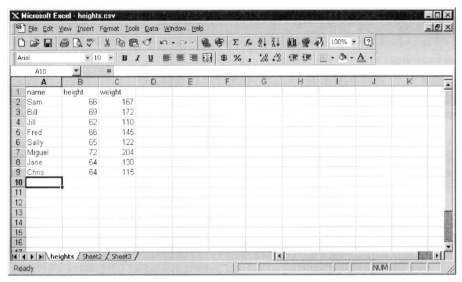

FIGURE 6.2. Entering data in Excel. Note that numerical data are right-justified and alphabetical data (the names) are left-justified. After typing each datum, push either *Enter* or *Tab*. This workbook was saved as *heights.xls*, and this worksheet was saved as *heights.csv*.

files do not contain all of the information that may be in a workbook. When you save as CSV, the program warns you that you may lose information. If you have already saved it as a workbook, you can go ahead and save as CSV.

To save a worksheet in CSV format, be sure you are looking at the worksheet you want to save (click the tabs at the bottom to switch from sheet to sheet). Then select *Save As* from the **File** menu. Next, choose *CSV* (*Comma delimited*) from the *Save as type* drop down list. Give the file the name *heights.csv* to distinguish it from the workbook *heights.xls*. Once you have saved the file, you can close it in Excel and open it in NotePad or another text editor. In the text editor, you will see that the file is a very simple text file with the variable names in the first line, and each case is on a separate line, as shown in Figure 6.3. In each line, commas separate the values.

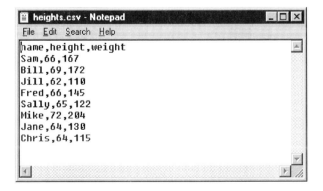

Figure 6.3. Appearance of the file *heights.csv*.

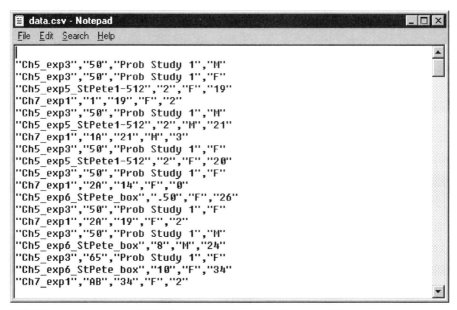

FIGURE 6.4. Appearance of file *data.csv* containing data from several experiments. Note that each value is in quotes and commas separate the values. This type of file can be imported to many spreadsheet and statistical programs.

DOWNLOAD THE DATA

If you use the generic script of Chapter 5, your data are sent to the file *data.csv* on the *psych.fullerton.edu* server. The next task, therefore, is to download these data and filter them to separate data from different studies.

First, use FTP to download the file *data.csv* from the *psych.fullerton.edu* server, using the method you learned in Chapter 2. Next, open the file in a text editor such as NotePad. Remember, when using NotePad (and other PC applications), you need to select "All files" (for *Files of type*), or the *Open file* dialog will not display files ending in *.csv*. The file *data.csv* changes as new experiments are added and as old data are cleaned out from time to time, so the appearance of the file may be different when you open the file from how it appears in Figure 6.4.

FILTERING WITH EXCEL

As you can see in Figure 6.4, there are data from different experiments in the same file. The next task, therefore, is to filter the data to separate data by experiments. You can do that easily with Excel. Start Excel and choose *Open* from the **File** menu. Then select *All Files (*.*)* from *Files of type* in the *Open* dialog, to see the files displayed as in Figure 6.5.

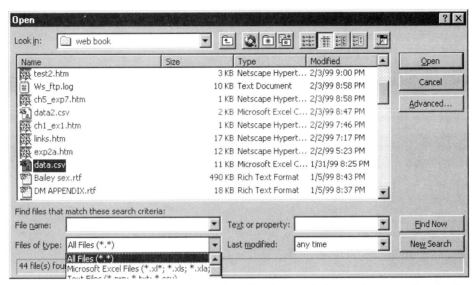

FIGURE 6.5.   *Open file* dialog in Excel. Note that *Files of type: All Files (*.*)* has been selected; otherwise, *data.csv* would not be displayed in the window.

The file appears as in Figure 6.6. The next step is to put variable names in the first row. Name the first column, **Exp,** for experiment, then type **X1** in the next column (in Cell B1). Press the Enter key. To make a cell entry bold, click on the cell and then click the **B** on the Formatting Toolbar. Now, click on **X1** and put your mouse pointer in the lower-right corner of cell B1 (with **X1** in it) until the arrow turns into a "**+**" (like a plus sign), then click and drag to the right for 31 columns. That trick is called *AutoFill*, and it allows you to name the variables **X1** to **X31** without having to type them all in.

The next step is to filter the data. Click in cell A1, then select from the **Data** menu *Filters*, then *Autofilters*, as shown in Figure 6.7. Drop-down filter arrows will appear in the first row. By clicking on one of these arrows and selecting one of the choices, the data are filtered to display only those records with the chosen value.

For example, you can look only at the data from *Ch5_exp3* by selecting that from the drop-down list in the first column. Recall that in *Ch5_exp3*, the problem was to judge the probability that the other coin is heads if Joe tossed two coins and said "at least one" is heads. The correct answer is 33 and a popular wrong answer is 50. By filtering now on the second column as well as the first, you will see how many people chose 33 as the right answer, or how many chose 50. Realize that the other data are still there; they are just hidden when filtered.

FILTER THE PROBABILITY DATA

The rest of this chapter is devoted to analysis of data from experiments in Chapter 5.

The next section presents an analysis of data that are included on your CD. You should follow along with your computer. From Excel, open the file *clean.csv* from the

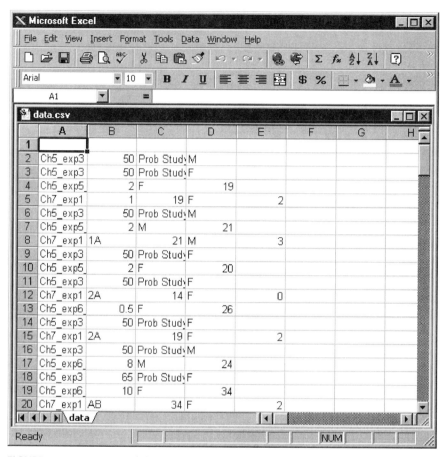

FIGURE 6.6.   Appearance of *data.csv* in Excel. The next step is to enter column labels in the first row.

folder of data files on the CD and save it on your hard drive (or Zip drive) as an Excel Workbook, using *Save As* from the **File** menu. It will now have the extension *.xls*. Remember where you put it. Notice that this file already has names in the first row (those names are used in Chapter 8). Now click in cell A1 and select *Filter, Autofilters* from the **Data** menu, as in Figure 6.7. In the first column, click on the filter arrow and select *Ch5_exp3* from the drop-down select list. That brings up the screen shown in Figure 6.8.

    Now click in the second row (labeled 52) in column A, and drag the mouse to the right and down to the lower-right corner of the data. That selects columns A through D and rows from the second row (row 52) through the end (row 1395)—it will look like ants crawling on the screen, showing what has been selected. Then select *Copy* from the **Edit** menu. Next, from the **Insert** menu, select *Worksheet,* and a new worksheet will appear. Click in cell A2 on the new worksheet, and then select *Paste* from the **Edit** menu. The data for the probability study should now appear in the new worksheet. Now type

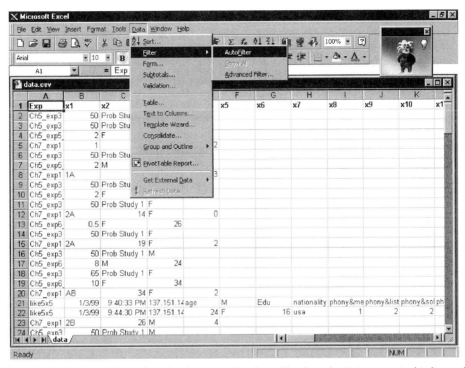

FIGURE 6.7. With cell A1 selected, select *AutoFilter* from *Filter* from the **Data** menu. In this figure, the assistant (cartoon of Einstein) has a light-bulb, indicating an offer of help. Click on the cartoon and you will receive advice that is often pertinent to your current actions. You can also click it anytime for help.

in the correct column labels for the probability experiment, which are **Exp, Answer, Title,** and **Sex.** The result is shown in Figure 6.9.

Next, double click on the tab at the bottom of the new worksheet, *Sheet1*, and rename it *Ch5_exp3*. A single click on the tab labeled *clean* takes you back to the sheet that contains all of the data. Repeat this process to select the data for the St. Petersburg study (*Ch5_exp4*, *Ch5_exp5*, and *Ch5_exp6*) and paste each set of selected data into a separate worksheet.

A PIVOT TABLE FOR THE PROBABILITY PROBLEM

The experiment title (*Prob Study*) in column C is always the same, so there would be no loss to delete it. You can delete column C by clicking on the **C** at the top of the column (which highlights the column) and then choosing *Delete* from the **Edit** menu. Be careful not to delete the whole sheet! If you do make a mistake in Excel, you can undo it (except in certain cases). To undo something, you can select *Undo* from the **Edit** menu (you can also click the Undo arrow, which curves to the left, from the toolbar; if that ar-

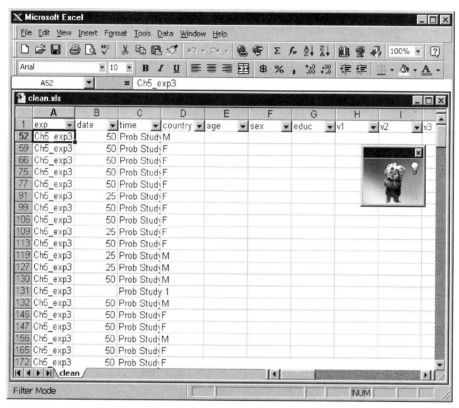

FIGURE 6.8. Open the file *clean.csv* and save it as an Excel workbook. Then select from the **Data** menu, *Filter...AutoFilters*. Then filter *exp* (column A) for *Ch5_exp3*. All records with *Ch5_exp3* in the first column are displayed, and other rows of data are hidden. Copy the displayed (filtered) data to a fresh worksheet.

row is dimmed, you cannot Undo). You can undo several steps by selecting *Undo* again and again. That might come in handy someday when you make a big mistake! For now, just undo deleting column **C** for practice. If you change your mind again, you can select *Redo* (to undo the undo) from the **Edit** menu. Try it. You can also use the arrow that curves to the right.

When examining data, you may find that some people did not respond at all. You can either analyze the data with these blanks in the file or you can go through and delete them row by row, using the same method as just described for the columns. To delete a row, click on the row number (which selects the row), then select *Delete* from **Edit** menu.

The nonresponse data mostly come from people who glance at the page and push the submit button to see what will happen. They get a "Thank you" and then they push the "Back" key to come back to actually read the instructions. In most cases, the very next line of data is from the same person. Later, you will learn methods for detecting

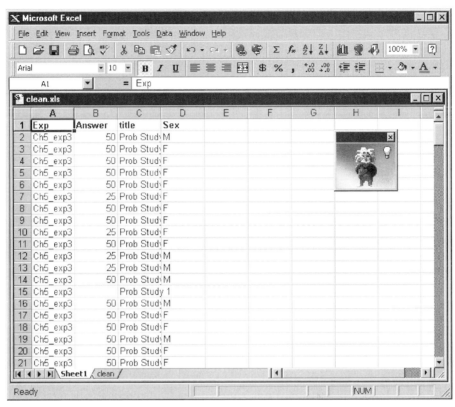

FIGURE 6.9. The data for the probability experiment have been copied and pasted into a fresh worksheet. Note the tab labeled *Sheet1* at the bottom of the worksheet. Double click on the tab and rename it *Ch5_exp3*. Clicking the tab marked *clean* returns to the (filtered) sheet of all data. Repeat the process to filter *Ch5_exp4, Ch5_exp5,* and *Ch5_exp6* to separate worksheets.

when this happens that will also help you spot when the same person sends the same data twice.

To analyze these data, you will construct a Pivot Table. First, click in cell A1. Then, from the **Data** menu, select *Pivot Table Report.* A Wizard will pop up with the ungrammatical message, "Where is the data you want to analyze?" (It should say, "Where *are* the data you wish to analyze?" The word "data," like the word "people," is plural; "datum" is singular, as is "person.") If *Microsoft Excel list or database* is selected (which it probably will be), then click *Next.* It will then say (again, ungrammatically), "Where is the data you want to use?" It will probably list the correct cell entries (A1:D209, unless you deleted column C, in which case it will say A1:C209). If needed, select the proper data with the mouse. When the "ants" show that the data are properly selected, click *Next* again.

In the third step, the screen in Figure 6.10 appears. With the mouse pointer, drag *Sex* from the right to the *COLUMN*, drag *Answer* from the right to the *ROW*, and drag *Answer* again from the right to the center of the table, labeled *DATA.* You may need to

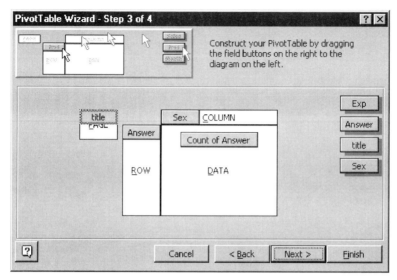

FIGURE 6.10. Step 3 of the *PivotTable Wizard*. In this panel, you can drag variables to the rows and columns, and drag the dependent variable to the center of the table. If the *DATA* field is labeled as *Sum of Answer* or some other function, double click on it, and select *Count of Answer* from the list, as shown in Figure 6.11.

double click on *Answer* in the *DATA* field, and then select *Count* from the menu, as shown in Figure 6.11. When this is done, click *Next*. It will say, "Where do you want to put the pivot table?" and you should select *New worksheet*. Click *Finish*, and Excel will then create the Pivot Table shown in Figure 6.12 on a fresh worksheet.

Note that there are a grand total of 200 participants who gave an answer. The bottom line shows that there were 112 females, 79 males, and 9 left *Sex* blank (59% of the 191 who gave their gender were female). The column on the right shows that 20 responded 25% and 175 responded 50%. Only 1 person gave the right answer, 33%, and 4 gave other answers. These results are what one usually finds among students who have not yet taken a course in critical thinking or elementary probability—very few get the correct answer until they have taken one of these classes.

Save your Excel file as a workbook with the filename *clean.xls* on your floppy or

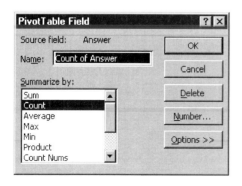

FIGURE 6.11.
Double clicking on the dependent variable in the *DATA* field brings up this dialog box. Select the statistic wanted (in this case, *Count*) and click *OK*.

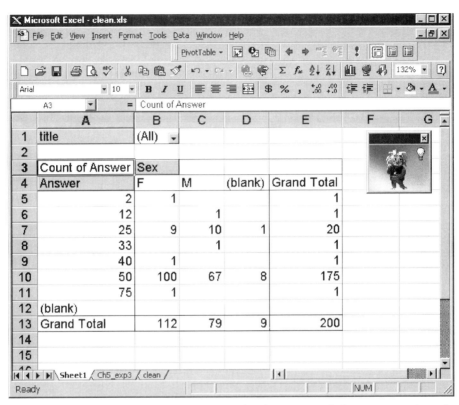

FIGURE 6.12. PivotTable of answers by sex. Note that there are a total of 200 responses, but only one person gave the right answer, which is *33*.

hard drive. Click on the tab for *Ch5_exp3* and save that worksheet as a CSV file for use later.

 ## ANALYSIS OF THE ST. PETERSBURG PARADOX

In Chapter 5, it was hypothesized that different response procedures (different select menus or a text box) might produce different results for the value of the St. Petersburg gamble. To examine the data, there are three steps. The first step is to use Autofilters to filter the data for each version of the St. Petersburg Paradox into separate worksheets. Second, you will find the mean and median value of the St. Petersburg gamble with each procedure. Third, you will learn to conduct a statistical test known as the "*t*-test" to see if the difference between two procedures is significant.

Click on the tab labeled *clean*, which is the original worksheet with all the data. Using *Autofilter* in the first column, *exp*, select *Ch5_exp4_StPete1-10*. Copy the data, insert a new worksheet, and paste the data. Then go back to the data, click the filter again, and select for *Ch5_exp5_StPete1-512*. Next, filter the data again, and copy the results for *Ch5_exp6_StPete_box*, which used a text box that allowed the participant to type an answer in the box provided. Recall that experiments 4 and 5 used selection lists with different response options.

Next, enter names for the variables in columns A, B, C, and D in row 1. Name these variables **Exp, Value, Sex,** and **Age.** Enter these names on all three worksheets. The first task will be to find the Mean **Value** of the St. Petersburg gamble in each of the three methods. To do this, select the sheet for *Ch5_exp4.* Then click in a cell below the data in column B (e.g., B68). Click the = sign in the formula line (or select *Function ...* from the **Insert** menu), and a list of functions appears. You may need to click *More functions* to find the function for *Average.* When you select it, the dialog box in Figure 6.13 appears. The dialog box (Figure 6.13) appears, asking you to specify the range of values for the average. You can either type in the range (B2:B66) or you can use the mouse to select the data you want averaged (which enters the appropriate range in the box). Check if everything looks correct, then click *OK.* Note that the answer is shown in this dialog box, before it is entered in the cell. When you click *OK,* the value is placed into the selected cell in the worksheet. In the neighboring cell, A68, type "mean=", to remind yourself that B68 contains the mean.

To find the median, follow the same steps except choose the *MEDIAN* function from the list of functions. Be careful to enter the same range of values from which to compute the median (do not include the mean as another number among the data). The median and mean are not necessarily equal, and in this case they are different. The mean is found by calculating the sum of the numbers and dividing the result by the number of cases. The median is the value of the response for which an equal number of cases give smaller and larger answers. The mean of 1, 4, and 10 is 5 (the sum is 15; divided by 3, the mean is 5); the median of the same three numbers is 4, because an equal number (one) is above and below 4. The mean and median calculations for *Ch5_exp4,* where response selection included responses from $1 to $10, are shown in Figure 6.14. Follow the same procedures to find the mean and median age of the participants in this condition.

Select Cells A68:B69, increase their font sizes, and click the **B** to make them bold. Next, click the drop-down selection arrow next to the paint can (Formatting Toolbar) and choose a yellow fill color to highlight the mean and median. Now click on the tab at the bottom of the screen to switch to *Ch5_exp5.* Find the mean and median of this condition. You will find that the median is still $2, but the mean on this sheet is $21.08, which is considerably higher than the mean for *Ch5_exp4,* which was $3.37! In both cases, about half of the subjects responded that the St. Petersburg gamble is worth $2 or less. Because the arithmetic average is computed by summing up all of the numbers

FIGURE 6.13. Select a cell, then select *Function* from the **Insert** menu. From the list of functions, choose *AVERAGE.* In this case, you want to average cells B2 to B66. Note that the *Formula result* at the bottom shows the calculation before you click *OK.* Clicking *OK* inserts the value in the selected cell. Clicking the question mark (lower left) provides more explanation about this step.

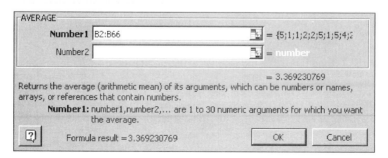

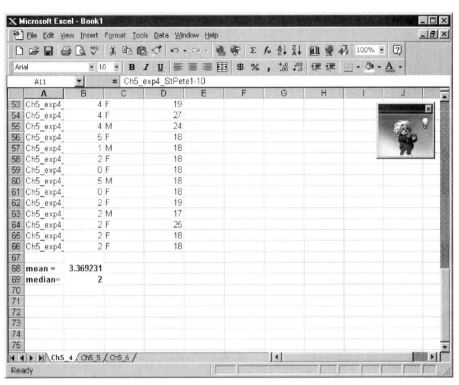

FIGURE 6.14.   Mean and median judgments of value of St. Petersburg gamble with the response selections from $0 to $10.

and dividing by the number of cases, it can be "pulled" toward a few large numbers. In this case, there are a few large numbers in Experiment 5. Examine the data and you see that a few people indeed said the gamble was worth $512. Those cases pull the mean upward.

Do the same for *Ch5_exp6,* and you will find that in the condition where the participants typed in their responses that the median is also $2, but the mean is $8.06.

To find out if means are significantly different in two conditions, we can calculate a *t*-statistic. To calculate a *t*-test between two conditions, click in a cell (where the *p*-value for the *t*-test will be inserted); next click the "=" sign in the Formula bar (or choose *Function* from the **Insert** menu), and select *t*-test from the list of functions. The dialog box of Figure 6.15 appears. Then select B2:B57 for *Array1,* or type in B2:B57 in the space provided. Click in the box for *Array2,* then click the tab at the bottom of the screen to select *Ch5_exp4.* Then select the data from that worksheet (B2:B66). Next click in the *Tails* box (Figure 6.15), and enter 2 for the number of tails, and then enter 2 in the *Type* box, to indicate that we have two independent groups with equal variances. Click *OK* and the computed value of *p* is inserted in the cell selected.

The value of the calculated *p* represents the probability that if you randomly selected two samples of data from the same population, the difference in sample means would be as large (or larger) than the difference observed. This is the probability of the observed difference in means given the null hypothesis. Note that *p* = .02. Because this

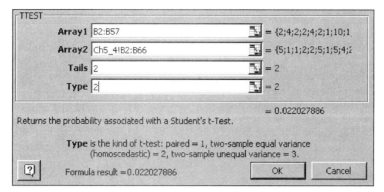

FIGURE 6.15.   The dialog box in Excel for a *t*-test. This function returns the probability level, rather than the value of *t* itself. Another function in Excel computes the *t* value itself from the probability.

value is less than $\alpha = .05$, the significance level, you can reject the hypothesis that the response format had no effect in favor of the theory that the numbers come from different distributions. Presumably, the difference in response procedures caused a significant difference in means.

Although the means differ significantly, the medians are the same in all three versions of the experiment. Most people are willing to pay very little for this gamble, even though it has infinite expected value (EV). Although the EV is infinite, most people say they would not pay more than $4 for the chance to play the St. Petersburg gamble. These judges, like those in the days of Bernoulli, apparently do not judge a gamble by its expected value.

INTRODUCTION TO SPSS

The Statistical Package for the Social Sciences (SPSS) is a popular program for statistical analysis, tables, and plotting of data. Whereas Excel is more widely used than SPSS in the business world, SPSS is more widely used in the academic world of psychology.

Start SPSS. You may get a dialog that asks what you want to do. If you are given the option of running the tutorial, run it and learn about SPSS. You can also run the tutorial from the **Help** menu. When you are done with the tutorial, close the tutorial screen and examine the data editor. (You will also get to the data editor if you close the box that offers you the tutorial, or if someone else has modified your lab copy to skip that dialog.)

The grid in SPSS looks similar to Excel's, and it is, except for a very important difference. Variable names in SPSS should *not* be entered into the grid (as they are in Excel); instead, you enter their names by double-clicking on the *VAR* at the top of each column. Unlike Excel, variable names are limited to eight characters and must not include spaces. When you double-click on VAR, the *Define Variable* dialog box appears. (You can also get to this dialog for a variable by clicking in its column and choosing *Define Variable* from the **Data** menu.)

To enter the heights data in SPSS, you need three variables: the person's name, height, and weight. A person's *name* is a String variable, a variable consisting of letters and numbers. To change the name of the variable in the *Define Variable* dialog, type in the variable name (in this case, *name*) over *Var001,* the default. To change the variable from numeric to String, click on *Type.* A new dialog appears. Click the radio button next to *String.* You could also change the number of possible characters. In this case, all of the names are eight characters or less, so if it shows eight, you can click *Continue.* Then click *OK.*

For the second variable, double-click on *VAR* at the top of the second column, and change the name (from *Var002*) to *height.* Change the *Type* to *Numeric* (eight columns with two decimals would do), click *Continue,* and change the measurement to *Scale.*

A nominal scale is a variable such as a list of names; an ordinal scale measures order, but does not retain interval information; a *scale* retains numerical information beyond the ordinal level. Height and weight are good examples of scales. An example of an ordinal scale would be a list of who took first, second, third, fourth, and so on in a race. If you knew the time it took each contestant to complete the race, however, you would have more than ordinal information because the times give information about the differences, or intervals, between the racers. The times also contain the ordinal information, because the person with the lowest time was first, the next lowest time was second, and so on.

Do the same for the third column, as for height, but give it the name, *weight.* Next, enter data in the same manner as in Excel. As in Excel, *Enter* drops the selected cell to the next row and *Tab* causes the selected cell to move to the next column. Save the data by selecting *Save As* from the **File** menu. Save it as an SPSS data file, with the name *heights.sav.* On PC, the extension *.sav* will be added for you; on the Mac, you can add the extension.

 ## IMPORTING CSV DATA TO SPSS

Start SPSS and view the data editor. From the **File** menu, select *Read Text Data.* Open *Ch5_exp3.csv.* To open a file in SPSS, it must not be open in another application. It is a good idea to close Excel before working with SPSS. Remember, you need to select *All Files(*.*)* in the open dialog box to see the file. When you select the file to open, the Data Import Wizard appears. The first screen is shown in Figure 6.16. The data are not in preformatted columns, so check "No." The data can be previewed in the mini-window. Click *Next.* The next steps are shown in Figures 6.17, 6.18, 6.19, 6.20, and 6.21; follow the steps suggested in the figure captions. When you press *Finish,* you may see a list of warnings in the Output window. From the **Window** menu, select the *data editor.*

 ## CROSSTABS IN SPSS

In general, to do a statistical analysis in SPSS, you select the type of analysis from the **Analyze** menu. If you have an earlier version of SPSS than 9.0 (or if you have SPSS 6.1 for Mac), this menu is labeled the **Statistics** menu. To do crosstabulations, from the **Analyze** menu select *Descriptive Statistics,* then *Crosstabs...,* as shown in Figure 6.22. Then follow the steps illustrated in Figure 6.23. The result is shown in Figure 6.24, after enlargement of the fonts. Note that this same table was created by Excel using the technique of Pivot Tables, as shown in Figure 6.12.

On the CD are data files that contain additional cases for the St. Petersburg ex-

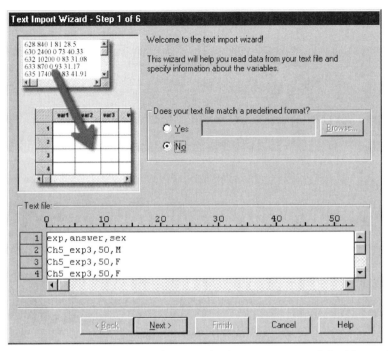

FIGURE 6.16. Text Import Wizard in SPSS. The data are not in a predefined format, in which each item is in the same number of columns, so check *No*. A preview of the file is shown in the mini-window. Click *Next*.

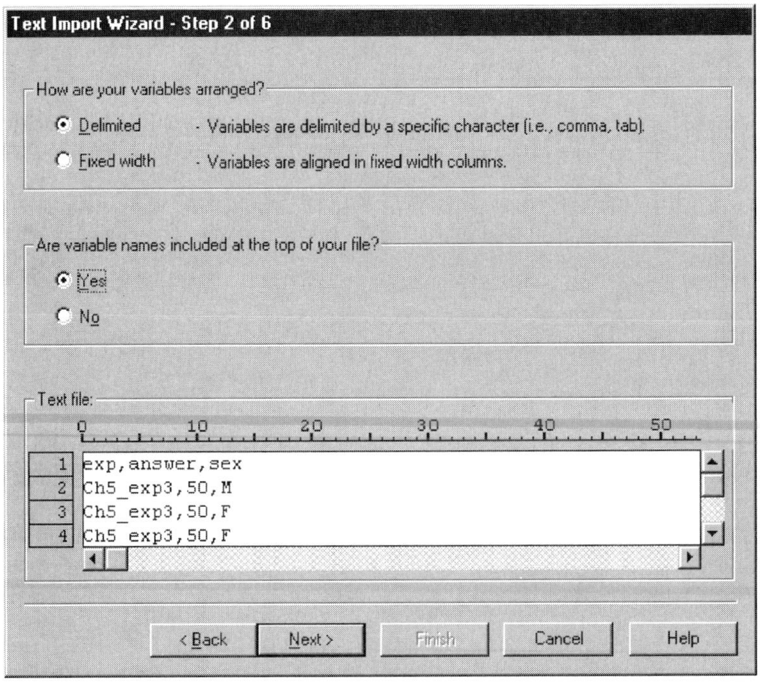

FIGURE 6.17. Step 2 of the Text Import Wizard. Click to indicate that the data are delimited (they are delimited by commas), and *Yes*, variable names are in the first row. Click *Next*.

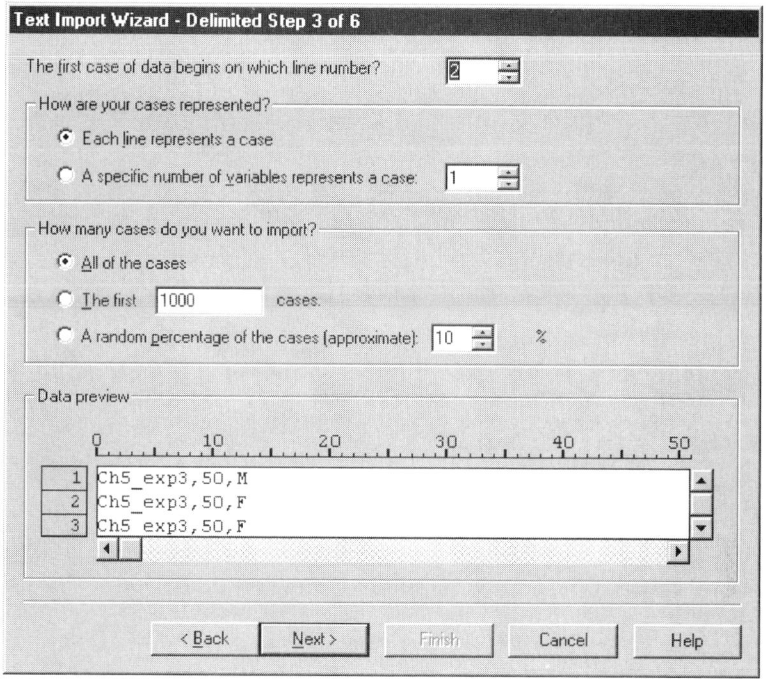

FIGURE 6.18. Step 3 of the Data Import Wizard. In this case, data begins in line 2, each line represents a case, and all of the cases should be imported. Click *Next.*

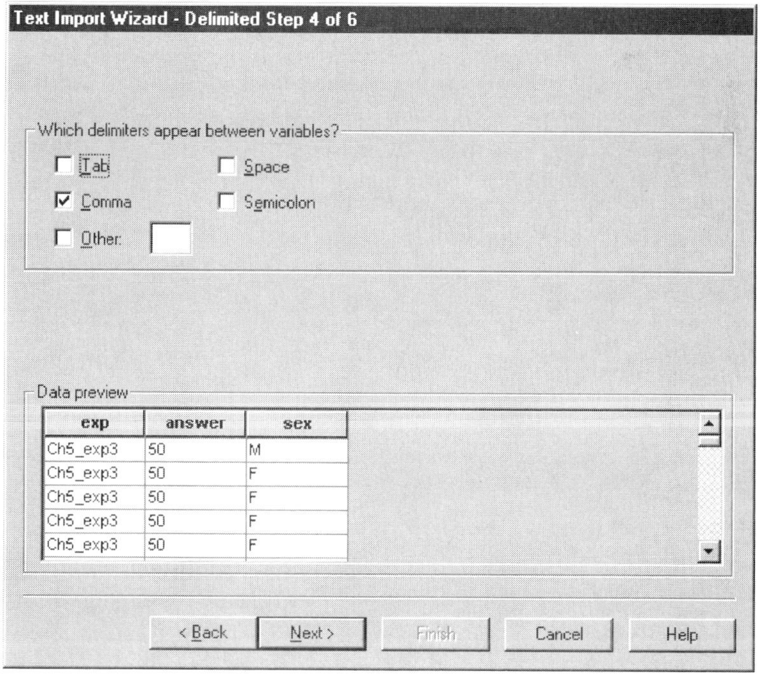

FIGURE 6.19. In step 4, indicate that a comma is used to separate values and examine the preview. If *Space* or *Tab* is checked, be sure to remove the checks. Click *Next.*

Specifications for variable(s) selected in the data preview

Variable name: Original Name:

answer   answer

Data format:

Numeric

Data preview

exp	answer	sex
Ch5_exp3	50	M
Ch5_exp3	50	F
Ch5_exp3	50	F
Ch5_exp3	50	F
Ch5_exp3	50	F

< Back   Next >   Finish   Cancel   Help

FIGURE 6.20.   In step 5, click on each variable and specify its name and data type. The *answer* is numeric, and *sex* is a string variable. When you have clicked on each variable and checked its name and type, click *Next.*

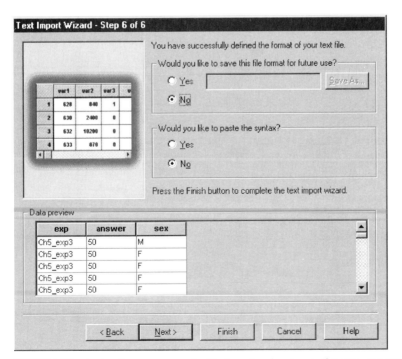

You have successfully defined the format of your text file.

Would you like to save this file format for future use?

○ Yes   Save As...

● No

Would you like to paste the syntax?

○ Yes

● No

Press the Finish button to complete the text import wizard.

Data preview

exp	answer	sex
Ch5_exp3	50	M
Ch5_exp3	50	F
Ch5_exp3	50	F
Ch5_exp3	50	F
Ch5_exp3	50	F

< Back   Next >   Finish   Cancel   Help

FIGURE 6.21.   In step 6, you can save the file format and syntax. In this case, just press *Finish.*

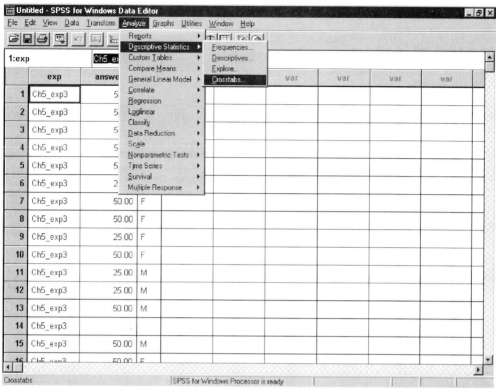

FIGURE 6.22. To do Crosstabs, select *Descriptive Statistics* from the **Analyze** menu, then *Crosstabs...* from the sub-menu.

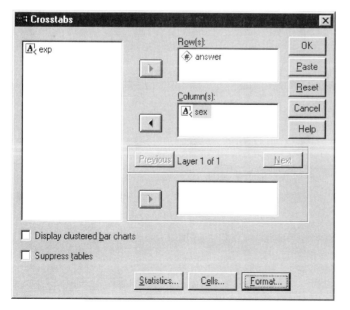

FIGURE 6.23.

To choose *answer* as Rows, click on its name in the left display to select, then click on the arrow to send it to *Row(s)*. Then select *sex* for columns by the same method, clicking the arrow to send it into the box for *Column(s)*, as shown. To undo an error, click on a variable and the arrow sends it back to the list of variables. Click on the buttons for *Statistics...*, *Cells...*, and *Format...* for other options. For now, press *OK* to produce the results shown in Figure 6.24.

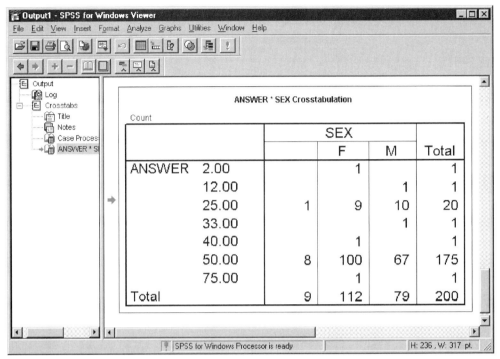

FIGURE 6.24. The ANSWER*SEX Crosstabulation table, produced by SPSS, provides the same results as the Pivot Table of Figure 6.12, produced by Excel. By double-clicking on the table, fonts can be enlarged and formats changed.

periment. These are labeled *StPeteAll.csv* and *StPeteAll.sav.* Open *StPeteAll.sav* in SPSS. To compute a *t*-test by SPSS, from the **Analyze** menu, select *Compare Means* and then select *Independent Samples T test.* Use a group variable (the experiment number, labeled group, is in column 5 of the data) to define the groups. The output in *StPeteAll.spo* gives the results of *t*-tests between each pair of groups by SPSS. You can compare your results with this output.

 ## SUMMARY

You should know how to open a data file (such as *data.csv*) in Excel, how to save it as an Excel workbook, and how to save a worksheet as a CSV file. You should know how to use *AutoFilters* to filter data from one experiment and how to insert them on a fresh worksheet. You should know how to construct a PivotTable report, how to find the means and medians, and how to construct a *t*-test of significance between two sets of data.

You should also know how to create a file of data in SPSS, open a CSV file in SPSS, and how to construct crosstabulations that are the equivalent of the Pivot Table of Excel.

EXERCISES

1. In SPSS, import the file *Ch5_exp3.csv*. Create a crosstabulation showing *sex* by *Answer* without referring to the book. Do the same in Excel, also without looking in the book. If you need to peek at the book, do so, then start over without the book and see if you can do it on your own.

2. On the CD is included a file, *StPeteAll.csv*, that contains additional data on the value of the St. Petersburg gamble. In this file are data from all three experiments, *Ch5_exp4*, *Ch5_exp5*, and *Ch5_exp6*, with the experiment listed in the first column. Import these data to Excel and perform the same analyses that were illustrated in the chapter. Hint: You can Cut and Paste the data for different experiments to arrange them in the same way as was done in the chapter. However, that is not really necessary. You can check your results against the results in *StPeteAll.xls*, which is also on the CD.

3. Import the file *StPeteAll.csv* to SPSS. Analyze the St. Petersburg data in SPSS. To compute a *t*-test in SPSS, define a new variable called *group*. Assign this new variable the value 6 for *Ch5_exp6* (box), assign the value 4 for *Ch5_exp4* (1–10), and assign the value 5 for *Ch5_exp5* (1–512). Now, from the **Analyze** menu, select *Compare Means*, then *Independent-samples T test*. In the dialog box, insert *Value* (the judgment of value of the gamble) as the *Test variable*, then insert *group* as the grouping variable. Click the button to define groups, and then select specified values. Let the values be 4 and 6 for groups 4 and 6, respectively. That compares the text box with the 1–10 scale. You can repeat the process to get each of three comparisons of means. Explain why the biggest mean difference is not necessarily the "most significant" according to the *p*-value.

4. In SPSS, create a crosstabulation of group (columns) by value (rows). This crosstabulation gives you an idea of how the numbers for the different groups were distributed.

5. Create the crosstabulation of experiment by value with Excel using Pivot Tables. Use *StPeteAll.csv*. Use *exp* as columns, *Value* as rows, and *Count of Value* as the data.

6. In Excel, also create a Pivot Table with the rows for *sex*, columns for *exp*, and put the mean (Average) *Value* in the data field.

Chapter 7

Images and Logical Thinking

This chapter reviews a study in logical thinking, and it covers everything from putting the experiment on the Web to analyzing the data. First, you learn how to incorporate images in your Web experiments and how to create an image map so that a mouse click on one part of a picture has a different action from clicking on another part. Second, you will learn how to set up and run a reliable psychological demonstration of a systematic flaw in human reasoning. Third, this chapter shows you how to analyze the data for the logic problem, which are included on the CD that accompanies this book.

 ## DISPLAYING IMAGES WITH HTML

The `IMG` tag, which displays images, is used in the following example:

```
<IMG SRC="cards.gif" ALT="4 cards showing..." ALIGN="left" WIDTH=160
  HEIGHT=120 BORDER=0>
```

The SRC gives the filename of the image, *cards.gif*. This image, shown in Figure 7.1, was created in PowerPoint. It represents four cards used in a classic study of human reasoning by Wason (1960).

The text in `ALT="4 cards showing: A, B, 1, and 2"` specifies a verbal description of the image that would be useful to a person who has images turned off.

 ## A PROBLEM IN LOGIC

Do people understand each other? Do people understand simple sentences of the form, "All A's are B," or "If A, then B?" Do people understand what it means if somebody says, "All dogs have noses." Load the experiment *Ch7_exp1.htm* and complete the task. The text of the experiment reads as follows:

> There is a deck of cards, each of which has a number on one side of the card and a letter on the other side. This fact is a given, and you can assume it is true. Four of these cards are dealt onto a table, showing the following face up: 1, 2, A, and B. Conjecture: "For these four cards, every card with an even number on one side has a vowel on the other." Question: What is the smallest set of cards that must be turned over to *test* the conjecture? Definitions: *Vowel* = a letter in the set {A, E, I, O, U}. An *Even Number* is divisible by 2 without remainder,{... −4, −2, 0, 2, 4,...}. *Test:* An experiment that would refute (disprove) the conjecture, if the conjecture were false.

There are 16 possible meanings of the sentence, "Every card with an even number on one side has a vowel on the other." These possible meanings are revealed by the experiments that test (might disprove) the sentence. For each card, one either needs to check it (turn it over) or not. Because there are four cards, there are $2^4 = 16$ possibilities. These 16 possibilities, from turning over none to turning over all four, are listed as choices in the selection menu. (In this case, a pull-down selection is appropriate, because there is a finite list of all possible answers.)

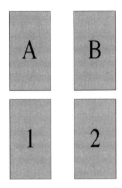

FIGURE 7.1.
The image in file *cards.gif*. This graphic was created in PowerPoint. The document was saved as HTML, and the image file was renamed.

In my introductory psychology classes, every student is required to "vote" for one of the 16 possible meanings. The correct answer is 2 and B. We need to turn over the 2 to see if there is a vowel on the other side; if not, then the conjecture is disproved. We also need to turn over the B, to check if there is an even number on the other side; if it is even (e.g., 2), the conjecture is also disproved because there would be an even number without a vowel on the other side. We do not need to turn over the 1 because a vowel or consonant would be compatible with the conjecture; similarly, we need not turn over the vowel because there may be either an odd or even number on the other side without contradiction.

In a class of 100 college freshmen and sophomores, about two or three people get the problem right, and the rest split up into many *different* ideas of what the sentence means. People not only do not understand the sentence the way a person trained in logic understands it, they also have many different opinions of its meaning. Demonstrations like this make one realize that communication is partly an illusion. The HTML (with abbreviated instructions) is given in Figure 7.2.

The new idea in Figure 7.2 is the use of an image. A version of the experiment that includes the environmental hidden variables (Appendix A) is in *Ch7_exp2.htm* on the CD. The correct answer is explained in *Ch7_ex1.htm*, which gives feedback on each card in order to construct an informal "truth table." A truth table is a systematic listing of the truth status of each possible situation. This online example illustrates the use of image maps.

 IMAGE MAPS

Figure 7.3 illustrates the use of an image map in *Ch7_ex1.htm*. When the user clicks on the image, the action depends on where the mouse pointer was when it was clicked. Try it out by loading *Ch7_ex1.htm* in your browser.

This example illustrates how one can define a map on an image and use the location of the mouse pointer to branch to one of several actions. The IMG tag now contains a notation (USEMAP="#mapdemo") linking to MAP with the same name. The coordinates are pairs of x (horizontal) and y (vertical). The coordinate system places (0, 0) at the upper left-hand side of the image. The x coordinate measures the horizontal distance to the right, and the y coordinate measures the vertical distance *downward*. The use of positive numbers to go *down* requires an adjustment for those trained in other coordinate systems.

```
<H3>Test of Reasoning</H3><P>There is a deck of cards, each of which has a
number on one side of the card and a letter on the other. Four of these
are:</P>
<IMG SRC="cards.gif" ALT="4 cards showing: A, B, 1, and 2" ALIGN="left"
WIDTH=160 HEIGHT=120 BORDER=0>
<P><B>Conjecture:</B> "For these four cards, every card with an even number
on one side has a vowel on the other."</P>
1.<B>What is the smallest set of cards that must be turned over in order to
test the conjecture? <BR>
Select your answer from the following pull-down menu:</B>
<INPUT TYPE="hidden" NAME="00exp" VALUE="Ch7_exp1">
<SELECT NAME="01ans">
    <OPTION SELECTED VALUE="">Pull down here to select
    <OPTION VALUE="0">None
    <OPTION VALUE="1">1
    <OPTION VALUE="2">2
    <OPTION VALUE="A">A
    <OPTION VALUE="B">B
    <OPTION VALUE="12">1 & 2
    <OPTION VALUE="1A">1 & A
    <OPTION VALUE="1B">1 & B
    <OPTION VALUE="2A">2 & A
    <OPTION VALUE="2B">2 & B
    <OPTION VALUE="AB">A & B
    <OPTION VALUE="12A">1 & 2 & A
    <OPTION VALUE="12B">1 & 2 & B
    <OPTION VALUE="1AB">1 & A & B
    <OPTION VALUE="2AB">2 & A & B
    <OPTION VALUE="12AB">ALL FOUR: 1 & 2 & A & B
</SELECT>
```

FIGURE 7.2. HTML for *Ch7_exp1.htm* (abbreviated).

The lines ending in HREF=SayA.htm are links that cause a click on a part of the image to link to different files, according to which part of the image is clicked. There are four files, each with the appropriate message for one card, and each page has a link to return to the page of feedback. Another example on your CD uses JavaScript alerts, which are discussed in Chapter 18.

```
<H3>Here is an Image Map</H3>
<B>Conjecture: All Cards with an Even Number on one side have a Vowel
on the Other.
<HR>
Click on the Cards to check which we need turn over to TEST this
conjecture</B>
<P>
<IMG SRC="cards.gif" ALT="4 cards showing A, B, 1, 2"  WIDTH=250
HEIGHT=200 USEMAP="#mapdemo">
<MAP NAME="mapdemo">
<AREA SHAPE="rect" COORDS="0,0,125,100" HREF="SayA.htm">
<AREA SHAPE="rect" COORDS="125,0,250,100" HREF="SayB.htm">
<AREA SHAPE="rect" COORDS="0,100,125,200" HREF="Say1.htm">
<AREA SHAPE="rect" COORDS="125,100,250,200" HREF="Say2.htm">
</MAP>
<HR>
```

FIGURE 7.3.   Illustration of the use of image maps. This HTML is part of *Ch7_ex1.htm.*

A PIVOT TABLE FOR THE LOGIC PROBLEM

Follow the steps in Chapter 6 to make a Pivot Table for these data. In this case, let the *Rows* depict the *Answer,* and move *Sex* and *Education* to the *Columns.* The example in Figure 7.4 shows how the Pivot Table appears in Excel. Try rearranging the table to explore the data. Try dragging *Education* up to the Page (that leaves *Sex* as the only column variable). Or try dragging *Sex* up to the page position, which leaves *Education* as the only column variable. No matter how you look at it, very few people understand the sentence *All A's are B.* Some authors consider this finding evidence of a positive bias— people have trouble with negative thinking. *All A's are B* is the same as *not B implies not A.* In other words, *If A then B* is the same as *if not B then not A.* This basic principle of logic or comprehension appears to be very difficult for college students untrained in logic.

SUMMARY

In this chapter, you learned about a systematic flaw in human reasoning. People have trouble understanding sentences of the form *if A then B.* You also learned about how to set up an experiment on this problem (incorporating images) and how to use an image map to give interactive feedback on the problem. The tags featured in this chapter are summarized in Table 7.1.

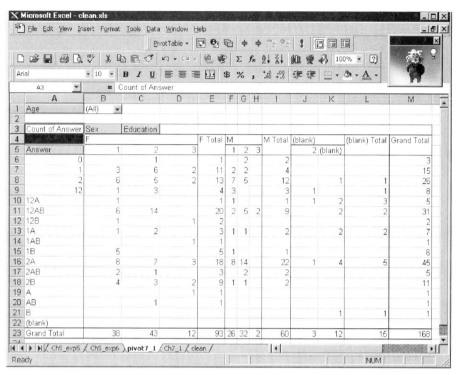

FIGURE 7.4. Pivot Table of Logic Problem. Only 11 of 168 chose the correct answer (2B). Four other answers were more popular (1, 2, 12AB, 2A) than the correct answer (2B). No answer is agreed on by more than 27% of the sample. Education is coded as follows: 1 = High school graduate; 2 = 1–3 years of college; 3 = college graduate; 4 = master's degree; 5 = doctorate. None of these participants had higher degrees.

TABLE 7.1. Summary of Tags used in Chapter 7

TAG	DESCRIPTION
`<IMG`	Places images in HTML file.
`  SRC="cards.gif"`	File name of image.
`  ALT="description"`	Verbal description of the image.
`  ALIGN="left"`	Specifies alignment.
`  WIDTH=160 HEIGHT=120 BORDER=0`	Specifies dimensions.
`  USEMAP="#ref">`	Reference to MAP #ref.
`<MAP NAME=ref></MAP>`	Define an image map.
`<AREA SHAPE="rect"`	Defines a portion of a map where
`  COORDS="x1,y1,x2,y2"`	mouse click will send to the link
`  HREF="filename.htm">`	specified in HREF.

EXERCISES

1. Load the file *Ch7_exp1.htm*. Look at the file in a text editor as well as in the browser. The only new technique in this experiment is the use of an image. Try changing the values of the HEIGHT, WIDTH, ALT, and BORDER attributes to see their effects on the display in the browser. Also try ALIGN=left, ALIGN=right, and ALIGN=middle to see their effects.

2. Open the file *Ch7_exp2.htm* in your browser and view the source HTML. This second version illustrates the use of hidden variables that were covered in Chapter 5 (see also Appendix A). Collect some data using this version of the program, examine the data file *data.csv,* and relate the HTML to your data.

3. Download software to create or convert images. Practice working with photographs and with graphic images in these programs. If you are interested in visual perception, motion perception, art, or multimedia, then these programs will be useful to you. If you are very interested in using visual images and animations in your experiments, you may want to acquire commercial software; however, check the free software first. More information on graphics is given in Chapter 14.

4. There are two sets of data on the logic problem on the CD in the file, *logic1.csv* and *logic2.csv.* Load these data into SPSS or Excel. Next, construct cross-tabulation tables in SPSS or PivotTable reports in Excel showing how the answer depends on education. Examine the HTML in *Ch7_exp1.htm,* and you will see that education is defined by a series of radio buttons as follows: 1 = High school graduate; 2 = 1–3 years of college; 3 = college graduate; 4 = master's degree; 5 = doctorate. You should be able to construct two tables analogous to that shown in Figure 7.4. How do the results for the second sample compare to the results from the first sample?

5. Project idea: Change the logic problem in systematic ways to investigate the effects of different logical questions. For example, it has been argued that "if then" statements are better understood as "permissions" than when stated as logical properties. For example, suppose someone says, "You are a bouncer at a bar. Your job is to make sure that nobody under 21 is drinking." Which people do you check: Over 21, under 21, drinkers, or nondrinkers? Or: "You work at the post office. All sealed letters must have first-class postage. Which envelopes do you need to turn over to check? Sealed, unsealed, those with first-class stamps, or those with less than first-class stamps?" The conjecture is that people understand the idea that *All A's are B* better when it is part of a statement of *permission* than when it is stated as *If A then B, all A's are B.* It is also observed that people are quite poor in understanding the problem when it is phrased as a causal proposition. For example, suppose someone conjectures that all abusers are themselves victims of child abuse. Suppose the police have four lists of people in their files: victims of abuse, perpetrators of abuse, people who are not victims, and people who are not abusers. Which cases do we need to check to find out if all abusers were victims? Try out these variations of the logic problems. Can you use permission language to rewrite the logic problem, "All even numbers have vowels," so that most people get it right? Can you find a way to get people to understand sentences of the form, *All As are B,* or *If A then B?*

Chapter 8

A STUDY OF DECISION MAKING

If you understand the material in Chapters 2–6, then you understand all of the computer techniques that were involved in the studies of Birnbaum (1999c, 2000a). If you have not done so already, load and run the decision-making experiment on your CD, *Ch8_exp1.htm*. This chapter reviews background in the psychology of decision making that helps you understand that study. You also practice some tricks of data processing and analysis and learn how to apply them to analyze the decision-making experiment.

 ## PSYCHOLOGY OF DECISION MAKING

Why do people do what they do? Psychology is the science of behavior, so it attempts to answer this question. As a science, it is the study of rival theories, or explanations, of behavior. One approach to understanding human behavior is to interpret what people do as the result of a decision to act. Normative decision theory prescribes how a rational person *should* decide, whereas descriptive decision theory is the empirical study of how people *do* make decisions. As you will see, people do not always do what theoreticians think they should do.

Consider the decision of whether to carry an umbrella tomorrow. The contingencies are described in the following matrix:

	RAINS	DOES NOT RAIN
Carry umbrella	Stay dry	Extra work
Don't carry umbrella	Get wet	Travel light

Clearly, if it is going to rain, then it would be better to carry your umbrella tomorrow because you will stay dry. However, if it is not going to rain, then it would be easier to leave the umbrella at home. The greater the probability of rain, the stronger the argument to carry the umbrella. If the weatherman says that there is a 50% chance of rain in the afternoon, would you carry your umbrella? What you decide to do would depend on your subjective values for staying dry, getting wet, for carrying an umbrella when it does not rain, and for traveling light. What you decide to do also depends on your beliefs concerning what will likely happen when the weatherman says, "The chance of rain is fifty percent."

Consider the following choice designed to create situations simpler than that of deciding to carry an umbrella. In this case, a fair coin is tossed and the consequences are monetary payoffs that depend on the outcome of the coin toss. If you choose alternative *A*, then if heads occurs, you win $50; if tails occurs, you lose $10. However, if you choose *B*, then if heads occurs, you lose $100; if tails occurs, you win $100. This choice seems simpler than the umbrella decision, because the probabilities of heads and tails are better defined than the likelihood (and strength) of rain when the weatherman says

"50%." It also seems simpler because the consequences are money rather than subjective feelings such as those of getting your hair wet. In this choice, most people would probably choose *A* over *B*.

	HEADS	TAILS
A	$50	−$10
B	−$100	$100

Now consider the following choice, which produces more disagreement.

	HEADS	TAILS
C	$40	$40
D	$100	$0

In Choice *C*, you win $40 whether Heads or Tails occurs, so it is a sure $40. For *D*, however, you might win $100 or $0. Some people prefer *C* and others will prefer *D*.

EXPECTED VALUE AND EXPECTED UTILITY

The expected value (EV) of a gamble can be thought of as the average amount that you would win if the gamble were played an infinite number of times. The EV is given by the following formula,

$$EV(G) = \sum_{i=1}^{n} p_i x_i \tag{8.1}$$

where $EV(G)$ is the expected value of gamble G, p_i and x_i are the probability and monetary value of consequence i, summed over all n mutually exclusive and exhaustive outcomes of the gamble. For *D*, $EV(D) = \$50$, because the two outcomes (heads and tails) have probabilities of .5, and the consequences are $0 and $100, so $EV(D) = .5(\$0) + .5(\$100) = \$50$. The EV of *C* is $40.

In terms of expected value, gamble *D* is better than gamble *C*; however, many people prefer *C*, because it provides a "safe and sure" $40, whereas gamble *D* seems more "risky." When people make choices like this—that is, they prefer a sure thing to a gamble with the same or even higher EV—their behavior is described as *risk averse*.

Risk aversion is inconsistent with the theory that people choose gambles by their EVs; however, Bernoulli realized that risk aversion could be explained by the theory that the psychological value of money is a nonlinear function of money. This theory of expected utility (EU) can be written as follows:

$$EU(G) = \sum_{i=1}^{n} p_i u(x_i) \tag{8.2}$$

where $u(x)$ is the utility, or *psychological value*, of a certain amount of money.

Bernoulli proposed Eq. 8.2 as an explanation for the St. Petersburg Paradox (see Chapter 5) and other violations of EV. If the utility of money is a nonlinear function of its cash value, then the cash value of the expected utility of the St. Petersburg Paradox can be finite. Bernoulli discussed the functions, $u(x) = \log x$, and $u(x) = \sqrt{x}$ as possible utility functions that would explain the St. Petersburg Paradox and would also explain risk aversion, such as a preference for choice *C* over choice *D*.

Suppose $u(x) = \sqrt{x}$. For gamble *D*, the EU is $.5\sqrt{0} + .5\sqrt{100} = 5$. For gamble *C*, $\text{EU}(C) = .5\sqrt{40} + .5\sqrt{40} = 6.32 > \text{EU}(D) = 5$; therefore, this theory predicts that a person would prefer *C* to *D*. In EU theory, *C* is better than *D* because the psychological value of $40 is better than half the psychological value of $100. In other words, this theory says that the subjective difference from $0 to $40 exceeds the subjective difference from $40 to $100.

 ## THE PRINCIPLE OF DOMINANCE

Some choices are relatively easy, and there is little disagreement, as in the choice between *E* and *F*:

	HEADS	TAILS
E	$100	$50
F	$65	$50

Notice that gamble *E* is strictly better than gamble *F* because for either heads or tails, the consequence of choosing *E* is always better than or equal to the consequence of *F*— for tails, the consequences are the same, but for heads, *E* gives $100 and *F* gives only $65. When one gamble is strictly better than another in this way, we say that *E dominates F*. If *G* and *H* are two distinct gambles such that $P(x > t \mid G) \geq P(x > t \mid H)$ for all *t*, then gamble *G* is said to *stochastically dominate* gamble *H*. This concept is also known as *first stochastic dominance*.

Many descriptive (psychological) theories of decision making, including expected utility theory, imply that people should obey stochastic dominance. These theories predict that people will choose the dominant gamble. The study described in this chapter tested conditions under which people satisfy and violate dominance. This study also tested other properties of choice (Birnbaum, 1999b, 1999c).

 ## DECISION-MAKING EXPERIMENT

If you examine *Ch8_exp1.htm* in a text editor, you find that the experiment makes use of hidden variables, text boxes, and radio buttons. There is no new computer technique here, just variations of things you have learned in previous chapters. Note that each choice between two gambles is constructed from a set of three radio buttons. By using three radio buttons, it is possible to distinguish preference for the first gamble (-1), preference for the second gamble $(+1)$, or a failure to respond (0). Note that the button for nonresponse is in the left margin, making it easy for the subject to see if she or he has completed all of the questions. A portion of the experiment is shown in Figure 8.1.

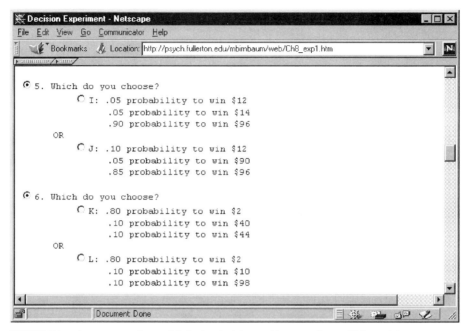

FIGURE 8.1.   Appearance of two trials in the decision-making experiment *Ch8_exp1.htm.*

When this experiment was actually run, some lucky participants were given a chance to play one of their chosen gambles for real. For the first 1900 people tested, there were 19 winners, including 11 who won $90 or more. The version on your CD does not offer prizes, but you can get an idea of what it was like to be a participant in the study.

One of the questions addressed in this study is as follows: When motivated by money, would people choose the dominant gamble? It is not only the rational thing to do, but it is also predicted to be what people would do if they satisfied Expected Utility theory or one of several modern utility theories (Luce & Fishburn, 1991; 1995; Tversky & Kahneman, 1992). However, configural weight models of Birnbaum and Navarrete (1998) imply that people will violate stochastic dominance in certain specially constructed choices.

 RANK-DEPENDENT EXPECTED UTILITY THEORY

The theories of Luce and Fishburn (1991, 1995) and of Tversky and Kahneman (1992) have the same representation as rank-dependent expected utility theory (Quiggin, 1993) when the gambles have strictly positive consequences. These theories represent the utility of such gambles as follows:

$$RDU(G) = \sum_{i=1}^{n} u(x_i)\,[\,W(P_i) - W(P_{i-1})\,] \tag{8.3}$$

where $RDU(G)$ is the rank-dependent expected utility of gamble G; $u(x)$ is the utility of consequence x; $W(P)$ is a strictly monotonic weighting function that assigns decumulative weight to decumulative probability, with $W(0) = 0$ and $W(1) = 1$; P_i is the (decumulative) probability of winning x_i or more and P_{i-1} is the probability of winning strictly more than x_i. If $W(P) = P$, then this theory reduces to EU theory. This theory can account for the Allais paradoxes, phenomena that violate EU theory (Quiggin, 1993). This theory also implies that if G stochastically dominates H, then the $RDU(G) > RDU(H)$, so people should choose G over H.

COMPARING RIVAL THEORIES

Use Netscape to load the decision calculator *taxcalculator.htm*, from the CD. This calculator uses JavaScript (presented in Chapters 17–19) to calculate predictions for three models of decision making. This calculator is also available at URL http://psych.fullerton.edu/mbirnbaum/taxcalculator.htm.

One model is the TAX model of Birnbaum and Navarrete (1998), the second is the cumulative prospect theory (CPT) model of Tversky and Kahneman (1992), and the third is EV. The CPT model is a special case of Eq. 8.3. Calculate the value of gambles *I* and *J* in choice 5 of Figure 8.1.

To use the calculator, first press the *Set Values* button. This action sets the parameters of the models to values published in the literature. Next, type *3* for the *number of outcomes*. Type the outcomes (the prizes) in order from the lowest outcome on the left to the highest. Leave spaces to the right blank. Enter the corresponding probabilities in the spaces provided. Press the *Compute* button and read off the values according to the CWT (configural weight, TAX model), CPT, and EV. Help and instructions are available in the file.

You will see that different theories make different predictions for this choice. Which gamble has the higher EV? (Answer: *I* is higher in EV than *J*: $87.7 to $87.3). Which gamble has the higher CPT value? (Answer: *I* is higher than *J*: $72.27 to $71.73). Which gamble has the higher TAX value? (Answer: *J* is higher than *I*: $63.10 to $45.77).

Which gamble did you pick? If you are like most undergraduates who served in this experiment, you probably chose *J*, as predicted by the TAX model. In the next sections, you analyze the data to find out which gamble most people preferred to see whether the CWT TAX model or CPT is more accurate.

DATA ANALYSIS OF DECISION EXPERIMENT

In the next sections, you import the data file into Excel to analyze the data. You could also use SPSS, as in Chapter 6.

Your CD includes files named *clean.csv* (Figure 8.2) and *clean.xls* that contain the data analyzed in this chapter. These files have been cleaned of identifying information such as email addresses that were used to notify winners. To follow along in this analysis, open the file *clean.xls* in Excel—either the one you created in Chapter 6, or the one provided on the CD.

The variable names have been entered already in *clean.csv*. If you examine the experimental form, *Ch8_exp1.htm*, you see that the *date* and *time* are inserted as hidden variables. Note that the time variable shows up as ######### in Figure 8.2. The times are too big to fit in the default display.

You can adjust the spacing of the columns in Excel by placing your arrow pointer

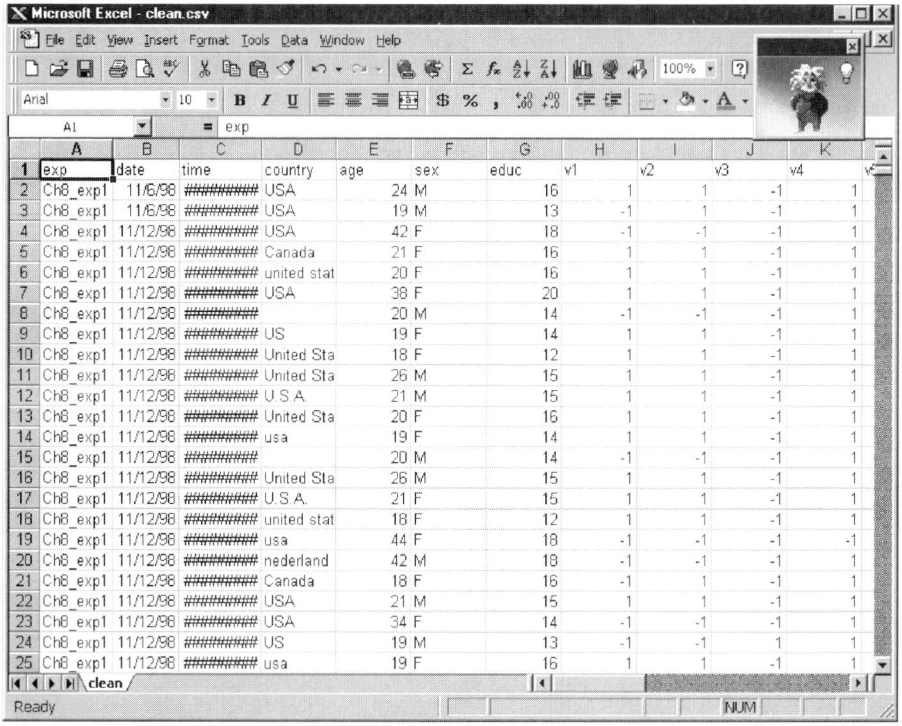

	A	B	C	D	E	F	G	H	I	J	K
1	exp	date	time	country	age	sex	educ	v1	v2	v3	v4
2	Ch8_exp1	11/6/98	#########	USA	24	M	16	1	1	-1	1
3	Ch8_exp1	11/6/98	#########	USA	19	M	13	-1	1	-1	1
4	Ch8_exp1	11/12/98	#########	USA	42	F	18	-1	-1	-1	1
5	Ch8_exp1	11/12/98	#########	Canada	21	F	16	1	1	-1	1
6	Ch8_exp1	11/12/98	#########	united stat	20	F	16	1	1	-1	1
7	Ch8_exp1	11/12/98	#########	USA	38	F	20	1	1	-1	1
8	Ch8_exp1	11/12/98	#########		20	M	14	-1	-1	-1	1
9	Ch8_exp1	11/12/98	#########	US	19	F	14	1	1	-1	1
10	Ch8_exp1	11/12/98	#########	United Sta	18	F	12	1	1	-1	1
11	Ch8_exp1	11/12/98	#########	United Sta	26	M	15	1	1	-1	1
12	Ch8_exp1	11/12/98	#########	U.S.A.	21	M	15	1	1	-1	1
13	Ch8_exp1	11/12/98	#########	United Sta	20	F	16	1	1	-1	1
14	Ch8_exp1	11/12/98	#########	usa	19	F	14	1	1	-1	1
15	Ch8_exp1	11/12/98	#########		20	M	14	-1	-1	-1	1
16	Ch8_exp1	11/12/98	#########	United Sta	26	M	15	1	1	-1	1
17	Ch8_exp1	11/12/98	#########	U.S.A.	21	F	15	1	1	-1	1
18	Ch8_exp1	11/12/98	#########	united stat	18	F	12	1	1	-1	1
19	Ch8_exp1	11/12/98	#########	usa	44	F	18	-1	-1	-1	-1
20	Ch8_exp1	11/12/98	#########	nederland	42	M	18	-1	-1	-1	1
21	Ch8_exp1	11/12/98	#########	Canada	18	F	16	-1	1	-1	1
22	Ch8_exp1	11/12/98	#########	USA	21	M	15	1	1	-1	1
23	Ch8_exp1	11/12/98	#########	USA	34	F	14	-1	-1	-1	1
24	Ch8_exp1	11/12/98	#########	US	19	M	13	-1	-1	1	1
25	Ch8_exp1	11/12/98	#########	usa	19	F	16	1	1	-1	1

FIGURE 8.2. Appearance of *clean.csv* when opened by Excel.

on the cracks between column labels at the top of the sheet, then clicking and dragging. Place the mouse pointer on the crack between C and D, at the top of the column. When the two-headed arrow appears, drag the crack to the right to make column C bigger. You can also double-click on the crack to adjust its width automatically to the data. Now the *times* can be read. Next, respace the columns for the choices (−1 and 1), to make them thinner so that you can see more of the data on one screen.

Before you go on, save the file as an Excel workbook, but so as not to erase the work of Chapters 6 and 7, save it this time on your hard drive as *clean2.xls.*

Check the variable names in the first row. These names have been entered for you, but in a new study, you would fill them in according to what is in the new experiment. The first variable identifies the experiment, "**exp,**" the next two variables are **date** and **time,** followed by **country** (nationality), **age, sex** (gender), and **edu** (education). After that, the next 20 variables (**v1** to **v20**) are the choices in the 20 decision problems, in the order that they appeared in *Ch8_exp1.htm.* The next item is a question that asked if the participant has read a scientific paper or book on the theory of decision making, which is called **Read DM** (read on decision making). The last value is a field for **Comments.** There had also been a box for the email address, which has been removed. Some of the subjects were students who were tested in the department's computer lab, and others were volunteers who took the experiment via the Internet. Select the first row, and click **B** icon on the formatting toolbar to make the variable names bold.

FILTERING THE DATA

Filter the data so that all records have "*Ch8_exp1*" in the first column. As in Chapter 6, select *Filter: AutoFilters* from the **Data** menu. A number of little pull-down arrows appear on the variable names. In the first column, select *Ch8_exp1*. The file will then appear as in Figure 8.3.

Selecting one value causes all other lines of data to be hidden from view. Now select all of the data showing—do this by clicking in cell A1 and dragging the mouse to the right to column AC and down the page until everything visible is selected (to row 1288). Next, choose *Copy* from the **Edit** menu and then select *Insert a new Worksheet* from the **Insert** menu. Paste the selected data into the new worksheet and you have filtered the data needed. This time, you are instructed to copy the first row because the variable names are correct for this study. It is a good idea to save the file again. The file now appears as in Figure 8.4. (Your CD also contains the file *DMaking.xls*, with which you can compare your results, and *DMaking.csv*, which you can load into SPSS without the filtering step.)

Notice that the original data are still on the worksheet called "*clean*" (see the tabs at the bottom of the worksheet). Clicking on a tab shows the data on that sheet. By double-clicking on the *Sheet 1* tab, you can rename it *Ch8_exp1*.

FIGURE 8.3. From the **Data** menu, select *Filter,* then select *Autofilters*. Drop-down filter arrows appear. The arrow in the first column has been clicked, showing a list of possible values in the first column. Select *Ch8_exp1*.

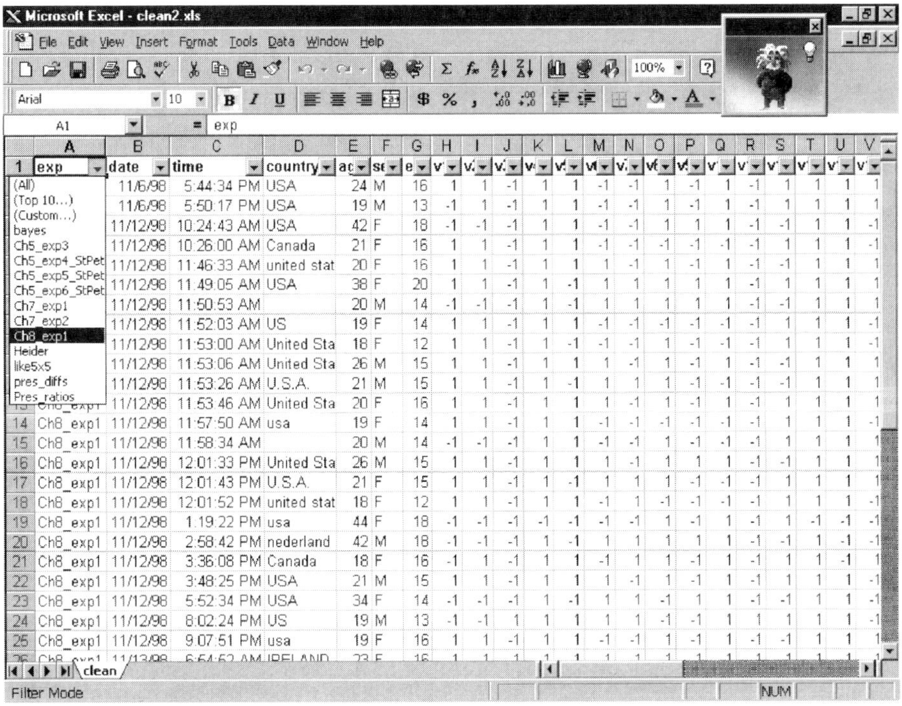

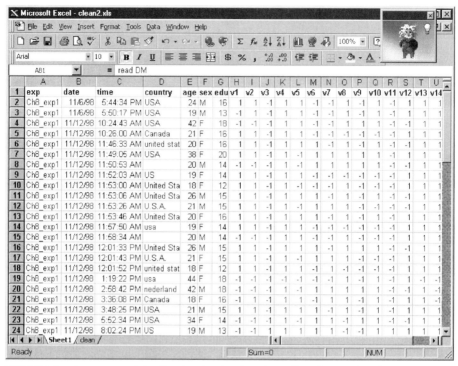

FIGURE 8.4.   Appearance of the file after the data have been filtered, copied, and pasted into a new, inserted worksheet.

 A PIVOT TABLE REPORT FOR DECISION MAKING

To address the original questions of the research, you will create cross-tabulations using the Pivot Table Report. To illustrate, consider choices 5 and 11 of the experiment. These choices are as follows:

5. Which do you choose?

I:	.05 probability to win $12	*J:*	.10 probability to win $12
	.05 probability to win $14		.05 probability to win $90
	.90 probability to win $96		.85 probability to win $96

11. Which do you choose?

U:	.05 probability to win $12	*V:*	.05 probability to win $12
	.05 probability to win $14		.05 probability to win $12
	.05 probability to win $96		.05 probability to win $90
	.85 probability to win $96		.85 probability to win $96

The responses were coded so that preference for the first gamble (shown here on the left) was coded as -1, and choice of the second gamble was coded as $+1$.

Note that gamble *I* is the same as *U* and that *J* is the same as *V*, except that iden-

tical consequences in *U* and *V* have been combined in choice 5 by adding their probabilities. Many decision theories, including the rank-dependent utility theory of Eq. 8.3,
imply that people will choose *I* over *J* and *U* over *V* because *I* dominates *J* and *U* dominates *V*. However, according to the configural weight TAX model, with parameters of
Birnbaum (1999a), people might choose *U* over *V*, and yet choose *J* over *I*. When you
used Netscape to load *taxcalculator.htm*, you found that the TAX model, unlike CPT and
EV, predicts that *J* has a higher value than *I*. You can enter the four outcome gambles
of *U* and *V* to check that the TAX model also predicts that people will choose *U*
over *V*.

The accuracy of this prediction can be examined in a Pivot Table Report of the
data. First, click the mouse in A1. Then, from the **Data** menu, select *Pivot Table Report*.
A series of "Wizard" dialogs appear, which are shown in Figures 8.5–8.9. The procedure
is similar to that described in Chapter 6.

After the pivot table has been constructed (Fig. 8.10), you can drag a variable from the ROW to COLUMN. You can drag it away, which eliminates it from the
table. Note that the "PAGE" variables—sex and education—list "all," indicating that
both sexes are included and all education levels. To see the results for just females, for
example, click on the down arrow and select F. The table then displays the results for
only females. You can do the same to examine the results for just males, or for different levels of education. You can also select *PivotTable Report* again and create another
table.

The table (Fig. 8.10) shows that of the 78 subjects, 54 chose *J* over *I* on choice 5,
representing 69% violations of stochastic dominance on this choice! These results are
similar to those reported by Birnbaum and Navarrete (1998), who tested undergraduates in a much longer study. However, on choice 11, 64 chose *U* over *V*; in other words,
82% *satisfied* stochastic dominance, and only 18% violated stochastic dominance. To ask
if the rate of 69% is significantly different from 18%, one can use the test of correlated
proportions.

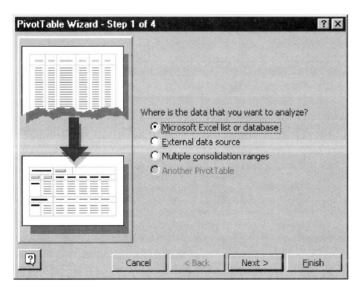

FIGURE 8.5.
PivotTable Wizard, Step 1. Choose *Mi-
crosoft Excel list or data base*, then click
Next.

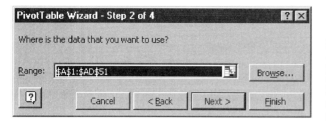

FIGURE 8.6.
A range box appears; the program may anticipate the range correctly. If not, enter the range
of cells, including all of the data, or click in the
box, and use the mouse pointer to select the
range in the worksheet. In this case, the 51
should be changed to 79. Click *Next.*

 STATISTICAL TEST OF CORRELATED PROPORTIONS

This test is a binomial sign test that compares the number who violated dominance on
choice 5 *and* satisfied dominance on choice 11 (49) against the number who had the
opposite preferences (8). The binomial sign test then asks the question, What is the
probability of getting this split (49 to 8) if those $n = 57$ who switched preferences were
equally likely to have switched in either direction? In other words, this equals the probability of tossing 57 coins and finding 49 or more are heads. The binomial distribution
has a mean, $\mu = np$, where n is the number of independent trials and p is the probability [in this case, $p = \frac{1}{2}$, so $\mu = (57)(\frac{1}{2}) = 28.5$], and it has a standard deviation,
$\sigma = \sqrt{np(1-p)}$. In this case, $\sigma = \sqrt{57(.5)(.5)} = 3.77$. For small n ($n < 30$), you can look
up the cumulative probabilities in a binomial table. As n gets larger, the binomial can
be approximated by the normal distribution, so $z = \dfrac{X - \mu}{\sigma}$ can be compared to the standard normal distribution, in which the probability is .95 that z will fall between -1.96

FIGURE 8.7.   In step 3 of the PivotTable Wizard, drag *sex* from the right to the PAGE box, drag *V11* to the
ROW, drag *V11* to the COLUMN, and drag *V5* again to the DATA field. If "Sum of V5" is
showing or another function besides "Count of V5," then double-click on it, which brings
up the dialog of Figure 8.8.

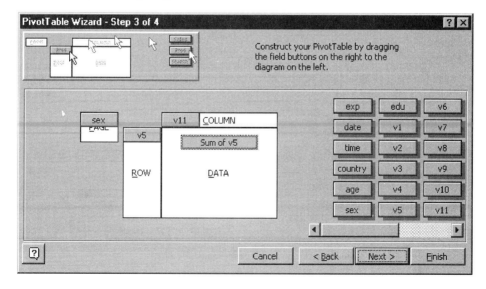

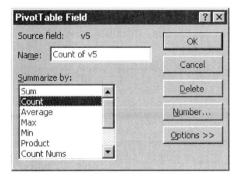

FIGURE 8.8.
Select *Count* from the menu and click *OK*. Then drag *edu* (education) to the PAGE box in Figure 8.7 and click *Next.*

and 1.96. For this case, $z = 5.43$ [$z = (49 - 28.5)/3.77$]; because such an extreme value of z is extremely unlikely by chance, one can reject the null hypothesis that these two types of violation of stochastic dominance are equally probable. Instead, this test shows that significantly more people violated stochastic dominance on choice 5 than on choice 11.

What is going on here? The configural weight TAX model assumes that people average the values of the information with weights that are affected by the probabilities and the ranks of the payoffs. Lower-valued consequences take weight (attention) from higher-valued consequences. Because *J* has two good outcomes ($90 and $96) whereas *I* only has one good outcome ($96), this configurally weighted average gives *J* a higher value than *I*. However, when the outcomes are split in choice 11, corresponding outcomes receive the same weight, so higher consequences produce higher averages. The TAX model satisfies dominance for choice 11 even though it violates it in choice 5.

Another way of looking at the results is to consider them evidence of event-splitting effects, which are violations of coalescing. Rank-dependent models imply that people should make the same choice in either choice 5 or choice 11, because the only difference is in how the events are split or coalesced. The data show significant violations of coalescing, which according to the configural weight model, are the cause of violations of stochastic dominance (Birnbaum & Navarrete, 1998).

Expected value, expected utility, and rank-dependent expected utility theory (including cumulative prospect theory) all predict that people should make the same decisions in choices 5 and 11. These theories imply that people should prefer the domi-

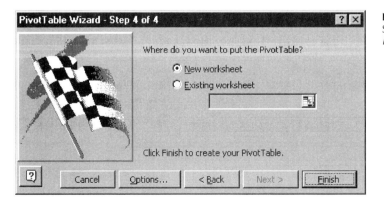

FIGURE 8.9.
Select *New worksheet* and click *Finish.*

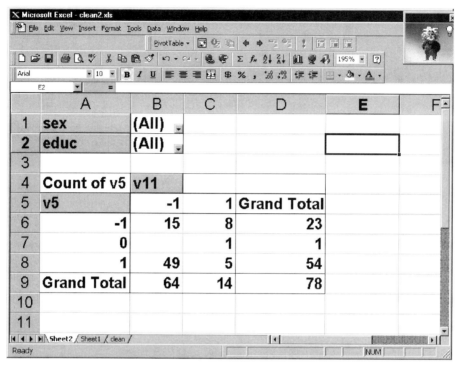

FIGURE 8.10.   The PivotTable for V5 and V11 of the decision-making experiment.

nant gamble in both choices. However, the configural weight TAX model predicts that people will violate stochastic dominance in choice 5, and that they will satisfy stochastic dominance in choice 11. These results thus refute the descriptive accuracy of a class of theories of decision making, but the configural weight TAX model remains a viable descriptive theory.

Birnbaum (1999c, 2000a) reported Web studies involving more than 1900 people in which systematic violations of stochastic dominance were observed; these studies yielded similar conclusions to those obtained from the sample of data included on your CD. Those studies also compared the results of highly educated people with the results of college students tested in the lab. People recruited from the Internet were better educated and less likely to violate stochastic dominance than those from the lab, but both studies reached the same conclusions regarding the viability of the theories compared. Because the Web sample was so large and diverse, it was possible to separate the data for analysis within genders by education levels. It was found that violations of stochastic dominance were correlated with education: Better-educated people are less likely to violate stochastic dominance.

SUMMARY

This chapter reviewed expected value, expected utility, and rank-dependent expected utility theories. These theories imply that decision makers should satisfy stochastic dominance. Procedures for conducting an experiment on decision making via the Web and for analyzing the data were described. An on-line calculator that can be used to calculate the predicted values of gambles from three theories was described. Data included on your CD were analyzed to show that people violate stochastic dominance on certain choices in which people are predicted to violate stochastic dominance by the configural weight TAX model of Birnbaum and Navarrete (1998).

 EXERCISES

1. Construct pivot table reports for other combinations of choices in the decision-making experiment. For example, choices 7 and 13 are like those of choices 5 and 11, except the position of the dominant gambles has been reversed to counterbalance position in the choice. Do choices 7 and 13 yield the same conclusions as choices 5 and 11?

2. When you have your own scripts, you can use different scripts for different experiments, in which case you will not need to separate data by filtering. However, when a separate script is used for each experiment, filtering can still be very useful for studying the data. For example, look at choices 3 and 4 of the decision experiment. If a person violated transparent dominance on these choices, maybe that person did not understand the instructions. To check how the results would be changed by filtering on choices 3 and 4, you could, for example, filter *v3* for −1 and *v4* for +1. How many people violated dominance on both choices 3 and 4?

3. Create a PivotTable of *v5* and *v7*. Look closely at the HTML, and you see that choosing *J* in choice 5 (+1) is a violation of stochastic dominance, and choosing *M* over *N* (−1) is a violation of stochastic dominance in choice 7. From your PivotTable of choices *v5* and *v7*, find out if significantly more people have two violations (+1 and −1 on *v5* and *v7*) than have no violations on those two trials (−1 and +1 on V5 and V7). The appropriate statistic in this case is the binomial test of correlated proportions. In this case, the statistic tests the proposition that the proportion of violations is .5; if significantly more people have two violations than have zero, it means that the overall probability of violations, averaged over V5 and V7, exceeds $\frac{1}{2}$.

4. Analyze the data by SPSS using crosstabs. You can import *Dmaking.csv* to SPSS.

5. Project idea: Can you think of some type of training that will cause people to have fewer violations of stochastic dominance? Design a between-subjects experiment in which different groups get different training. Then have both groups complete the experiment. See if the rate of violations is lower in the group with special training.

6. Project idea: Read Birnbaum (1999c, 2000a) and try to devise new choices that distinguish CPT from the configural weight TAX model. Before you run your experiment, use the calculator to make sure that at least two theories make different predictions.

Part II

MAKING SURVEYS, TESTS, AND EXPERIMENTS

Chapter 9

MAKING SURVEYS WITH SURVEYWIZ

This chapter explains how to use surveyWiz, a Web page that makes it easy to put simple surveys and questionnaires on the Web (Birnbaum, 2000c). The program embedded in the Web page is written in JavaScript. The program is included on the CD that comes with this book. SurveyWiz allows you to add questions with either text boxes for input or scales composed of a series of radio buttons, whose number and endpoint labels can be specified.

The use of this program will be illustrated by an example experiment on judgments of the "size" of numbers. How big a number is 221? How big is 9? The results will surprise you, because the data show that 9 is judged a significantly "bigger" number than 221! As you might guess, there is a trick. The trick is to collect ratings in a between-subjects design. As you will see, it can be tricky to interpret judgments collected from different groups of subjects who receive different treatments.

 HOW TO USE SURVEYWIZ

Load *surveyWiz.htm* in your browser (Figure 9.1). Type in a title for the study in the box labeled *Survey Name*. For the first example, type *Judging the Size of Numbers*. This title will be placed both as the title of the page and it will also be printed as a heading in the file. Press *Tab* and give the experiment a *Short Name*. In the first example, the short name will be *numbers221*. The *Short Name* will be the first variable in the data file, included as a hidden variable, *00exp*. Next, push the button labeled *1. Start Form*, which starts the HTML form. The screen appears as in Figure 9.1.

Note that the HTML includes the usual tags to start an HTML page, and it also starts a FORM whose ACTION is the URL of the generic script that you have used before. This script sends the data to the file, *data.csv*, which you can download by FTP. When you have your own script, you can replace that URL with the address of your own script. Hidden variables are also created, including the study's condition name (i.e., the short name, *numbers221*), the *date, time,* and *remote address*. The remote address is useful for detecting multiple submissions by the same person—if two lines of data come in on the same day from the same remote address, they are probably multiple submissions by the same person.

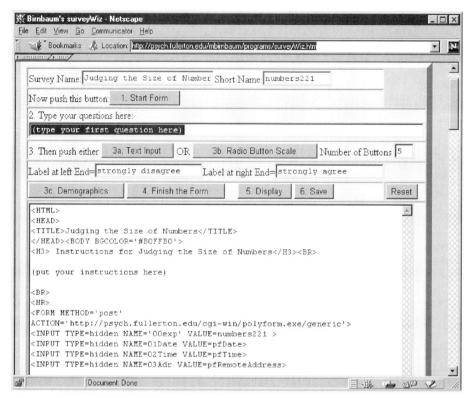

FIGURE 9.1.   Appearance of the Web page *surveyWiz.htm* after the first step. Note the HTML that the program inserted into the window within the text area. The text for the second step is selected automatically so that you can type each question without another keystroke.

The next line after *2. Type your questions here,* says, "(*put your first question here.*)" It is selected after you press button 1. If it is not selected, then select it, and replace it with the following question: *How big a number is 221?*

Now, define the radio button response scale. First, enter 7 for the *Number of Buttons.* Next, change the *Label at left End* to "very very small" and the *Label at right End* to "very very large." Then push the button labeled *3b. Radio Button Scale.* The screen now appears as in Figure 9.2.

You could now continue to add questions in this way, up to 90 questions. You can mix items with a text box response field instead of a scale of radio buttons. After you entered each question, you would press the button for either *3a. Text Input* or *3b. Radio Button Scale.* For this example, however, the next step is to add demographic questions.

To add preset demographic questions, push the button labeled *3c. Demographics.* The demographics might be placed in the beginning, middle, or end of the form. Finally, push the button labeled *4. Finish the Form,* and the final HTML tags are added to close the form and the HTML page.

Scroll through the HTML to the beginning and replace (*put your instructions here*) with "This is a study of the psychological size of numbers." That editing can be

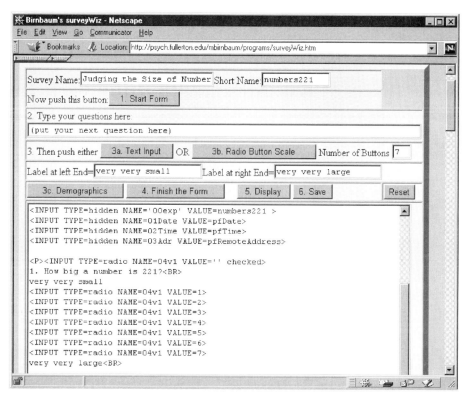

FIGURE 9.2. In this step, a series of radio buttons has just been created, as shown in the HTML. The new question line is automatically selected, and you are ready to enter the next question.

done directly in the text area within the window, or it can be done later in a text editor such as NotePad. You can change the color of the background by changing `BGCOLOR="B0FFB0"` to another color, which might be `"teal"`, `"cyan"`, or whatever. In Chapter 14 you learn more about specifying colors.

You can now push the *5. Display* button to view the file in the browser. The *Display* button works with Netscape 3 and above for Mac or PC, and with Internet Explorer 4.0 and above for PC and 4.5 and above for Mac. If you do not have Netscape Navigator for Mac, you may have to proceed to the next step to view and save the new page.

COPY HTML TO A TEXT EDITOR AND SAVE

The next step is to scroll to the bottom of the text area window of HTML and use the mouse to select upward until you have selected the entire contents of the window. Be sure to select everything from `<HTML>` to `</HTML>`. Select *Copy* from the **Edit** menu. The screen will appear as in Figure 9.3. Now open a text editor such as NotePad or Simple-Text and paste the HTML into a new file. Save it with the name *numbersA.htm*, to indi-

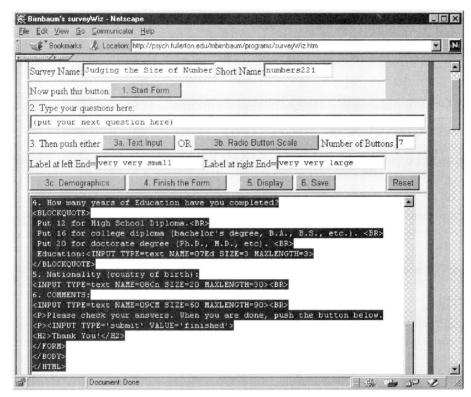

FIGURE 9.3. Appearance of surveyWiz window after completing third step. The entire window of HTML has been selected, and it is copied and pasted into a text editor and saved. Pressing the *Save* button will not save it, but it will remind you of this step. In some browsers, you can also press *Display* and save the source HTML from the browser.

cate that this is condition A. The appearance of the HTML in NotePad is shown in Figure 9.4.

NotePad may try to add a *.txt* ending to your filename. In the *Save As* dialog box, for *Files of type*, be sure to select *All files(*.*)*, and give the filename an ending of *.htm* or *.html*. Keep the text editor open until you are finished with the editing. After you have saved the file in the text editor, you can also load the same file in the browser. If you see an error or if you see an adjustment you want to make to the appearance of the page, make your changes in the text editor, save it in the editor, then reload the page in the browser. Recall that you must save your changes *and* reload the page in the browser in order to see the changes. Figure 9.5 shows the appearance in the browser of the page created.

The next task is to make another experimental page, *numbersB.htm*, that will be identical to *numbersA.htm* except that it asks for a judgment of the number 9. Press the reset button. Repeat the steps used to make *numbersA.htm*, except the question should be, "How big is the number 9?" Give this one the same *Survey Name*, but give it a *Short Name* of *number9* and save the HTML as *numbersB.htm*. Make another experiment with

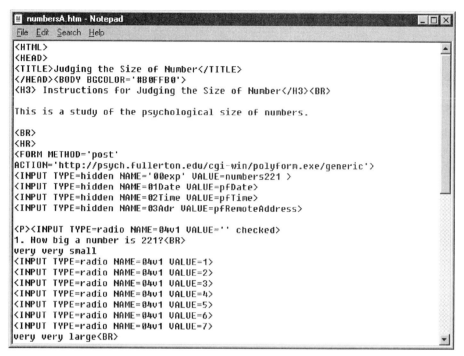

```
numbersA.htm - Notepad
File  Edit  Search  Help
<HTML>
<HEAD>
<TITLE>Judging the Size of Number</TITLE>
</HEAD><BODY BGCOLOR='#B0FFB0'>
<H3> Instructions for Judging the Size of Number</H3><BR>

This is a study of the psychological size of numbers.

<BR>
<HR>
<FORM METHOD='post'
ACTION='http://psych.fullerton.edu/cgi-win/polyform.exe/generic'>
<INPUT TYPE=hidden NAME='00exp' VALUE=numbers221 >
<INPUT TYPE=hidden NAME=01Date VALUE=pfDate>
<INPUT TYPE=hidden NAME=02Time VALUE=pfTime>
<INPUT TYPE=hidden NAME=03Adr VALUE=pfRemoteAddress>

<P><INPUT TYPE=radio NAME=04v1 VALUE='' checked>
1. How big a number is 221?<BR>
very very small
<INPUT TYPE=radio NAME=04v1 VALUE=1>
<INPUT TYPE=radio NAME=04v1 VALUE=2>
<INPUT TYPE=radio NAME=04v1 VALUE=3>
<INPUT TYPE=radio NAME=04v1 VALUE=4>
<INPUT TYPE=radio NAME=04v1 VALUE=5>
<INPUT TYPE=radio NAME=04v1 VALUE=6>
<INPUT TYPE=radio NAME=04v1 VALUE=7>
very very large<BR>
```

FIGURE 9.4.   HTML created by surveyWiz has been copied to the text editor, NotePad, and saved as *numbersA.htm*.

two items, called *numbersC.htm*, which asks for judgments of the sizes of both 221 and of 9.

Finally, create a page that asks the participant to click on his or her month of birth, as was done in the St. Petersburg experiment in Chapter 5. Set it up so that four months are assigned to condition A, four to condition B, and four to condition C. This assignment page is on the CD as *Ch9_exp1.htm*. (A random assignment page in JavaScript from Chapter 17 is also included on the CD, which assigns people to condition A or B by a computer-generated random number.)

RESULTS OF NUMBERS STUDY: BETWEEN-SUBJECTS AND WITHIN-SUBJECTS DESIGNS

Whenever you set up a new survey or experiment, it is a good idea for you to complete the task yourself, to be sure that you understand how the survey or experiment feels and also to be certain you know how the data will return in the file.

The variables appear in the order in which they were entered to surveyWiz. You can, however, cut and paste to rearrange them in the HTML page. If you do so, the data will still return in the order in which they were entered in surveyWiz, because the script places them in the file in the order of the numbers that precede the variable names (i.e., 00exp, 01date, 02time, etc.).

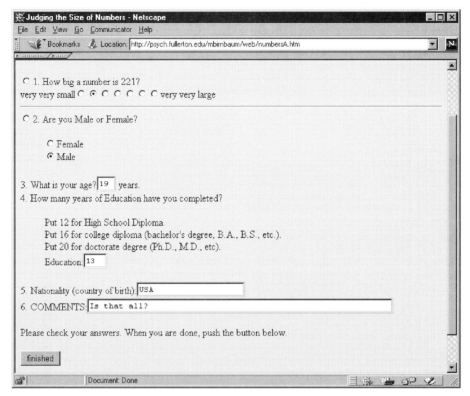

FIGURE 9.5.   Appearance of the page *numbersA.htm* created by surveyWiz.

When this simple experiment is done in a *between-subjects* design (i.e., different subjects serve in the 9 and 221 conditions, as in conditions A and B), 9 receives a significantly higher mean judgment than 221 (Birnbaum, 1999a). That probably surprises you because it is pretty obvious that 221 is actually bigger than 9!

Why would the results show that 9 is rated "bigger" than 221? In a *between-subjects* design, each subject only experiences one treatment and makes judgments in the context of the stimuli presented. Judgments are always made in some context (Parducci, 1968, 1995). The experiment provided "no" context other than the number presented for judgment, so our judges supplied their own contexts. In this case, when the judges do not know of the other possible numbers, so the context is *confounded* with the stimulus. When people are asked to judge the number 221, people apparently think of bigger numbers, perhaps as high as 999, among which the number 221 seems "small." However, when judging the number 9, people think of smaller numbers, among which 9 seems "average" or even "large."

In the *within-subjects* design, *numbersC.htm*, judges receive a context that includes both the numbers 9 and 221, so they give larger judgments for larger numbers. In condition C, where each person judges both numbers, 221 is judged larger than 9.

This experiment illustrates that every numerical judgment is made with respect to some context, and that in a between-subjects design, the context for judgment may be confounded with the stimulus. One must be very cautious when trying to interpret judgments obtained in between-subjects experiments.

RANGE-FREQUENCY THEORY OF CONTEXTUAL EFFECTS

Parducci (1968, 1995) developed a theory that gives a good account of contextual effects judgments of magnitude of psychophysical, social, and hedonic stimuli. He believes that happiness is also determined by the same principles that determine judgments of magnitude, so to Parducci, understanding the principles of judgment is the key to understanding how to lead a happy life. According to his theory, known as *range-frequency theory*, happiness is a negatively skewed distribution.

Range-frequency theory asserts that people compare stimuli to two standards. First, where does the stimulus fall with respect to the endpoints? The relative position of a stimulus to the endpoints is known as the *range* effect. Second, what is the relative position of the stimulus compared to the frequency distribution of the stimuli? In other words, what is the percentile rank of the stimulus compared to all stimuli in the person's context? That position is the *frequency* effect. Range-frequency theory says that people judge stimuli by a compromise between these two systems of relative judgment.

For example, to determine the stimulus that would be judged "average," the result would be the stimulus that falls between the psychological midpoint (range) and the median (frequency). In a negatively skewed distribution, more than half of the stimuli exceed the mean; in a positively skewed distribution, most stimuli fall below the mean. To be happy, you should arrange your life so that most experiences are better than the midpoint experience. If you have an opportunity to experience a unique, rare, and wonderful event *once,* you should avoid it, because it will make the rest of your life dull and mundane, if not unpleasant. A rare and wonderful experience will cause the midpoint to increase, which might cause the rest of your experiences to seem poor in comparison to that one moment of ecstasy.

Numbers experiments *D* and *E* contain two contexts such as have been used by Parducci to investigate contextual effects in judgments of the size of numbers. The experiment labeled *numbersD.htm* has numbers from 108 to 992 in a positively skewed distribution. The experiment labeled *numbersE.htm* has numbers that are negatively skewed with the same endpoints. According to range-frequency theory, judgments of the same numbers (108, 257, 324, 435, 550, 621, 776, 833, and 992 are common to both conditions) should be higher in the positively skewed distribution (*D*) than in the negatively skewed distribution. It takes a larger number to be judged "average" in the negatively skewed distribution.

If you use different groups of subjects in each context, you are using a *systextual design* in which the context of the experimental design has been systematically manipulated (Birnbaum, 1974b). Draw a graph that shows the mean judgment of the common numbers with a separate curve for each between-subjects context. Compare judgments obtained with conditions *D* and *E*. You will see that within groups (within each curve), people give higher judgments to bigger numbers. However, between groups, a smaller number can receive larger judgments in the positively skewed context than does a larger number in the negatively skewed context.

DISCUSSION AND SUMMARY

This chapter explained how to use surveyWiz to make simple tests and surveys. This program can save time in creating the HTML for a simple survey, questionnaire, or test, especially if you have many items with the same type of scale of radio buttons. You should understand the HTML created by surveyWiz, even if you do not yet understand the JavaScript program that makes the HTML. This chapter also discussed the problem of comparing judgments obtained in between-subjects designs. Range-frequency theory explains how context can be manipulated between subjects.

SurveyWiz makes it easy to make simple surveys, questionnaires, and tests. Now that you know HTML, you can modify the survey to change its appearance or add something (for example, a TEXTAREA) that surveyWiz does not make for you.

SurveyWiz is also available on-line at the URL:

http://psych.fullerton.edu/mbirnbaum/programs/surveyWiz.htm

You can check this site for the latest version of the program. The program is entirely self-contained in one file. To download the latest version, visit the Web site and select *View Source* from your browser. Then copy and paste the source into a text editor and save it. SurveyWiz may be copied and used for noncommercial, scholarly purposes without charge. As you should with any resource (published in a journal or on the Web) that benefits your papers, you should acknowledge credit for the help.

Another program that has a similar purpose is WWW Survey Assistant by Schmidt (1997b), which can also be used freely by noncommercial, educational users. It is available online from the URL:

http://survey.psy.buffalo.edu/

Survey Assistant has advantages over commercial programs. You may find the program harder to use than surveyWiz for making a simple questionnaire, but the program supports a greater variety of question formats, and it also supports development of server-side scripts that allow preprocessing of the data.

 EXERCISES

1. Use surveyWiz to make a 10-item true–false test of knowledge of some situation. Use two radio buttons for "True" and "False."
2. Use surveyWiz to make a 10-item short-answer questionnaire or quiz. If the answers will exceed the defaults, you may need to increase the SIZE and MAXLENGTH attributes of the text boxes from SIZE=8 MAXLENGTH=25 to SIZE=60 MAXLENGTH=100.
3. Use surveyWiz to make a 5-item multiple-choice quiz of questions for Introductory Psychology. Use the scales of radio buttons, and after the form is complete, edit the HTML to place each button (except the one in the margin) on a separate line (use <BR>). You will need to add the multiple-choice alternatives in the editing stage. For example, create the following item:

> Pavlov conditioned his dogs to salivate when they heard the sound of a bell. In Pavlov's terminology, the bell is:
> a. A conditioned stimulus
> b. An unconditioned stimulus
> c. A conditioned response
> d. An unconditioned response
> e. Both a and c

To create the item, type in the first line of the question, and use a 5-point scale with blank endpoint labels. Then edit the item to complete the question, add the response choices, and put <BR> at the end of each line. As you edit, you can use the *Display* key to see how the item will look. You can also add `<BLOCKQUOTE></BLOCKQUOTE>` tags to indent the choices.

4. Project idea: Collect data for the numbers experiments *D* and *E*. Set up a page that assigns people to one of these conditions. See if you can explain why the same number gets different judgments in the different conditions. If you understand range-frequency theory, you can understand what numbers to present people so that you maximize (or minimize) their judgments of size. What numbers would you present people so that the average of all judgments is as large as possible? Relate this problem to Parducci's goal of arranging a life to maximize happiness.

Chapter 10

PERSONALITY TESTING

This chapter shows how to construct a simple personality test with surveyWiz. SurveyWiz is well suited to making personality tests. You could also make the HTML directly by the methods explained in Chapters 2–5, but surveyWiz saves you a lot of tedious typing. This chapter also reviews basic concepts of psychological testing and illustrates these ideas with analyses of data for the personality test. These data are included on the CD that accompanies this book.

In a personality test, the participant's task is to evaluate him- or herself. Rather than judging the sizes of numbers (as in Chapter 9), the participant judges his or her own personality traits and behaviors. This chapter describes the construction of a simple personality test to measure shyness and masculinity/femininity. The survey permits you to correlate personality measures with students' grades, heights, and genders. You also learn how to use SPSS to calculate a correlation matrix and perform a factor analysis.

 CONSTRUCTING A SIMPLE PERSONALITY TEST

First, push the *Reset* button on surveyWiz to erase everything from your previous use, such as the exercises in Chapter 9. (Be sure to save any work you need to save first.) Type in the name *Personality Questionnaire* for the *Survey Name* and *personality* for the *Short Name*. Next, push button *1. Start Form*. Then enter the questions that follow; for each of the items, use the default 5-point radio button scale with labels of "strongly disagree" to "strongly agree." Type the following questions and press the *3b. Radio Button Scale* key after each item:

> *I am a shy person.*
> *I am an extrovert.*
>
> *Those who know me say I'm extroverted.*
> *Those who know me say I'm shy.*
>
> *For a person of my gender, I'm considered masculine.*
> *For a person of my gender, I'm considered feminine.*
>
> *I think I'm masculine in my personality compared to people of both genders.*
> *I think I'm feminine in my personality compared to people of both genders.*

For the next items, use text box inputs; press the *3a. Text Input* button after you enter each item:

> *What is your grade point average? (4 = A, 3 = B, 2 = C, 1 = D, 0 = F; if you have a perfect A average, your GPA would be 4.0)*
> *What is your height in inches? (5 feet = 60 inches; 6 feet = 72 inches; if you are 5'4", then put 64 in the box)*

Next, push the *3c. Demographics* button. Then push the *4. Finish the Form* button.

Study the HTML in the textarea, and replace (*put your instructions here*) with the following instructions: *Please rate how well each item describes your personality*. Look at the

HTML at the end of the document and carefully change the value of Male from "M" to 1; change "F" to 0. This coding allows you to correlate gender with other numerical variables such as height and the masculinity items. Remember: On this scale of gender, a positive correlation with gender means that males are higher on the scale than females. One expects a positive correlation between gender and height with this coding, because on average, males are usually taller than females. Copy the HTML to a text editor and save it as *personality.htm*. Compare your version with *personalityA.htm* on the CD. This questionnaire is pretty easy to make with surveyWiz.

Be sure to print out a copy of the questionnaire (and the HTML). Make a record of the variables, including the "hidden" variables, so that you know exactly how the variables will be returned to the data file. At this point, when you are sure that you know the order of the variables, you could cut and paste the HTML to make a new ordering of the items in the questionnaire. A copy of this questionnaire is included on the CD as *personalityA.htm*. A slightly more advanced version (which presents feedback) is also included on the CD as *personalityB.htm*. Load and complete the questionnaire in *personalityB.htm*. The more advanced version is explained in Chapter 19.

When you get the data, you can import them into Excel and filter by the techniques described in Chapter 6, saving the data as a CSV file. The CD contains data for *personalityB.htm* in the file *personality.csv*. To compute correlation coefficients between columns of data in Excel, you click in a cell where the correlation will be placed, and then select *Function* from the **Insert** menu. From the *Functions* dialog box, choose *Correlations*. Select the two columns that you want correlated, and click *OK*.

A later section teaches you how to use SPSS to calculate correlation coefficients and to perform a simple factor analysis. To prepare data for SPSS, it is a good idea to filter them first in Excel, copy them to a fresh page worksheet, and use *Save As* to save the data as a *Comma Separated File (.csv)*. Also included on the CD is an SPSS data file, *personality.sav*. Before you analyze the data, however, it is important that you understand a few things about personality, correlation, and test theory.

CAUSATION AND CORRELATION

A personality test is an instrument designed to measure individual differences. Some people are tall and others are short; some are thin and some are heavy. Just as people differ in these physical characteristics, people differ in dimensions or traits of personality: some are shy and some are outgoing; some are emotionally calm and others seem nervous or anxious; some people are socially conservative and others are nonconformists; some are honest and some are not. The idea is that people are different, and if we could measure aspects of their personalities, we might be able to predict who would behave one way and who would behave differently when placed in the same situation.

If we could predict behavior from a test of personality, it does not mean that personality caused the behavior. Finding a correlation between gender and height does not mean that gender causes height, or that height causes gender. Finding a correlation between shyness and GPA would not mean that being shy causes people to spend more time with books, thereby increasing their GPAs; nor does it mean that being smart causes people to be shy. It would merely mean that one can predict GPA from our measure of shyness or predict shyness from GPA.

If two variables are correlated, then you can predict one from the other. *Causation* means you can change things. Causation and correlation are two completely different concepts, but people often confuse them and think that evidence of correlation somehow is related to causation. One of the hardest ideas to get freshmen in psychology to give up is the fallacy that causation and correlation are somehow related. To understand the distinction between causation and correlation, it helps to consider two studies of the relationship between antibiotics and death.

If one conducts a *survey* and correlates the amount of antibiotics taken last year with death (whether a person is alive or dead this year), one finds that people who took a lot of antibiotics last year are more likely to be dead this year than people who took no antibiotics last year. Thus, antibiotics are *positively* correlated with death—the use of more antibiotics is associated with being more likely dead. However, if you do an *experiment* on the effect of antibiotics, you find the opposite relation—people who were *randomly assigned* to receive antibiotics instead of placebo are more likely to be *alive* this year. In the experiment, antibiotic treatment is negatively correlated with death—the use of more antibiotics means less likely to be dead. Thus, these two types of studies yield opposite relations.

What happens in an experiment is often the opposite of what happens in the so-called real world of confounded variables. That is why scientists who want to understand causation prefer to do experiments in controlled situations. In the so-called real world, antibiotics predict death because sick people in wealthy countries are given antibiotics, and medicines do not always work. If you are in the life insurance business, you do *not* want to sell life insurance to people who have been taking a lot of antibiotics because they are sick and likely to die. However, from double-blind experiments with random assignment, we learn that taking antibiotics has the causal effect of *decreasing* the likelihood of death. So, if you already insure a person who gets sick, you would advise that person to take antibiotics because that treatment *causes* a decrease in the death rate. Thus, correlation and causation can be and often are opposites.

As another example, ask yourself the following question: Would students learn more in a small or large class in high school? However, what is the correlation between class size and scholastic performance? Think of your high school. Which students are enrolled in the smallest classes? The mentally or behaviorally challenged students are in the smallest classes. Which was larger in your high school, the class of AP (advanced placement, or honors) English, or the class for people with learning disabilities? So, if an investigator correlated a scholastic achievement test with class size, the investigator would find that larger class sizes are positively correlated with better performance. Does that mean that we should make all classes larger? No, because correlation does not imply causation; it might help to reduce class size, just as it might help to give antibiotics. Do not be confused by correlation and confounded variables. Remember: correlation and causation are two different ideas; they are not related to each other, and they can and will easily yield opposite relations. Surveys are used to assess correlation, and experiments are used to assess causation.

Here is a test item that all students of psychology receive in one form or another.

> If A and B are positively correlated, it means:
> a. A causes B
> b. B causes A
> c. Some third factor C causes both A and B
> d. We know that a, b, or c is true, but we do not know which
> e. None of the above

The correct answer is e, None of the above. From correlation, we know nothing about causation. It is possible that A caused B; it is possible that B caused A; it is possible that A causes B *and* B causes A; it is possible that a third factor, C, causes both A and B. However, it is also possible that there is *absolutely no causal relation at all.* Just as alchemists tried to make gold by mixing lead and sulfur, there are statistical alchemists who try to draw causal inferences from correlation. Do not be fooled.

ASSESSING TESTS: INTERNAL CONSISTENCY, RELIABILITY, AND VALIDITY

Any test or measure can be analyzed for internal consistency, reliability, and validity (Anastasi, 1982; Nunnally, 1978). *Internal consistency* is measured by correlations among items that make up the scale. In our personality test, there were four items that were intended to measure introversion/extroversion (*I am a shy person; I am an extrovert; Those who know me say I'm extroverted;* and *Those who know me say I'm shy*). The first two items should correlate negatively because a person who is an extrovert is not likely to be shy. Similarly, a person who describes him- or herself as shy would also tend to think that acquaintances would describe them in the same way, so the first and fourth items should be positively correlated. To construct a *total shyness* measure, we can add the responses to the two shyness items and subtract the responses to the two items measuring extroversion. This scale would have high internal consistency if the items making up the scale correlate properly with each other. The higher the average interitem correlation and the more items there are in the scale, the higher the internal consistency. If the items all measure the same construct, then higher internal consistency means higher reliability.

If a test is reliable, then one can predict from one assessment of the measure to another assessment. Test–retest reliability is the correlation between scores of a test and the scores obtained when the same people are tested again with the same test on another occasion. If the same personality test is given twice, the person who is shy today should be shy next week. The *alternate-forms* definition of reliability is measured by the correlation between two different versions of the same test.

If a scale is unreliable, then it is not a useful measure. For example, suppose you got on a bathroom scale and it gave a reading of 125 lb. Suppose you stepped off and on again and got a measure of 367 lb. Suppose you get on again and it reads 41 lb., and next it reads 212 lb. If a scale gives different readings each time the same measure is taken, that scale is unreliable. You certainly would not want to use that scale to measure the outcome of a diet study, nor would it be fair to use that scale to weigh in fighters before a prizefight. If a test is not reliable, then it is not valid.

If a test is reliable, it may or may not be a valid measure of what the test is supposed to measure. *Validity* is the correlation between a test and the construct that the test is supposed to predict. A test of marital satisfaction should predict which couples will get divorced and which will stay together. A behavioral test of drunkenness used by the police should predict how well a driver could operate his or her vehicle. A test of law school aptitude should predict who will succeed and who will flunk out or fail the bar exam. If a test is valid, then it can be used to predict what the test is supposed to measure.

Consider a behavioral measure of shyness, measured by a student's willingness to give a presentation to a class. Students might be paired to work on a project, with the assignment that one student from each pair must give a presentation to the class. Which person do you think will volunteer to give the talk? One expects those students with higher extroversion (less shyness) should be more likely to volunteer to give a talk. If the measure correctly predicts which student would give the talk, then such a correlation would be an index of the *convergent validity* of the test. At the same time, the test of masculinity/femininity should not predict this same behavior. Thus, the test battery should *discriminate* between behaviors that are and are not measures of a given construct.

Ask yourself: Which test (shyness/extroversion, or masculinity/femininity) should more accurately predict if a woman is wearing pants or a skirt? Which test should predict if a person is willing to perform in a skit for the class? Which test should predict if a person likes to play football? Which test should predict if a person prefers to socialize with many friends or with only one? These studies would be ways to assess the convergent and discriminant validity of the personality scales on the test.

Another approach to validation of personality tests is to examine if the test discriminates between *criterion groups* that should differ systematically on the test. For example, a test of mental illness should distinguish patients in mental hospitals from people who work there. Which group do you think would score higher in masculinity: Navy Seals or interior decorators? Which group should score higher in shyness: members of the drama club or members of the computer club? Buchanan (2000) discussed how newsgroups on the Internet (groups of people who subscribe according to specific interests) can be used as criterion groups to validate personality tests.

After measuring extroversion/shyness and masculinity/femininity, one could ask how each of these scales correlates with GPA. These relationships are not really measures of validity; they are measures of empirical relationships.

ANALYSIS OF PERSONALITY DATA IN SPSS

Start SPSS and open the file *personality.sav.* For SPSS, the variable names must be short, so the item *I am a shy person* has been given the variable name *Im_shy;* similarly, the item *For a person of my gender, I'm considered masculine* has been given the variable name *con_masc.* The variables are in the same order in the data file as in the questionnaire, starting with the hidden variables of *experiment* (short name), *date, time, remote address* (which has been deleted), and ending with the person's judgment of *accuracy* and their *comments.*

The first task is to compute the matrix of correlation coefficients among all of the variables in the study. To do this, select *Correlations* then *Bivariate* from the **Analyze** menu, as shown in Figure 10.1. That brings up the dialog of Figure 10.2.

In the dialog of Figure 10.2, select all of the numerical variables with the mouse, then click the right-pointing arrow to send the selected variables to the list of variables to be intercorrelated. Variables can be added or removed from the list by selecting them individually and clicking the arrow to send them back to the list of variables omitted from the analysis or to the list chosen. For this analysis, include all of the numerical variables. Check the box beside *Pearson correlations*, then click *OK.* SPSS displays the results in a screen of output. You can double-click on parts of the output to adjust the fonts and appearance of the tables, and you can save or print the output.

Means and standard deviations are shown in Figure 10.3, and the table of correlations is shown (in part) in Figure 10.4. The correlation between the response to the statement *I am a shy person (IM_SHY)* and the statement *Those who know me say I'm shy (SAY_SHY)* is .698. That means that from one answer you can predict what the answer to another item will be; those people who describe themselves as shy also think that others who know them tend to say they are shy. The correlation between *IM_SHY* and the statement *I am an extrovert (IM_EXTR)* is −.597. The negative correlation means that those who respond high on *IM_SHY* respond low on *IM_EXTR*, and vice versa. You can predict from one to the other, but the direction of the relationship is negative.

The next task is to construct a score of total shyness from the responses to these four items. First, you must reverse the scales of the two items measuring extroversion to convert them to scales of introversion; you can do that by reflecting their signs. Thus,

![personality – SPSS for Windows Data Editor screenshot showing the Analyze menu expanded with Correlate > Bivariate selected, and a data grid with columns exp, date, noteip, im_shy, im_extr, say_extr, say_shy]

	exp	date	noteip	im_shy	im_extr	say_extr	say_shy	c
2	Personality_	4/2/99		2.00	4.00	4.00	2.00	
3	Personality_	4/2/99		5.00	1.00	3.00	5.00	
4	Personality_	4/3/99	ted)	3.00	3.00	3.00	3.00	
5	Personality_	4/4/99	ted)	4.00	1.00	1.00	4.00	
6	Personality_	4/4/99	ted)	4.00	3.00	5.00	2.00	
7	Personality_	4/4/99	ted)	4.00	2.00	1.00	5.00	
8	Personality_	4/5/99	11:35:48 AM	(deleted)	4.00	3.00	4.00	2.00
9	Personality_	4/5/99	2:19:14 PM	(deleted)	2.00	4.00	4.00	2.00
10	Personality_	4/6/99	9:16:56 AM	(deleted)	3.00	3.00	3.00	3.00
11	Personality_	4/6/99	2:43:04 PM	(deleted)	2.00	2.00	2.00	2.00
12	Personality_	4/7/99	8:57:10 PM	(deleted)	1.00	4.00	1.00	1.00
13	Personality_	4/7/99	9:50:42 PM	(deleted)	3.00	4.00	4.00	3.00
14	Personality_	4/7/99	10:05:49 PM	(deleted)	2.00	2.00	4.00	2.00
15	Personality_	4/8/99	12:07:45 PM	(deleted)	2.00	5.00	5.00	2.00
16	Personality_	4/8/99	6:02:19 PM	(deleted)	1.00	5.00	5.00	1.00
17	Personality_	4/8/99	6:35:38 PM	(deleted)	5.00	1.00	1.00	5.00

FIGURE 10.1.   To compute a matrix of correlations in SPSS, select *Correlate* then *Bivariate* from the **Analyze** menu.

we can add the responses to the two shyness items and subtract the responses to the two extroversion items, which produces a total score that measures shyness and introversion.

To compute a composite score in SPSS, do the following steps. From the **Transform** menu, select *Compute*. That brings up the dialog box shown in Figure 10.5. In the

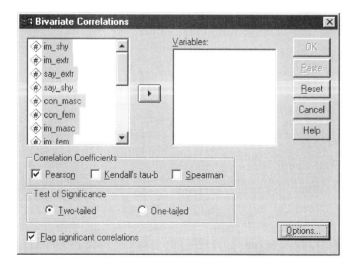

FIGURE 10.2.
The Bivariate Correlations dialog box. Select the numerical variables by clicking with the mouse and dragging. Then click the arrow, which moves the selected variables to the list to be correlated. From the *Options* key in the lower right corner, you can also obtain other statistics, including means and standard deviations. When everything is completed, click *OK*.

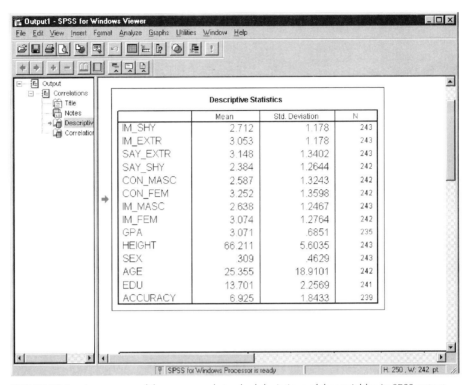

FIGURE 10.3. Appearance of the means and standard deviations of the variables in SPSS output.

Target Variable box (which will be the name of the new variable), type *TOT_SHY* (for To-tal Shyness). In the numeric expression box, you can specify the calculations that SPSS will make. To insert a variable name, select it in the box on the left, and use the arrow to send it to the expression box. Type or use the mini-keyboard to enter the minus and plus signs between the variables. Explore this box to see the variety of function calcula-tions available. Press *OK,* and SPSS creates a new column of values from the requested computation. Notice that the scores on this new scale can be positive or negative. A pos-itive sign indicates more shyness than extroversion, and a negative sign represents the opposite. Use the same approach to compute a scale of total masculinity.

The internal consistency of total scores can be computed from the Spearman–Brown prophecy formula (Nunnally, 1978, p. 211),

$$r_{kk} = \frac{k\bar{r}_{ij}}{1 + (k-1)\bar{r}_{ij}} \tag{10.1}$$

where r_{kk} is the internal consistency (theoretical reliability) of the total test score, k is the number of items in the total ($k = 4$ in these examples), and $\bar{r}_{ij}$ is the average in-teritem correlation. For the shyness total, the average interitem correlation (after re-flection of the scales) is .631, so the internal consistency is .872. For the masculinity to-tal, the average interitem correlation is .624, so the internal consistency is .869. This formula assumes that each item in a total is measuring the same true score with homo-geneous, independent error. If all of the items are measuring the same factor, then in-ternal consistency, r_{kk}, is an estimate of reliability.

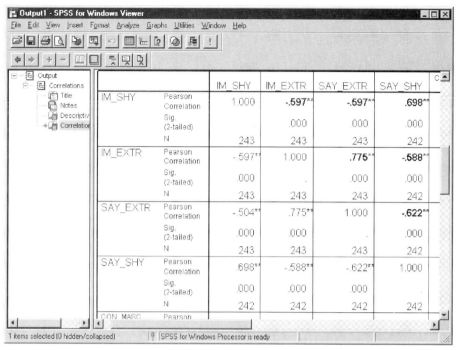

FIGURE 10.4.   Correlations among items that relate to shyness/extroversion, as shown in SPSS viewer. To see the rest of the matrix, you must scroll on the screen or print the output. By double-clicking on the table and selecting cells, you can change fonts and formats.

FIGURE 10.5.   *Compute Variable* dialog. In this case, a new variable, *TOT_SHY*, will be computed by adding the responses to *im_shy* and *say_shy*, and subtracting the responses to *im_extr* and *say_extr*. *Compute Variable* can also be used to create a scale of total masculinity, *TOT_MASC.*

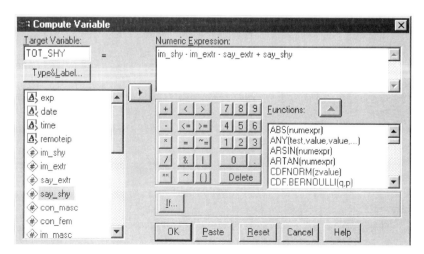

You can also use factor analysis to examine the structure of correlations (Anastasi, 1982; Nunnally, 1978). To run factor analysis from SPSS, from the **Analyze** menu, choose *Data Reduction,* then *Factor. . . .* In the *Factor Analysis* box, move the eight personality items to the list of variables to be factored. Then, click the *Extraction* button and choose *Principal Axes* as the method, *Analyze* the *correlation matrix,* and *Extract Eigenvalues over 1.* (These settings are probably the defaults, as they are the settings that historically have been most often used in factor analysis.) Click the *Continue* button. Then click the *Rotation* button and choose *Varimax* as the method, and *Display the Rotated Solution.* Click *Continue.* Explore the other dialog boxes, and then click *OK.* The results indicate that there are two factors in the data. Among the results is the rotated component (factor loading) matrix, shown in Figure 10.6.

Factor analysis is a method for exploring correlations among variables. A more general method that includes factor analysis as a special case is the approach known as *linear structural equations analysis.* Personality test developers use such methods to investigate how many factors of personality might underlie a set of items and explore the dimensions of individual differences among people.

In the little personality test used here, there were eight items designed to assess two personality factors. Factor analysis indicated that shyness and masculinity are nearly independent factors. To check this in another way, perform another correlation analysis in which the total scores for shyness and masculinity are included with the other nu-

FIGURE 10.6.   The rotated factor loading matrix. Note that this exploratory factor analysis yielded two factors that when rotated can be interpreted as extroversion and masculinity. (Note that shyness items load negatively on the first component and that femininity items load negatively on the second component.) These results confirm the hypothesized structure.

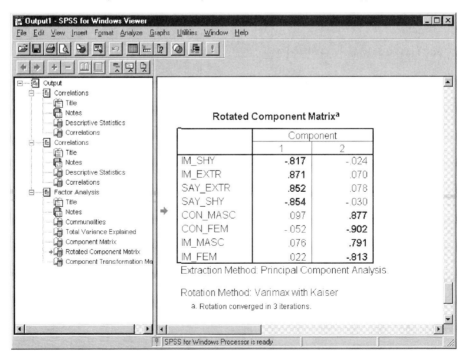

meric variables. If the two scales were independent, then they would have a correlation of zero. The two total scores correlate only $-.107$, indicating that the two scales are nearly independent.

In larger studies of personality, other factors or dimensions of personality have been developed and measured. The real challenge to personality testing is to develop tests that have high validity when used to predict interesting behavioral criteria. Intelligence tests can predict success in school (as measured by grades or scholastic achievement tests) with correlations above .5. Personality tests have not yet achieved validity coefficients as high as those reported for IQ tests.

Some social psychologists dispute the basic premise of personality testing; they argue that people are not very different in personality, and behavior is determined more by the social situation than by individual differences. This debate is long from settled.

SUMMARY AND DISCUSSION

In this chapter, you learned to use surveyWiz to construct a simple personality test. You also learned how to use SPSS to compute correlations, make computations with the data (find total scores), and conduct a simple factor analysis. You also learn that evidence of correlation and causation are not necessarily related in any simple manner, and that you should not confuse the results of correlational surveys as evidence of causation.

A number of articles discuss individual differences testing via the Internet. For discussions of online personality testing, see Buchanan (2000), Buchanan and Smith (1999), and Pasveer and Ellard (1998). Bailey, Foote, and Throckmorton (2000) present the results of a comparison of online and in-class tests of sexual attitudes, knowledge, and behaviors. Mueller, Jacobson, and Schwarzer (2000) present a study that correlates a personality test of self-efficacy with experience in computer programming. Perhaps people who learn to control a computer also learn to control other aspects of their lives. Pagani and Lombardi (2000) examine individual differences in the communication of emotions in pictorial stimuli that are correlated with cultural differences.

EXERCISES

1. For the data included, what is the correlation between height and gender (sex)? What does this correlation mean? What is the correlation between the total masculinity score (*TOT_MASC*) and gender? Would you consider this correlation evidence of validity of the scale? What is the correlation between *TOT_MASC* and height? How would you interpret this correlation?
2. Suppose you wanted to predict GPA. Can you predict GPA from shyness or masculinity? (Hint: Look at the correlation matrix to see what variables are most highly correlated with GPA.) What can you predict GPA from? How would you interpret the correlations with GPA? What personality scales should correlate with GPA?
3. What happens if you include gender (sex), height, and GPA as well as the eight personality items in the factor analysis? Can you interpret the factors?
4. Use surveyWiz to construct a personality test designed to measure two of the following personality dimensions: social conformity, neuroticism, order, depression, extroversion, and locus of control.
5. Project idea: Have everyone in a class take a personality test twice. Compute the test–retest reliability of each scale on the test.
6. Project idea: Devise a personality test to measure authoritarian personality. Devise a procedure to validate the test. Construct your questionnaire using surveyWiz or by writing your own HTML.
7. Project idea: Have everyone in a class take the personality test. Also ask each person if they would like to give a speech to the class. Correlate the test scores to see if you can predict how much a person would like to give a speech from their measure on the test of shyness.

Chapter 11

USING FACTORWIZ FOR FACTORIAL DESIGNS

An old question in psychology is: Is the whole equal to the sum of its parts? Imagine someone who might be described as *sincere and mean*. How much do you think you would like that person? Is the personality impression of the combination just a sum or weighted average of the separate impressions produced by the separate words?

In contrast with the early mental chemists, who thought that complex psychological ideas could be analyzed into their elements, Gestalt psychologists argued that psychological impressions and perceptions were more than just the sums of their parts. The term *Gestalt,* which means "form" or "configuration" in German, was used to indicate the idea that in addition to the elements were the relationships among the component stimuli that make up the integrated impression.

Factorial designs allow you to assess if the data can be represented as the sum of the main effects of the separate factors, or if there is also an interaction, or *nonadditivity*, in the data. A factorial design has two or more independent variables manipulated by the experimenter. In a factorial design, every level of each independent variable is paired with every level of the other variables (see also Chapter 1).

This chapter shows you how to use factorWiz, a Web page included on your CD, to set up within-subjects factorial designs that allow you to test for interactions. The chapter uses an experiment on impression formation to illustrate how to make an experiment with factorWiz. The example experiment is designed to test if judgments of liking of a person are the sum (or weighted average) of the liking of the person's traits. This study replicates via the Web an experiment by Birnbaum (1974a) that was done in the lab. Birnbaum found systematic violations of additivity, contradicting the conclusions of Anderson (1962), who disputed the Gestalt ideas of Asch (1946). Results of the study are analyzed in Chapter 12.

In this experiment, the factorial design combines the effects of two adjectives. Each factor has five levels, corresponding to a set of adjectives. The factorial design is displayed in Table 11.1.

The factorial design in Table 11.1 contains 25 different combinations of row and column adjectives (5 rows × 5 columns), each of which describes a person. How much would you like each one? To do the experiment, you need to randomize the order of presentation of the pairs. Also, in Chapter 9, you learned that there should be a warm-up of trials to allow the judge to become accommodated to the response scale and the range and distribution of stimuli. The next section shows you how to set up this experiment with factorWiz.

 HOW TO USE FACTORWIZ

To make the HTML for a factorial design with factorWiz, carry out the steps in the following example. Load *factorWiz.htm* in your browser. Give the experiment a name (which will be printed as the title of the page) and give it a short name (which will be inserted as the first variable in the data file). Name the row and column factors. In this case, name the experiment *Impression Formation* and give it the short name *like5x5*. The

TABLE 11.1.   Factorial Design of Adjective 1 by Adjective 2

ADJECTIVE 1	ADJECTIVE 2				
	Mean	*Listless*	*Solemn*	*Light Hearted*	*Trustworthy*
Phony	Phony & mean	Phony & listless	Phony & solemn	Phony & light-hearted	Phony & trustworthy
Squeamish	Squeamish & mean	Squeamish & listless	Squeamish & solemn	Squeamish & light-hearted	Squeamish & trustworthy
Blunt	Blunt & mean	Blunt & listless	Blunt & solemn	Blunt & light-hearted	Blunt & trustworthy
Informal	Informal & mean	Informal & listless	Informal & solemn	Informal & light-hearted	Informal & trustworthy
Sincere	Sincere & mean	Sincere & listless	Sincere & solemn	Sincere & light-hearted	Sincere & trustworthy

factors are *Adjective 1* and *Adjective 2*. Type in the number of levels of the row and column factors in the spaces provided (5 and 5, in this example). Then enter the stimuli that define rows and columns. In this case, type in the adjectives as shown in Figure 11.1.

Each person is described as a combination of one of the adjectives from the first set (row = *phony, squeamish, blunt, informal, sincere*) with one from the second set (column = *mean, listless, solemn, light-hearted, trustworthy*). Each subject receives all possible combinations, in random order. Replace the separator (default is " & ") with " and "; be careful to leave a space before and after the word "and" and do not type in the quotes. The separator will be printed between the row and column adjectives; in this case, a person might be described as *sincere and mean*, for example. Figure 11.1 shows the appearance of the window.

Now push the *Make the Form* button to make the stimuli, randomize the trials, and write the HTML, which appears in the text window. If you use Netscape Navigator or the latest version of Internet Explorer (4.5 or above), you can display the form at this point by pushing the *Display* button. Next, scroll to the end of this text window and select all of the HTML, being sure to get the beginning of the document. Choose *Copy* from the **Edit** menu. The window now appears as in Figure 11.2.

 ## COPY THE HTML TO A TEXT EDITOR AND SAVE

Next, paste the entire contents of the window into your text editor and save it with an extension of *.htm*. In this case, illustrated in Figure 11.3, the file was named *like.htm*.

 ## ADD INSTRUCTIONS AND WARMUP TRIALS

In the text editor, replace the phrase *(put your instructions here)* with appropriate instructions for the task (see Figure 11.3) and also copy a few more of the trials from the main experiment to the warmup, changing their trial numbers. In Figure 11.4, the number of warmup trials has been increased from four to seven. It is a good practice to include not only the four extremes, which are automatically inserted by factorWiz as warmups, but also to include at least one trial with each of the levels of each factor, so that the participant will experience all of the adjectives before the main experiment. The warmup trials must be placed within the first FORM, as shown in Figure 11.4.

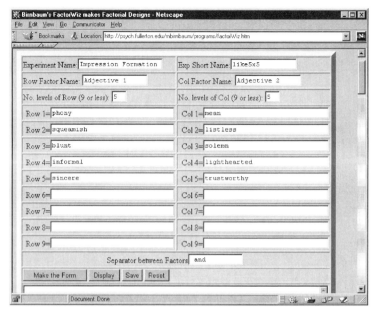

FIGURE 11.1. Making a factorial design for impression formation experiment by means of factorWiz. There are spaces around the word "and" in the *separator* box.

FIGURE 11.2. Pressing the button *Make the Form* creates the trials, randomizes them, and displays the HTML page in the textarea within the window. The *Display* key opens a new window, showing how the page displays in the browser. Note the scroll bar on the textarea window. Be sure to select the entire contents and copy it to a text editor; save it as *like.htm*. The *Save* key reminds you to copy to a text editor. The *Reset* key erases everything from the form. To get another random order of the same design, press *Make the Form* again (without pushing the *Reset* button).

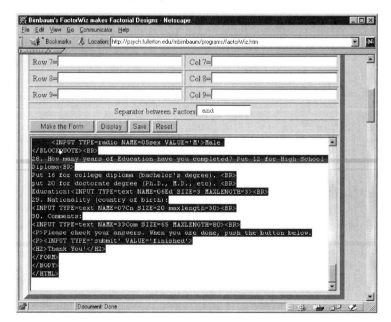

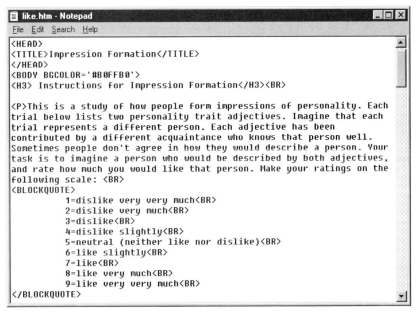

FIGURE 11.3. Appearance of the HTML, copied from factorWiz to NotePad. The instructions were added, replacing the sentence *(put your instructions here).*

FIGURE 11.4. Add warmups. Four warmups are automatically created by the program; here, three additional warmups were made to include at least one presentation of each of the adjectives in the warmup. Note that the warmup trials are nested in a FORM that has no action. The warmups accustom the judge to the stimuli and the response scale.

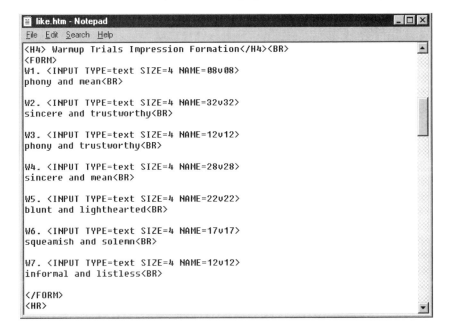

Note that these warmups guarantee that the participant will see in the warmup the best combination, the worst combination, and each of the adjectives in the study. The names given to the variables in the warmup are not important, because none of the variables in this FORM will be sent to the data file (there is no ACTION for the warmup form, nor is there a submit button). The purpose of the warmups is to allow the subject to become acquainted with the stimuli and the response scale.

VIEW THE FILE WITH YOUR BROWSER

Now open the file from the browser to see how it looks. (It is not necessary to close the file in the text editor; in fact, it is easier to make corrections and modifications if you keep the file open in the text editor as well as the browser.) You can edit the file to modify instructions or adjust formatting if needed. When you have a script on your local server, you can also change the URL in the ACTION of the form to that of your local script.

In Netscape, the file created appears as in Figure 11.5. You can load this file from the CD, where it is named *like.htm.*

You could have created everything in this file from what you learned in Chapters 2–5, but this program makes your task much easier. Because you understand the HTML,

FIGURE 11.5. Appearance of the Impression Formation experiment in Netscape.

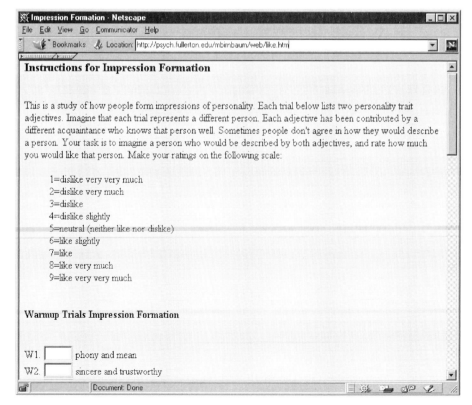

you also know how to adjust it to add another variable, change the format, or make some other modification. You can change the background color, fonts, formats, or add graphics as appropriate for your experiment.

CHECK THE EXPERIMENT AND DATA FILE CREATED

Test the experiment in your browser to make sure it works properly. Download your data. An FTP link to the data file is included in the examples for this chapter. You may need to select *Page Source* from the **View** menu to see the file in your browser.

Be sure that you understand how the data are arranged in the data file. Note that factorWiz randomized the trials, but the data appear in the file in their proper factorial order. The first variables sent by the script will be as follows:

> *Experiment short name*
> *Date*
> *Time*
> *Remote address* (the IP address identifies the computer network that sent the data. Two successive entries from the same address probably mean that the same person pushed the "submit" button twice; you can thus spot and delete multiple submissions.)
> *Age*
> *Gender* (M or F for male or female)
> *Education*
> *Nationality*

The next variables are the judgments, in the following order:

> (*row 1, col 1*), (*row 1, col 2*)…(*row 1, col c*)
> (*row 2, col 1*), (*row 2, col 2*)…(*row 2, col c*)
> …
> (*row r, col 1*), (*row r, col 2*) …(*row r, col c*)

Finally, the last variable is for *Comments*.

To make sure that you know how the data are arranged, you should now "run" yourself on the experiment by typing in the *stimuli* you see on each trial; that is, the text of each question instead of your judgment. For example, instead of judging how much you would like someone who is *sincere and mean,* you type *sincere & mean,* or an abbreviation. Type the word "*age*" when you are asked for age, and type "*edu*" when asked for education. You will then have a record in your data file of exactly how the experiment and the data are organized. Figure 11.6 shows how the data file appears for the impression formation experiment.

Two records are shown in Figure 11.6. The first is the "reminder" created by the experimenter who typed in the stimuli on each trial. It is a good idea to do this once for each new experiment so that you will not be confused later when it is time to analyze your data. The identifying line can also be imported with the data to Excel, where it can be pasted to the first line to define the variables. In Figure 11.6, you should also replace "like5×5", "1/3/99", "9:40:33" and "137.151.149.110" with the words *exp, date, time,* and *address.* The second record shows a typical set of judgments.

ADDING OTHER RANDOM ORDERS

It is easy to add other random orders. Once created, the trials could be cut and pasted within the form and their trial numbers changed. The data are returned by the script according to the numbers that precede the variable names, so they return in the factorial order.

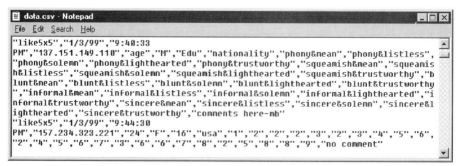

FIGURE 11.6.   Data produced by typing the stimuli into the response box to properly decode the experiment in the data file. In the first record, the experimenter "took" the experiment by typing the stimuli; in the second record, a subject took the same study, entering her judgments of liking.

FactorWiz also allows you to make new orderings with the push of a button. After you have created one form and saved it to disk, just push *Make the Form* again, and you have another random order of the same experiment. (Do not press *Reset* until you have all of the orders you want.) You can put several of these orders on the Web and use a page in which the subject clicks on his or her birth month to be assigned to one of the random orders. You can then analyze the effects of trial order with analysis of variance, or you can just combine the data to average across different random orders.

You can insert graphics, sounds, or lengthy material for the row and column factors with search and replace. To do this, type an abbreviation for the row and column factor levels. For example, you can type rx1, rx2, rx3 and so on for the rows and cx1, cx2, and so on for the columns. Then use *Search and Replace* in the text editor to replace these symbols with the appropriate HTML tags to insert the more complex or lengthy material. This procedure is illustrated in Chapter 14.

SUMMARY

This chapter explained the use of factorWiz to make within-subjects factorial experiments. A variety of experiments created with this tool will be analyzed in Chapters 12–16. In Chapter 12, you learn how to analyze data from a factorial experiment, using data for the impression formation study.

EXERCISES

1. Use factorWiz to create the following 3 × 5 design in which the factors are the length of acquaintance (rows) that the source has with the target person described and the adjective (columns) that the person has provided. You can use the same instructions, except add the following:

    "In this study, your task is to rate how much you would like the person described if that person has been described by someone who has known the person for *one meeting*, for *one month*, or for *years*. A person who has only met the person once may not be as accurate as a person who has known the person for months or years."

Use the following levels for row factor:
Acquaintance of 1 meeting says the person is
Acquaintance of 1 month says the person is
Acquaintance of years says the person is

Use the same adjectives for the column adjectives as used in the example of this chapter.

2. Set up the following experiment, which is similar to one by Shanteau (1975b). The instructions are as follows:

This is a study of the value of gambles. Suppose you reach into a jar that contains 200 marbles, some of which are red and some of which are white. If you draw a red marble, you win the designated prize. If you draw a white marble, you receive nothing. A friend of yours has looked at the jar and estimated your chances of winning. Your friend has not actually counted the marbles, but has shaken the jar, viewed the marbles, and informally judged your chances.

The two factors are the prize (columns) and your friend's estimate of your chances (rows). Set up a 6 × 6 factorial experiment with the following prizes and chances. Prizes are a new toothpick, a six-pack of your favorite drink, a scientific calculator, a CD player (with included tape deck, speakers, and radio), a bicycle, and a computer. Your friend's estimates of your chances: "No chance," "Very unlikely to win," "Probably won't win," "Tossup—fifty–fifty," "A good chance to win," and "Nearly sure thing." A typical trial should read as follows: "A good chance to win a bicycle." Make the chances the row factor, because that factor is printed first. Use " to win " as the separator.

According to the model of Shanteau (1975b), the judged value of such a gamble can be represented as the product of the subjective weight of the probability phrase times the subjective value of the prize. Thus, Shanteau's model implies a multiplicative interaction between the chance to win and the subjective value of the prize. In this experiment, both the probability phrase and the prizes are described verbally.

3. How large a tip would you leave if the service was slow and you did not get everything as ordered? Design a study to find out how large the tip would be if the bill was $5, $10, $15, $20, $25, or $30, and the service was "lousy," "mediocre," "acceptable," or "excellent." The two factors are size of bill (rows) and quality of service (columns).

4. A classic article by Cliff (1959) presented a model in which adverbs are multipliers. For example, if "*very*" has the multiplicative value of 1.32, then "*very neat*" is 1.32 times as neat as *neat*. A person who is "*very charming*" is also 1.32 times as likeable as a person who is *charming*. You can use factorWiz to set up a partial replication of Cliff's research. Use similar instructions as for the experiment on judgments of liking, as follows:

"This is a study of how people form impressions of personality. Each trial below lists a description of a person. Assume that the description has been contributed by an acquaintance who knows that person well. Your task is to imagine a person who would be so described and rate how much you would like that person. Make your ratings on the following scale:" (Insert the same scale as for impression formation).

Set up a 4 × 6 design with the following adverbs: *slightly, (no adverb), very*, and *extremely*. Let the six adjectives be *evil, bad, inferior, charming, pleasant*, and *good*. For the *no adverb*, just leave the space blank. The separator between factors should be just a space (to separate the adverb and adjective). The CD contains two experiments for the adverb*adjective experiment, *adjadv.htm* and *adjadv2.htm*, that were created by factorWiz, as illustrated in Figure 11.7. The CD also contains data for one of these studies.

5. A cab was involved in a hit-and-run accident at night. A witness said it was a blue cab. What is the probability that it was blue, as the witness testified? FactorWiz can be used as illustrated in Figure 11.8 to set up an experiment on this cab problem. Follow the figure and use factorWiz to make the same experiment, which is included and analyzed in Chapter 16.

6. How much do you think you will like John if you love Bill and Bill hates John? Set up a factorial experiment on social balance, following Figure 11.9. This experiment is analyzed in Chapter 13.

7. Study Figure 14.3 in Chapter 14. It illustrates how to use factorWiz to create a factorial design of graphic images. Each image was created in a graphics program and named F0L1.JPG to F5L5.JPG. This experiment is detailed in Chapter 14.

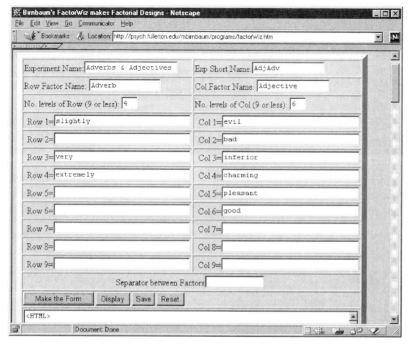

FIGURE 11.7. Using factorWiz to set up a replication of Cliff's (1959) experiment on adverbs as multipliers. The separator contains a single space. This experiment is named *AdjAdv2.htm* on the CD.

FIGURE 11.8. How to set up an experiment on the Cab Problem of Bayesian inference. This experiment is analyzed in Chapter 16.

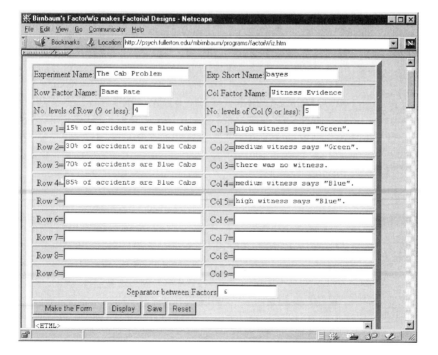

FIGURE 11.9.   This figure shows how to use factorWiz to set up a factorial design to test Heider's Social Balance theory. This experiment is analyzed in Chapter 13.

Part III

APPLICATIONS WITH DATA

Chapter 12

ANALYSIS OF IMPRESSION FORMATION

The question posed in Chapter 11 is as follows: Is the impression of the whole equal to the sum (or average) of the impressions of the parts? For example, does the effect of one adjective depend on the adjective with which it is paired? Chapter 11 showed how to use factorWiz to construct a Web-based replication of a study by Birnbaum (1974a, Experiment 1) that addressed this question.

This chapter analyzes new data from the Web version of the experiment assembled in Chapter 11. The chapter shows how to find means in Excel, and how to draw a graph to see if there is an interaction between two independent variables. This chapter also describes how to use SPSS to conduct an analysis of variance (ANOVA) to test statistical significance of interactions in a factorial design.

CHECKING THE DATA

First, open the data file *clean.xls*. Then click the pointer in cell A1 and select *Filter … Auto Filter* from the **Data** menu. Then click on the first column's filter arrow and select *like5x5*, using the procedure described in Chapter 6. The screen appears as in Figure 12.1.

Now select the data by clicking on cell A1 and dragging to the last column (AG1), then down to the last row. Next, choose *Copy* from the **Edit** menu. Now, select *New* from the **File** menu. Open a new workbook. Then click in cell A1 and choose *Paste* from the **Edit** menu. This pastes a copy of the liking data into a new workbook. You can save this workbook as *Liking.xls*. On the CD is a copy of this workbook, which you can compare with your work.

In the first row, you must rename the variables appropriately for this experiment. The first variables are *exp* (experiment name), *date, time, age, sex, education*, and *nationality*, then cells (1,1), (1,2), and so on up to (5,5), which have been named $v(1,1)$ to $v(5,5)$. (If you collect additional data with the liking experiment *like.htm*, remote address will also appear as a variable; it has been removed here.)

Next, click the cursor on the cracks between column headings above the sheet and adjust the width of the columns. The screen now appears as in Figure 12.2.

It is a good idea to examine data for values that are "out of bounds." The instructions specified ratings from 1 to 9. Thus, if someone responded with a number like, say, 3333333, it must be some error. If you find such a number, you should set that subject's data aside for separate analysis, because one strange number in the data can have a dra-

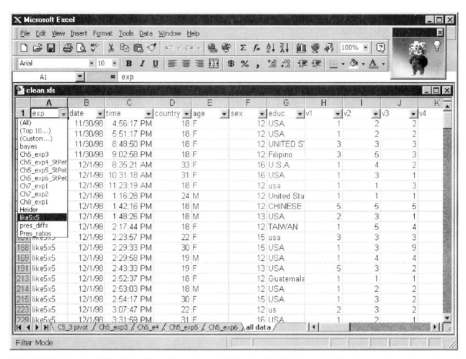

FIGURE 12.1. Load the data file, *clean.xls,* and filter for *like5x5* to select the impression formation data.

FIGURE 12.2. Data have been filtered, copied to a new workbook (*liking.xls*), and variable names have been typed in row 1, which has also been formatted in bold with a larger font.

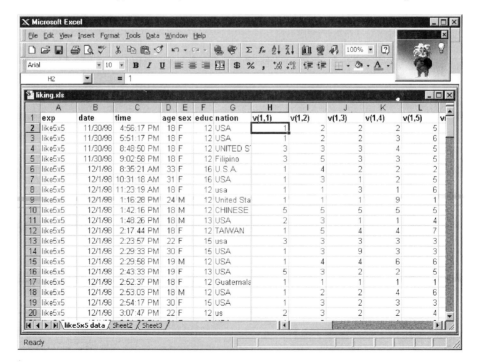

matic effect on the means. If the experiment had used a row of radio buttons instead of a text input box, no one could have entered out of range numbers even if they wanted to, and this check would be unnecessary.

Procedures used to clean data should be planned in advance of the analysis and should be independent of the hypothesis of the study. You should keep a record of any changes and report them in the method section of your paper. Otherwise, there is a danger that an experimenter may try to "help" the hypothesis along by deleting data that do not conform to the experimenter's theory. The purpose of checking is to ensure that a few strange numbers do not produce a wrong conclusion, and checking in this study should be strictly to see if there are numbers that violate the instructions.

Whenever you have a question about data processing, you can analyze the data with the questionable data excluded and included, to see if it makes a difference. In this case, the conclusions would not be affected.

To *easily* spot numbers that are out of range, you can use Excel's *Conditional Formatting*. First, select the judgments (columns H to AF), then from the **Format** menu, select *Conditional Formatting*. Figure 12.3 shows the dialog box that appears.

By using the little drop down menus, you should make a conditional format for cells whose value is *not* between 1 and 9. You can format such numbers in red font with a yellow background, so that a quick look through the data will spot them.

Another potential problem to check is multiple submission of data by the same person. In rows 36 and 39 are records that came in at 10:15 and 10:32 of the same day from a 19-year-old male from Taiwan. Other identifiers (which have been removed) indicated that the same person gave both records. Apparently, he finished his judgments, then rethought the instructions, and repeated the experiment, giving different answers. The first time, he gave mostly neutral judgments (judgments near 5); however, the second time, he gave judgments indicating that he expected to dislike most people, except for those with the most favorable traits.

One should follow a consistent rule for how to handle multiple submissions. For example, one might delete the first record on the supposition that the person corrected his answers. However, some studies may be focused on first reactions, so subsequent data should be removed. Completely blank records, which happens when someone scrolls to the end of the form without doing anything and clicks the submit button, should be deleted. To delete an entire line, click on the row number to select the entire line, select *Delete* then from the **Edit** menu. The whole line will vanish.

One student put "ba" for education. That student was probably trying to say she had a BA degree, which should be recorded as "16" years of education according to the

FIGURE 12.3. Dialog box for Conditional Formatting. In this case, cells have a special format if the cell value is not between 1 and 9. Clicking the *Format...* button allows one to set the format for such cases, which would be inconsistent with the instructions.

original instructions, so change "ba" to 16. You should make any such corrections on the copy, keeping the original data for possible reanalysis, and make a record of all changes.

 ## FINDING MEANS

Now that you have examined and cleaned the data, the next steps are to find the means and plot the data. Click the cursor in the row after the last row of data (i.e., in cell H182). Then, select *Function* from the **Insert** menu (you can also click the function icon, f_x, on the toolbar). The dialog box in Figure 12.4 appears.

Select *AVERAGE* and click *OK.* That brings up the dialog box shown in Figure 12.5. The program will try to guess what you want averaged. When there is a missing value in the column, Excel may guess wrong. In this case, it guessed correctly. That range is H2:H181. If the range is incorrect, you type in the range of cells that should be averaged. You can also select this range by first clicking in the box for *Number1*, then clicking and dragging in the workbook to select what should be averaged. Note that the dialog box also shows the tentative result (1.90556). If everything is okay, click *OK* and the value will be entered in the cell that was originally selected. Now, fill in all of the means with *Autofill*. To do this, click in the cell and position the cursor in the lower right of the cell (until you see **+**); next, drag to the right to spread the same idea (find column means), to all of the columns. Whenever you use the *Autofill* feature, you should

FIGURE 12.4. Click in a cell, then choose *Function* from the **Insert** menu. This dialog box appears. Select *AVERAGE* from the list and click *OK.*

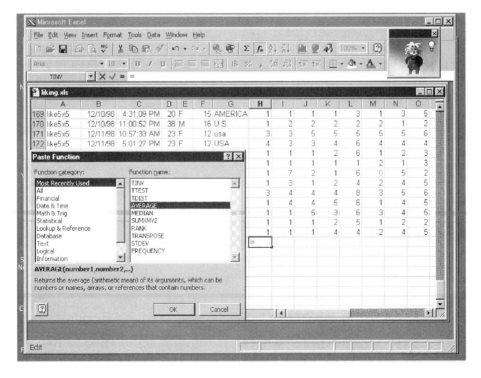

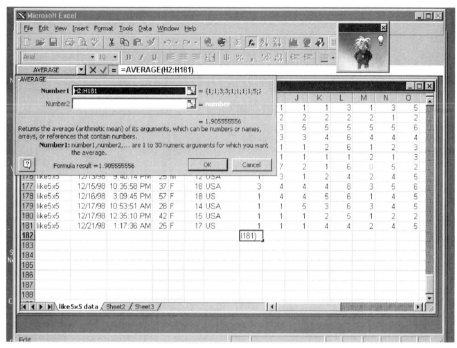

FIGURE 12.5. Type in the range of data to be averaged in the *Number1* box. The range will also be supplied if you click in this box, then select the data on the sheet.

check to make sure that Excel properly generalizes the idea you want applied to fill in the cells.

Next, highlight these cells in yellow. To make the cells stand out, select them, and then click on the drop-down arrow next to the paint can on the Formatting toolbar to make their backgrounds yellow. You can also change formats and background colors by selecting the cells and then choose *Format cells* from the **Format** menu. That brings up the dialog box in Figure 12.6.

Note that there are several tabs, for *Number, Alignment, Font,* and so on. The *Patterns* tab has been clicked, which brings the *Cell shadings* to the front. Click on one of the yellow cells to give the cells the appearance of yellow highlighting. Click *OK,* and when you click outside the selected cells, you see that the background is now yellow.

 ## ARRANGING THE MATRIX OF CELL MEANS

The next step is to copy the means to another worksheet. First, select the means (be sure to get the entire row of 25 means), then choose *Copy* from the **Edit** menu, then click on *Sheet 2* tab on the bottom of the worksheet. Now click in cell B2, and from the **Edit** menu, select *Paste Special*. The dialog box in Figure 12.7 appears.

Click the *Paste Link* button in the lower right of this dialog. You might have copied just the values (by clicking the *Values* button and then *OK*); however, if you later make a change in the data page, you would have to redo your work. With *Paste Link,* any change in the data is automatically reflected in the matrix that you construct. Pasting a

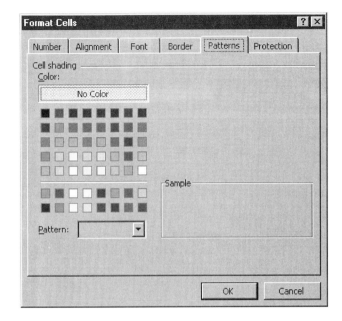

FIGURE 12.6.
Dialog box of *Format Cells.* Note the different tabs.

link means that the data on this page are linked to the means on the previous page. If you changed the data, it would change the means, and because of the link, it would change the means on this page as well.

The next task is to arrange the data into a matrix of rows and columns. Click in cell G2 and drag until all of the 20 cells to the right are selected. Then choose *Cut* from the **Edit** menu (or click the *Cut* icon—the little scissors—from the toolbar), then click in cell B3 and choose *Paste* (or click the *Paste* icon in the toolbar). That moved 20 cells. Then do the same thing to *Cut* and *Copy* the next 15 cells into row 4. (Select from cell G3 to the right, cut, click in cell B4 and paste. Row 4 of the Excel worksheet holds the

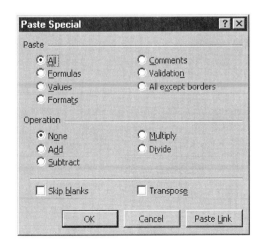

FIGURE 12.7.
Paste special dialog box. In this case, select *All* for *Paste,* and click the *Paste Link* button.

third row of the data matrix.) Then *Cut* the next 10 cells to construct row 5; finally *Cut* and *Copy* the last five cells into Row 6 (the fifth row of data). When done, the matrix will appear as in Figure 12.8.

Next, type in the adjectives, to clearly label each entry. Recall from the last chapter that the adjectives for rows were *phony, squeamish, blunt, informal,* and *sincere;* for columns, they were *mean, listless, solemn, light-hearted,* and *trustworthy.* Type these in the labels for row and column. Next, select the adjectives in row 1, and then from the **Format** menu select *Cells....* The dialog in Figure 12.9 appears.

Click on the *Alignment* tab; then, in the box on the right, click and drag the red diamond from horizontal to vertical, showing 90° of rotation of the text. Click on the *Font* tab, and make the font bold and size 12. Also make the row adjectives bold and size 12, but leave them horizontal. Then select the numbers in the matrix, then **Format Cells...,** and from the *Number* tab, select *Number,* then select 2 for *Decimal places,* as shown in Figure 12.10.

The formatted matrix should now appear as in Figure 12.11. Next, double-click on the tab at the bottom of the page labeled *Sheet2* and rename it "matrix."

MAKING A GRAPH OF THE DATA

The next task is to draw a graph of the data to examine the interaction. First, however, look at the data and think about them for a few moments. A person who is described by

FIGURE 12.8.   The matrix of means on *Sheet2*. These are copied and *Paste Special* is used with a *Paste Link* from the means on *like5x5 data* sheet.

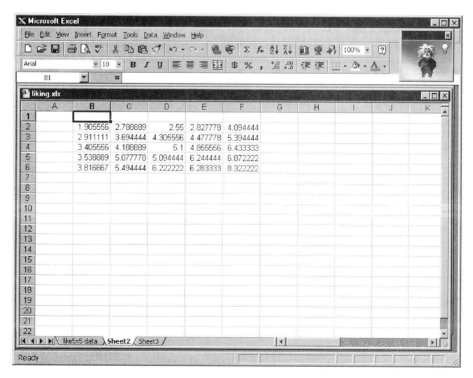

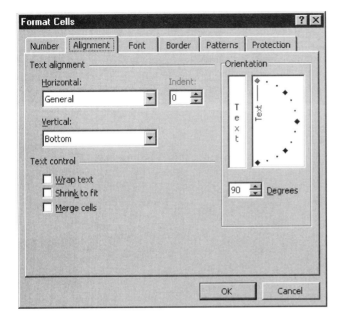

FIGURE 12.9.
Format cells, *Alignment* tab is used to make text align to vertical. Use the mouse to click and drag the colored diamond from horizontal to the desired angle.

FIGURE 12.10.   Use *Format Cells* to change the number of decimal places in the display. First select the cells, then from the **Format** menu, select *Cells,* then click the *Number* tab. In the select list, click *Number,* then change *Decimal places* to 2.

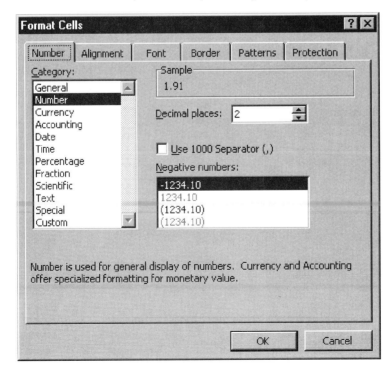

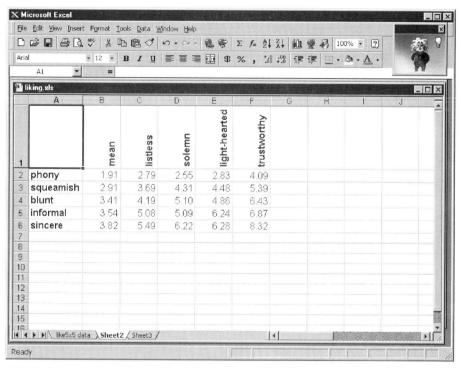

FIGURE 12.11.   Matrix of formatted mean judgments of likeableness.

one source as *phony* and by another source as *mean* gets a mean rating of 1.91, which on the 1 to 9 scale is close to 2 = *dislike very much*. A person described as *sincere* and *trustworthy* is rated 8.32 (close to 8 = *like very much*). Half-way between 2 and 8 would be 5 = *neutral*. However, notice that if a person is described by one source as *phony* and by another as *trustworthy,* then the mean rating is 4.09 (close to 4 = *dislike slightly*). Similarly, a person described as *sincere* and *mean* is rated 3.82 on the average. Thus, when there is disagreement, the "benefit of the doubt" goes to the lower trait—not really a benefit! You will be able to see this interaction visually in the graph that is drawn next.

To draw a graph of the data, select the whole table, adjectives and all (A1:F6). Then select *Chart* from the **Insert** menu (or click the *Chart* icon on the standard toolbar). The *Chart Wizard* appears, as shown in Figure 12.12.

Select *XY (Scatter)* as the chart type, then click the icon showing points connected by straight lines, as shown in Figure 12.12. At this point, you can press on the bar marked "Press and hold to view sample," which shows a preview of the graph. Then click *Next,* bringing up Step 2, shown in Figure 12.13.

Try clicking on the "Columns" button. If you look closely at the graph, you see that it plots each column of data as a curve instead of plotting each row of data as a curve. Plotting the same data in different ways gives your eye a chance to see them from another viewpoint. After studying the data in the other format, click back on *Rows,* and then click *Next,* which brings up Figure 12.14.

In the dialog in Figure 12.14, there are several tabs. On the *Titles* page, enter a title for the graph. Then label the *X*-axis (abscissa) as "Column adjectives"(remember, 1

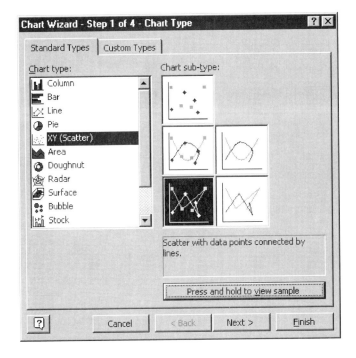

FIGURE 12.12.
Step 1 of the *Chart Wizard*. Click *XY (Scatter)* for *Chart type* and choose *Scatter with data points connected by lines* as the *Chart sub-type,* as shown.

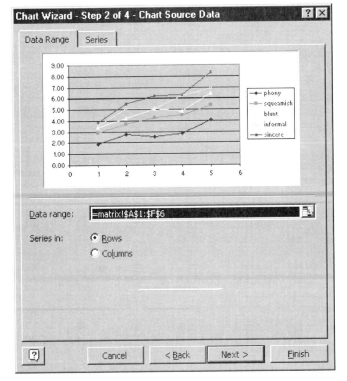

FIGURE 12.13.
In step 2, try viewing the series in *Columns,* but click *Rows* again before you press *Next.*

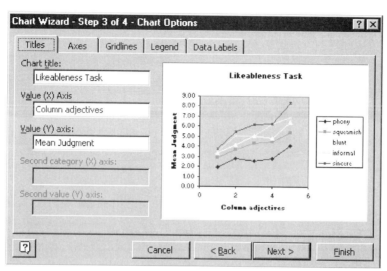

FIGURE 12.14.   Step 3 of the *Chart Wizard*. Give the chart a title and labels for the *X* and *Y* axes. Note the tabs for *Axes, Gridlines, Legend,* and *Data Labels.* Click the tab for *Gridlines,* and remove gridlines.

is *mean,* 2 is *listless,* etc.). Next, label the *Y*-axis (ordinate) as "Mean judgment." After a few seconds, these labels appear in the little figure. Click the tab for *Gridlines,* and click to remove the check, removing the horizontal lines. You can experiment with adding horizontal and vertical gridlines, but when you are done exploring these features, uncheck them. Explore the other tabs (for example, look at the effect of adding values or adding labels—adding labels puts the adjectives on the graph; adding values puts the data means on the graph). When you are done trying those options, click *Next,* which brings up the box shown in Figure 12.15.

Click the button next to *As new sheet;* otherwise, it would put the graph on the same worksheet as the data matrix. Then click *Finish* (you are not yet finished, but you are done with the wizard). The graph appears as in Figure 12.16.

To edit elements in the chart, point and double-click on them; then make adjustments in the dialog boxes. For example, to increase the fonts of the axis labels, double-click on the axis labels, then change the font size to 16. Make all of the fonts size 16. To change data symbols or lines, point to the right-most symbol for a given line and double-click. Then make the changes in the symbol type, the color of the foreground and background, and so on. Make all of the symbols 9 or 10 in size, and make all colors black or white. After adjustments to increase fonts, make the background white, and other modifications, the graph appears as in Figure 12.17. In addition to double-clicking on a graph element, you can right-click (PC) or CTRL-click (Mac) on a graph element, and a drop-down menu of choices appears.

If there were no interaction, the curves would be parallel. Instead, the slope of each line increases as the row adjective improves: The curves diverge to the right. The slope for the lowest curve (*phony*) is the smallest. If a person is *phony,* then the increase in liking produced by changing the column adjective from *mean* to *trustworthy* is only about 2 points on the scale. However, if the row adjective is *sincere,* it makes more than 4 points difference to be *trustworthy* instead of *mean.* Similarly, the vertical gaps between curves represent differences between the rows. The difference between being *phony* and *sincere* (the vertical gap) depends on whether the person was also *mean* or *trustworthy.* If

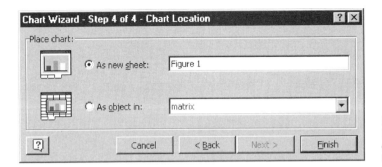

FIGURE 12.15.
In step 4, select *As new sheet*. Otherwise, the figure will appear on the same page as the data.

the person was *mean*, it makes little difference; if the person was *trustworthy*, it makes twice the difference.

If these curves had been parallel (no interaction), then the slopes of each segment would be the same for all rows, and the vertical gaps between any two rows would be the same for all columns.

The nonparallelism of the curves (the divergence, or spreading out of the curves) shows an interaction, or nonadditivity. Ratings are not just the sum or average of the separate impressions of the adjectives. Something else is happening. The divergent interaction suggests that the worst trait gets more weight than the best trait in a person. Some

FIGURE 12.16.   Appearance of the graph on its new sheet. The fonts and data symbols are small.

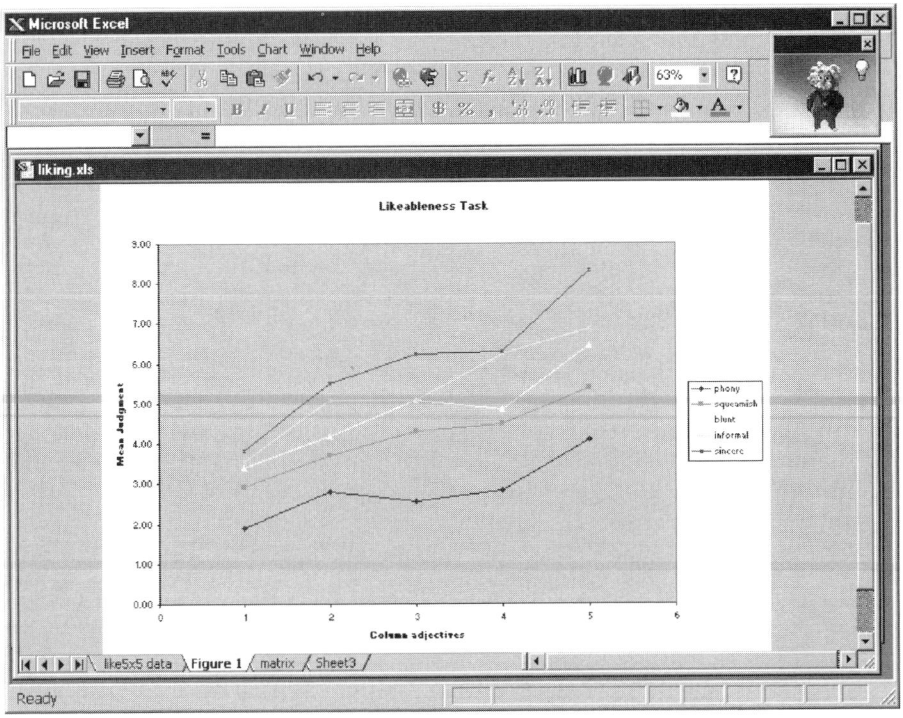

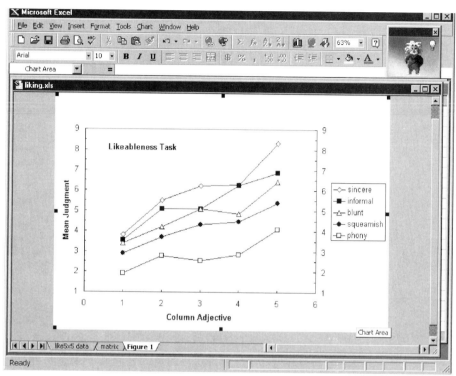

FIGURE 12.17.   Appearance of the graph after adjustments to font sizes, symbol markers, lines, and background color.

people may forgive another person their faults, but the average person puts the most weight on another's worst trait. These results are similar to those observed by Birnbaum (1971a, Experiment 1).

 ## EXAMINING INDIVIDUAL DATA

To investigate individual differences, you could draw a graph like Figure 12.17 for each person; you could also calculate the difference between *sincere and trustworthy* and *sincere and mean* and compare it to the difference between *phony and trustworthy* and *phony and mean*. If the first difference is greater than the second difference, then this person has the same type of divergent interaction as the mean judgments shown in the graph of Figure 12.17. If the second difference is greater than the first, then this individual has the opposite type of interaction; that is, one that is convergent instead of divergent.

To do this analysis in Excel, return to the worksheet showing the data (click on the tab for *like 5x5 data*). Now, click the cursor in cell AH2. Then click the equal sign on the formula line (above the worksheet and below the icons). To take the difference between cell $v(5,5)$ and cell $v(5,1)$, type AF2 − AB2, then hit return. A number appears in the cell, and you should verify that it is correct. Then click your cursor in the lower-right corner of cell AH2 (the + appears) and use *AutoFill* to drag down the column to fill in the whole column of differences. Drag all the way down, including the column means.

Name this variable *dif2.* Then, click in cell AI2, and click the equal sign on the formula line. Here, find *v(1,5)−v(1,1),* as shown in Figure 12.18 (L2 − H2).

Now, use *Autofill* to drag down this column. Name the second column *dif1.* For each subject, if *dif2 > dif1,* then that person has a divergent interaction, like the means. Note in the last row, that the mean *dif2* = 4.51, which is more than twice the mean of *dif1,* which is 2.19.

You could look at *dif2−dif1* for each participant and count by hand how many people show positive differences. However, you can use Excel to do the counting. Use the logical function *IF.* Click in cell AJ2, and then click the equal sign in the formula line (or choose *Function* from the **Insert** menu).

The *Paste Function* dialog comes up, as shown in Figure 12.19. Paste the logical function, *IF,* which brings up the display in Figure 12.20. Enter the logical expression shown in Figure 12.20.

Then type in the logical test, AH2 > AI2 (or click in those boxes to supply their locations). Type in 1 as the *value_if_true,* and 0 for the *value_if_false,* then click *OK.* Then click in the lower right-hand corner (of AJ2) to get the *Autofill* handle, and drag down to the last subject, but do not include here the line of means. Now, in the next line (the line of the means), click in the cell and then click the *AutoSum* button (cap sigma Σ on the standard toolbar). Hit return, and the sum will appear (you can also se-

FIGURE 12.18. Excel can be used to calculate an interaction for each participant. Click in cell AI2, press =, and type the expression. In this case, *dif1* is *v(1,5) − v(1,1),* or L2 − H2.

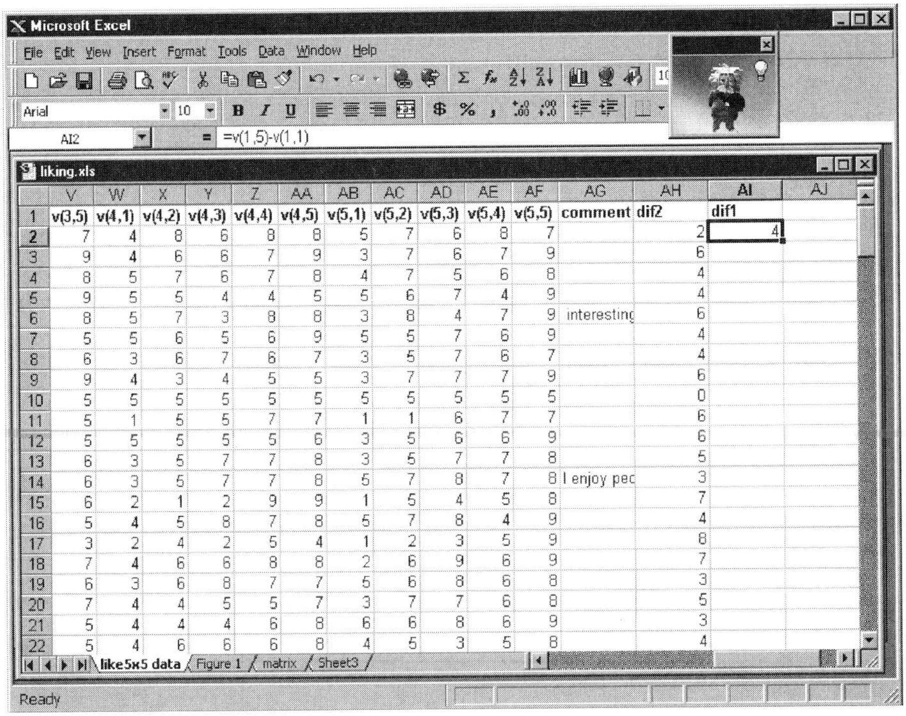

	V	W	X	Y	Z	AA	AB	AC	AD	AE	AF	AG	AH	AI	AJ
1	v(3,5)	v(4,1)	v(4,2)	v(4,3)	v(4,4)	v(4,5)	v(5,1)	v(5,2)	v(5,3)	v(5,4)	v(5,5)	comment	dif2	dif1	
2	7	4	8	6	8	8	5	7	6	8	7		2	4	
3	9	4	6	6	7	9	3	7	6	7	9		6		
4	8	5	7	6	7	8	4	7	5	6	8		4		
5	9	5	5	4	4	5	5	6	7	4	9		4		
6	8	5	7	3	8	8	3	8	4	7	9	interesting	6		
7	5	5	6	5	6	9	5	5	7	6	9		4		
8	6	3	6	7	6	7	3	5	7	6	7		4		
9	9	4	3	4	5	5	3	7	7	7	9		6		
10	5	5	5	5	5	5	5	5	5	5	5		0		
11	5	1	5	5	7	7	1	1	6	7	7		6		
12	5	5	5	5	5	6	3	5	6	6	9		6		
13	6	3	5	7	7	8	3	5	7	7	8		5		
14	6	3	5	7	7	8	5	7	8	7	8	I enjoy pec	3		
15	6	2	1	2	9	9	1	5	4	5	8		7		
16	5	4	5	8	7	8	5	7	8	4	9		4		
17	3	2	4	2	5	4	1	2	3	5	9		8		
18	7	4	6	6	8	8	2	6	9	6	9		7		
19	6	3	6	8	7	7	5	6	8	6	8		3		
20	7	4	4	5	5	7	3	7	7	6	8		5		
21	5	4	4	4	6	8	6	6	8	6	9		3		
22	5	4	6	6	6	8	4	5	3	5	8		4		

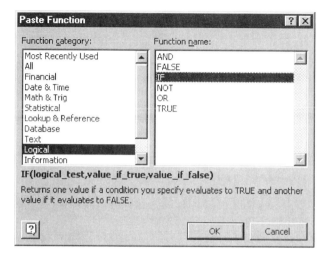

FIGURE 12.19.
Paste the logical function, *IF*. Then click *OK*. That brings up Figure 12.20.

lect *Sum* from the list of functions from **Insert** *Function*). Use the same procedures to find out how many did the opposite.

Results show that of 180 subjects, 135 (75%) show the same trend as the means, 22 (12%) show the opposite, and 23 had both differences equal. The binomial sign test (Chapter 8) can be used to test if the difference is significant. There were 157 who showed some difference, so the null hypothesis has a mean of 78.5 (157/2) and a standard deviation of 6.26. Therefore, $z = (135 - 78.5)/6.26 = 9.02$, which is significant (recall that $z > 1.96$ is significant at the $\alpha = .05$ level). This result shows that significantly more subjects showed a divergent interaction than showed a convergent interaction.

These results show that impressions of personality are not just the sum or a simple average of the likeablenesses of the separate traits. Instead, these results replicate previous findings that suggest that impression formation follows a configural process in which people place more weight on the lower valued of two traits (Birnbaum, 1974a; Birnbaum & Jou, 1990).

FIGURE 12.20. Type in AH2 > AI2 for the *logical_test,* 1 for the value if true, 0 if false.

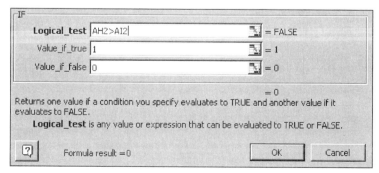

ANOVA WITH SPSS

Another approach to testing the significance of interactions is by analysis of variance, also known as ANOVA. SPSS is fairly easy to use to compute ANOVA. To import the CSV data into SPSS, select *Read Text Data* from the **File** menu. Indicate *All files* for *Files of Type*, and open *liking.csv*. The Wizard appears. In step 1, indicate that the data are not in pre-defined format. In step 2, indicate that the data are *Delimited*, and check *Yes* to indicate that the variable names are at the top of the file. In step 3, indicate that the first case is on line 2, that each line represents a case, and to import *all cases*. In Step 4, check that the *delimiter* is a comma. Remove any other checks here. (For example, *Space* may be checked. Uncheck it if it is checked. You do not want to declare "United States" to be two different variables, just because there is a space in the middle.) In step 5, click on each of the variables to make sure that SPSS has correctly identified all of the v11 to v55 variables as numeric. Click *Finish* in step 6, and you see some warnings that long comments and long nationalities have been truncated.

To do an analysis of variance, from the **Analyze** menu, select *General Linear Model*, then *Repeated Measures*, as shown in Figure 12.21. (When each participant receives all of the treatment combinations in a within-subjects design, the design may also be given the term *repeated measures*.) The dialog box of Figure 12.22 appears. In this box, name the row factor *adj1* (adjective 1) with 5 levels, and name the column factor *adj2*, also with 5

FIGURE 12.21. To do ANOVA, from the **Analyze** menu, select *General Linear* Model, then *Repeated Measures.*

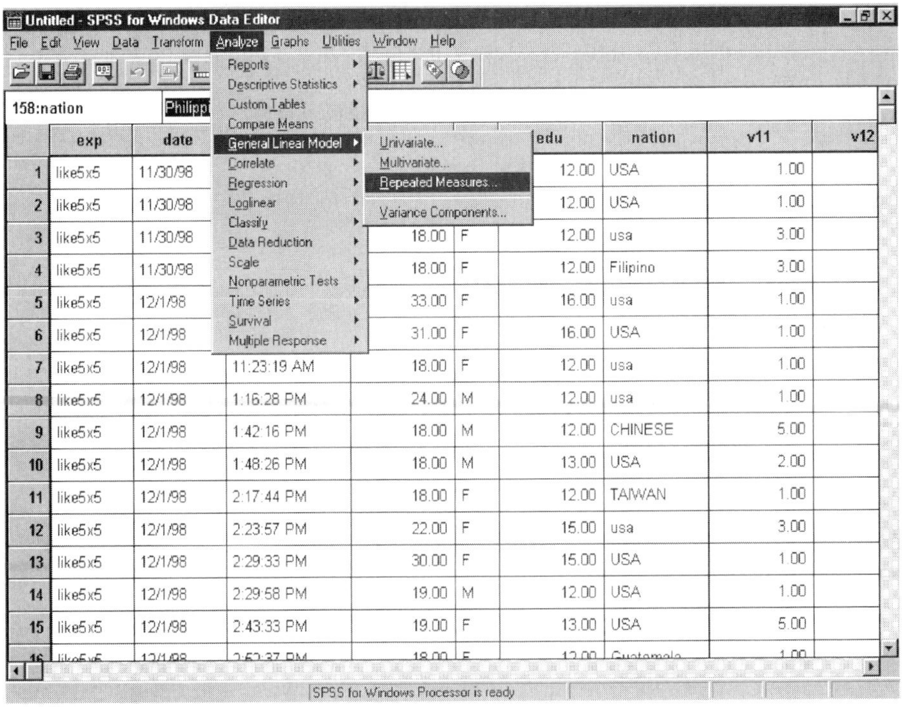

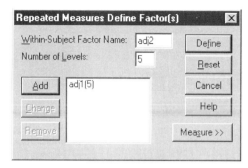

FIGURE 12.22.
Define the row factor (adjective 1) as *adj1* with 5 levels; then define the column factor, *adj2,* with 5 levels. Press *Add* to add each factor. When both factors have been added, press *Define.*

levels. Click *Add* to add each variable. Then click *Define,* which brings up the box in Figure 12.23.

Select all of the within-subjects variables, *v11, v12, ..., v55.* Then click the right-facing arrow to send these variables to the box. Click *Model* at the bottom left of this dialog box, and click the button for *Full factorial.* Click *Continue,* then click the button for *Plots.* Insert *adj1* in *Horizontal axis,* and *adj2* for *Separate lines.* Then click *Add* to add the graph. You can request another graph, with *adj1* for separate lines and *adj2* on the *Horizontal axis.* Press *Continue.*

Explore the *Post Hoc* and *Save* dialogs, but do not make any changes. Now, click

FIGURE 12.23. Select all of the variables, *v11* to *v55,* and click the right-facing arrow, which sends them to the box for *Within-Subjects Variables.* Because the data are organized in factorial order, this step can be done with one click of the arrow.

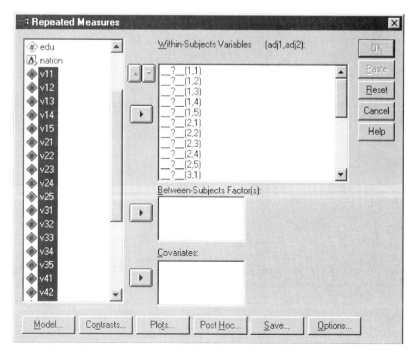

Options, and make the selections shown in Figure 12.24. The descriptive statistics option prints cell means and standard deviations. Click *Continue*. Then click *OK* on the *Repeated Measures* screen shown in Figure 12.23. After a few moments, the output will be available for viewing. Standard errors of means can be found by dividing standard deviations by the square root of n. In this case, $n = 180$. Thus, the standard error for a standard deviation of 1.5 would be .11. Thus, an observed mean can be considered an estimate of the population means with a 95% confidence interval of .22. In other words, the confidence interval for a sample mean of 2.00 would be 1.78 to 2.22. One could add error bars to Figure 12.17 to show these standard errors.

The ANOVA table from the output is shown (in part) in Figure 12.25. The main purpose of the analysis was to test the significance of the interaction. The ANOVA has been done by several methods. The interaction is statistically significant, $F(16, 2864) = 22.37$. SPSS provides additional results for more conservative procedures; in this case, the result is significant by all procedures. Examine the rest of the output from SPSS, including the graphs, which you can compare with Figure 12.17.

Therefore, we can reject the hypothesis that the deviations from parallelism are due to chance in favor of a theory in which the true means are not parallel.

 ## SUMMARY

In this chapter, you learned how to analyze data from a within-subjects factorial design. You learned how to use conditional formatting in Excel to find values that violate the instructions. You also learned how to format cells to make the Excel spreadsheet easier to read. You used Excel to find means, and you learned how to use *Autofill* to find all of

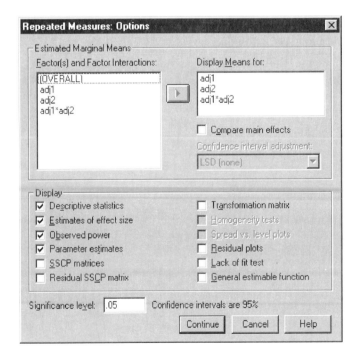

FIGURE 12.24.
Options dialog. Here, select the main effects and interactions shown, and click the right-facing arrow to send them to the *Display Means* box. Also check the box for *Descriptive statistics* and the other options shown. Click *Continue*.

Source		Type I Sum of Squares	df	Mean Square	F	Sig.
ADJ1	Sphericity Assumed	5377.030	4	1344.258	471.491	.000
	Greenhouse-Geisser	5377.030	3.024	1777.995	471.491	.000
	Huynh-Feldt	5377.030	3.082	1744.655	471.491	.000
	Lower-bound	5377.030	1.000	5377.030	471.491	.000
Error(ADJ1)	Sphericity Assumed	2041.370	716	2.851		
	Greenhouse-Geisser	2041.370	541.334	3.771		
	Huynh-Feldt	2041.370	551.678	3.700		
	Lower-bound	2041.370	179.000	11.404		
ADJ2	Sphericity Assumed	4565.379	4	1141.345	380.338	.000
	Greenhouse-Geisser	4565.379	3.476	1313.352	380.338	.000
	Huynh-Feldt	4565.379	3.553	1284.799	380.338	.000
	Lower-bound	4565.379	1.000	4565.379	380.338	.000
Error(ADJ2)	Sphericity Assumed	2148.621	716	3.001		
	Greenhouse-Geisser	2148.621	622.227	3.453		
	Huynh-Feldt	2148.621	636.055	3.378		
	Lower-bound	2148.621	179.000	12.003		
ADJ1 * ADJ2	Sphericity Assumed	494.636	16	30.915	**22.369**	.000
	Greenhouse-Geisser	494.636	12.678	39.015	22.369	.000
	Huynh-Feldt	494.636	13.709	36.082	22.369	.000
	Lower-bound	494.636	1.000	494.636	22.369	.000
Error(ADJ1*ADJ2)	Sphericity Assumed	3958.164	2864	1.382		
	Greenhouse-Geisser	3958.164	2269.394	1.744		
	Huynh-Feldt	3958.164	2453.874	1.613		
	Lower-bound	3958.164	179.000	22.113		

a. Computed using alpha = .05

FIGURE 12.25.   Analysis of variance table for impression formation experiment. The *F*-ratio for adj1*adj2 interaction is $F(16, 2854) = 22.37$, shown in bold type. Both main effects are also significant. Different rows within each source are tests that take into account correlations among the repeated measures. Even by the most conservative procedure, the interaction is significant, $F(1, 179) = 22.37$, $p < .001$.

the cell means easily. These means were copied using *Paste Special* (*Paste Link*) to a new sheet and arranged in a matrix. You learned to make a graph of the data in which the curves for each row would be parallel if there had been no interaction. You learned how to compute the interaction for each person to see if the pattern of means is also representative of the majority of individuals. Finally, you learned how to conduct an analysis of variance for a repeated measures factorial design by means of SPSS. This program

TABLE 12.1.   Review of Techniques for Analysis of Data

CONCEPT	TECHNIQUE
Data filtering	Autofilters in Excel (from **Data** menu)
Data checking	*Conditional Formatting* in Excel
Means	*Insert* function in Excel (AVERAGE)
Repeating operation	*AutoFill* in Excel
Arrange matrix	*Copy* and *Paste Special* in Excel (*Paste Link*)
Graph	*Insert Chart* in Excel
Interaction	Deviations from parallelism in graph
Statistical tests in factorial design	ANOVA by SPSS (*General Linear Model*)

finds means and standard deviations and computes *F*-tests of significance of the effects of rows, columns, and interaction. The data showed a significant systematic interaction, which means that impressions of personality are not just the sum of the impressions of the parts. The techniques covered in this chapter are reviewed in Table 12.1.

 ## EXERCISES

1. In the data file, delete the data for those participants who gave numbers out of range. Reanalyze the data (or examine the results in Excel, which should update automatically). Does it make a difference?

2. Separate the data by Excel into Males and Females. Analyze the data for males only or females only, replicating the analyses of this chapter. Try to do the reanalysis without looking at the book. Are the conclusions different when the data are analyzed in this way?

3. Separate the data by age (subdivide the data into those who are below the median in age and those above the median in age). Do all of the analyses of this chapter separately on those who are younger or older than the average. Do the results and conclusions depend on age?

4. Suppose the matrix of means in Figure 12.11 were as shown in Table 12.2.
   a. Is there an interaction in these data? (Draw a graph as in Figure 12.17 to decide.)
   b. What would you conclude about impression formation if the data consistently yielded this pattern of results?

5. If people gave the benefit of the doubt to higher-valued traits (instead of to lower-valued traits), how would the data of Figures 12.11 and 12.17 appear? Draw a graph to show your answer.

6. Project idea: Use factorWiz to set up an experiment that applies a scale-free test of the interaction. Use the following six combinations as levels of both row and column: *phony & mean, phony & solemn, phony & trustworthy, sincere & mean, sincere & solemn,* and *sincere & trustworthy*. The task is to judge differences in likeableness between each person, each described by a pair of adjectives (see Birnbaum, 1974a, Experiment 4).

TABLE 12.2. Hypothetical Data for Impression Formation

	MEAN	LISTLESS	SOLEMN	LIGHT-HEARTED	TRUSTWORTHY
Phony	1.00	2.00	3.00	4.00	5.00
Squeamish	2.00	3.00	4.00	5.00	6.00
Blunt	3.00	4.00	5.00	6.00	7.00
Informal	4.00	5.00	6.00	7.00	8.00
Sincere	5.00	6.00	7.00	8.00	9.00

Chapter 13

Analysis of Social Balance

This chapter reviews an experiment on social balance theory. You learn how to analyze a simple algebraic model in Excel and how to fit such a model to empirical data. The results show excellent agreement between the model and data obtained in a Web experiment.

The multiplying model predicts a crossover interaction. This is an excellent example of a model in which there can be no main effects and yet there is a very strong interaction. This chapter illustrates this type of interaction with the social psychology of Heider's balance theory (Heider, 1946).

You have probably heard the expressions, "Any friend of my friend is a friend of mine," or "My enemy's enemy is my friend." These statements are expressions of social balance (Heider, 1946). A social structure would be balanced if there were two cliques, in which everyone within each clique likes everybody else in that clique and dislikes everyone in the rival clique (Cartwright & Harary, 1956).

When there is not balance, the results are tragic, in both literature and life. For example, in *Romeo and Juliet*, the Capulets all loved each other and hated the Montagues, and the Montagues all loved each other and hated all the Capulets. Then, Romeo (Montague) and Juliet (Capulet) fell in love, and you know the story—it ends in grief. A real tragedy that occurs all too often is when children are caught in a bitter divorce. The child loves both mom and dad, but the parents now hate each other—to restore balance, the child must take one side or the other, because being caught in the middle causes distress and dismay.

Load the file *heider.htm*, which was created with factorWiz, and complete the experiment, if you have not done so already. In this experiment, there are three people, You, Bill, and John. The independent variables are how much You like Bill and how much Bill likes John. The dependent variable is the judgment of how much you think You will like John.

The diagram in Figure 13.1 can be used to represent the social situation of this experiment.

You might love or hate Bill, and Bill might love or hate John, and the question is, How much will You like John? According to balance theory, if You love Bill, then if Bill loves John, You will love John. Those who endeavor to sell basketball shoes say, "Michael Jordan likes these shoes." So, if you like Mike, you should like these shoes.

If You love Bill, and if Bill hates John, then balance occurs if You hate John. However, if You hate Bill, and Bill loves John, You also suspect You will dislike John. (Any friend of your enemy is probably your enemy as well. When people try to convince somebody that something is bad, they say, "Oh, yes, that's what Hitler liked.")

Let positive numbers represent liking and negative numbers represent disliking. The following equation represents a balanced situation:

Your liking of John = (Your liking of Bill) × (Bill's liking of John)   (13.1)

In a state of balance, the product of the signs going around the diagram in Figure 13.1 would be positive. Therefore, the sign of You liking of John should be the product of the other two.

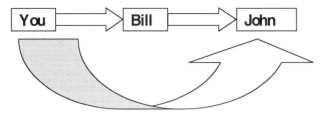

FIGURE 13.1.   The experiment asked You to judge how much You expect to like John based on Your liking for Bill and Bill's liking for John. According to balance theory, the diagram will be balanced if the product of the three signs is positive. This chapter investigates a stronger hypothesis—namely, that Your liking of John is the product of Your liking for Bill times Bill's liking of John.

Think of how the multiplication works. The product of two positives is positive (a friend of a friend is a friend of mine), and the product of two negatives is positive (my enemy's enemy is my friend). However, the product of positive and negative is negative (my friend's enemy is my enemy) and the product of a negative and a positive is negative (my enemy's friend is my enemy).

GRAPH OF MULTIPLICATION

You can follow the same procedures used in Chapter 12 to test if there is an interaction between two factors. The dependent variable in this experiment is the judgment of liking. The independent variables are (row) Your liking of Bill and (column) Bill's liking of John.

The theory is multiplicative, so it predicts a special kind of interaction between two factors. This interaction is sometimes called a linear by linear, or bilinear interaction. Imagine a graph of the function $y = ax$. When $a = 1$, $y = ax$ plots a straight line that goes through the origin, with a slope of 1. When $a = 2$, the graph of $y = ax$ is a straight line whose slope is 2. The two lines intersect at the origin [i.e., at $(0, 0)$]. Now add a line with $a = -1$; this line decreases, but all three lines still intersect at the origin.

To get an idea what the graph of $y = ax$ looks like, you can draw a graph in Excel. Start on a fresh workbook, and enter the numbers -2, -1, 0, 1, 2 in cells A2 to A6 and also in cells B1 to F1. Next, select the cells A2 to A6. Name these cells LB (for your liking of Bill). To name the selected cells, type in LB in the *Name Box* (directly above cell A1 on the formula line). Then hit return. If you had cells A2 to A6 selected, then you have just renamed the collection as LB, as illustrated in Figure 13.2.

Next, select B1 to B6, and name them BLJ (for how much Bill likes John). Next, click in cell B2, and type "=LB*BLJ" (without the quotes), as shown in Figure 13.3.

When you hit the *Enter* key, the number 4 appears in the cell. What has happened is that you have multiplied -2 times -2 and gotten 4. However, you used a formula, so now you can use *AutoFill* to fill in the entire array. After hitting return in cell B2, put the cursor in that cell (B2) again, and move it to the lower right until the *AutoFill* handle ($+$) appears, then drag down to fill the column; next (with the column selected), drag the whole column to the right to fill the entire array. The array will match Figure 13.4.

Notice that each entry in Figure 13.4 is the product of LB and BLJ. The next task is to graph it. Select the whole matrix (i.e., select A1: F6), then click the chart icon on the toolbar (or select *Chart* from the **Insert** menu). Then use the Wizard to make the figure following the procedures described in Chapter 12, and insert it as a new worksheet. After formatting lines and styles, the figure appears in Figure 13.5.

Figure 13.5 shows what you can expect to see if the two independent variables

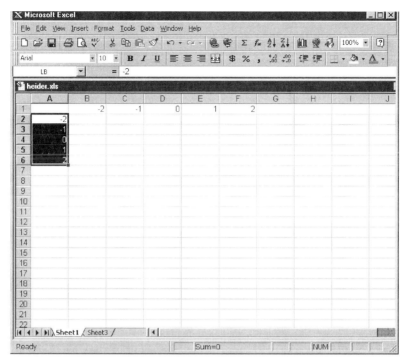

FIGURE 13.2. Name the row factor LB, by selecting A2:A6 and typing LB in the *Name Box* (shown here above the filename, above cell A1). Hit *Enter*.

FIGURE 13.3. Type = LB*BLJ in cell B2 and hit return; the number 4 appears in cell B2.

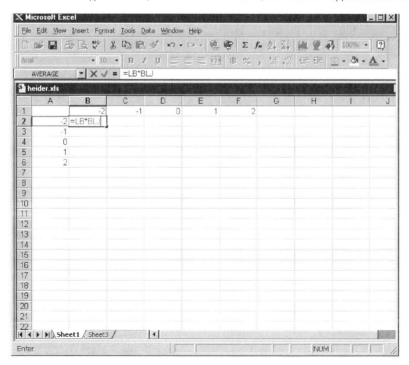

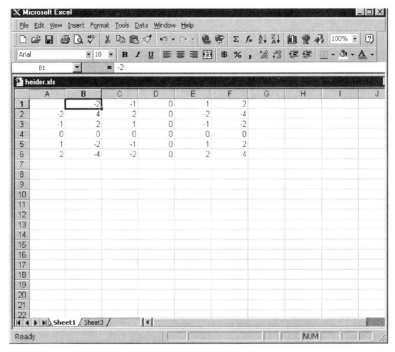

FIGURE 13.4. Click in cell B2, move the cursor to the lower right corner until the + appears. Drag down, using *AutoFill* to complete the column. With the column still selected, drag to the right, filling in the entire matrix. Each entry is the product of the entries in the first row and the first column (i.e., the product of LB*BLJ).

FIGURE 13.5. Intersecting lines representing multiplication form a "spider" pattern.

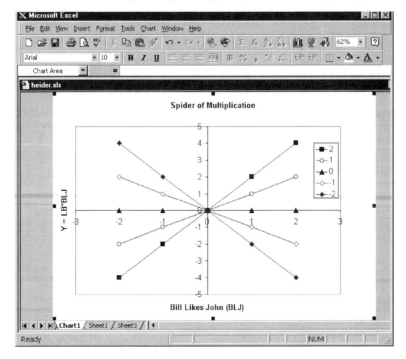

154

combine by multiplication. The graph shows $y = ax$ with $x = -2$ to 2 and $a = -2$ to 2. This fan of crossing lines is sometimes called the "spider" of multiplication. However, notice that within the domain of positive numbers (the upper right quadrant of Figure 13.5), multiplication appears as a diverging fan of curves, and in the domain of negative values of x (lower left quadrant), it produces converging curves.

Double-click on the tab of *Sheet1* and rename this sheet *theory*. Now that you understand what the theory predicts, you must examine the data to see if they resemble these predictions. The next two sections allow you to practice techniques that were explained more fully in Chapter 12, to analyze the data from this experiment.

FILTER THE DATA AND FIND COLUMN MEANS

Follow the same procedures here as in Chapter 12 to filter and clean the data. First, open *clean.xls* or *clean.csv*, turn on *AutoFilters*, and choose "heider" from the list of experiments in the first column. Second, select *Copy* and *Paste* the data to a new sheet in the workbook containing the predictions of multiplication. Add column labels. Third, use conditional formatting for the judgments to find values outside of the range from 1 to 9. Fourth, find the column mean in the first column of data, and then use *AutoFill* to get means for all of the 25 columns of data (see Chapter 12). Save this workbook as *heider.xls*. A copy of the completed file is on the CD for you to compare with your work; a cleaned version of the data, corrected for out-of-range responses and other violations of instructions, is on a separate sheet in this file labeled *clean data*. The file now appears as in Figure 13.6.

COPY THE MEANS AND *PASTE SPECIAL* TO MAKE THE MATRIX

Next, copy the means to a new worksheet, and *Paste Special* into B2. Be sure to use *Paste Link;* that way, any change to the data is reflected in this matrix. Then cut and paste the data in segments until the 5×5 matrix is completed. Next, add labels for the rows and columns. Procedures to do these tasks are explained in greater detail in Chapter 12. The result is shown in Figure 13.7.

The next step is to draw a graph of the data. To draw the graph, select the matrix of means (Figure 13.7), including the labels (A1: F6), and click the chart icon on the toolbar (or select *Chart* from the **Insert** menu). Then follow the chart Wizard (as in Chapter 12). Insert the chart on a separate sheet. To alter a chart element, recall that you can double-click on it to bring up a menu, or right-click on it on a PC to bring up a menu (on the Mac, Ctrl-click does the same). The graph is shown in Figure 13.8.

Note that we have a set of lines that intersect at a point near "neutral" on the liking scale. There is an obvious similarity between Figure 13.8 (showing data) and Figure 13.5 (showing predictions of the model). The next section fits the model to the data to solve for subjective values.

HOW TO FIT A MULTIPLICATIVE MODEL

Notice that the lines in Figure 13.8 are not exactly linear. Also, the negative slope when *you hate Bill* is not simply the negative of the (positive) slope when *you love Bill*. In addition, being *neutral* produces a slightly positive slope, so being *neutral* is slightly positive.

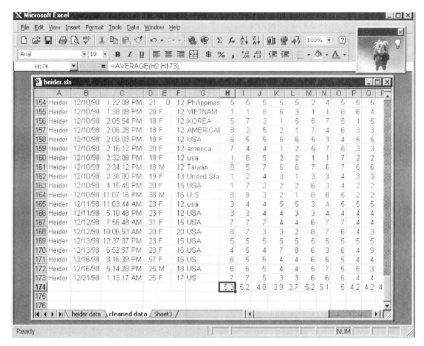

FIGURE 13.6. After copying the heider data from *clean.xls*, compute the means of the first column. Then use *AutoFill* to find the means of all columns.

FIGURE 13.7. Labeled matrix of mean judgments, after formatting of cells.

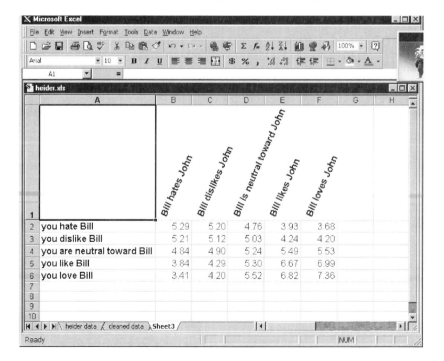

	Bill hates John	Bill dislikes John	Bill is neutral toward John	Bill likes John	Bill loves John
you hate Bill	5.29	5.20	4.76	3.93	3.68
you dislike Bill	5.21	5.12	5.03	4.24	4.20
you are neutral toward Bill	4.84	4.90	5.24	5.49	5.53
you like Bill	3.84	4.29	5.30	6.67	6.99
you love Bill	3.41	4.20	5.52	6.82	7.36

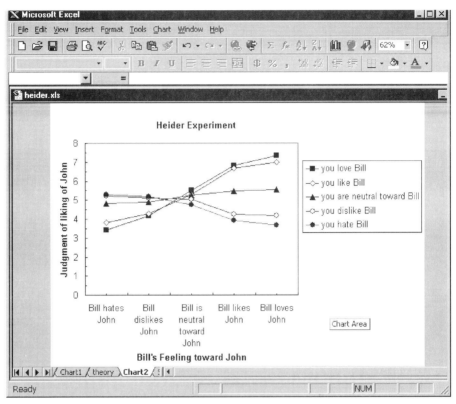

FIGURE 13.8. Mean judgments of your liking of John, plotted as a function of Bill's liking of John, with a separate curve for each level of how much you like Bill. The mean judgments show a similar interaction to that shown in Figure 13.5.

By fitting a model, you estimate numerical values from the data that represent the subjective values of such terms as *like, love, neutral,* and *hate.* The model is as follows:

Liking of John = (*liking of Bill*)*(*Bill's liking of John*) + *b*

Notice that this model requires estimates for the rows (*liking of Bill*), the columns (*Bill's liking of John*), and the additive constant, *b*. From the graph, we see that *b* (the projection of the point where the curves cross onto the ordinate) is approximately 5, the point that was labeled *neutral* on the response scale.

The next step is to modify the calculations at the beginning of the chapter and use them to fit the multiplicative model to the data. Click on the tab for those calculations, named *theory.* In cell A1 of the theory matrix, type the number 5, then click in the *Name Box,* and name it B; hit return. Then click in cell B2, and enter =LB*BLJ +B. Hit return, and cell B2 should be 9. Then use *AutoFill* to complete the matrix by dragging the first column, and then dragging the column to fill the matrix. The matrix should now appear as in Figure 13.9.

The next step is to calculate the sum of squared differences between the mean data and the theory matrix. To do this, copy the matrix of mean judgments (B2:F6) and

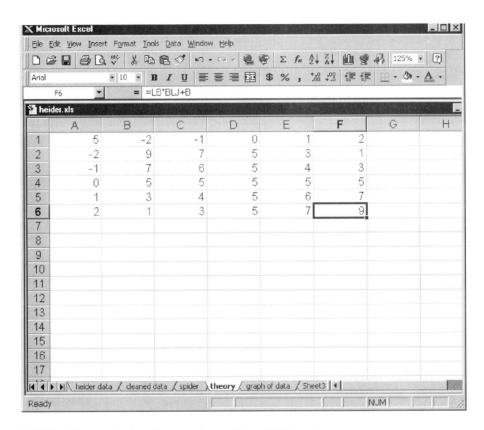

FIGURE 13.9. Matrix of predictions, calculated from LB*BLJ + B.

use *Paste Special* to paste the data matrix in cells B8:F12 of the sheet for *theory*. From the *Paste Special* dialog, click *Paste All*, then click *Paste Link*. The screen is shown in Figure 13.10.

The next task is to put the sum of squared differences between the arrays in cell G13. To do that, click in cell G13, and click the *Function* icon on the toolbar (or select *Function* from the **Insert** menu). Choose *SUMXMY2* from the list of functions in the dialog box shown in Figure 13.11.

Then select the cells B2:F6 (either by typing or by using the mouse to select the cells) for *Array_x*, then click in the box for *Array_y* and select (or type) the cells B8:F12. The dialog appears in Figure 13.12.

Notice that the function dialog box describes what the function does and also gives the numerical value. (If you have further questions about a function, you can click the question mark in the left lower corner of the box.) When everything looks right, click *OK*. Cell G13 now contains a measure of how far the theoretical predictions are from the data means.

Now click on G13 (the cell containing the sum of squared differences) and select *Solver* from the **Tools** menu. The *Solver* dialog box appears (Figure 13.13). Note that the *Set Target Cell:* is cell G13. If it is not, then type G13 in the box. Next click the button for *Min*, which minimizes the value in cell G13. Now click in the box labeled *By Chang-*

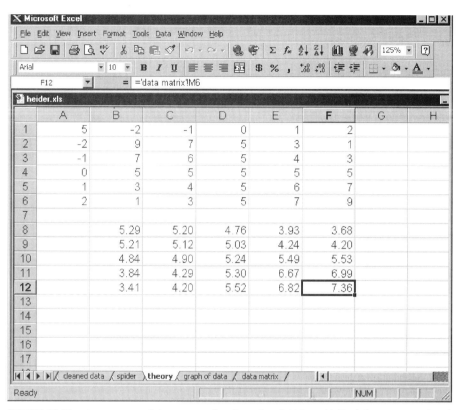

FIGURE 13.10. Appearance of the screen after *Paste Special* (*Paste Link*) of the means to the *theory* worksheet.

FIGURE 13.11. Paste Function dialog box. Choose *SUMXMY2*.

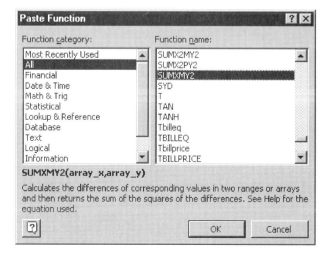

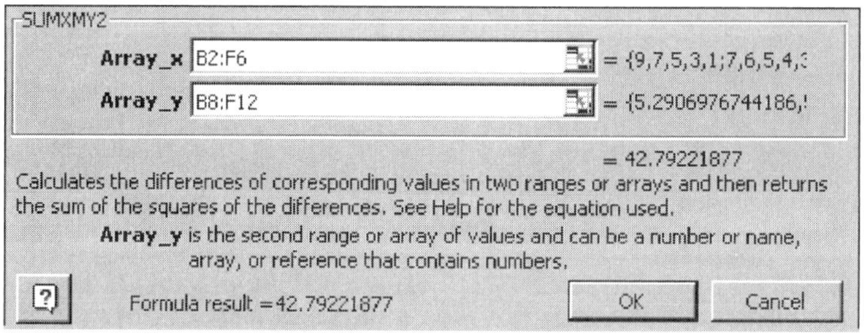

FIGURE 13.12.   *SUMXMY2* dialog requires specification of *Array_x* and *Array_y,* which can be done by typing in the cell ranges or by selecting the cells with the mouse.

ing Cells: and select cells $A1: $F1 and, while holding down the *Control* key, select $A2:$A6. These cells hold the parameters for the row and column and the additive constant. You could also type in this box the names of these parameters: LB, BLJ, and B, separated by commas.

When everything looks right in this dialog (Figure 13.13), click the *Solve* button in the upper right of the dialog box. Pushing the *Solve* button brings up the dialog in Figure 13.14. You can explore these options later; for now, click *OK*. The window of the *theory* sheet should now appear as in Figure 13.15.

Solver caused four things to happen on this sheet: First, the value of G13, which measures the sum of squared differences between the entries in the theory matrix and the data matrix, decreased from 42.7 to 0.35. In other words, the fit has improved. Second, the numbers -2, -1, 0, 1, and 2, which were set as initial row values (representing how much *you like Bill*), changed to $-.74$, $-.46$, .37, 1.36, and 1.60 for *hate, dislike, neutral, like,* and *love,* respectively. Notice that if you are *neutral* toward Bill, the value is slightly positive (.37). Third, the column values, which were originally -2, -1, 0, 1, and 2, have changed to $-.82$, $-.44$, .31, 1.26, and 1.54 for the levels of *Bill's liking of John: hates, dislikes, neutral, likes,* and *loves,* respectively. Again, if Bill is neutral toward John, it is slightly positive. Fourth, the value of B has changed from 5 to 4.92.

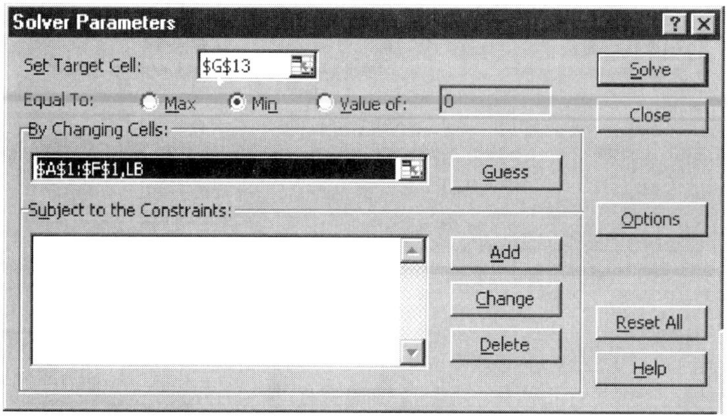

FIGURE 13.13.
The Solver Parameters dialog. Set the target cell (G13), click *Min* (for minimize), and specify the list of cells to change in order to minimize the value in G13.

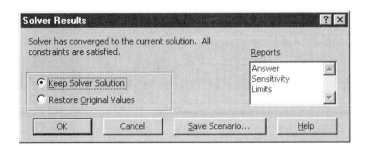

FIGURE 13.14.
Solver Results dialog box. Click *OK*.

 ## GRAPHING THE PREDICTIONS AND THE DATA

To see how well a model fits the data and allow the eye to search for systematic deviations, it is helpful to plot both the predictions and mean judgments on the same graph. To do this, select B1:F6 and, while holding down the *CRTL* key, select B8:F12. (Hold-

FIGURE 13.15. Results of Solver Solution. Compare the numbers in bold with corresponding initial values in Figure 13.10. The sum of squared differences between theory and data is only 0.35.

	A	B	C	D	E	F	G	H
1	4.924345	-0.81517	-0.43812	0.313472	1.255287	1.542076		
2	-0.7411	5.528466	5.249036	4.692032	3.994056	3.781518		
3	-0.46016	5.299457	5.125953	4.780097	4.346708	4.214739		
4	0.373557	4.619831	4.760681	5.041445	5.393266	5.500398		
5	1.359084	3.816457	4.328899	5.35038	6.630384	7.020155		
6	1.604206	3.61664	4.221505	5.427219	6.938083	7.398152		
7								
8		5.29	5.20	4.76	3.93	3.68		
9		5.21	5.12	5.03	4.24	4.20		
10		4.84	4.90	5.24	5.49	5.53		
11		3.84	4.29	5.30	6.67	6.99		
12		3.41	4.20	5.52	6.82	7.36		
13							0.351738	
14								
15								
16								
17								

G13 = =SUMXMY2(B2:F6,B8:F12)

ing down the *Control* key allows you to select several sections that may be separated on the sheet.) Then click the *Chart* icon (or select *Chart* from the **Insert** menu). Select *XY scatterplot* and click the icon *showing data points connected by lines.* When you press and hold to preview in the first step of the Wizard, the graph may appear strange, but keep the faith and continue. Click *Next,* and on the second step of the Chart Wizard, click the button that designates that data series are in rows—the figure will now look much better.

On the same step (step 2) of the Chart Wizard, click the tab labeled *Series.* Each row of the theory or data matrix is one series. For example, the first row of the first matrix contains the predictions for "You hate Bill." The sixth series is the first row of actual data. Rename *Series* 1 to *Series* 5: *You hate Bill prediction, You dislike Bill prediction, . . .* to *You love Bill prediction,* respectively. Rename Series 6 to Series 10: *You hate Bill data, You dislike Bill data, . . . You love Bill data.* This step is illustrated in Figure 13.16.

Click *Next.* Complete the graph, which brings up Figure 13.17. As we did in Chapter 12, make the background white and eliminate the gridlines. Increase the font size of the axis labels to 16.

The next task is to make the prediction markers (point symbols) disappear (leaving the lines) and make the data lines disappear (leaving the data point markers). Point the mouse arrow to the last data marker in each row. If you aim the pointer exactly at a point, a small box appears with a label for the series. When it shows a data series, double-click, which brings up the dialog box shown in Figure 13.18.

Notice that four things have been done in Figure 13.18. First, the *Line* has been

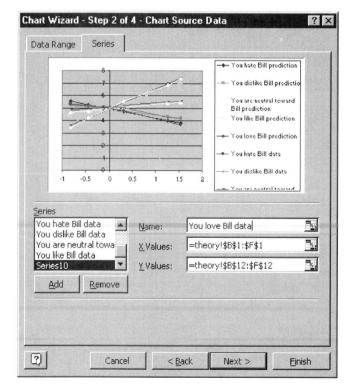

FIGURE 13.16.
On step 2 of the Chart Wizard, click the *Series* tab. Rename Series 1 to 10 with descriptive (informative) labels. This step requires clicking on the Series label on the left, then clicking in the *Name* box and typing the name of the series. These names are displayed on the graph.

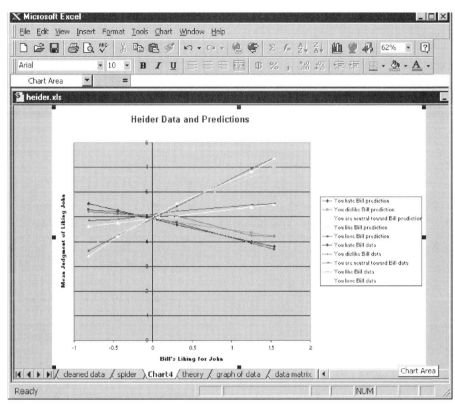

FIGURE 13.17. Predictions and data are plotted as a function of the estimated scale values of Bill's liking for John. There are separate curves (and markers) for data and predictions and for each level of how much you like Bill. Remove the markers for curves of theoretical predictions and remove the lines for empirical data.

changed to *None*. (Its color does not matter because there is no line.) Second, the *Marker* has been increased to *Size* 10. Third, the Marker *Style* has been selected as a filled circle. Fourth, the colors of both foreground and background of the Marker have been set to black. Click *OK*. Repeat this step for each series of data, using different Marker styles for each curve.

Next, select one of the series of predictions and double-click. It brings up the same dialog box, but this time for a series of predictions. The trick now is to choose a black line, and choose "None" for Marker. Do the same for each series of predictions. The finished graph appears in Figure 13.19.

Figure 13.19 shows that the theory (lines) does a good job of fitting the data (markers). The largest discrepancies between the data and theory occur when Bill hates John. When you hate Bill and Bill hates John, the mean rating is only 5.29, so these data suggest that your enemy's enemy is not much of a friend.

Despite these discrepancies, the multiplicative representation of this social inference task appears to provide an excellent fit to the mean judgments.

The social inference task of Heider illustrates an extreme form of interaction. This interaction shows that the effect of one variable (how much Bill likes John) can be reversed by changing another variable (how much you like Bill). Although an interac-

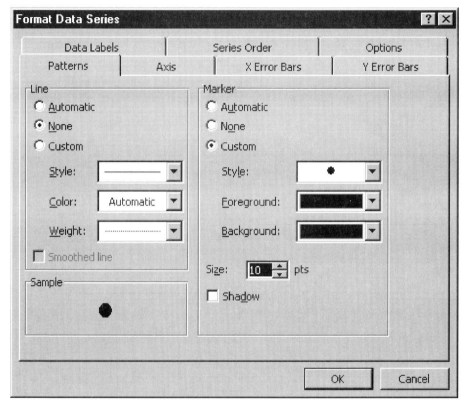

FIGURE 13.18.   Format Data Series dialog. For each series of data, choose *None* for line (left side of the
Patterns panel) and increase Marker size (right side of the same panel) to 10. Also, make
the foreground and background color black to create a filled symbol. Make the background white to make an unfilled symbol. For each series of predictions, choose *None*
for *Marker* and make the line black. Thus, each series of data will have markers without
lines, and each series of predictions will have lines without markers.

tion may seem a complicated idea, these data also show that a simple algebraic model
(multiplication) predicts this pattern quite well. The model represents a process that
people do without having to calculate on paper or count on their fingers. People do not
need to make any calculations, nor are people aware that they made any calculations,
because their brains make this calculation (which can be well approximated by multiplication) without interferring with speech or verbal trains of thought. Thus, multiplication in this case represents how the mind works to produce judgments, but not necessarily what people report of their verbal thoughts.

 SUMMARY

In this chapter, you learned how to graph a theory, fit it to the data, and plot both theory and data on the same graph. You analyzed data from an experiment on social balance and found that a multiplicative model provides an excellent fit to the data.

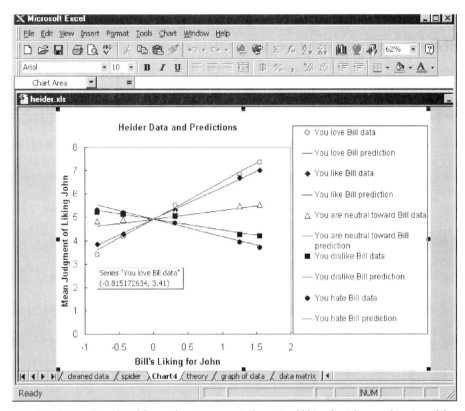

FIGURE 13.19. Completed figure showing mean judgments of liking for John as a function of the estimated scale values for *Bill's liking of John* with separate lines for predictions for each level of *your liking for Bill,* and markers for corresponding data. This figure also illustrates the small box that appears when the pointer aims at one of the series.

 **EXERCISES**

1. Subdivide the data for males and females using Excel's *AutoFilters.* Analyze the data separately for males and females, repeating the same analyses presented in this chapter. Do the conclusions of this study depend on gender?

2. Create a theoretical matrix of ratios. Use the integers from 1 to 7 as the levels of both row and column. Label the rows SR and label columns SC. Then compute SC/SR. Use *AutoFill* to complete the array. Plot this matrix twice: once with data in rows and once with data in columns.

3. Use SPSS to calculate an ANOVA for the Heider data (the methods are described in Chapter 12). Are main effects and interactions statistically significant?

4. How many individuals show the same crossover interaction as shown in the means? Use Excel to count (see Chapter 12 for the techniques).

5. If you understand the analyses of this chapter, then you should be able to analyze the data for adverbs and adjectives, replicating the Cliff (1959) experiment. Cliff's theory is that adverbs multiply the value of adjectives. If adverbs have all positive values, then the data should appear as a subset of the "spider" of multiplication (Figure 13.5 with positive slopes). The experimental materials are included on the CD as *AdjAdv.htm.* The experiment was created with the help of factorWiz. On the CD that accompanies this book is included a data file, *AdjAdv.csv.* These data were collected with a 4 × 5 design, in which the four adverbs (*slightly, no adverb, very,* and *extremely*) were paired with five ad-

jectives (*mean*, *noisy*, *blunt*, *practical*, and *understanding*). Because the adverb*adjective combination is theorized to follow multiplication, you should be able to apply the same techniques of this chapter to analyze these data.

6.   Project idea: Think of judgment tasks that might conform to a multiplicative relationship between the independent variables. Here are some examples: Shanteau (1975b) used a multiplicative model to describe how probability phrases combine with the values of prizes to determine the combined value. How much tip should you leave as a function of the size of the bill and the quality of the service? How nervous would you be to present a talk, based on the size and status of the audience? (Would you be more nervous to give a talk to a concert hall holding 200 professors or to a small class of 5 undergraduates?) How credible would an accusation against a defendant be as a function of the number and status of the witnesses who accuse him? (The witnesses might be convicted felons, factory workers, schoolteachers, or medical doctors.) Design an experiment on one of these tasks (or another that you think might fit multiplication), construct the experiment with factorWiz, collect the data, and analyze them for a project.

Chapter 14

PRESENTING PSYCHOPHYSICAL STIMULI

Psychophysics is the study of the relationships between physical measures of stimuli and the psychological experiences that they produce. Researchers in psychophysics use precisely calibrated equipment to control sound levels, visual stimuli, olfactory stimuli (smells), vibrations, and other dimensions. They typically present these stimuli to a small number of trained observers (participants) in labs whose precise conditions can be controlled; for example, experiments with auditory stimuli are usually conducted in sound-proof chambers. Because online researchers do not know what type of computer monitor, browser, or speakers (if any) their Internet participants are using, they really do not have the kind of control that those in psychophysics prefer to have in their research. In addition, some stimuli (e.g., smells, tastes, tactile stimuli) simply cannot be sent yet via the Web.

However, despite difficulties, you can illustrate principles of psychophysics with demonstrations on the Internet and obtain reliable results, even with auditory stimulation (Welch & Krantz, 1996). This chapter teaches a few easy ways to include psychophysical materials in Web pages. At the same time, this chapter also gives some ideas of how to work with frames, tables, graphics, and sounds.

A BIT OF HISTORY

Gustav Fechner lay in bed on the morning of October 22, 1850, wondering how to measure psychological magnitudes. He was not a psychologist, for there was no such department at universities in those days. He was a physicist and a philosopher, but he was thinking about ideas that have become the domain of psychology. Fechner thought that if he could measure psychological values, then a science of psychology might be developed that would have the kinds of laws one finds in physics. Could psychology have laws in which one can make accurate predictions by making computations with psychological measures? Fechner thought that if one could specify the relationship between the physical measure of a stimulus and its psychological impact, then a quantitative science of psychology would be possible.

Fechner considered Bernoulli's idea that the utility of money is a logarithmic function of its cash value. If Bernoulli were right, a poor man with $1000 would be as happy to gain $500 as a rich man with $100,000 would be to gain $50,000. He also thought about Weber's finding that the change in stimulus intensity that is just noticeably different is proportional to the standard stimulus. A *just noticeable difference* refers to the change in stimulation required to be recognized correctly 75% of the time. The just noticeable difference in weight is 5 g (the weight of one nickel) for a standard weight of 100 g. For weights, people judge that the weight of 21 nickels is heavier than the weight of 20 nickels 75% of the time. Weber's law, as Fechner called it, implies that it would take a 10 g increment to be just noticeably greater than 200 g; that is, it would take the weight of 42 nickels to be judged heavier than the weight of 40 nickels 75% of the time. For a standard of 400 g, the increase would have to be 20 g to be noticed equally often.

In 1860, Fechner published *Elements of Psychophysics,* a book that connected his theories with methods for quantifying psychological values. Fechner theorized that subjective values of stimuli are logarithmically related to physical values, a principle known as *Fechner's law.*

The logarithmic psychophysical law means that equal physical ratios produce equal psychological differences. For example, the psychological difference in heaviness between 100 g and 105 g equals the psychological difference between 200 g and 210 g. To test the idea, Fechner suggested methods for quantifying the psychological values of stimuli.

Since the days of Fechner, psychologists have applied Fechner's methods and suggested new methods for measurement of psychological values. The *Psychological Review* published a centennial issue in 1994, celebrating contributions to psychological theory. Thurstone's (1927) law of comparative judgment, which built on Fechner's ideas, was selected as one of the most important contributions of the century (Luce, 1994; Dawes, 1994). Thurstone noted that his methods could be applied to stimuli without a physical measure; for example, they could be used to measure attitudes toward crimes.

A paper by Stevens (1957) on the psychophysical law, which criticized Thurstone's and Fechner's ideas, was also found to be one of the 20 most widely cited papers in the first century of *Psychological Review* (Kintsch & Cacioppo, 1994, p. 198). Stevens (1957) advocated another approach to psychological measurement based on "direct" judgments of magnitude. Stevens concluded that subjective values are a power function of physical values. This relation, known as *Stevens' law*, implies that equal physical ratios produce equal subjective ratios.

Psychologists have used techniques of psychological measurement to measure many different types of psychological values including heaviness of lifted weights, loudness of tones, brightness of lights, roughness of sandpaper, sweetness of drinks, intensity of odors, and the darkness of grays. They have also measured more complex stimuli such as the annoyance of traffic noises, experiences of pleasure and pain, beauty of women and men, the stressfulness of life changes, goodness or badness of moral deeds, and the prestige of occupations.

A TABLE OF NEUTRAL COLORS

Suppose you wanted to present squares of varying darkness on the screen of the monitor and ask people to judge relations among their experiences of darkness. The HTML in Figure 14.1, *Ch14_ex1.htm* on the CD, creates a table of such stimuli.

The trick used in this example is to create a table and change the background color of each cell of the table. The `<TABLE></TABLE>` tags identify that material between is a table. Within a table there are rows, defined by `<TR>` and `</TR>`. Each cell in a table is defined by the table data tag, `<TD>table data</TD>`. Tables can include text, numbers, pictures, buttons, and `<INPUT>` devices such as text boxes. In *Ch14_ex1.htm,* the table contains spaces, which in HTML are written ` `.

Borders allow one to create lines of trim or "picture frames" about material. By setting `BORDERS` to zero, one can use tables to align text and pictures in columns. The second example, *Ch14_ex2.htm,* illustrates how variations of `BORDER` can be used to create a frame around the panels of gray. CELLSPACING separates the table cells, eliminating the Mach Bands (contrast illusions) where adjoining colors meet.

The colors in the table are defined by the `BGCOLOR="color"` in each `<TD>` tag, which sets the background of each table cell. These are specified in hexadecimal.

There are several very useful Web sites for computing colors in hexadecimal, which are linked from the list of examples for this chapter.

```
<HTML><HEAD><TITLE>Use of a Table to Create Gray Stimuli</TITLE>
</HEAD>
<BODY BGCOLOR="ffffff" text="000000">
<TABLE BORDER=0 CELLPADDING=0 CELLSPACING=0>
<TR >
<TD WIDTH=50 HEIGHT=50 BGCOLOR="dddddd"> </TD>
<TD WIDTH=50 HEIGHT=50 BGCOLOR="bbbbbb"> </TD>
<TD WIDTH=50 HEIGHT=50 BGCOLOR="999999"> </TD>
<TD WIDTH=50 HEIGHT=50 BGCOLOR="777777"> </TD>
<TD WIDTH=50 HEIGHT=50 BGCOLOR="555555"> </TD>
<TD WIDTH=50 HEIGHT=50 BGCOLOR="333333"> </TD>
<TD WIDTH=50 HEIGHT=50 BGCOLOR="000000"> </TD>
</TR>
<TR ALIGN=center>
<TD WIDTH=50 HEIGHT=50 BGCOLOR="ffffff"> A</TD>
<TD WIDTH=50 HEIGHT=50 BGCOLOR="ffffff"> B</TD>
<TD WIDTH=50 HEIGHT=50 BGCOLOR="ffffff"> C</TD>
<TD WIDTH=50 HEIGHT=50 BGCOLOR="ffffff"> D</TD>
<TD WIDTH=50 HEIGHT=50 BGCOLOR="ffffff"> E</TD>
<TD WIDTH=50 HEIGHT=50 BGCOLOR="ffffff"> F</TD>
<TD WIDTH=50 HEIGHT=50 BGCOLOR="ffffff"> G</TD>
</TR></TABLE>
</BODY></HTML>
```

FIGURE 14.1.   Use of table and color values. Try varying the BORDER and color values. When this stimulus is viewed, Mach Bands (psychological contrast edges) also appear at the edges between areas of different color. Try CELLSPACING=10 to remove the Mach Bands; also try BORDER=10. A space in HTML is written as .

Hexadecimal means that there are sixteen possible values, which are *0, 1, 2, 3, 4, 5, 6, 7, 8, 9, a, b, c, d, e,* and *f.* The decimal number 10 is represented in hexadecimal by *a,* and *f* is fifteen; the hexadecimal number *10* is the decimal number 16. Two-digit numbers in hexadecimal include *11,* which is 17 (1 in the 16 place plus 1), and *ff,* which is 255 in decimal. There are three colors, (red, green, and blue), each of which takes on 256 possible values from 00 to ff (i.e., 0 to 255, in decimal).

You can designate colors by name; for example, <BODY BGCOLOR="blue">. You can also designate colors by a six-digit number, as in the following example: <BODY BGCOLOR="0000ff">. This hexadecimal code says red = 00, green = 00, and blue is 255 (ff), which produces a dark blue. It is dark because two of the lights (red and green) are turned off. If you are used to mixing paints, you know that as you "add" more colors, the mix becomes darker. That occurs because you are adding pigments, each of which absorbs some of the light. Mixing lights is different from mixing pigments—the more lights you add, the lighter the mix. Big numbers (ffffff) are bright, and small numbers (000000) are dark.

So, BGCOLOR="ff0000" produces a dark red and BGCOLOR="00ff00" produces a dark green. Mixtures of lights produce other colors, which you can explore in Web sites such as ColorCenterTM (http://www.hidaho.com/colorcenter/cc.html), or by trying different combinations yourself.

Colors in which red, green, and blue are equal are sometimes called "neutral" colors, forming the gray scale from 000000 (black), through 888888 (gray), to ffffff (white). Not all colors display the same on every monitor or with every browser. If someone's monitor looks "green" when it is displaying 666666, then that monitor needs adjustment. In the example, notice that all of the digits are the same within each color. These are neutral colors because the red, green, and blue components are equal. A row of squares of different colors is produced.

Colors that work best with browsers are those in which both digits are equal within each color (red, blue, and green). The color Web sites also give information on how different browsers differ in their color values. The "Web-Safe" colors are those 216 in which the red, green, and blue components take on 6 levels: *00, 33, 66, 99, cc,* and *ff.*

 ## AN APPLICATION OF FRAMES

As you learned in Chapter 4, the technique of frames allows you to divide the window into portions that can contain different files. In the next example, frames are used to keep the stimuli visible throughout the experiment while the participants answer questions about them in another frame.

Consider *Ch14_ex3.htm,* which is listed in Figure 14.2.

This HTML page uses the FRAMESET and FRAME tags and has no BODY tag. This FRAMESET tag divides the window into two rows. The first row is set to 100 pixels, and the * designates that the rest of the window is the second frame (see Chapter 4). The FRAME SRC tags designate that the first frame will contain the table of stimuli from the first example of this chapter. The second frame will contain an experiment that was made with surveyWiz. The observer (i.e., the participant) can now view the gray stimuli in the upper frame while making the judgments requested in the form, which shows in the lower frame. In most browsers, the user can adjust the size of frames by clicking the mouse on the frame divider and dragging it to the desired position. Try this in *Ch14_exp1.htm.*

The method illustrated in *Ch14_exp1.htm* is called the *method of equal appearing intervals,* one of Fechner's techniques for measuring psychological value. It is also called the *method of category rating.* Another technique for judging the magnitude of psychological experiences is called *magnitude estimation* (Stevens, 1957). That technique is illustrated in *Ch14_exp2.htm,* which was also created by surveyWiz. The technique of magnitude estimation contains instructions that state that the numbers should be proportional to psychological magnitudes. If ratings are linearly related to subjective value, and if magnitude estimations are proportional to the same subjective values,

FIGURE 14.2. Illustration of FRAMESET and FRAME tags of HTML.

```
<HTML><HEAD><TITLE>Frameset Illustration</TITLE></HEAD>
<FRAMESET ROWS="100,*">
<FRAME SRC="tablegray.html">
<FRAME SRC="RateGray.htm">
</FRAMESET></HTML>
```

these two scales should be linearly related to each other. The two techniques yield results that are not linearly related, which was a long-standing problem in psychological measurement (Birnbaum, 1982). The issue of judgments based on "intervals" and "ratios" of subjective value is taken up in more detail in Chapter 15.

Frames can be a useful technique when it is desired to display two Web pages at once on the screen. However, they can also be annoying when used inappropriately. One problem with frames is that once a page opens with a frame, then if a link from one frame selects another page with frames, the screen becomes subdivided into smaller and smaller pieces. To escape the "tyranny of frames" it can be helpful to use one of the following types of links from pages to be displayed in frames (see also Chapter 4).

```
<A HREF=AnyPage.htm TARGET="_top">click here</A>
<A HREF=AnyPage.htm TARGET="_blank">or click here</A>
```

The former link TARGET will cause the new page to display at the top of the window, even if it is called by a page displayed within a frame. The latter link creates a new Web browser page, which also displays at the top. These tricks are illustrated in *Ch14_ex3b.htm,* which also uses *Ch14_ex3c.htm.*

 ## WORKING WITH GRAPHICS

Another way to make stimuli is to create them in a program that supports drawing, such as Adobe Illustrator, or even programs like MS Word or PowerPoint, and then save as HTML to create JPEG (*.jpg*) or GIF (*.gif*) files. For example, you can make similar stimuli to the grays in *Ch14_ex1.htm* by means of MS Word. Word supports the creation of drawing objects. You can convert these drawing objects to pictures, and then you can *Save As HTML,* which creates files that can be displayed from HTML pages on the Web. MS Word was used to create the graphic shown in *Ch14_ex4.htm.*

Here are four pointers for this approach. First, you should save your files containing drawing objects *before* you convert them to pictures and before you save as HTML. Once you convert drawing objects to pictures, you have much less control over the separate elements of the picture. Thus, if you decide you want to change something later (e.g., if you move a graphic element from here to there), you will be glad you saved your work as a drawing object in a separate file. Save files of drawing objects and pictures with separate names so that you can make revisions later on those files. Second, when you are happy with your drawing object, group the elements of your drawings and copy them to another file. When you copy them, use *Paste Special* and paste the graphics in the new document as *pictures.* Save this file under a second name. Third, from the **File** menu, select *Save As HTML* (or *Save As a Web Page*) and save the HTML under a third name. If your document contained several pictures, these are saved in a folder with names such as *image001.gif, image002.gif,* and so on. You should be aware of the fact that when you convert from a drawing object to a picture, and then from a picture to JPEG or GIF, that the appearance of colors and figure elements may change. Fourth, realize that the appearance of a file as displayed by the program that created it may not be the same as its appearance when viewed in a browser.

Examples of similar sets of gray stimuli that were created with MS Word are included in *Ch14_ex4.htm.* If you look closely at these stimuli in the browser, you will see that the gray colors are not uniform in color, but are in fact grainy. The color values used in the creation of the stimuli are slightly different in the two sets displayed in the example.

A set of dot patterns, similar to those used by Thurstone (1929) in his classic study of Fechner's law, and by Birnbaum (1978; 1982), is also included on the CD. These seven figures were created as drawing objects in MS Word. Each figure was then grouped and copied to a new file, where they were pasted special as pictures, and the new file containing seven pictures was saved as HTML. The seven images were then re-named from *image001.gif, image002.gif,* and so on to *dots1.gif, dots2.gif,* and so on.

Next, factorWiz was used to create an experimental file containing symbolic values for the rows and columns (*r1, r2, r3,* etc., for rows; and *r1, r2,* etc., for columns). Then, with Search and Replace, each "*r4*" was replaced with the tag to insert the appropriate stimulus:

```
<IMG SRC=dots4.gif width=50 height=50 align=middle>
```

This process was repeated six times until all of the stimuli (i.e., *r1, r2, ... r7*) had been replaced by the appropriate tags. The stimuli and materials for factorial experiments of "ratio" and "difference" judgments are included on the CD. The trick of using Search and Replace would also work for extensive blocks of text that would not fit in the boxes of factorWiz. The analysis of this type of experiment is taken up in Chapter 15.

Also included on your CD is an experiment on the Mueller–Lyer illusion, a classic perceptual illusion. Click the link in the examples and complete the experiment. The method of creating the experiment, which was also done with the help of factorWiz, is explained next.

 ## MUELLER-LYER EXPERIMENT

The Mueller–Lyer experiment uses a 5 × 6 factorial design of Horizontal Line length by Fin type. The five levels of horizontal line length were 98, 99, 100, 101, and 102 mm. The six levels of fins were no fins, in-going fins at 30°, in-going at 60°, right angle (90°), outgoing fins at 120°, and outgoing fins at 150°. These 30 figures were made in Adobe Illustrator 5.0 and saved as *.jpg* files. They were given names of *L1F0.jpg* to *L5F5.jpg*, where the number following the letter *L* indicates the level of line length (from *L1* = 98 mm to *L5* = 102 mm). The number following the *F* indicates the level of fin type (*F0* = no fins, *F1* = in-going fins at 30° to *F5* = outgoing fins at 150°).

In this experiment, the fins do not join the lines and are clearly distinct from them. Some theories of the illusion hold that there should be no Mueller–Lyer illusion in these figures.

Realize that to display a figure requires an HTML tag such as the following:

```
<IMG SRC=L5F5.jpg ALIGN=MIDDLE>
```

Because the figures have been named in a factorial form, you can use factorWiz (Chapter 11) to make the experimental Web page for this experiment. The trick is to enter the first part of the HTML tag up to the designation of the lines for the row factor and enter the second part, including the fins for the column factor. There should be no separator, so be sure to delete any spaces in the separator field. Also be sure that there are no extra spaces after the row designations. The screen appears as in Figure 14.3. It should be clear that the stimuli were made in a graphics program, and the HTML for creating the factorial design and randomizing the trials was created by factorWiz.

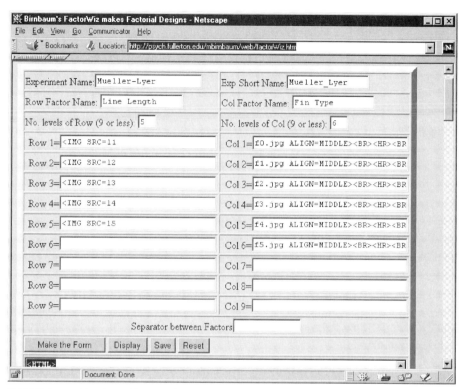

FIGURE 14.3.   This figure illustrates how to use factorWiz to set up a factorial design involving graphic stimuli. In this study, a series of stimuli have been created, named L1F0.JPG to L5F5.JPG. Each combination of row and column creates the image tag to present one image. Tags are also included to separate each trial with a horizontal rule. There are no spaces in the separator field.

 INCLUDING SOUNDS IN A WEB PAGE

A Web site described by Welch and Krantz (1996) contains many interesting auditory demonstrations; this site has the URL:

http://www.music.mcgill.ca/auditory/Auditory.html

This site permits the downloading of copies of the files and is linked to the list of examples on the CD.

If you want to create or record your own sound files, you will need the equipment and software. That means you need a computer equipped with a microphone and software to record sounds, or you will need software to synthesize sounds. To search for software, try www.download.com and www.shareware.com, and search for *audio* and *audio, recorder*. A good deal of freeware and shareware software is available for you to try out.

The HTML in *Ch14_ex5.htm* uses the Anchor tag (`<A HREF=sound.wav></A>`) to load the sound.

```
<HTML><HEAD><TITLE>Presenting Sounds</TITLE>
</HEAD><BODY>
<H1>Using a link to Sound in a .WAV file</H1>
<P>
<A HREF=A.wav>Click here</A>
</BODY></HTML>
```

The next example, *Ch14_ex6.htm*, works in Netscape but not in Internet Explorer. Netscape allows one to use JavaScript to control the playing, pausing, and stopping of sounds. (Explorer uses a different procedure.) This example illustrates how to control the volume levels of sounds, sound G should be louder than sounds C or D. Despite this apparent ability to control sound levels, the listener can still readjust them.

Sound files can be saved in many formats. Until recently, sound files had to be sent before they could be played, which meant that you had to be very patient to wait for large sound files to arrive. New software has been developed for compression and transmission of sounds. This software speeds up the process considerably, with only a small reduction in quality for such stimuli as music and speech. The software can be downloaded free, including both the RealPlayer plug-in, which plays the music, and RealEncoder, which allows you to convert standard sound files to "streaming audio" files. In streaming audio, you can begin playing the start of a musical selection, for example, while the rest of the file is loading. A link to [http://www.real.com/] is included on the CD.

If you want to send music as compressed files for an experiment, you need to ensure that your participants have the proper plug-in to play it. *Ch14_ex7.htm* compares a 10 MB WAV file with a 120K RealAudio file of the same music. You must download the RealPlayer plug-in to hear the compressed music. The 10 MB file, which represents about 1 minute of music, may give you "out of memory error." It could take a long time to download 10 MB file from the Internet. The music sounds almost as good in RealAudio as it does in the uncompressed format, but it arrives and plays much faster.

The transmission of sound via the Web lags behind the transmission of visual images; one can expect improvements in both in the next few years. Besides the long waits to load sound files, another difficulty with using sound in experiments is that there is a great variety of sound systems in use by the potential audience, from no sound to poor-quality speakers to advanced stereo systems. The problem is that you have to either limit your experiment to people with certain equipment or hope that these differences in equipment do not make a difference to your research topic. If that is a concern to your research, you should certainly include items asking the participants what type of hardware and software they are using so that you can analyze the data separately for people with different systems.

Compression of music in MP3 format is currently becoming quite popular, and this standard will probably dominate music coding for the next few years. MP3 is short for Moving Pictures Experts Group Layer 3. It refers to a standard for sound compression that takes advantage of the perceptual system to present only a fraction of the actual sound information in a way that will still sound good to a human ear. Further information on MP3 can be obtained from sites linked from the examples to this chapter.

 **SUMMARY**

This chapter reviewed methods for including visual and auditory stimuli within a Web page for psychophysical studies and demonstrations. HTML provides methods for controlling the colors presented on a monitor via the browser. Visual stimuli can also be created in programs that support drawings. This technique requires one to create the stimulus in the drawing program, then convert the graphic to a format such as GIF or JPEG that can be supported on the Web. The construction of sounds is currently more complex, requiring a recorder or synthesizer, the software for encoding the sound files to a format that can be handled by browsers (or their plug-ins), and the player programs or plug-ins to play back the sounds. Sites with more information, where you can download the needed software, are linked in the examples.

 EXERCISES

1. Use HTML tables to create a screen of horizontal black bars (`color=000000`) and horizontal red stripes (`color=ff0000`). Then create another table of vertical black bars separated by vertical green stripes (`color=00ff00`). Create two more tables, with horizontal bars separated by white stripes (`color=ffffff`), and the other with vertical black bars separated by white stripes. You can create an interesting illusion by alternately viewing these two-colored stimuli for 15 sec. each, repeating for a total of about 3–5 min, then look at a screen of horizontal or vertical black bars separated by white stripes. These stimuli create an orientation-specific after effect. You will see after-effect illusory contrasting colors between the black bars. The illusory colors depend on the orientation of the black bars.

2. Make a 5 × 5 table in which every cell has the same color except the one in the center. This table could be used to show contrast illusions with neutral or chromatic colors. Make a second 5 × 5 table with the same center square and different values for the color of the surround. (One solution is given in *Ch14_ex8.htm*.)

3. Create a test of the horizontal–vertical illusion by dividing the screen into frames. In the upper frame, place a horizontal line of 75 mm. In the lower frame, place vertical lines of 50 to 100 mm, labeled with letters. Ask the observer to choose which of the vertical lines is equal in length to the horizontal line. Measure the strength of the illusion by computing the difference between lengths of the two lines that are supposedly equal for each person.

4. Use a graphic program to create figures for a visual illusion such as the Ponzo illusion, Poggendorf illusion, Baldwin illusion, or another. Manipulate two factors in the construction of the figures. For example, in the Ponzo illusion, one could manipulate the angle of the "railway lines" and the vertical separation between the two horizontal lines. Use factorWiz to randomize and create the HTML form for the study.

5. Try out the "extra" examples on the CD with Netscape. You will need to install RealPlayer to hear the compressed musical selection. The file *melissa4.wav* is about 10 MB in size. This file was compressed to *melissa4.rm*, which is only 120K, by RealEncoder. To play the larger file, you must be patient to allow it to load.

6. Project idea: Collect data with *Ch14_exp1.htm* and *Ch14_exp2.htm*. Plot the median magnitude estimation of each stimulus against the mean category rating of the same stimulus. Is the function linear? Compare your results to those of Birnbaum (1982). If your results agree with typical results of such "direct" scaling, your magnitude estimations are a nonlinear, positively accelerating function of category ratings. This nonlinear relationship puzzled psychologists for many years.

7. Project idea: Download software to record, encode, and play back sounds. Create your own sounds and include them in a Web page. Be sure to include a link within your Web page so that the reader can figure out how to download any needed player or plug-in to play back the sounds.

8. Project idea: Collect data for the Mueller–Lyer experiment and see if there is an illusion with this variation of the figure in which the lines do not join the fins.

9. Project idea: Collect data for "ratios" and "differences" of darkness of dot patterns. Compare your Web research results with the results of the two lab procedures of Birnbaum (1978, 1982).

Chapter 15

Psychological Scaling with "Ratios" and "Differences"

Does it make sense to describe how you feel? Can one measure psychological impressions such as those of heaviness of lifted weights, darkness of a patch of color, the loudness or pitch of a tone? If subjective values of psychophysical stimuli can be measured, there is hope that psychology can become a science in which it is meaningful to discuss subjective experiences for other concepts such as pain, pleasure, hunger, perceptions, emotions, and judgments. In Chapter 14, you learned about the presentation of psychophysical stimuli, and in this chapter you learn about the scaling of psychological values of stimuli that do not necessarily have physical measures.

Previous chapters analyzed single experiments. In this chapter, you learn to analyze two different experiments that are linked in the same study. The concept that links them is the assumption that subjective experiences can be measured, and that these subjective values are independent of the comparison task.

If you have not done so already, participate as a judge in the two experiments on "ratios" and "differences" of prestige of occupations. Is the difference in prestige between the occupations of *doctor* and a *factory worker* greater than the difference in prestige between the occupations of *college professor* and *architect*? Most people think so. If such judgments can be represented by intervals on a numerical scale, it is possible to assign numbers to represent the separations in prestige between occupations. In other words, we can scale subjective values on an interval scale of social prestige.

These experiments were constructed with the help of factorWiz. The row and column stimuli are names of occupations. The experiments are available on the CD from the list of examples. These experiments illustrate how such judgments can be used to test models of comparison and also to measure subjective value. In this example, the studies scale the prestige of different occupations. Data are included on CD for two experiments that form a Web-based partial replication of the experiments by Hardin and Birnbaum (1990).

Thurstone (1927) argued for a subtractive model of comparison. However, Stevens (1957) argued that one should use "ratio" judgments and a ratio model. Taking judgments of "ratios" at face value, he thought category ratings and judgments of intervals were "biased and invalid." Early research, comparing the method of magnitude estimation with the method of equal-appearing intervals, such as described in Chapter 14, could not resolve these rival theories. The fact that these two procedures did not yield the same scale was known, but could not be resolved by single studies.

Modern research allows us to test not only these models, but also theories having implications for the results of two or more different types of experiments. Evidence with judgments of "ratios" and "differences" has been consistent with the theory that people use only one operation, that the operation is subtraction, and that psychophysical functions come closer to the predictions of Fechner than to those of Stevens (Birnbaum, 1980, 1982). This chapter teaches you how to analyze such research.

SUBTRACTIVE MODEL

Imagine three points on a straight line, *A, B,* and *C.* The distance from *A* to *C* equals the distance from *A* to *B* plus the distance from *B* to *C.* If all of the differences between points are known, one cannot only assign numbers to the points (measure), but can also test the model, which assumes these points are on a line.

In a test of the subtractive model, the experimenter presents pairs of stimuli, such as squares varying in darkness, weights varying in heaviness, or tones varying in loudness, and asks people to judge the psychological "differences" between the stimuli. Quotation marks are used to distinguish the instruction to judge "differences" or numbers produced by people under such instructions from actual (computed) or theoretical differences. Judgments of "differences" or "ratios" may or may not obey the mathematical properties of numeric or theoretical differences or ratios. As explained later in this chapter, evidence is consistent with the theory that people actually judge "ratios" by computing subjective differences (Birnbaum, 1980, 1982).

The subtractive model of "difference" judgments can be written as follows:

$$D_{ij} = a_D(s_i - t_j) + b_D \tag{15.1}$$

where D_{ij} is the predicted judgment of "difference" between two stimuli, having subjective values, s_i and t_j; a_D and b_D are constants that depend on the response scale. This model implies that there should be no interaction between two factors in which the stimuli are varied. For any set of four stimuli, the following should hold:

$$D_{ij} - D_{im} = D_{kj} - D_{km} \tag{15.2}$$

For example, the "difference" in prestige between *physician* and *factory worker* minus the "difference" between *physician* and *college professor* should equal the "difference" between *police officer* and *factory worker* minus the "difference" between *police officer* and *college professor.* Judgments in any two rows should be linearly related to each other, with the same slope. In other words, there should be no interaction between rows and columns in analysis of variance.

 ## RATIO MODEL

The ratio model of "ratio" judgments can be written as follows:

$$R_{ij} = a_R (s_i / t_j)^m + b_R \tag{15.3}$$

where R_{ij} is the predicted "ratio" of stimuli with the same scale values as in Eq. 15.1, and where a_R, b_R, and m are constants that depend on the response scale. When a_R and m are both 1, and $b_R = 0$, we say that judgments of "ratios" can be *taken at face value;* so, if a person says that one job is "three times" as prestigious as another, we assume the subjective ratio is 3. If $m = 2$, for example, it means that if a person says the "ratio" is "four times," we assume the subjective ratio is 2 (because $2^m = 4$).

Equation 15.3 implies that judgments of "ratios" should form a divergent, bilinear fan in which any two rows are linearly related and all pairs of curves intersect at the same point on the ordinate. This pattern is like that of the multiplicative model examined in Chapter 13, restricted to positive numbers.

TWO-OPERATION THEORY

The two-operation theory assumes that when people are instructed to judge both "differences" and "ratios," that Eqs. 15.1 and 15.3 describe both sets of judgments with the same scale values (same values of s and t) in both tasks. Actual ratios and differences are not monotonically related to each other. For example, $2 - 1 = 3 - 2$ but $2/1 > 3/2$. Similarly, $2/1 = 4/2$, but $2 - 1 < 4 - 2$. Therefore, if people used two operations, one predicts that judgments of "ratios" and "differences" will not be monotonically related to each other, but instead show the theoretical pattern of interrelations of actual ratios and differences.

ONE-OPERATION THEORY

The one-operation theory assumes that people use the same scale values and the same comparison operation for both tasks (Torgenson, 1961). The subtractive theory of Birnbaum (1980; 1982) postulates that "ratio" judgments are governed by the following subtractive model instead of Eq. 15.3:

$$R_{ij} = a_R \exp(s_i - t_j) + b_R \tag{15.4}$$

where $\exp(x)$ represents the exponential function. This theory predicts that "ratio" and "difference" judgments will be monotonically related to each other, $R_{ij} = \mathfrak{M}(D_{ij})$, where $\mathfrak{M}$ is a strictly increasing monotonic function, because both are based on the same underlying operation computed on the same scales of subjective value. In other words, if "ratios" and "differences" are each monotonically related to the same intervals of subjective value, then they should be monotonically related to each other.

By collecting data for two experiments, "ratios" and "differences," employing the same stimuli, it is possible to test between the one- and two-operation theories.

CLEAN AND FILTER "RATIOS" AND "DIFFERENCES" OF OCCUPATIONAL PRESTIGE

To analyze the data on CD, follow the steps described in previous chapters to filter the data, then copy them to a new workbook. In this case, the steps are as follows: From Excel, open the data file *clean.xls*. Type variable names in the first row (if you have not done so already). Then click in cell A1, and choose *Filter: AutoFilters* from the **Data** menu. Click on the drop-down selection arrow in A1, and select *pres_diffs* from the list of experiments. Drag the mouse from the second row in column A to column AG, then continue to drag down to select all of the data (excluding the first row of variable names). Select *Copy* from the **Edit** menu (you should now see the "ants" crawling around to show your selection). From the **File** menu, select *New* to create a new workbook. Click in cell A2 of the new workbook, and choose *Paste* from the **Edit** menu (or press *CTRL* and V). You have now pasted the judged "differences." Save the new workbook as *RD.xls* (select *Save As* from the **File** menu).

Now, return to *clean.xls* (from the **Window** menu, select the filename *clean.xls*). Click again in cell A1 on the drop-down selection, and now select *pres_ratios*. As before, click in the second row of column A and drag to the right to column AG then drag down to select all of the rows of data (excluding the first row). Choose *Copy* from the **Edit** menu. Then return to the file *RD.xls* by clicking on that filename in the **Window** menu.

Now click the tab at the bottom of the sheet labeled *Sheet2*. Click in cell A2, and choose *Paste* from the **Edit** menu. You now can double-click on the tab and rename *Sheet2* to *R* (for judgments of "ratios"). Double click on the tab *Sheet1* and rename it *D* (for judgments of "differences").

Now look at the last row of sheet *R("ratios")*. That row contains a list of variable names. That list was created by the trick (described in Chapter 11) of completing the experiment by typing in the stimuli instead of responses; then in an editor replacing the date, time, and gender with "date," "time," and "sex." Select that row and cut it from the last row, then paste it into the first row of both worksheets (with "ratios" and "differences.") You may need to delete a blank row. To delete a row, click on the row number (to the left of the grid), which selects the row. Then from the **Edit** menu, select *Delete* (but be careful not to delete the whole sheet!). Make the variable names bold by selecting the first row and clicking on the **"B"** for bold on the toolbar (or select *Cells* from the **Format** menu, and click the *Font* tab). Now copy them to sheet *D* ("differences") as follows: Select the first row, then select *Copy* from the **Edit** menu, then click on the tab for *D* and paste in the first row. You should edit the first entry, now in cell A1, to say *Differences* instead of *pres_ratios.*

The column labels for the judgments can be rotated to vertical as follows. Select columns G through AF in the first row, select *Cells* from the **Format** menu, then click the tab for *Alignment,* and drag the red dot to turn the text sideways.

The data file appears as in Figure 15.1. If you examine the file, you see that on

FIGURE 15.1. Appearance of the data file *RD.xls*. Check the value in cell K17. Instructions were to use integers from 1 to 9; thus, 3,333,333 must be an error.

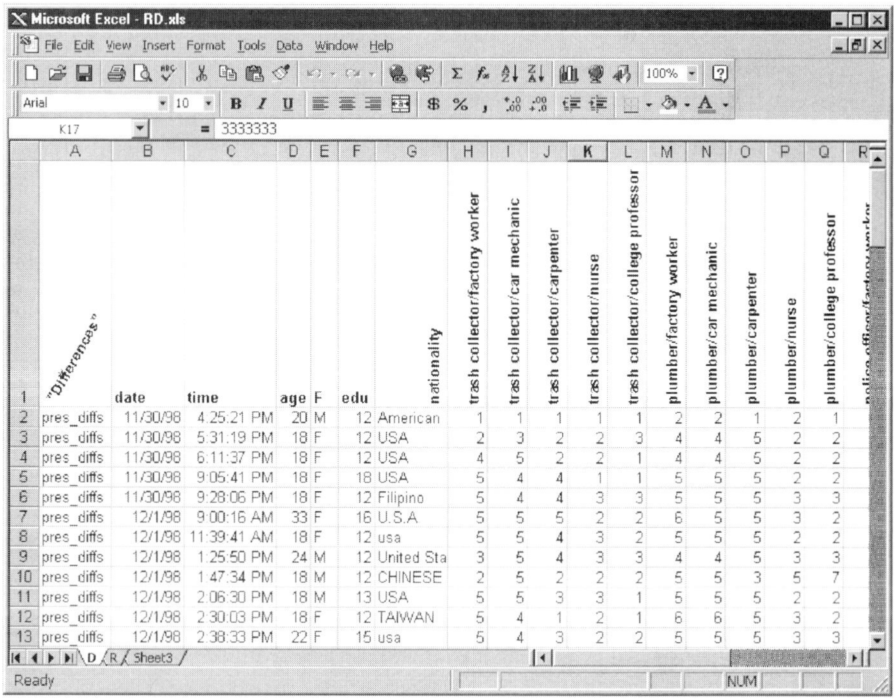

	A	B	C	D	E	F	G	H	I	J	K	L	M	N	O	P	Q
1	"Differences"	date	time	age	F	edu	nationality	trash collector/factory worker	trash collector/car mechanic	trash collector/carpenter	trash collector/nurse	trash collector/college professor	plumber/factory worker	plumber/car mechanic	plumber/carpenter	plumber/nurse	plumber/college professor
2	pres_diffs	11/30/98	4:25:21 PM	20	M	12	American	1	1	1	1	1	2	2	1	2	1
3	pres_diffs	11/30/98	5:31:19 PM	18	F	12	USA	2	3	2	2	3	4	4	5	2	2
4	pres_diffs	11/30/98	6:11:37 PM	18	F	12	USA	4	5	2	2	1	4	4	5	2	2
5	pres_diffs	11/30/98	9:05:41 PM	18	F	18	USA	5	4	4	1	1	5	5	5	2	2
6	pres_diffs	11/30/98	9:28:06 PM	18	F	12	Filipino	5	4	4	3	3	5	5	5	3	3
7	pres_diffs	12/1/98	9:00:16 AM	33	F	16	U.S.A	5	5	5	2	2	6	5	5	3	2
8	pres_diffs	12/1/98	11:39:41 AM	18	F	12	usa	5	5	4	3	2	5	5	5	2	2
9	pres_diffs	12/1/98	1:25:50 PM	24	M	12	United Sta	3	5	4	3	3	4	4	5	3	3
10	pres_diffs	12/1/98	1:47:34 PM	18	M	12	CHINESE	2	5	2	2	2	5	5	3	5	7
11	pres_diffs	12/1/98	2:06:30 PM	18	M	13	USA	5	5	3	3	1	5	5	5	2	2
12	pres_diffs	12/1/98	2:30:03 PM	18	F	12	TAIWAN	5	4	1	2	1	6	6	5	3	2
13	pres_diffs	12/1/98	2:38:33 PM	22	F	15	usa	5	4	3	2	2	5	5	5	3	3

FIGURE 15.2. The conditional formatting dialog box. In this case, the cell will have a yellow cell background and red font if the value is not between 1 and 9. The instructions for the "difference" task instructed people to use a 1 to 9 scale, so values outside of this range are "out of bounds."

12/1/98, at 3:03 PM, a 30-year-old female made a judgment of 3,333,333. Because the instructions specified responses from 1 to 9, this response is completely out of range. Perhaps she put her finger on the 3 and held the key long enough to produce a string of repeated 3's. As noted earlier, you should follow a preplanned scheme to put aside data of subjects who do not follow instructions for separate analysis. It would be misleading to average such out-of-bounds values with the rest of the data. When finding means, one error that large makes quite a difference in the result. In this case, the column mean would be 22,224.72 instead of 2.52.

To find such out-of-range numbers, use conditional formatting. Select the data (in row 2, select H through AF, then drag down to include all rows, aside from the first). When the data are selected, choose *Conditional formatting . . .* from the **Format** menu. The dialog box is shown in Figure 15.2. Specify that values that are not between 1 and 9 will have a yellow background and red font. Examining the file, you find a subject who left six trials blank. That row of data should also be removed for separate analysis. From identifying information (not shown), it was found that person "A" repeated the task, submitting two sets of data. That person's data are labeled. To avoid giving too much weight to data from those who submit multiple copies, you should follow a predetermined rule to use only one set of data per person.

Repeat the process with the judgments of "ratios," looking for numbers less than or equal to zero. You will discover a few typos. Change '00 to 100, and change 8O0 to 800—the letter "oh" was used instead of zero. These cases can also be spotted because they are left-justified, like text, instead of right-justified, as are numbers in Excel.

FIND AVERAGES AND ARRANGE DATA MATRICES

The next step is to find means. Click in cell H111 (just after the end of the data) in sheet R ("ratios"). Choose *Function* from the **Insert** menu, then select *AVERAGE* from the list of functions. Select H2:H110 for the range of numbers to be averaged (Excel will probably anticipate this correctly for you). Then hit Enter. Next, use *AutoFill* to fill in the means for all of the columns by dragging the *AutoFill* handle (+) from H111 to AG111.

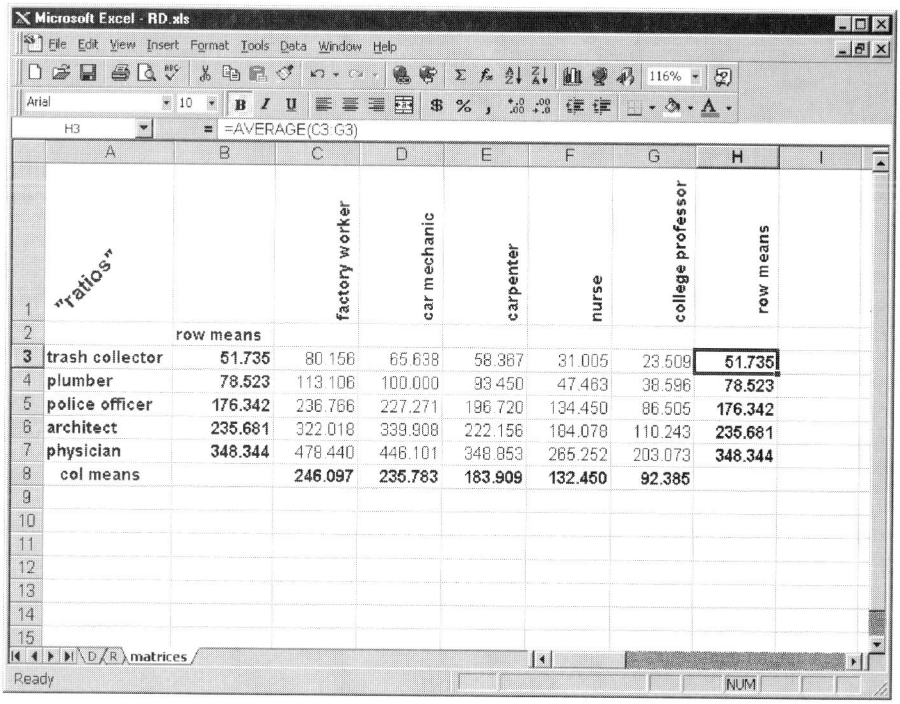

"ratios"		factory worker	car mechanic	carpenter	nurse	college professor	row means
	row means						
trash collector	**51.735**	80.156	65.638	58.367	31.005	23.509	**51.735**
plumber	**78.523**	113.106	100.000	93.450	47.463	38.596	**78.523**
police officer	**176.342**	236.766	227.271	196.720	134.450	86.505	**176.342**
architect	**235.681**	322.018	339.908	222.156	184.078	110.243	**235.681**
physician	**348.344**	478.440	446.101	348.853	265.252	203.073	**348.344**
col means		**246.097**	**235.783**	**183.909**	**132.450**	**92.385**	

FIGURE 15.3. Appearance of the matrix of mean "ratios" of prestige of the row occupation divided by the column occupation. For example, it is 4.78 times as prestigious to be a *physician* than it is to be a *factory worker* (recall that judgments are 100 times the "ratios"), and it is 2.03 times as prestigious to be a *physician* as it is to be a *college professor.* The row means were copied from H3:H7 to B3:B7 to facilitate drawing the graph.

The next step is to arrange the column means in an array. From the **Insert** menu, choose *Worksheet.* Name this new worksheet *matrices.* Now, copy the mean "ratio" judgments into cell C3 of the new worksheet (use *Paste Special* and be sure to click *Paste Link*). Then cut the last 20 cells and paste them in cell C4. Next cut off the last 15 cells and paste in cell C5. Continue cutting and pasting groups of five in this way until you have a 5 × 5 matrix. Then type in the names of the occupations in the rows and columns. Next, find the row and column means of the matrix using the *AVERAGE* function and, using *AutoFill* to speed up the process, copy the row marginal means into column B using *Copy* and *Paste Special* (*Paste Link*). After making the labels and marginal means bold, and after formatting the cells to show three decimals, the matrix appears as in Figure 15.3.

Find the means of the "difference" judgments using *AVERAGE. Copy* and *Paste Special* (*Paste Link*) these means to cell L3 in the worksheet "matrices." Cut and paste them to arrange them in a similar matrix of average (arithmetic mean) judgments. Figure 15.4 shows the matrix of mean "differences" after the marginal means have been computed.

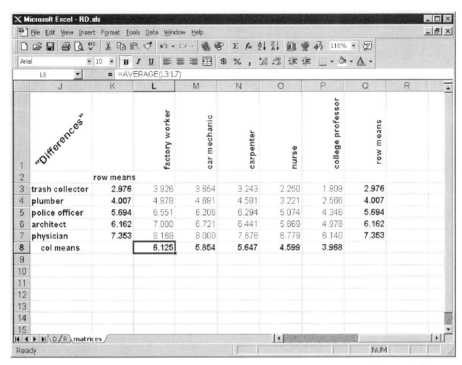

FIGURE 15.4.   Matrix of mean "differences" in occupational prestige. The scale ranged from 1 to 9, with 5 indicating "no difference" in prestige. The data show that it is very much more prestigious to be a *physician* than it is to be a *factory worker*. The entry in P3 is less than 5, showing that it is more prestigious to be a *college professor* than it is to be a *trash collector*.

 MAKE GRAPHS OF "RATIO" AND "DIFFERENCE" JUDGMENTS

Graph the "ratio" judgments against the row marginal means. To do this, select B3:G7 and click the chart icon, or select *Chart* from the **Insert** menu. From the Chart Wizard, select *XY (Scatter)* and select . . . *points connected by straight lines.* In step 2, click that data series are in *Columns*. In step 3, click *Titles* and add appropriate labels for the abscissa and ordinate; also click gridlines and uncheck any gridlines. In step 4, insert the graph as a *New sheet*. To adjust the appearance of the figure, point and double-click on chart elements to modify them (you can also bring up menus with the right mouse button on PC or CTRL and click on Mac). After changing the colors of the points and lines, adjusting the font sizes of the labels and formatting the numbers, the "ratio" data appear as in Figure 15.5.

Follow the same procedures to make a figure of the "difference" judgments, plotting them in the same way as the "ratio" judgments. The resulting graph is shown in Figure 15.6.

Notice that the "ratio" judgments are not parallel, but show divergence. The "difference" judgments are nearly parallel and linear. At first look, the data appear to conform to the theory that people compute ratios when instructed to judge "ratios" and that they compute differences when instructed to judge "differences." That is, each data matrix appears consistent with the idea that people followed the directions for that

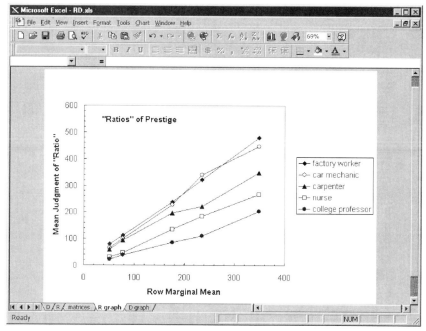

FIGURE 15.5. Mean judgments of "ratios" of occupational prestige as a function of the row marginal means, with a separate curve for each "denominator" occupation. The successive "numerator" occupations were *trash collector, plumber, police officer, architect,* and *physician.*

FIGURE 15.6. Mean judgments of "differences" plotted as in Figure 15.5.

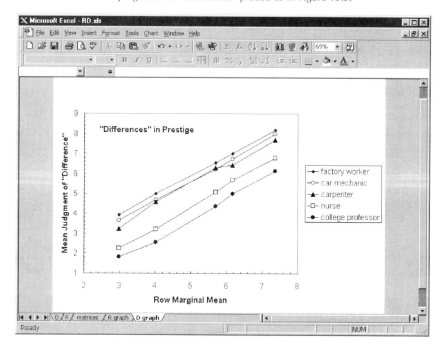

task. However, another way of looking at the data contradicts that theory and suggests that they are using the same computation in both tasks.

 ## FIT OF THE TWO-OPERATION THEORY

The two-operation theory assumes that people compute both ratios and differences on the same scales of subjective value. To fit the theory, we must estimate the subjective values of the prestige of the occupations. We can use the *Solver* in Excel to estimate the parameters of the theory.

To fit the two-operation theory, click on the tab for *matrices*, then carry out the following steps:

1. Select cells A10:A11 and click the *Merge and Center* icon on the toolbar (it looks like the letter "a" with arrows in a box). Type the title "Two Operations."
2. In cells A11, A12, and A13, type the parameter labels aR=, bR=, and m=.
3. In cells B11, B12, and B13, type the corresponding initial values of these parameters; that is, type 100, 0, and 1, respectively.
4. Click in cell B11 and give it the name A_R by replacing B11 in the Name Box (the Name Box is directly over column A in the spreadsheet), and then hit enter. Give B12 the name B_R; next, give B13 the name M_.
5. Next, type the label "scale values" in B14.
6. In B15 through B19 type the initial row scale values; that is, type the numbers 1, 2, 3, 4, and 5. Select these cells (B15:B19) and rename them s_i.
7. Now, type the initial values for the column scale values in cells C14:G14 and name them t_j.

Now, in cell C15, type the following:

=A_R*(s_i/t_j)^M_ + B_R

Then hit return. The value 1 will appear in C15. Next, click in C15 and use *AutoFill* to fill the first column, then while the first column is selected, drag to the right to fill the entire matrix of predicted ratios. The matrix now appears as in Figure 15.7.

The next step is to construct the matrix of theoretical differences. First, use *Copy* and *Paste Special* (*Paste Link*) to copy the row scale values from B15:B19 to K15:K19. Second, use *Copy* and *Paste Special* (*Paste Link*) to copy the column scale values from C14:G14 to L14:P14. Name the row scale values in K15:K19 s_iD; name the column scale values in L14:P14 t_jD. In J11 and J12, type the labels aD= and bD=. In K11 and K12, type the initial estimates; that is type 1 and 5, respectively. Assign the name a_D to K11 and assign the name b_D to K12. In L15, type the following formula for the subtractive model:

=a_D*(s_iD − t_jD) + b_D

Hit return, and 5 appears in L15. Select L15 and use *AutoFill* to fill in the first column, then the entire 5 × 5 matrix.

Next, compute the sum of squared differences between the judgments of "differences" and the predicted differences by typing =SUMXMY2(L3:P7,L15:P19) in cell Q21. (You can also do this by clicking in cell Q21 and select *function* from the **Insert** menu. Then select the SUMXMY2 function and specify the matrix of data and the matrix of predictions.) To the left of Q21, select cells M21:P21 and click the *Merge and Center* icon (looks like a little "a" in a box). Then type in that large merged cell "Sum of squared deviations =". The predictions appear as in Figure 15.8.

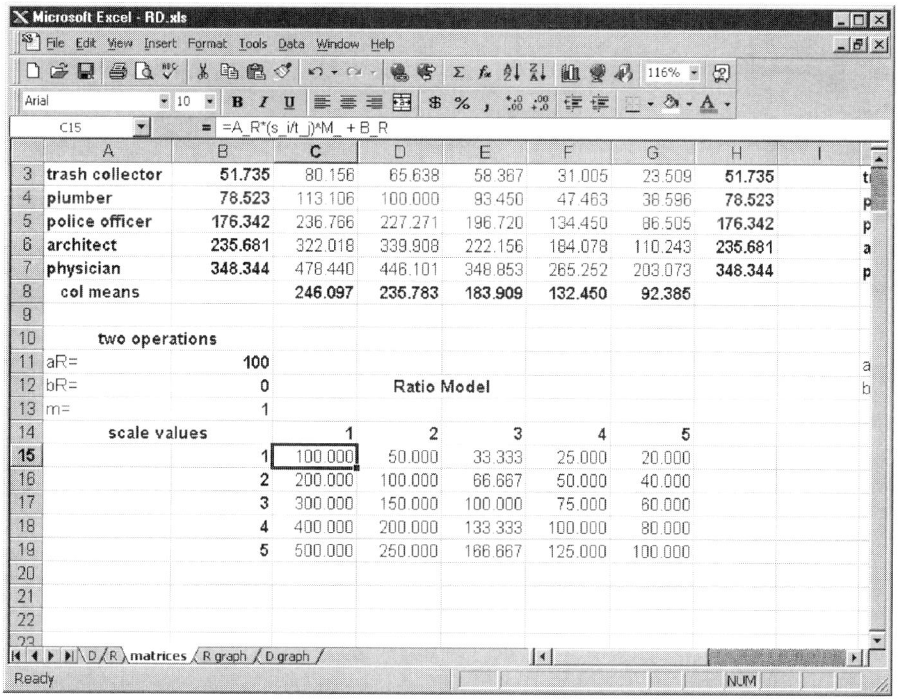

	A	B	C	D	E	F	G	H
3	trash collector	51.735	80.156	65.638	58.367	31.005	23.509	51.735
4	plumber	78.523	113.106	100.000	93.450	47.463	38.596	78.523
5	police officer	176.342	236.766	227.271	196.720	134.450	86.505	176.342
6	architect	235.681	322.018	339.908	222.156	184.078	110.243	235.681
7	physician	348.344	478.440	446.101	348.853	265.252	203.073	348.344
8	col means		246.097	235.783	183.909	132.450	92.385	
9								
10	two operations							
11	aR=	100						
12	bR=	0		Ratio Model				
13	m=	1						
14	scale values		1	2	3	4	5	
15		1	100.000	50.000	33.333	25.000	20.000	
16		2	200.000	100.000	66.667	50.000	40.000	
17		3	300.000	150.000	100.000	75.000	60.000	
18		4	400.000	200.000	133.333	100.000	80.000	
19		5	500.000	250.000	166.667	125.000	100.000	

FIGURE 15.7. Theoretical matrix of ratio model constructed below the "ratio" data.

In H21, compute the sum of squared deviations between the judged "ratios" and theoretical ratios by the same method. This time, however, divide the sum of squared residuals by 10000 (i.e., in cell H21, type =SUMXMY2(C15:G19,C3:G7)/10000). The reason to divide by the square of 100 is to put the "ratio" deviations on a scale comparable to that for "differences" (recall that "ratio" judgments are 100 times the subjective "ratio"). Next, in H22, add the sum of H21 and Q21 (type =H21+Q21 in cell H22 and hit enter). Label this as the "total sum of squared residuals." The number in cell H22 measures the badness of fit of the model to both arrays of data. The larger the number, the worse the fit. We can use the *Solver* to make this number smaller (Figure 15.9).

The next step is to use the *Solver* to estimate the parameters. Click in H22. Then, select *Solver*... from the **Tools** menu. Be sure that cell H22 is selected as the Target. Click the radio button to *Minimize*. Select the scale values and parameters of the model. These values are located in cells B15:B19, C14:G14, K11:K12, and B11:B13. To select these, click the *By Changing Cells:* box; then, while holding the Ctrl button, use the mouse to select the cells that contain parameters of the model. These cells hold the row and column scale values, and the constants of Eqs. 15.1 and 15.3. Next, click the *Add* button on the Solver Parameters dialog. This button is used to add constraints. Constrain the first row scale value to 1 by selecting B15 = 1. Similarly, initially take "ratios" at face value by constraining the ratio model constants to be 100, 0, and 1, respectively. The instructions also specified that if there was "no difference" that the "difference" judgment was to be 5, so constrain K12 to be 5. This dialog box is shown in Figure 15.10.

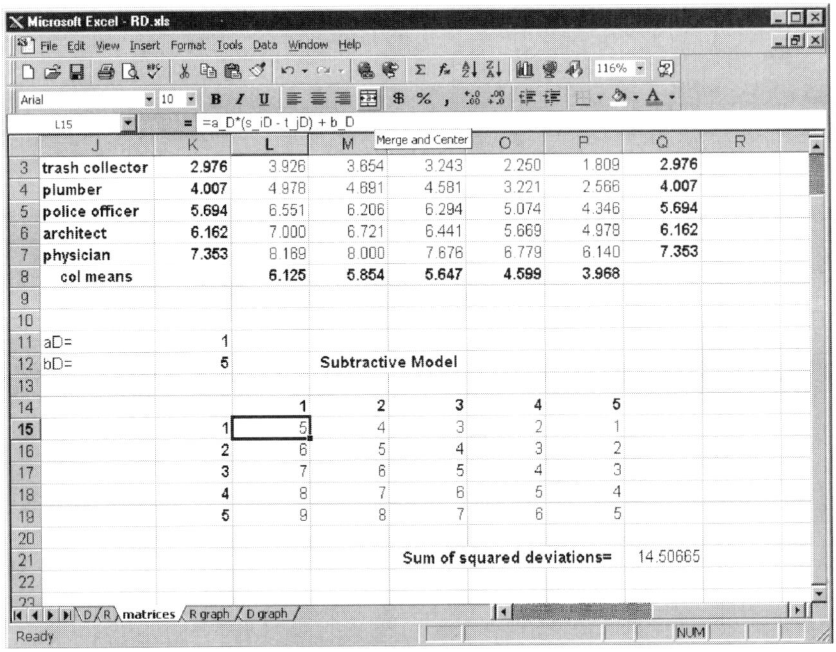

FIGURE 15.8. Matrix of theoretical predictions of subtractive model. The formula line shows the equation typed into cell L15. The *Merge and Center* icon is above the formula line, above column M in this picture.

FIGURE 15.9. Sum of Squared Differences between judged "ratios" and theoretical ratios and the total measure of fit.

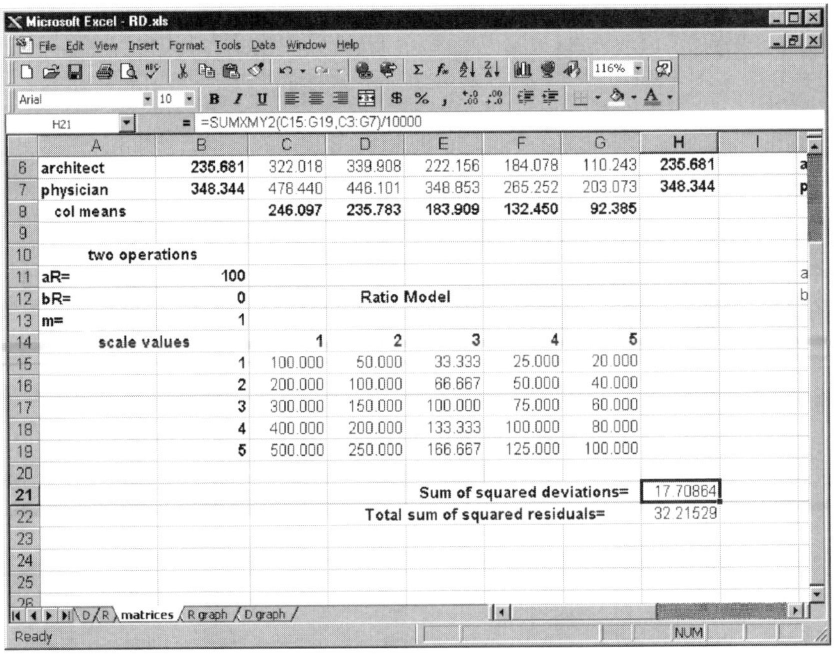

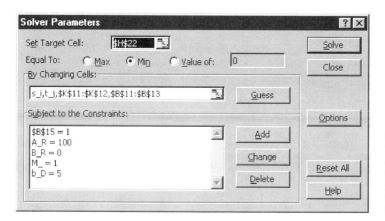

FIGURE 15.10.
The *Solver* Parameters dialog box. This setup is used to fit the two-operation theory with "ratios" at face value and assuming that "5" on the "difference" scale corresponds to no difference. Later, fit the theory that allows *m* to be free.

Click *Solve* on the button, and the values in the theoretical matrix change. Excel has varied the parameters of the model to try to make the theory fit the data as well as possible. Clicking *OK* to keep the solver solution shows the changes in Figure 15.11. The total sum of squared residuals dropped from 32.22 (for the initial estimates) to 4.83 for the two-operation theory. This fit is better, but we can do much better still.

FIT OF THE ONE-OPERATION THEORY

To fit one-operation theory, you must create two new theoretical matrices. Put them below the matrices for two-operation theory. Follow the same steps as before to construct the ratio model predictions, but this time give the row and column scale values the names s1_i (rows) and t1_j (columns) instead of s_i and t_j. The new names are used to distinguish these one-operation scale values from the two-operation scale values estimated previously. The equation in C29 is now:

=A1_R*2^(s1_i − t1_j)+B1_R

where the values of A1_R and B1_R are stored in cells B25 and B26, respectively. Note that this equation is a subtractive model with an exponential transformation; in this case, the base is 2. This work is shown in Figure 15.12.

Construct the predictions for the "difference" judgments according to the subtractive model, as was done previously, but give new names to the row and column scale values and parameters, to allow Excel to distinguish between the one- and two-operation models. Then compute the sum of squared residuals between the theory and the data and add them together as before, putting the total in Cell H36.

Click in cell H36 and select *Solver* from the **Tools** menu. Click *Reset All*, and specify the new row and column scale values and parameters as before. Also, constrain the parameters and one of the scale values to 1, as before. The *Solver* Parameter dialog is shown in Figure 15.13. Click the *Solve* button, click *Continue* if necessary, then click *OK* to keep the solution.

The one-operation theory fits better than two-operation theory if ratios are taken at face value. The total sum of squared residuals is 1.74, less than half as large as 4.83. The solution is shown in Figure 15.14.

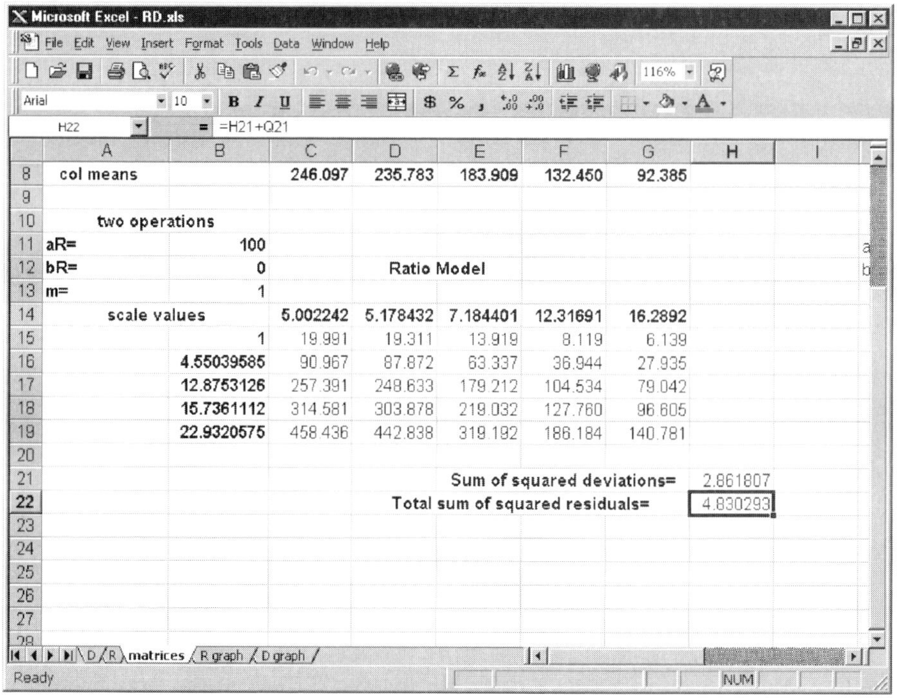

FIGURE 15.11 spreadsheet (Microsoft Excel - RD.xls), cell H22 = =H21+Q21

	A	B	C	D	E	F	G	H
8	col means		246.097	235.783	183.909	132.450	92.385	
9								
10	two operations							
11	aR=	100						
12	bR=	0		Ratio Model				
13	m=	1						
14	scale values		5.002242	5.178432	7.184401	12.31691	16.2892	
15	1		19.991	19.311	13.919	8.119	6.139	
16	4.55039585		90.967	87.872	63.337	36.944	27.935	
17	12.8753126		257.391	248.633	179.212	104.534	79.042	
18	15.7361112		314.581	303.878	218.032	127.760	96.605	
19	22.9320575		458.436	442.838	319.192	186.184	140.781	
20								
21					Sum of squared deviations=			2.861807
22					Total sum of squared residuals=			4.830293

FIGURE 15.11. The results of the fit to two-operation theory with $m = 1$.

FIGURE 15.12. Subtractive model of "ratio" judgments for the one-operation theory.

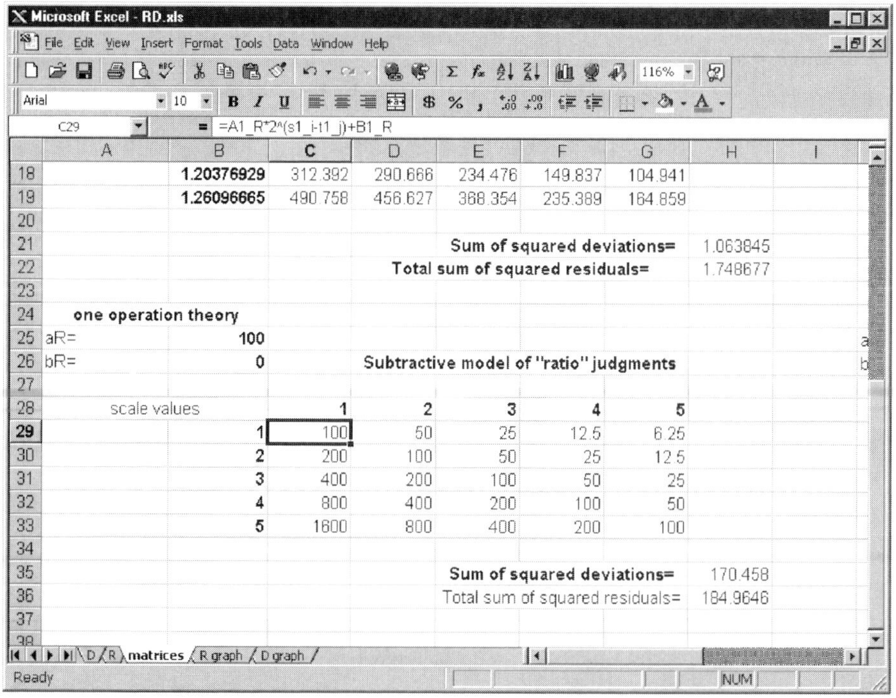

FIGURE 15.12 spreadsheet (Microsoft Excel - RD.xls), cell C29 = =A1_R*2^(s1_i-11_j)+B1_R

	A	B	C	D	E	F	G	H
18		1.20376929	312.392	290.666	234.476	149.837	104.941	
19		1.26096665	490.758	456.627	368.354	235.389	164.859	
20								
21					Sum of squared deviations=			1.063845
22					Total sum of squared residuals=			1.748677
23								
24	one operation theory							
25	aR=	100						
26	bR=	0		Subtractive model of "ratio" judgments				
27								
28	scale values		1	2	3	4	5	
29		1	100	50	25	12.5	6.25	
30		2	200	100	50	25	12.5	
31		3	400	200	100	50	25	
32		4	800	400	200	100	50	
33		5	1600	800	400	200	100	
34								
35					Sum of squared deviations=			170.458
36					Total sum of squared residuals=			184.9646

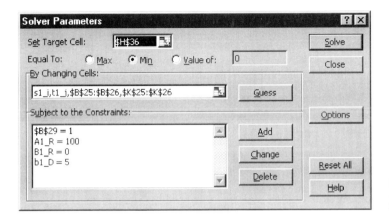

FIGURE 15.13.
Solver dialog box for one-operation theory.

FIGURE 15.14.   Solution to one-operation theory. This theory fits better than two-operation theory with *m* fixed to 1. According to these data, one-operation theory provides the following scale values for occupations: *trash collector* (1.0), *plumber* (1.78), *factory worker* (1.86), *car mechanic* (1.96), *carpenter* (2.26), *nurse* (2.89), *college professor* (3.41), *architect* (3.49), and *physician* (4.15). Both "ratios" and "differences" are based on differences in these values.

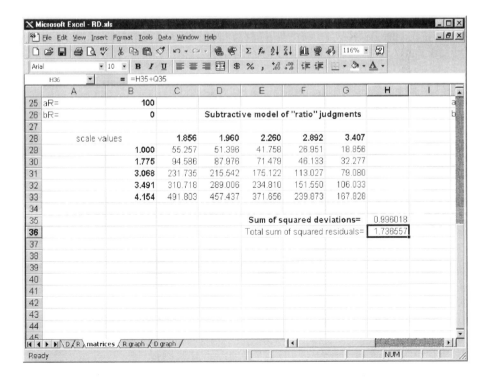

We can improve the fit of the two-operation theory if we allow m to be free. Indeed, as m gets larger, the two-operation theory can be made to approximate the predictions of one-operation theory (Birnbaum, 1980). To fit the two-operation theory with m free, repeat the previous steps, except delete the constraint that $m = 1$. This model, which has one extra parameter, fits with a total sum of squared residuals of 1.75, about the same as the fit of one-operation theory. The best-fit value of $m = 9.73$. This solution implies that it is only 26% more prestigious to be a *physician* than a *trash collector,* and the ratio of prestige of a *physican* to a *factory worker* is 1.178, but people report this "ratio" to be about "five" because of the exponent $m = 9.73$ ($1.178^{9.73} = 4.92$).

Because the extreme value of m seems inelegant and because the best-fit solution of two-operation theory is basically an approximation of one-operation theory, the one-operation theory seems a better representation of these data. It is simpler to assume that people use one operation than to assume that they use two, but due to an extreme value of an extra parameter, the data appear to be produced by one operation. Certainly, the one-operation theory fits better than the theory of two operations with the assumption that ratios can be taken as face value. This conclusion is similar to that reached in previous research, where it has been found that for heaviness, loudness, pitch, and a variety of other continua, one-operation theory describes judgments of "ratios" and "differences" in subjective value (Birnbaum, 1980, 1982; Hardin & Birnbaum, 1990; Mellers, Davis, & Birnbaum, 1984).

SUMMARY

Judgments of "ratios" and "differences" can be used separately to scale subjective magnitude. By studying both tasks in the same study, it is possible to test theories of how people compare stimuli. Data of many studies suggest that both judgments are mediated by subtraction, indicating that subjective value can be measured on an interval scale.

This chapter explained how to do a type of meta-analysis in which two or more studies are combined. The usual application of meta-analysis in psychology is to combine similar experiments to estimate the size of an effect. In contrast, in this chapter, the purpose of combining two studies is to test theories that can only be tested with two or more different experiments. By combining data from "ratio" and "difference" tasks, you found that one-operation theory gave a better account of the data than two-operation theory. You also derived a scale of the prestige of occupations that reproduces judgments in two tasks.

EXERCISES

1. Use Excel to draw a graph of the predicted "differences" according to one-operation theory. Do the predictions resemble the data in Figure 15.6?
2. Use Excel to draw a graph of predicted "ratios" according to one-operation theory. Do the predictions fit the observed judgments in Figure 15.5?
3. Draw a scatterplot connected by straight lines that shows the row marginal means of "ratios," $\overline{R}_{i\bullet}$ plotted against the row marginal means of "differences," $\overline{D}_{i\bullet}$. This graph will have 5 points. Draw this graph for:
    a. Mean judgments
    b. Predictions of one-operation theory
    c. Predictions of two-operation theory with "ratios" taken at face value ($m = 1$)
    d. Predictions of two-operation theory with parameters free

4. Draw a scatterplot that shows R_{ij} on the ordinate plotted against D_{ij} on the abscissa. For this experiment, each scatterplot will have 25 points. Plot this graph for:
   a. Mean judgments (of "ratios" and "differences" of occupational prestige)
   b. Predictions of one-operation theory
   c. Predictions of two-operation theory with "ratios" taken at face value; that is, constrain $m = 1$, $a = 100$, and $b = 0$.
   d. Predictions of two-operation theory with m, a, and b free
5. Project idea: Devise a study in which people will show evidence of two operations for "ratios" and "differences." Consider using intervals between stimuli ("distances") as the stimuli.
6. Project idea: Ask Ss to judge "ratios" and "differences" of intervals of prestige. Analyze the data for evidence of one or two operations.

Chapter 16

BAYESIAN INFERENCE AND HUMAN INFERENCE

In this chapter, you learn about Bayes' theorem, a rational procedure for revising beliefs. You learn how to set up a Web-based experiment that tests if the theorem is descriptive of human inference, and you also learn how to analyze the data from such an experiment.

If you toss a coin, what is the probability that it will be heads? What is the probability that a major league baseball player will hit more than 68 home runs in the next baseball season?

The first question dealing with tossing a coin refers to an experiment that can be repeated. You can assume that the coin has no memory and that it will behave in the same way from day to day and year to year. You can develop and test a physical theory that the two sides of the coin are equally likely to fall facing up, independent of the coin's history and the actions of other coins. Evidence from the past can be used to infer the probability of what will happen in the future. The second question (home runs) refers to a unique event that either will or will not happen, and there is no way to calculate a proportion that is clearly valid. You might look at what other ball players have done and ask if those who are likely to accomplish the feat seem healthy, but players and conditions (e.g., pitchers) change, and it is never really the same experiment. This type of situation is sometimes referred to as one of *uncertainty*, and the term *subjective probability* is sometimes used to refer to the psychological strength of belief that the event will happen.

Nevertheless, people are willing to use the same term, *probability*, to express both types of ideas. People are willing to gamble on both types of predictions—on repeatable, mechanical games of chance (like dice, cards, and roulette) and on unique events (like horse races and sporting contests). In fact, people are even willing to use the same language *after* something has happened (a murder, for example) to discuss the "probability" that a particular event occurred (e.g., this defendant committed the crime).

The Rev. Thomas Bayes (1702–1761) derived a theorem for inference from the mathematics of probability. Philosophers recognized that this theorem could be interpreted as a calculus for rational thought. Psychologists have investigated if Bayes' theorem also describes how people form and revise their beliefs (Birnbaum, 1983; Birnbaum & Mellers, 1983; Edwards, 1968; Gigerenzer & Hoffrage, 1995; Koehler, 1996; Massaro & Stork, 1998; Novemsky & Kronzon, 1999; Shanteau, 1975a; Troutman & Shanteau, 1977; Wallsten, 1972).

BAYES' THEOREM

To illustrate how Bayes' theorem works, it helps to work through an example. Suppose there is a disease that infects 1 person in 1000, completely at random. Suppose also that there is a blood test for the disease that yields a *positive* test result in 99.5% of cases of the disease and gives a false *positive* in only 0.5% of people who do not have the disease. Suppose a person in this study tests *positive;* what is the probability that he or she has the disease? Think for a moment and see if you can intuitively arrive at a judgment of the likelihood that a person who tests *positive* is actually sick with the disease in this case. The solution, according to Bayes' theorem, may surprise you.

Before you read on, you should load the experiment *Bayes.htm* from the CD and participate as a judge in the experiment on the *Cab Problem*. This experiment was constructed with the help of factorWiz. Later in this chapter, you learn to analyze data from this experiment and compare them with the theory of Bayes.

Suppose there are two hypotheses, *H* and not-*H* (denoted *H'*). In the previous example, they are the hypothesis that the person is sick with the disease (*H*) and the complementary hypothesis (*H'*) that the person does not have the disease. Let *D* refer to the datum that is relevant to the hypotheses. In the example, *D* would refer to a *positive* test result, and *D'* would be a *negative* result from the blood test.

The problem stated that 1 in 1000 have the disease, so $P(H) = .001$; that is, the prior probability (before we test the blood) that a person has the disease is .001, and the probability that the person is not sick with the disease is $.999 = P(H') = 1 - P(H)$.

The problem also gave information about the diagnostic value of the test. The conditional probability that a person will test *positive* given that person has the disease is written as $P(positive \mid H) = .995$, and the conditional probability that a person will test *positive* given he or she is not sick is $P(positive \mid H') = .005$. These two probabilities are also called the *HIT RATE* and *FALSE ALARM RATE* in signal detection, and they are also known as *power* and *significance* (α) in statistics. We need to calculate $P(H \mid D)$, the probability that a person is sick given the test was *positive*. This calculation is known as an *inference*.

The conditional probability of *A* given *B* is not the same as the conditional probability of *B* given *A*. For example, the probability that someone is male given he or she is a member of the U.S. Senate is quite high because there are few women in the senate. However, the probability that a person is a member of the U.S. Senate given that person is male is quite low because there are so few senators and so many males. Conditional probability is defined as follows:

$$P(A \mid B) = \frac{P(A \cap B)}{P(B)}$$

(16.1)

$$P(B \mid A) = \frac{P(A \cap B)}{P(A)}$$

(16.2)

So, if *A* is the set of U.S. senators (of which there are 100) and *B* is the set of males (of which there are billions), we see that the probability of *A* given *B* is quite small, but the probability of *B* given *A* can be quite high.

The situation is as follows: we know $P(H)$, $P(D \mid H)$, and $P(D \mid H')$, and we want to calculate $P(H \mid D)$. From the definition of conditional probability:

$$P(H \mid D) = \frac{P(H \cap D)}{P(D)}$$

(16.3)

Also, from the definition of conditional probability, $P(H \cap D) = P(D \mid H)P(H)$. In addition, *D* can happen in two mutually exclusive ways, either with *H* or without it, so $P(D) = P(D \cap H) + P(D \cap H')$. Each of these conjunctions can be written in terms of conditionals, so, by substitution, the formula is as follows:

$$P(H \mid D) = \frac{P(D \mid H)P(H)}{P(D \mid H)P(H) + P(D \mid H')P(H')}$$

(16.4)

Equation 16.4 is known as Bayes' theorem. Substituting the values given for the blood test problem yields the following result:

$$P(sick \mid positive) = \frac{(.995)(.001)}{(.995)(.001) + (.005)(.999)} = .166$$

Does this result surprise you? Think of it this way: Among 1000 people, there is only 1 sick person. If all 1000 were given the test, the test would probably give a *positive* test result to that 1 person, and it would also give a *positive* test result to about 5 others (of the 999 healthy people, 0.5% should test positive). Thus, of the 6 people who test *positive*, only 1 is really sick, so the probability of being sick given a *positive* test result is only about 1 in 6. Another way to look at the .166 is that it is 166 times larger than the probability of being sick given no information about the blood test (.001), so there has indeed been considerable revision of opinion given the positive test.

 ## BAYESIAN CALCULATOR

The calculations of Eq. 16.4 can be facilitated by the Bayesian calculator included on your CD. You can load it from the index of examples for this chapter. To use the calculator, first you need to define H and D. Then identify and type in $P(H)$, $P(D \mid H)$, $P(D \mid H')$ into the first column. (Leave the second column and the last row value blank.) Press the calculate button, and the answer, $P(H \mid D)$, appears in the last row. Test the calculator with the disease problem. Instructions are also given in the Web page for the calculator.

If you view the page source of the calculator, you see that the first half uses HTML forms to define the table, and the second half is a JavaScript program that does the calculations. JavaScript is explained in Chapters 17–19. The appearance of the calculator is shown in Figure 16.1.

 ## THE CAB PROBLEM

The experiment on the Cab problem is based on a problem used by Tversky and Kahneman (1982; see also Kahneman & Tversky, 1973). Instructions for the Cab problem on your CD read (in part) as follows:

> A cab was involved in a hit-and-run accident at night. There are two cab companies in the city, the Blue and Green. Your task is to judge (or estimate) the probability that the cab in the accident was a Blue cab. You will be given information about the percentage of accidents at night that were caused by Blue cabs and the testimony of a witness who saw the accident.
>
> The percentage of night-time accidents involving Blue cabs is based on the previous 2 years in the city. In different cities, this percentage was 15%, 30%, 70%, or 85%. The rest of night-time accidents involved Green cabs.
>
> Witnesses were tested for their ability to identify colors at night. The witnesses were presented 100 Blue and 100 Green cabs to identify at night.
>
> The MEDIUM witness correctly identified 60% of the cabs of each color, calling Green cabs "Blue" 40% of the time and calling Blue cabs "Green" 40% of the time.
>
> The HIGH witness correctly identified 80% of each color, calling Blue cabs "Green" or Green cabs "Blue" on 20% of the tests.

When you have completed the task, use the calculator to find the Bayesian calculations assuming that the prior probabilities are $P(H) = .15, .30, .70,$ or $.85$, where $H =$

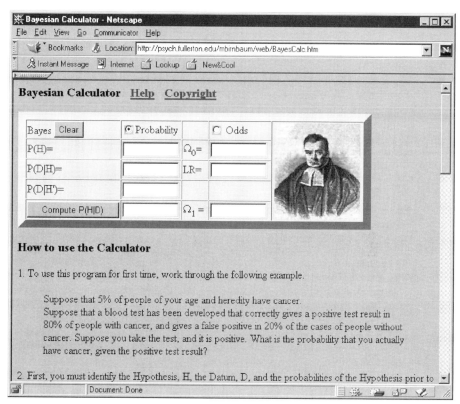

FIGURE 16.1. The Bayesian calculator. This calculator is written in JavaScript, which is explained in Chapters 17–19. Rev. Thomas Bayes is pictured on the calculator.

the hypothesis that the cab was Blue. Suppose the Medium credibility witness has $P(``B" \mid H) = .6$ and $P(``G" \mid H') = .4$; and suppose the High credibility witness has $P(``B" \mid H) = .8$ and $P(``B" \mid H') = .2$. For example, if 15% of accidents involve Blue cabs and the High credibility witness says the cab was a "Green" cab, the Bayesian probability that it was a Blue cab is only .04. The datum that the witness said the cab was "Green" tends to exonerate the Blue cab. To find that value, realize that the probability that the witness would say "Green" given the cab was Blue is only .2 and the probability that the witness would say "Green" given it was Green is .8. In the calculator, enter .15 for $P(H)$, .2 for $P(D \mid H)$, and .8 for $P(D \mid H')$.

Suppose there are 15% Blue cabs and the High credibility witness said "Blue." In this case, the posterior probability (probability it was Blue given witness said "Blue") is .413.

There are additional complications to the Bayesian solution to the Cab problem. One involves the extrapolation of the witness's performance during the test to the conditions on the night of the accident (Birnbaum, 1983). Another involves the inference from the percentage of accidents caused by Blue cabs in some period to the prior probability that the cab was Blue. In a later section, a more general, subjective Bayesian model is presented that allows such complications.

EXTRACT THE DATA FOR THE CAB PROBLEM AND FIND MEANS

The first step is to filter the data. In Excel, open the data file *clean.xls* from the CD. Type variable names in the first row, if you have not done so already. Click in cell A1 and select *Filter: Autofilter* from the **Data** menu. Then click the drop down selection arrow in the A1 and select *bayes*. Copy the data to a new file, and save the file as an Excel Workbook with the name *bayes.xls*. (A completed file of *bayes.xls* is included on the CD to allow you to check your work.)

The variable names are included at the end of the *bayes* data, so cut and copy them in the first row. To make the variable names, take the experiment and type in the stimuli rather than answers. Then, in NotePad, replace the date, time, and sex with the names of these variables.

The second step is to remove blank lines and multiple submissions from the data and find means. Use conditional formatting to check for responses that are out of bounds (e.g., negative numbers or values above 100). The techniques for conditional formatting are described in Chapter 12. The resulting data file is shown in Figure 16.2.

To find means, click in the row after the last row of data in column H and from the **Insert** menu select *function: Average* to find the mean judgment of probability for the case of 15% Blue cabs in accidents at night and a High credibility witness says that the cab was "Green." Then use *AutoFill* to find the other column means, using the technique described in previous chapters.

The third step is to use *Copy* and *Paste Special* to copy the means to a new work-

FIGURE 16.2. Appearance of data in file *bayes.xls*.

	exp	date	time	age	Sex	Edu	Nationality	15% and H says G	15% M says G	15% and no witness	15% M says B	15% H says B	15% H says G	30% M says G	30% no witness	30% and M says B	30% H says B	70% and H says G
2	bayes	11/30/98	4:10:24 PM	20	M	12	American	60	70	20	60	50	40	20	50	30	30	30
3	bayes	11/30/98	4:48:35 PM	18	F	12	USA	50	15	50	50	50	50	30	30	50	90	50
4	bayes	11/30/98	5:46:17 PM	18	F	12	USA	20	30	50	60	80	20	60	50	30	80	20
5	bayes	11/30/98	8:44:13 PM	18	F	12	UNITED ST	80	40	15	60	80	20	40	30	60	80	80
6	bayes	11/30/98	8:53:46 PM	18	F	12	Filipino	3	6	7	9	12	12	12	15	18	24	14
7	bayes	12/1/98	8:29:49 AM	33	F	16	U.S.A.	80	60	15	60	80	72	75	30	60	80	80
8	bayes	12/1/98	11:08:51 AM	20	F	12	america	50	70	50	70	80	40	70	80	75	80	50
9	bayes	12/1/98	11:19:42 AM	18	F	12	usa	85	55	15	75	25	70	70	30	90	70	30
10	bayes	12/1/98	1:12:45 PM	24	M	12	United Stat	3	3	15	10	13	7	12	30	20	25	15
11	bayes	12/1/98	1:40:41 PM	18	M	12	CHINESE	56	45	56	45	78	45	56	56	67	66	56
12	bayes	12/1/98	1:44:06 PM	18	M	13	USA	13	40	50	70	79	45	75	30	75	20	20
13	bayes	12/1/98	2:12:49 PM		0	12	TAIWAN	40	60	20	20	50	30	30	60	50	20	50
14	bayes	12/1/98	2:18:52 PM	22	F	15	usa	12	9	8	60	12	12	18	15	18	24	56
15	bayes	12/1/98	2:25:00 PM	30	F	15	USA	12	9	15	9	12	24	18	30	18	24	56
16	bayes	12/1/98	2:27:38 PM	19	M	12	USA	8	10	15	30	30	15	50	30	60	60	35

Sum=11700.5

sheet in the same workbook. Be sure to keep the means linked so that any change in the data is reflected in the rest of the workbook. Then cut and paste to arrange the means in matrix form. (This process was also described in Chapter 12.) Next, add labels for the rows and columns. The matrix of means is shown in Figure 16.3.

 ## GRAPH THE DATA

To graph the data, select cells A2:F6, then select *Chart* from the **Insert** menu. From the Chart Wizard, choose *XY scatter*, with data points connected by lines. In the second step of the Chart Wizard, specify that the data are in columns (that plots the data as a function of the prior probability, or base rate, of Blue cabs). After suitable labels have been added for the axes and adjustments have been made in the fonts, marker styles, and other features of the graph, the graph appears as in Figure 16.4.

Clearly, people use both the base rate and the witness information. The spread between curves represents the effect of the witness testimony, and the slopes of the curves represent the effects of the base rate. Research on the "base rate fallacy" contended that people neglect base rates (Kahneman & Tversky, 1973), based on a nonsignificant result in a between-subjects design. If people did not attend to the base rate, the curves in

FIGURE 16.3.   Mean judgments of the probability (expressed as a percentage) that the cab was Blue, given the base rate (of Blue cabs involved in accidents at night) and the testimony of a witness (who said the cab was either "Blue" or "Green.") H = high credibility witness; M = medium credibility witness.

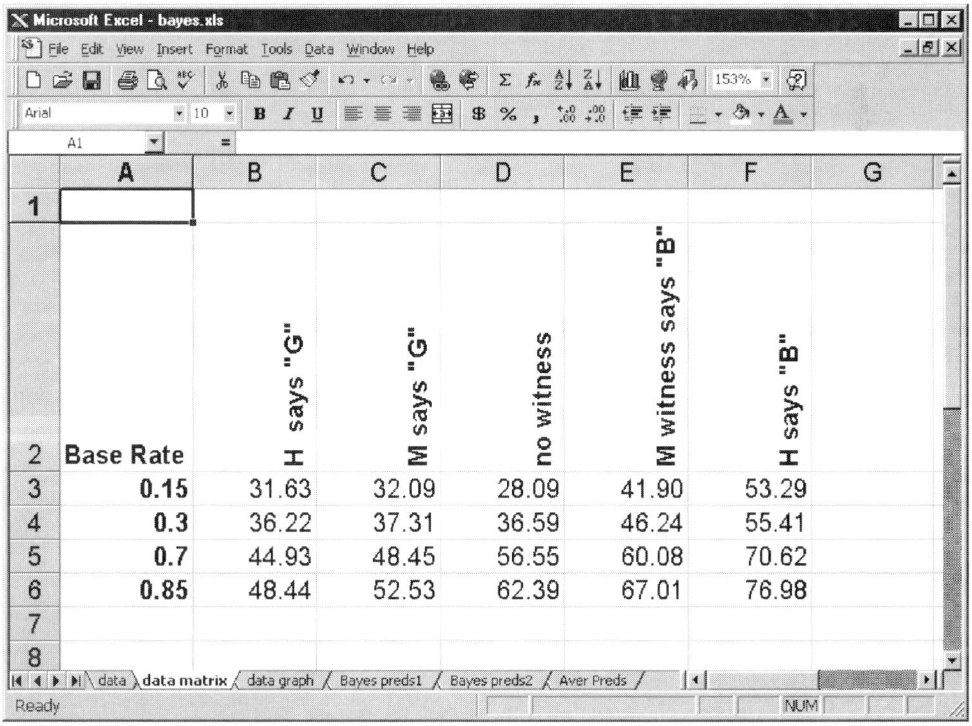

Base Rate	H says "G"	M says "G"	no witness	M witness says "B"	H says "B"
0.15	31.63	32.09	28.09	41.90	53.29
0.3	36.22	37.31	36.59	46.24	55.41
0.7	44.93	48.45	56.55	60.08	70.62
0.85	48.44	52.53	62.39	67.01	76.98

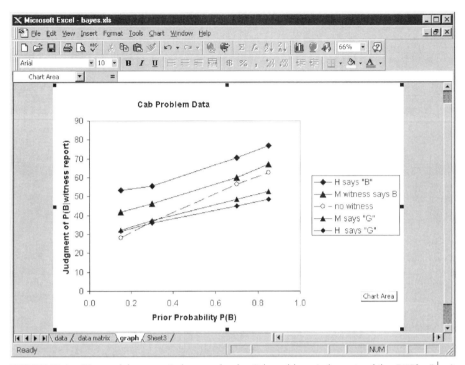

FIGURE 16.4. Figure of the mean judgments for the Cab problem. Judgments of the *P*("Blue" | witness testimony) are plotted as a function of the prior probability of Blue, with a separate curve for each level of the witness testimony.

Figure 16.4 would have slopes of zero; that is, they would be horizontal lines. However, Figure 16.4 shows that people do attend to base rate, even in the Cab problem, when base rates are manipulated within subjects. As noted in Chapter 9, it can be tricky to compare judgments between groups of subjects who judge different stimuli. Birnbaum and Mellers (1983) studied the same Bayesian problem within and between subjects and found quite different results. The data in Figure 16.4 are within subjects, and they show that people use the base rate.

Note that the curve for *no witness* is steeper than the other curves, and even crosses over two of the other curves. As shown in a later section, this crossover is not consistent with additive models, including a subjective version of Bayes' theorem (Novemsky & Kronzon, 1999; Wallsten, 1972). Instead, the crossover is indicative of an averaging model. To understand how the data differ from Bayesian theory, graph predictions for Bayes' theorem.

 ## COMPUTE BAYES' THEOREM

To construct predictions for Bayes' theorem, type in the base rates, .15, .3, .7, and .85, in cells H3:H6 of the worksheet with the matrix of means. Select those cells, and type in the name *BR* (for base rate) in the name box and hit enter. Then type in cells I2:M2 the values of $P(D \mid H)$ = .2, .4, .5, .6, and .8 for the *H* witness who says "Green," for M witness who says "Green," no witness, M witness who says "Blue," and H witness who says "Blue." Select all cells in I2:M2 and type *PDGH* in the *Name Box* (Probability of the Datum Given the Hypothesis), then hit enter. Next, in cells I1:M1, type the values of $P(D \mid H')$ = .8, .6, .5, .4, and .2; name them *PDGNH* (for Probability of the Datum Given Not the Hypothesis). In cell I3, type the following expression (Bayes' theorem):

$$= (PDGH * BR)/(PDGH * BR + PDGNH * (1 - BR))$$

Next hit enter, and the value .042 appears in cell I3. Next, click the mouse pointer in the lower right corner of cell I3 until you see the AutoFill "+". Drag down to fill in the first column, and while the column is selected, drag to the right to *AutoFill* the matrix. If you did everything right, the matrix will appear as in Figure 16.5. If you have a problem, check to see the names you gave the variables, and check the expression typed in cell I3 very carefully. You can undo your most recent steps with the *Undo* function (**Edit** menu); so when you catch an error, keep selecting *Undo* until you have removed the error. Then retype the correct expressions.

FIGURE 16.5. Bayesian calculations. Each entry is Excel's calculation according to Bayes' theorem (the expression typed in cell I3, shown in the formula line). Check these calculations with the Bayesian calculator.

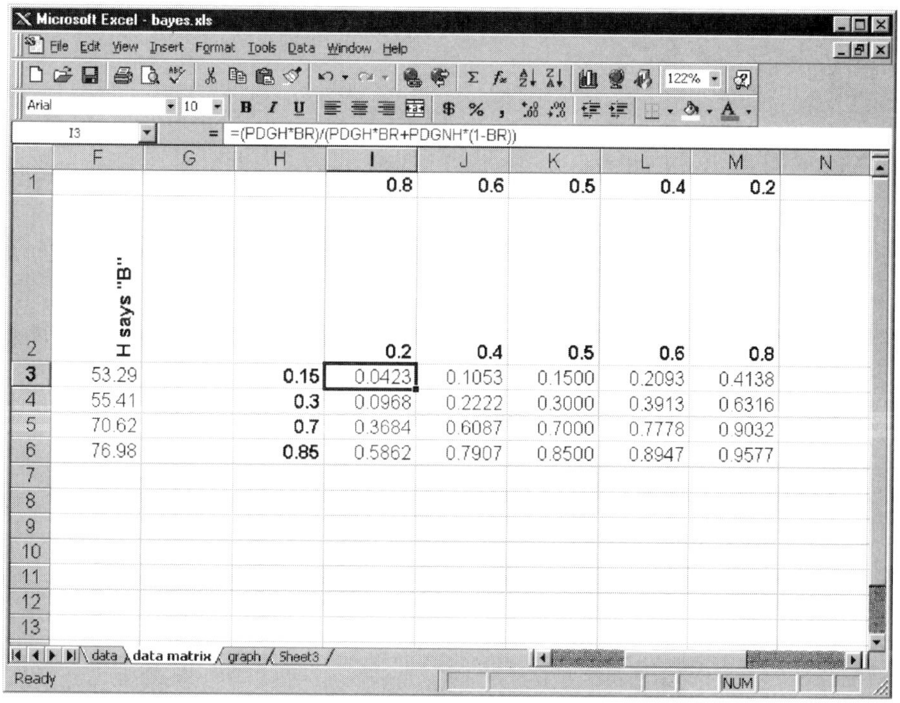

	F	G	H	I	J	K	L	M	N
1				0.8	0.6	0.5	0.4	0.2	
2	H says "B"			0.2	0.4	0.5	0.6	0.8	
3	53.29		0.15	0.0423	0.1053	0.1500	0.2093	0.4138	
4	55.41		0.3	0.0968	0.2222	0.3000	0.3913	0.6316	
5	70.62		0.7	0.3684	0.6087	0.7000	0.7778	0.9032	
6	76.98		0.85	0.5862	0.7907	0.8500	0.8947	0.9577	
7									
8									
9									
10									
11									
12									
13									

GRAPH PREDICTIONS OF BAYES' THEOREM

The next step is to plot the predictions in the same manner as was done for the data. The predictions are shown in Figure 16.6. The predictions shown in Figure 16.6 can be compared to the data shown in Figure 16.4. This comparison shows that judgments are "conservative" relative to Bayes' theorem. If 85% of night time accidents are caused by Blue cabs and the High witness says the cab was "Blue," Bayes' theorem predicts a value of .96, but the mean judgment is only 78% (.78). Only 7 of 153 people gave responses greater than .95 for this case. Probabilities predicted to be close to zero [when $P(B) =$ .15 and the High witness said "Green"] are also regressed toward .5. The Bayesian prediction is .04 and the mean response is 31.6% (.32). This failure to give judgments as extreme as those calculated by Bayes' theorem was described as "conservatism" in early literature, reviewed by Edwards (1968).

Another aspect of the data can be seen in the following comparisons. When the base rate is .85 and the High witness says "Green," the prediction is .58; when the base rate is .15 and the H witness says "Blue," the prediction is .41; Bayes' theorem says the .15 base rate outweighs a High credibility (.8) source. However, the mean judgments in these two cases have the opposite relation (48% to 53%). This pattern might be indica-

FIGURE 16.6.   Predictions of Bayes' theorem, assuming that $P(B)$ are the values for the previous 2 years and that $P(D|H)$ and $P(D|H')$ are the same as the values in the previous 2 years. The comparison of predictions like these and data as shown in Figure 16.4 led to the conclusion that people are "conservative" relative to Bayes' theorem. In other words, people deviate less from .5 than they are predicted to do by use of these values.

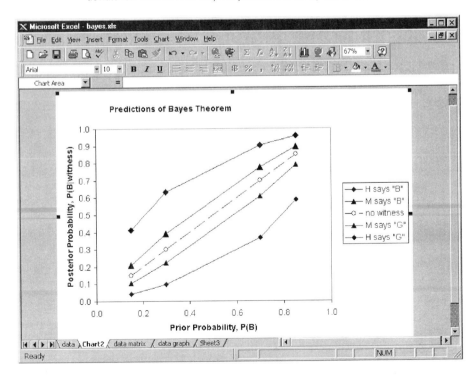

tive of underweighting of base rate information, a less extreme form of the type of base rate neglect argued for by Tversky and Kahneman (1982).

 ## SUBJECTIVE BAYESIAN THEORY

Perhaps people use Bayesian reasoning, but they do not assign their subjective priors to the values given in the problem for Blue cabs involved in accidents at night. In addition, they may use different subjective values for the hit rate and false alarm rates of the witnesses from the values specified in the problem. Indeed, the test used an equal number of Blue and Green cabs, but on the night of the accident, the witness may have been aware of the base rate and taken that into account. Wallsten (1972) suggested such a subjective version of the Bayesian model. A monotonic transformation converts the subjective Bayesian model into an additive model (Birnbaum & Mellers, 1983; Novemsky & Kronzon, 1999).

We can represent a Bayesian process with subjective values by using the equation of Bayes' theorem and solving for the values of the evidence. To do this, multiply the predictions by 100 (to express them as percentages, comparable to the data) and take the difference between data and predictions. Next, use the *solver* to minimize the sum of squared differences between data and predictions. In cells A9:F14, construct the same theoretical matrix as in the previous analysis, except multiply each entry by 100. Next, click in cell G15 (any convenient cell would do), and choose *Function* from the **Insert** menu. Select SUMXMY2, the function that computes the sum of squared differences between two arrays. Select the data for the first array (B3:F6). Then specify the predictions for the second array (B11:F14). The sum of squared differences is 6334.4. This step is shown in Figure 16.7.

The next step is to select *Solver* from the **Tools** menu. Select cell G15 as the target cell; choose to *Minimize* (click the radio button next to *Min*); click in the box for *By changing cells* and select the prior probabilities; hit and false alarm rates (i.e., cells A11:A14 and B9:F10). After the *Solver* has worked, the cells change and the sum of squared differences changes, as shown in Figure 16.8. The new predictions, shown in Figure 16.9, are closer to the data, but still do not predict the crossover of the dashed curve, representing judgments when there was *no witness*.

 ## AVERAGING MODEL OF SOURCE CREDIBILITY

Another theory is that people aggregate probabilistic information by an averaging process rather than by Bayes' theorem in either the objective, subjective, or additive form (Anderson, 1974; Shanteau, 1975a; Birnbaum & Mellers, 1983). An averaging model can be written as follows:

$$R = \frac{\sum_{i=0}^{n} w_i s_i}{\sum_{i=0}^{n} w_i} \tag{16.5}$$

where R is the subjective impression of probability, w_i and s_i are the weight and scale value of source of information i, and w_0 and s_0 are the weight and scale value of the initial impression. The base rate information should have a single weight and scale values that depend on the percentage of Blue cabs in accidents at night. The scale value and weight of the sources depend on the hit rates and false-alarm rates of the sources (Birn-

Microsoft Excel - bayes.xls — G15 =SUMXMY2(B3:F6,B11:F14)

Row	A	B	C	D	E	F	G	H	I	J	K
2	Base Rate	H says "G"	M says "G"	no witness	M witness says B	H says "B"			0.2	0.4	0.5
3	0.15	31.63	32.09	28.09	41.90	53.29		0.15	0.0423	0.1053	0.1500
4	0.3	36.22	37.31	36.59	46.24	55.41		0.3	0.0968	0.2222	0.3000
5	0.7	44.93	48.45	56.55	60.08	70.62		0.7	0.3684	0.6087	0.7000
6	0.85	48.44	52.53	62.39	67.01	76.98		0.85	0.5862	0.7907	0.8500
7											
8											
9		0.8	0.6	0.5	0.4	0.2					
10		0.2	0.4	0.5	0.6	0.8					
11	0.15	4.23	10.53	15.00	20.93	41.38					
12	0.3	9.68	22.22	30.00	39.13	63.16					
13	0.7	36.84	60.87	70.00	77.78	90.32					
14	0.85	58.62	79.07	85.00	89.47	95.77					
15							6334.362	Sum of squared differences			

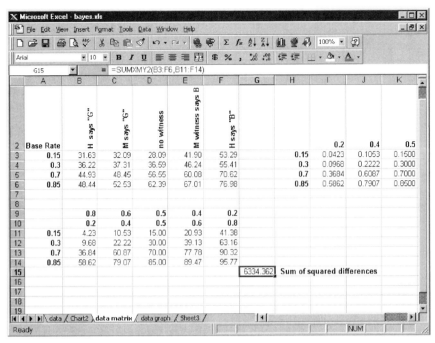

FIGURE 16.7. Predictions and Data. The selected cell shows the sum of squared differences prior to use of the *Solver.*

FIGURE 16.8. Solution to the Subjective Bayesian Theory, after the *Solver* has done its work. Note that the subjective values of the priors are .26 to .49. Note also the contrast between the subjective values of the hit and false-alarm rates and the objective values in Figure 16.7.

Microsoft Excel - bayes.xls — G15 =SUMXMY2(B3:F6,B11:F14)

Row	A	B	C	D	E	F	G	H	I	J	K
2	Base Rate	H says "G"	M says "G"	no witness	M witness says B	H says "B"			0.2	0.4	0.5
3	0.15	31.63	32.09	28.09	41.90	53.29		0.15	0.0423	0.1053	0.1500
4	0.3	36.22	37.31	36.59	46.24	55.41		0.3	0.0968	0.2222	0.3000
5	0.7	44.93	48.45	56.55	60.08	70.62		0.7	0.3684	0.6087	0.7000
6	0.85	48.44	52.53	62.39	67.01	76.98		0.85	0.5862	0.7907	0.8500
7											
8											
9		0.428308	0.388225	0.47277	0.277469	0.21487					
10		0.487798	0.490972	0.694635	0.563377	0.677064					
11	0.2586467	28.44	30.61	33.89	41.46	52.37					
12	0.3014672	32.95	35.31	38.80	46.70	57.63					
13	0.4344924	46.67	49.28	53.03	60.94	70.77					
14	0.4895173	52.20	54.81	58.49	66.07	75.13					
15							127.636	Sum of squared differences			

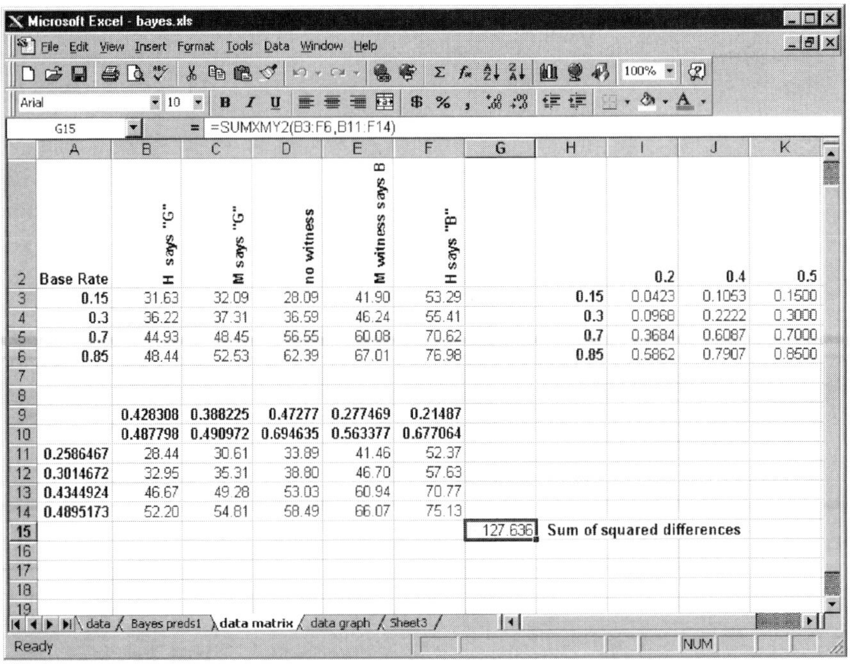

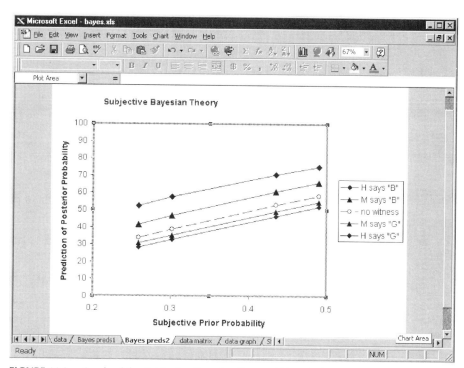

FIGURE 16.9.   Graph of the Subjective Bayesian Theory. Although these predictions are closer to the data than the previous predictions, they do not explain the curve for *no witness.*

baum & Mellers, 1983). The greater the difference between hit rate and false-alarm rate, the greater the weight. The scale value depends on whether the source said the cab was "Blue" or "Green" and the tendency of the witness (bias) to say cabs are "Blue" or "Green" (the sum of hit rate and false-alarm rate, which was constant in this study). When no witness is presented, the weight of the witness is zero. The averaging model predicts that the effect of the base rate is greater when there is no witness because the weight of the witness drops out of the denominator, increasing the relative weight of the base rate.

You can also use Excel to fit this theory. Figure 16.10 shows the spreadsheet set up with weights and scale values. Note that the equations in the cells are different, depending on whether the source said "Green," "no witness," or "Blue." The variable names assigned in Excel are $w_0 = W\_0$; $s_0 = S\_0$, the weight of a source is W_S. The scale value of "Green" is S_G, the scale value of "Blue" is S_B, scale value of the base rate is S_BR, and the weight of the base rate is W_B. The expression when the source says "Green" is as follows:

$$=100*(W\_0*S\_0+W\_B*S\_BR+W\_S*S\_G)/(W\_0+W\_B+W\_S)$$

when the source says "Blue," the expression is the same, except the scale value of S_B is substituted, as follows:

$$=100*(W\_0*S\_0+W\_B*S\_BR+W\_S*S\_B)/(W\_0+W\_B+W\_S)$$

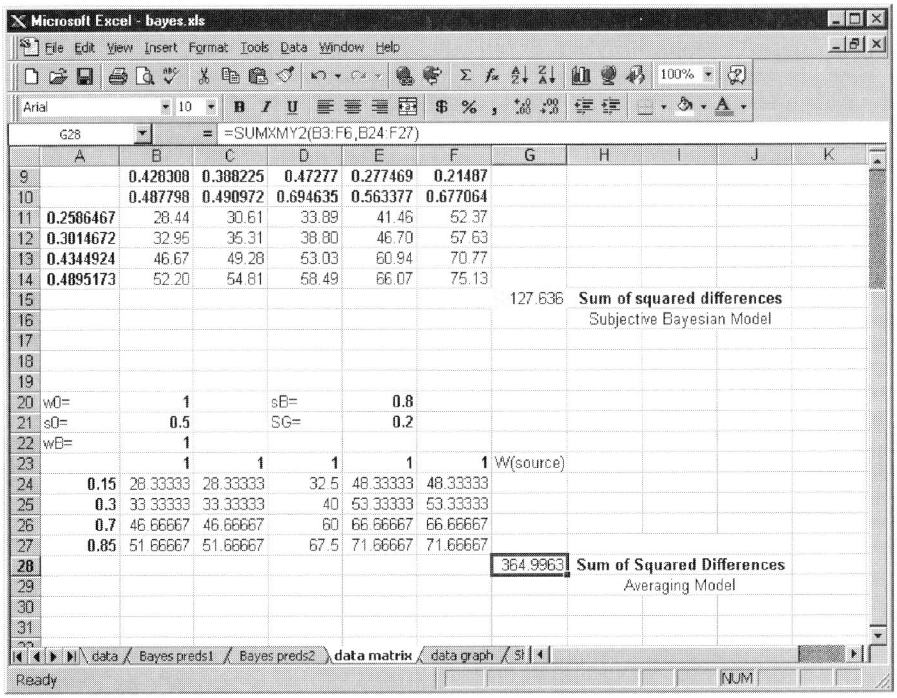

Microsoft Excel - bayes.xls

File Edit View Insert Format Tools Data Window Help

Arial   10   B I U

G28 = =SUMXMY2(B3:F6,B24:F27)

	A	B	C	D	E	F	G	H
9		0.420308	0.388225	0.47277	0.277469	0.21487		
10		0.487798	0.490972	0.694635	0.563377	0.677064		
11	0.2586467	28.44	30.61	33.89	41.46	52.37		
12	0.3014672	32.95	35.31	38.80	46.70	57.63		
13	0.4344924	46.67	49.28	53.03	60.94	70.77		
14	0.4895173	52.20	54.81	58.49	66.07	75.13		
15							127.636	**Sum of squared differences**
16								Subjective Bayesian Model
17								
18								
19								
20	w0=	1		sB=	0.8			
21	s0=	0.5		SG=	0.2			
22	wB=	1						
23		1	1	1	1	1	W(source)	
24	0.15	28.33333	28.33333	32.5	48.33333	48.33333		
25	0.3	33.33333	33.33333	40	53.33333	53.33333		
26	0.7	46.66667	46.66667	60	66.66667	66.66667		
27	0.85	51.66667	51.66667	67.5	71.66667	71.66667		
28							364.9963	**Sum of Squared Differences**
29								Averaging Model
30								
31								

data / Bayes preds1 / Bayes preds2 / data matrix / data graph / S!

Ready   NUM

FIGURE 16.10. Spreadsheet set up to fit the Averaging Model.

When there is no witness, the weight of W_S is set to zero, so the expression simplifies as follows:

$$=100*(W\_0*S\_0+W\_B*S\_BR)/(W\_0+W\_B)$$

Type in these expressions and use *AutoFill* again to compute the predictions in each respective subportion of the matrix. Next, compute the sum of squared differences between the data and the predictions, as before. The initial values of the parameters are set as follows: the weights are all set to 1, scale values of the prior probabilities are set to their objective values, S_B is set to .8, and S_G is set to .2. Based on these initial estimates, the predictions are as shown in Figure 16.10.

Next, use the *Solver* to find the best-fit solution to the averaging model. The sum of squared discrepancies between data and theory is only 22.96 for this model, which is a much better fit than for the Subjective Bayesian model. The solution is shown in Figure 16.11, and the predictions are graphed in Figure 16.12.

The averaging model provides a better fit to the data than either version of the Bayesian model. Apparently, people combine information by averaging the prior estimate with the evidence of the witness. When there is no witness, the relative weight of the prior information is greater than when there is a witness. This change in relative impact of information is evidence against the additive models and the subjective Bayesian models as well.

These results for the Cab problem agree with the results and theory of Birnbaum and Mellers (1983) and Birnbaum and Stegner (1979). Birnbaum and Mellers (1983) asked judges to estimate the probability that a used car would last a certain period of

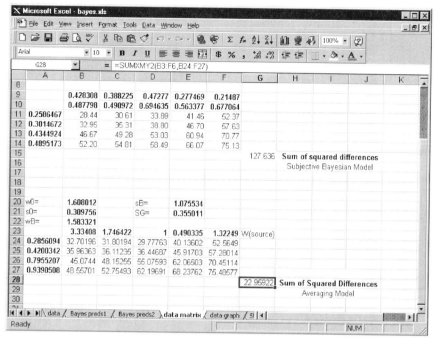

FIGURE 16.11. Spreadsheet after *Solver* has found best fit to the averaging model. Note that the sum of squared deviations for the Subjective Bayesian model are more than five times greater (worse) than the fit for the averaging model.

FIGURE 16.12. Predictions of the Averaging Model. Note that this model correctly predicts the crossover of the *no witness* curve.

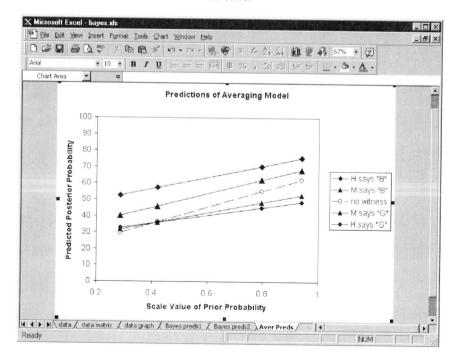

time given the opinion of a mechanic who examined the car and base rate for that type of car. They also found that the effect of a source of information was inversely related to the number and credibility of other sources of information. These phenomena are evidence of averaging rather than additive models. Their study also investigated the effect of bias of witnesses, a factor not studied in the Cab problem.

SUMMARY

In this chapter, you learned about Bayes' theorem as a mathematical theory of how people *should* revise their beliefs and also as a descriptive theory attempting to predict how people *do* make inferences. The chapter reviewed a Web experiment, constructed with the help of surveyWiz, which replicated previous results obtained in the lab. People attend to the base rate, contrary to the claim of a base rate fallacy; however, people do not combine base rates with witness evidence by a Bayesian or additive process. Instead, they appear to average evidence. You should know how to construct such an experiment and how to analyze the results.

EXERCISES

1. Examine the materials for the Cab problem in a text editor. Use factorWiz to create another variation of the Cab problem with different base rates: .20, .50, and .80. Use HIGH sources that have hit rates of .85 and false-alarm rates of .15. This manipulation reverses the numerical relationship between the witness and base rate; the source is now more diagnostic than the base rate. Also include a "source" of no witness.
2. Calculate predictions of Bayes' theorem for the above 3 × 4 design using the Bayesian calculator.
3. Calculate predictions of Bayes' theorem for the 3 × 4 design from Question 2 using Excel.
4. Project idea: Construct the materials for a replication of the Cab problem study with the Lawyer/ Engineer problem. In this problem, the judge is given the relative frequencies of lawyers and engineers in a sample, and is asked to infer if Tom is a lawyer or engineer based on a thumbnail description. For example, suppose Tom "likes jazz, and enjoys playing chess." What is the probability that Tom is a lawyer rather than an engineer? The proportion of lawyers or engineers is one factor (base rate), and the testimony and credibility of the thumbnail descriptions is the other factor.
5. Project idea: Construct the materials for an experiment on the bookbags and poker chips problem. An experimenter draws a sample of chips from one of two bookbags. Bag *R* has 80 red chips and 20 white ones. Bag *W* has 20 red chips and 80 white ones. The experimenter decides randomly which bag to choose, and presents a random sample of chips from that bag to the judge. The judge's task is to infer which bag the sample came from. For example, suppose the experimenter flipped a coin, and chose one of the bags; suppose the sample of chips was 4 Reds and 1 White chip. Which bag do you think was chosen? What is the probability that the bag sampled was Bag *R*? There are many parameters that can be manipulated in this situation, making many interesting studies that can be done.

Part IV

PROGRAMMING TECHNIQUES

Chapter 17

INTRODUCTION TO JAVASCRIPT

JavaScript is a programming language that allows you to design complex, interactive Web pages. The language is one of several scripting languages that permit a Web page to interact with the user. This book includes enough JavaScript to allow you to add considerable power to your experiments. However, a complete treatment is beyond the scope of this book. There are many books available that teach JavaScript, and if you like programming and enjoy these chapters, you may want to study these books. Links to on-line tutorials and books about JavaScript are included in the examples to this chapter.

Even if you do not plan to become a programmer, there are useful things that you can add to your experiments with a little JavaScript. For example, this chapter develops a small script that you can use in your HTML experiments to accomplish the useful task of random assignment to conditions. In previous chapters, participants were assigned to conditions by clicking on their birthday or birth month, and horoscope was counterbalanced by a Latin Square. In this chapter, you learn how to use a random number generator to assign participants to conditions.

JavaScript is a scripting language that should not be confused with the Java language, which is a distinct language. The intended goal of both languages is to support programs that run on anyone's computer, whether they have a Windows PC or Mac.

JavaScript programs can be included in the HTML document, and the server delivers them to the remote computer along with the HTML. Because JavaScript runs on the client's (the participant's) machine, it frees the server from having to make computations. It also frees the participant from waiting for a remote computer to compute something and send an answer. Thus, when JavaScript is delivered with the Web page, it runs on the participant's computer, not your server.

JavaScript is fairly new and still growing, but it is the oldest and most widely used scripting language of its type on the Web, so it is well worth learning. Ideally, JavaScript would run on Netscape and Explorer, and on Mac or PC in the same way. In practice, however, not all of the differences have yet been ironed out, so you must test your JavaScript program on several different browsers to make sure that your script behaves properly on them all; often you can find a way to make the program work on the major browsers. Because JavaScript was developed by Netscape, it tends to run better on Netscape than on early versions of Microsoft Internet Explorer.

Another consideration in the use of JavaScript (or Java, Shockwave, Active-X, or other advanced techniques) is that not all people are using browsers that support it (some have it turned off). Therefore, any experiment that uses these techniques will lose some of its potential audience. Of these "extras," JavaScript is the one available to more users than any other, followed closely by Java.

A SIMPLE JAVASCRIPT

The HTML page in Figure 17.1, *Ch17_ex1.htm,* illustrates how to include a JavaScript program in a Web page.

There are four things in this example that you will likely use in all of your JavaScripts. First, note the <SCRIPT LANGUAGE="JavaScript"> </SCRIPT> tags. These identify that the material between them is JavaScript. Second, notice the two lines that have the HTML comment tag; that is, <! ...>. All of the JavaScript is hidden from older browsers because it is within this giant HTML comment. It will soon become unnecessary to hide the JavaScript as more people shift to modern browsers. Third, anything that follows // on a line is a JavaScript comment, and does not affect JavaScript. Note that a JavaScript comment hides the close of the HTML comment from JavaScript. Fourth, to include a comment that covers several lines, begin it with /* and end it with */.

The // comment can begin on a line or it can follow an actual JavaScript statement, as on the line that writes *Hi!* The material that precedes the // is not a comment. It is a good idea to include comments in your scripts to remind yourself how your script works or to help others understand what you are doing. The computer, of course, does not read or interpret your comments.

There is only one JavaScript statement illustrated in the example. As you might guess, document.writer() (called a *method*) writes the contents within the quotes in the parentheses to the document. In the first case it writes *Hi!,* and in the second instance, it places a link in the document. Because the document is HTML, you can put HTML tags inside the quotes in the document.write() command, and the browser will interpret and display them correctly. The HTML will not be

FIGURE 17.1.   How to incorporate JavaScript in an HTML page. This is a listing of *Ch17_ex1.htm.* Load this example in your browser.

```
<HTML><HEAD><TITLE>First JavaScript Example</TITLE>
</HEAD><BODY>
<H3>TheFollowing is from JavaScript</H3>
<P><PRE>

<SCRIPTLANGUAGE="JavaScript">
<!--this comment hides the script from older browsers
//this is a comment. It has no effect.
/*This is also a comment. This one can
  stretch over several lines. It also has no effect */

document.write("Hi!")  // writes to the page
document.write("<A HREF='Ch5_exp6.htm'>Click here</A>")

//JavaScript comment hides the end of HTML comment -->
</SCRIPT>

</PRE></BODY></HTML>
```

displayed literally, but becomes part of the Web page itself. As shown in Chapter 18, this allows you to dynamically change the contents of a Web page.

In JavaScript, each statement is placed on a separate line. Multiple statements can be placed on the same line if they are separated by semicolons. JavaScript commands and key words are case sensitive. Try changing `document.write()` to `Document.Write()` and you get an error message. Because HTML is unaffected by capitalization, it may be difficult to get used to JavaScript's sensitivity to case.

 ## ILLUSTRATION OF RANDOM NUMBERS

The script in *Ch17_ex2.htm*, listed in Figure 17.2, illustrates the use of variables, mathematical computations, and random numbers.

Load the page *Ch17_ex2.htm* in your browser. Then push the *Reload* button (or *Reload* from the **View** menu). You will see that the values of *x* and *y* are not only different from each other, they are also different every time you reload the page. JavaScript has a package of mathematical functions available. These are collectively known as the *Math Object,* and the functions are called *methods.* `Math.random()` produces a random number that is uniformly distributed between 0 and 1.

FIGURE 17.2.   Load this example, *Ch17_ex2 .htm,* in your browser. Each time you reload, the values of *x* and *y* change, but *z* is always the sum of *x* and *y.*

```
<HTML><HEAD><TITLE>Illustrates math.random()</TITLE></HEAD><BODY>
<H3>RandomNumbers.</H3>
<H4>Reload this program--it will be different each time.</H4>
<P><PRE>


<SCRIPT LANGUAGE="JavaScript">
<!--this HTML comment hides the script


var x=0 // these lines establish the variables
var y=0
var z=0
//The following code illustrates use of Math.random()
//Math.random() produces a pseudo random number, uniform (0,1)


x = Math.random()
y = Math.random()
z = x + y  // adds x and y and puts sum in z


document.writeln("x = "+x+" y = "+y+" z = "+z)


//JavaScript comment hides end of HTML comment -->
</SCRIPT>
</PRE></BODY></HTML>
```

The first three lines of the program establish that *x, y,* and *z* are numeric variables and set their initial values to zero. In JavaScript, unlike BASIC, the symbols *x, y,* and *z* might refer to numbers or strings (sequences of letters and numbers) such as "Hi", "2-10-97", or "137.157.14". When strings are added, they are concatenated. For example `"HiThere" = "Hi" + "There"`. When numbers are added, their numeric values are added, $4 = 2 + 2$; however, if the variables were strings, `"2" + "2"` is `"22"`. If you see such arithmetic in one of your scripts and you did not intend it, you should probably declare the variable with the `var` expression.

If you are unfamiliar with computer programming, it helps to read this statement,

```
z = x + y
```

from right to left. The statement is sometimes called an "assignment" statement because it adds *x* to *y* and assigns the resulting value to the variable, *z*. The assignment statement should not be misunderstood as an algebraic equality—it is not! For example, consider the statement `y = y + 2`. If $y = 1$ before the statement, then after the statement, `y = 3`; if y had been zero, then it is now 2. The computer statement `y = y + 1` means to add 1 to the value of *y* and store the result in *y*. In algebra, the statement is certainly a puzzle. Unlike algebra, the JavaScript statement `z = x + y` is *not* the same as `y = z - x`. In the former case, *z* is changed; in the latter case, *y* is changed.

The expression `y = y + 2` can also be written `y += 2`; the expression `y = y + 1` can also be written `y++`.

Unlike some programming languages and unlike HTML, JavaScript variables are case sensitive. That means that `x` is different from `X`, and `cow` is different from `COW`.

The arithmetic operations of addition, subtraction, multiplication, and division are represented by the symbols `+`, `-`, `*`, and `/`. Try replacing the `+` with `*` or `/` to see different computations in this example. Operations that are enclosed in parentheses are performed first. For example, `x + y/z` produces a different result from `(x + y)/z`. To raise *x* to the *y* power requires the power function in the Math Object. The expression is `z = Math.pow(x,y)`, which computes x^y. You learn more about the Math methods in Chapter 19.

RANDOM ASSIGNMENT TO CONDITIONS USING JAVASCRIPT

This section develops a simple JavaScript to assign participants to one of two or more conditions. This assignment occurs randomly in a way that no one can predict. Suppose there are two experimental groups and the experiments are in files *numbersA.htm* and *numbersB.htm.* Suppose you want half of the subjects to complete *numbersA.htm* and half to complete *numbersB.htm.* The script in Figure 17.3, *Ch17_ex3.htm,* accomplishes that.

The script in *Ch17_ex3.htm* uses a new idea: the *if* branch. The general expression is as follows:

```
If (Boolean expression)
    {statements; statements }
else {statements;
        statements}
```

If the Boolean (logical) expression is `true`, then the first block of statements in braces is executed; if the statement is `false`, then the second block of statements is executed.

```
<HTML><HEAD><TITLE>RANDOM ASSIGNMENT TO CONDITIONS</TITLE>
</HEAD><BODY>
<H3>RANDOM ASSIGNMENT TO TWO CONDITIONS</H3>
<H4>Reload this program. Reload each time to see different actions.</H4>
<P>
<PRE>


<SCRIPTLANGUAGE="JavaScript">
<!--this HTML comment hides the script from older browsers


var x=0
//       if x > .5, subjects get A, otherwise B
x = Math.random()
if(x > .5)
     {document.write("<A HREF='numbersA.htm'>Click to continue</A>")}
else {document.write("<A HREF='numbersB.htm'>Click to continue</A>")}


//JavaScript comment hides the end of HTML comment -->
</SCRIPT>
</PRE></BODY></HTML>
```

FIGURE 17.3.   JavaScript to randomly assign participants to two conditions, *Ch17_ex3.htm*. Reload this example several times and click on the link to verify that it behaves differently on different occasions of being loaded.

In the example of *Ch17_ex3.htm*, there is only one statement in each block. The only difference is that the <A HREF> tag points to a different file when x > .5 from that when x <= .5. If the random number generator works properly, then subjects are assigned equally likely in either direction.

Because instances of a random sequence rarely come out evenly, do not expect an exactly equal number of people in each condition. The example *Ch17_ex4.htm* shows how to assign to three conditions, which are the three conditions for obtaining responses for the value of the St. Petersburg paradox. If there were four between-subjects conditions, you could use two random variables, *x* and *y*, to assign people to conditions. Alternatively, you could assign to group 1 if x < .25, to group 2 if .25 <= x < .5, to group 3 if .5 <= x < .75, and to group 4 otherwise.

Note also in the example that there are nested quote marks. When quotes are nested, use single quotes to distinguish matching quotes. In this case, the outer quotes indicate that the material inside is a string literal to be printed in the document. The inner quotes show the filenames of the <A HREF="URL"> tag.

A Boolean expression is either true or false. Here is a list of the Boolean relations: (<, >, >=, <=, ==, !=); these refer to less than, greater than, greater than or equal, less than or equal, equal, and not equal, respectively. For example, if a == 3 and b == 4, it is true that a < b, and it is true that a != b. However, it is false that a >= b or that a == b. Note the use of double equal (==) for logical equal. The Boolean operators of AND, OR, and NEGATION are represented by &, |, and !. For example,

```
if (x < .5 & y < .5) {document.write("x and y are both less than .5")}
```

This statement writes its string only when both conditions are true.

SELECTING A RANDOM NUMBER FROM 1 TO *n*

Consider the following expression:

```
y = Math.floor(n*Math.random()) +1
```
(17.1)

The `Math.floor()` method truncates a number to the next lower integer. For example, `Math.floor(3.1)` is 3, and `Math.floor(3.99)` is also 3. If *n* is an integer, `n*Math.random()` will be uniformly distributed on $(0, n)$. Therefore, `Math.floor(n*Math.random())` yields integers from 0 to $n - 1$ with equal probability. Adding 1, the expression gives integers from 1 to *n* with equal likelihood. This expression is at the heart of *Ch17_ex6.htm*. In *Ch17_ex6.htm* there are six conditions, but it should be clear that *n* could be changed to any number. Expression 17.1 is also used in examples 7 and 8 of Chapter 17 to randomly select the outcome of a rolled die. Examples 7 and 8 also illustrate how to manipulate which of several images will be displayed from JavaScript.

REVIEW OF JAVASCRIPT FUNDAMENTALS

The concepts introduced in Chapter 17 are summarized in Table 17.1.

TABLE 17.1.   Summary of HTML and JavaScript Commands in Chapter 17

COMMAND	DESCRIPTION
`<SCRIPT></SCRIPT>`	HTML tags indicating script; `<SCRIPT LANGUAGE="JAVASCRIPT">`
`//`	JavaScript one line comment
`/*  */`	JavaScript multiple line comment
`<! anything. . .>`	HTML comment, used to hide JavaScript from older browsers
`document.write()`	Writes to the document
`Var x = 1`	Variable initialization and initial numerical assignment
`Var y = "goodBye"`	*y* initialized to a string variable and assigned a string
`Math.random()`	Random number, uniformly distributed between 0 and 1
`Math.pow(x,y)`	Computes *x* to the power of *y*
`+,−,*,/`	Addition, subtraction, multiplication, division
`z = x + y`	Computation and assignment (right to left)
`if (Boolean) {statements}` `else {statements}`	Logical branching. If the Boolean condition is true, executes the first block of statements; otherwise, executes the second.
`Math.floor(x)`	Truncates *x* to the largest integer less than *x*; `Math.floor(2.9)` is 2

EXERCISES

1. Try the following JavaScript, and see what it does:

```
var x = "2"
var y = "3"
z = x + y
document.write("x= "+x+" y = "+ y+ "z = "+z)
```

2. Now remove the quotes in the script used in Question 1; next, try changing the + to a -, *, or /. Try adding parentheses to evaluate the following:

```
z = x + y/x
z = (x + y)/x
z = x/x + y/x
```

3. To get power functions, replace the third line in Question 1 with the following:

```
z = Math.pow(x, y) (this assigns, z = x^y)
```

4. Try the following to calculate the area (A) of a circle with radius (r).

```
A = Math.PI*Math.pow(r, 2)
```

(`Math.PI` is the value of π; note that `PI` is in ALL CAPS.)

   Develop a script that calculates the area of a pizza whose diameter is 12 inches. It should print the result.

5. Make the JavaScript for a page that assigns subjects to one of four conditions based on two random variables, x and y. It should assign to condition 4 if $x > .5$ and $y > .5$. Also, do the same using one random variable, x.

6. Alter *Ch17_ex6.htm* so that it randomly assigns people to one of five conditions. Delete the printing of the random integer. Also, change the filenames to five variations of the Heider experiment, *heider1.htm to heider5.htm*. If you understand how to modify this example, you can handle random assignment to conditions.

Chapter 18

Interactive Web Pages with JavaScript

JavaScript supports communication and interaction with the reader of HTML pages. It allows you to make calculations and actions that are tailored to the individual responses that a person makes. In this chapter, you learn how to use four new methods of communication, how to measure time intervals, and how to use loops to make otherwise difficult calculations. An illustration is developed that uses these techniques to calculate the learning curve predicted by a replacement model of learning.

 ## ALERT, PROMPT, AND CONFIRM

The next examples illustrate three principles of JavaScript. First, JavaScript can be intermixed in an HTML page, not just in a separate section of code. Second, JavaScript can react to Events, such as loading or unloading a Web page, clicking on a button, moving the mouse over a link, or moving by tab or mouse click from one point of focus to another (e.g., moving from one text input box to another). Third, JavaScript provides new ways to communicate with the reader in addition to printing results in the Web page.

Consider the following example (*Ch18_ex1.htm*).

```
<HTML><HEAD><TITLE>Illustration of Forms and Event Handler</TITLE>
</HEAD>
<BODY>
<FORM>
<INPUT TYPE="button" VALUE="Push Me" OnClick="alert('Hey! Cut it
     out!')">
</FORM>
</BODY></HTML>
```

This example includes a form with a button that says, "Push Me." The *Event* that must be *handled* in this case is clicking of the button. When the reader clicks `OnClick="statements"` causes the statements in quotes to be executed. In this example, pushing the button causes the following JavaScript statement to be executed:

```
alert("Hey! Cut it out!")
```

The `alert` statement produces a JavaScript alert box, in which is printed whatever is inside the parentheses. In this case, the parentheses contain a literal message. Note that this example uses quotes within quotes; in these cases, use the double quotes for the outer pair and use single quotes within. When using quotes, pay special attention to words like "don't" that contain an apostrophe, which may cause errors that will be hard for you to figure out. To include an apostrophe, use \ ', as illustrated in *Ch18_ex1b.htm*.

The confirm statement allows you to ask a question that has a yes (true) or no (false) answer so that you can take action depending on the answer. The following example (*Ch18_ex2.htm*) illustrates its use:

```
<HTML><HEAD><TITLE>Illustration of Confirm</TITLE>
</HEAD>
<BODY>
<FORM>
<INPUT TYPE="button" VALUE="Click Here to Begin the Experiment"
     OnClick="if (confirm('As you have read, you must be over 18 and
     are free to quit at any time. Are you over 18 and wish to
     continue?')) alert('You may continue'); else alert('Sorry.')">
</FORM>
</BODY></HTML>
```

This example shows that a number of JavaScript statements can be placed within the quotes. When there are multiple statements on the same line, they should be separated by semicolons. The confirm command returns true or false, depending on the response of the reader. In this case, the program merely presents an alert to inform the reader. However, you could also send the reader to different files depending on the reader's response, by writing different links to the page with the techniques used in Chapter 17.

You can also use the confirm command in a regular link, as follows:

```
<A HREF="examples.htm" onClick="if(confirm('Are you sure you want to
     go back to the list of examples?'))return true; else return
     false"> Return to list of examples</A>
```

The prompt command is like an input text box and is illustrated with the following example (*Ch18_ex3.htm*):

```
<HTML><HEAD><TITLE>Illustration of Prompt</TITLE>
</HEAD><BODY>
<FORM>
<INPUT TYPE="button" VALUE="Click Here" OnClick="answer=prompt('what
     is your name?','(type here)');alert('Hi! ' + answer)">
</FORM>
</BODY></HEAD>
```

This example also illustrates how the answer can be used as a variable and then used in the alert. Note that there are two fields in the statement z = prompt(x, y) command: x is the message printed in the box and z is the value (or text) that the reader types in the box as an answer to the prompt.

A fourth way to communicate with the reader is to use the window status line. That line shows along the bottom of the browser's window. Consider the following:

```
<BODY OnLoad="window.status='Move your mouse over the links'">.
```

When the page loads, the status bar will show the message in status=message. Consider the following example:

```
<P><A HREF="examples.htm#eighteen"
     onMouseOver="window.status='Click here to return to examples for
     Chapter 18'; return true"
     onMouseOut="window.status='OK Try it again'">
Return to list of examples</A>
```

This example also illustrates the onMouseOver and onMouseOut events (the mouse pointer is over the link or it leaves the link). Try the example on your browser and move the mouse over each link and away from each link. If you missed it, you need to reload *Ch18_ex4.htm* to see the status after OnLoad. This example behaves slightly differently on different browsers. You should realize that messages placed in the status line are less likely to be noticed by the reader of the page than is an alert.

A fifth way to communicate is to open a new window (and create a new page "on the fly"), which is described in Chapter 19.

 ## DATE AND TIME INFORMATION

JavaScript provides the *Date* object, which can be used to put the date and time in Web pages and experiments. It can also be used to control the timing of an experiment or to measure response times in an experiment. The following example (*Ch18_ex5.htm*) illustrates the basic technique used to measure time intervals:

```
<HTML><HEAD><TITLE>Illustration of Date Object</TITLE>
</HEAD><BODY>
<FORM>
<INPUT TYPE="button" VALUE="Click Here to Begin"
     onClick="startTime=new Date()">
<INPUT TYPE="button" VALUE="Click Here to Stop"
     onClick="finishTime=new Date();
seconds=(finishTime.getTime()-startTime.getTime())/1000;
alert('Your time interval='+ seconds +' seconds')">
</FORM>
</BODY></HEAD>
</HTML>
```

The JavaScript statement startTime = new Date() creates a new instance of the Date Object. When the reader presses the first button, startTime contains a record of that time (and date). When the reader presses the second button, finishTime = new Date() creates another new instance of the Date Object, which stamps the time that the second button was pushed. The Date Object (like the Math Object mentioned in Chapter 17) has a number of methods (functions) associated with it that allow you to express the details of date and time. The getTime() method used in this example calculates and returns the number of milliseconds (.001 sec) since January 1, 1970. By taking the difference between two such times (in milliseconds) and dividing by 1000 (to convert to seconds), this program computes time intervals in seconds. Each interval is presented to the viewer with the `alert` command.

Some of the other Date Object methods are `getDate()`, `getDay()`, `getHours()`, `getMinutes()`, `getMonth()`, `getSeconds()`, and `getYear()`, which get the date of the month, day of the week, hour of the day, minutes after the hour, month of the year, seconds after the minute, and the year, respectively. You can also set the time and date by set methods (replace `get` with `set`) such as `setDate(n)`, in which n equals an integer from 1 to 31, which sets the date of the month; `setHours(h)`, in which h equals the hours (0 to 23), which sets the hour of the day, and so on.

In Chapter 19, you learn how to measure how much time was spent on a test or experiment and send the time measure back via the CGI script to your experiment's data file.

 ## LOOPS AND LEARNING MODELS

If you have done any computer programming before, you know that one of the most powerful techniques available is the use of loops to repeat computations. A loop causes a section of code to be executed repeatedly a specified number of times, or more generally, until a condition is satisfied.

Consider the following example (*Ch18_ex6.htm*), which calculates the amount owed after 15 years if a person borrowed $10,000 at 8% interest per year and made no payments until the last year:

```
var rate = .08      // set the interest rate (8%)
var debt = 10000    // set the initial amount owed
for (i=1;i<=15;i++)
    { debt = debt + debt*rate
    document.writeln("year = "+i+" Debt =  "+debt+ "\n")
    }
```

The variable `i` is the loop counter, or loop "index." The first expression in the parentheses after `for` represents the starting value of the index, which is the start of the first year. The second expression (`i<=15`) is the terminal condition; the loop continues as long as the condition is true and exits when this condition is false. The third expression (`i++`) indicates that the counter will be increased by 1 in each loop cycle (`i++` is the same as `i = i + 1`). Note that braces (`{}`) are used to designate all of the statements in the loop. In this case there are two statements in each cycle of the loop. The first one calculates the new debt, which is the old debt plus the interest, where the interest is the debt times the interest rate. The second statement is to print out the year and the debt. The statement `document.writeln(text)` writes to the document and adds a line return. The results show that a $10,000 loan at 8% will cost a total of $31,721.69 after 15 years. Now, try the same loan at 13% (i.e., change .08 in the program to .13).

Computer programs can help you understand very large numbers, such as the size of a nation's national debt. When the amount of money that a government spends exceeds the money it receives through taxes and other sources of revenue, the government borrows money to make up the deficit. The total amount of money owed by the government is called the *national debt*. The government pays interest on the money it borrows. Suppose a country has a population of 250 million citizens and a national debt of $5 trillion. If the government decided to assign its debt equally to all citizens, the debt per person would be about $20,000. A family of four would owe $80,000. Suppose instead that the government borrowed at 8%, ran no further deficits (aside from the interest), and then assigned the debt to the same sized population. How much would that debt be per citizen in 15 years? Suppose interest rates rose to 13% instead of 8%? You can modify the previous program to make the calculations. The modifications for 8% are in *Ch18_ex7.htm.*

The computer technique of loops is extremely powerful. In general, the `for` loop expression is as follows:

```
For (initial expression; final condition; update expression)
{statements}
```

The initial expression specifies the starting conditions of the loop. The loop continues to iterate (executing all of the statements in braces) as long as the final condition is true. After each iteration, the expression is updated by the update expression. When the condition becomes false, the loop ends, and the program continues to the next statements after the loop. (Each of the statements should be on a separate line; multiple statements may be on the same line if they are separated by semicolons.)

Loops provide a convenient way to calculate the predictions of mathematical learning models. A paper by Estes (1950, 1994) has been judged one of the most important contributions to psychology since the end of the nineteenth century (Bower, 1994) because it led to great advances in understanding how people learn. In each trial of a learning experiment, the learner gives a response to a stimulus situation that is either correct or incorrect. A reinforcement is then presented that enables the learner to improve his or her performance. As the learner has more and more trials, the performance (probability of a correct response) increases. The proportion correct can be plotted as a function of the number of reinforcing trials presented. This graph is known as the *learning curve.*

Do people learn by accumulating more and more information, or do they learn by replacing old ideas with new ones? Estes proposed stimulus sampling theory, a theory in which one can formalize these intuitive ideas to test predictions of specific models. For a brief introduction to simple versions of these models, see the Web page "Marbles and Memory" included on your CD. When the reinforcements are always correct and the learners are capable of eventually learning the task perfectly, the replacement model implies the following learning curve:

$$P(n) = P(n - 1) + \Theta[1 - P(n - 1)] \tag{18.1}$$

where $P(n)$ is the probability of being correct on trial n, $P(n - 1)$ is the probability of being correct on the previous trial, and Θ is the learning rate parameter. This model implies that the improvement on any trial is a constant proportion of the difference between performance on that trial and asymptotic (in this case, perfect) performance.

Bower (1961) conducted a paired-associates learning task in which data were remarkably well fit by the replacement model of Eq. 18.1. Subjects were presented with 10 stimuli, such as BX, and asked if each is a "1" or a "2." Because there are two possible answers and the letter combinations were randomly paired with responses, the learners are right only 50% of the time on the first trial. However, after each test trial, they are given the correct answer, so eventually they learn the associations, such as whether BX is a "1" or a "2." Bower found that on each trial, Stanford undergraduates learn about one-third of the items they have not yet learned on that trial. After about 10 trials, they are nearly perfect on all 10 pairs. Bower's data also permitted a test of the theory that people learn each item in an all-or-none fashion against the theory that people learn gradually. The data were consistent with predictions of the all-or-none model.

The example *Ch18_ex8.htm* shows how to calculate the learning curve for Bower's (1961) experiment. The program is a straightforward application of a loop. In each iteration, the probability correct on the next trial is calculated from the previous probability of being correct and the learning rate parameter. The probability of being correct on the first trial (before any reinforcements) is also called the *guessing rate* in this model.

 ## FUNCTIONS IN JAVASCRIPT

Suppose you were to repeat Bower's experiment with people who learn more slowly than Stanford students? This would require a change in the value of the learning rate parameter. Suppose you did an experiment in which there were three possible answers (e.g., "1", "2", or "3")? In such a case, people would be right on the first trial only one-third of the time instead of one-half the time. To allow the user to input different values of the guessing rate and learning rate, one could use the prompt commands, as illustrated in *Ch18_ex9.htm*. Another way to do it is to use INPUT tags within forms, which, as you learned in Chapter 5, is a good way to get information from the reader. That technique is used in *Ch18_ex10.htm*.

These examples illustrate two new aspects of JavaScript. Both use JavaScript functions to calculate the curve. Both examples also show that a Web page can be changed dynamically, based on the input provided by the user. This is especially clear in *Ch18_ex10.htm*, in which the window's title and background color are also changed inside the function.

Functions are defined as in the following form:

```
function myFunction(parameters) {statements; return}
```

where there may be many statements in the brackets. Functions (and methods) have parentheses that may contain a list of parameters separated by commas. The name of the function in this example is myFunction(). Functions can be called by other functions or they can be called by an event handler. In *Ch18_ex9.htm*, a button is pressed that calls the function [onClick="calcCurve()"]. The function calcCurve() in turn contains prompts to ask the reader for the learning rate and guessing rate (try .33 and .50; then try .33 and .33). Note that the prompt command receives a text input. This text input must be changed to numerical information, which can be done with the eval() function. The eval() function is a built-in, global function of JavaScript that is very useful. In the next section, you will learn that eval() can do much more than just convert text to numbers. The reader can enter an expression, such as 2+2*3/7, and eval will correctly evaluate it.

In *Ch18_ex10.htm*, the transfer of parameters from a form to a function is illustrated. Note the following section of this example:

```
<FORM NAME="test">
Guessing Rate (G): <INPUT TYPE=text NAME="guess" SIZE=5 value=".5">
Learning Rate (<FONT FACE="symbol">Q</FONT>):
<INPUT TYPE=text NAME="theta" SIZE=5 value=".335">
Compute the Curve:<INPUT TYPE=button VALUE="compute"
     OnClick="calCurv(test.theta.value,test.guess.value)">
</FORM>
```

This section of the code shows that when the button is clicked, the function `calCurv()` is executed with parameters `test.theta.value` and `test.guess.value`. Note the construction of these variables. They are placed within a form, which is the active object. The form name is `test`, the variable names are `theta` and `guess`, and the `"value"` contains the text that was typed in the box by the viewer. Because these responses are supposed to be numbers (but JavaScript considers them text), when they arrive in the function they are processed by `eval` to make sure that JavaScript recognizes them as numbers. Try entering 2/7 in one of the text boxes (literally). The `eval` function evaluates it correctly.

The techniques of `alert`, `confirm`, and `prompt` have the advantage that they command the reader's attention, and the reader must respond to them before anything else can happen. In *Ch18_ex9.htm*, for example, the reader must respond to the prompt for theta before he or she can enter the guessing rate. However, it may be restrictive to the reader to be forced to decide one issue before seeing the next question. The use of Input text boxes, as in *Ch18_ex10.htm*, allows the reader to change the parameters in either order and to view them both while deciding how to change them.

PROBABILITY LEARNING

In the Bower learning experiment, the learner always receives the correct answer on each trial, so the undergraduates eventually perform perfectly. What happens if the feedback is probabilistic? Many situations in life are not perfectly predictable. For example, store A might usually have lower average prices than store B, but on a given day a certain item might be cheaper at store B than at store A.

One implication derived from stimulus sampling theory was the prediction of probability matching. Probability learning experiments found evidence of probability matching, as predicted by the model. If a person is reinforced 60% of the time for one choice and 40% of the time for the other, people tend to respond 60% of the time to the choice that was reinforced 60% of the time. To experience a probability learning test, load the experiment *ProbLearn.htm* from the list of examples. When the experiment starts, your task is to click on button R1 or R2, attempting to predict whether R1 or R2 will be correct on the next trial. Try to predict whether the next reinforcement will be on the left or the right, by clicking on one of the two buttons, R1 or R2. At first, you have no idea what is coming next, so you must guess. Eventually, you learn to do better than chance. See how well you can predict the next event.

After you have completed 100 trials, you will receive an alert with feedback on your performance. You can compare your percentage of choosing R2 with the percentage of reinforcements of R2. A finding in the literature on this paradigm found that people "match," even though that behavior is not optimal. For example, if R2 is correct 60% of the time, then R1 is correct 40% of the time. If a person chooses R2 60% of the time (assuming that person does not have ESP), that person will be correct on R2 36% of the time (.6*.6) and correct on R1 16% of the time (.4*.4). Therefore, the person is correct a total of only 52% of the time. By *always* choosing R2, the person would have been right 60% of the time. For more information on this topic, including references to the literature, see Bower (1994). Data for the Web version of the experiment are included on the CD.

SUMMARY

The concepts introduced in Chapter 18 are summarized in Table 18.1.

TABLE 18.1.   JavaScript Statements Covered in Chapter 18

STATEMENT	DESCRIPTION
`alert(message)`	Presents message in a box
`confirm(question)`	Box with yes or no question is displayed. Returns `true` or `false`, depending on answer.
`prompt(x, y)`	Presents message x. Reader enters y in the textbox of the prompt message.
`onClick="javascript statements"`	Event handler. Executes the statements when the event occurs.
`window.status=message`	Contents of the status bar at the bottom of the browser window.
`for (i = 1; i <= n; i ++)`	Loop that repeats the block of statements, incrementing `{statement` i by one each time until $i > n$.
`eval(expression)`	Evaluates an expression such as $2^*(3 - 2)$.
`timeNow = new Date()`	Creating an instance of the `Date()` object. Methods of the
`y = timeNow.getTime()`	Date Object include `getTime()`, which returns time since 1–1–70 in milliseconds.
`function funName(parameters)` `{statements}`	JavaScript function. When the function is called, statements in brackets are executed.

  EXERCISES

1. Create the script to replace "?" in the following statement so that when the link is clicked, it sends an alert that says "o.k., you're an ambulance." `<A HREF="filename.htm" onClick="?">Call me an ambulance!</A>`
2. Create a Web page that includes at least one example of alert, prompt, and confirm.
3. Create a JavaScript that records the time from when a page is loaded until the reader clicks a button. Use `<BODY OnLoad="startTime=New Date()">` to record the time when the page loads. When the button is pressed, calculate the number of minutes. (Hint: Find seconds and convert to minutes.)
4. Use loops to calculate the first 20 Fibonacci numbers. Each Fibonacci number is the sum of the two preceding numbers. $f_1 = 1$, $f_2 = 1$, $f_3 = f_1 + f_2 = 2$, $f_4 = f_2 + f_3 = 3$, ..., $f_n = f_{n-2} + f_{n-1}$.
5. Use loops to calculate the learning curve according to the accumulation model that implies that $P(n) = \dfrac{G + \theta(n - 1)}{1 + \theta(n - 1)}$. Make one version with prompts for G and θ; make another variation with forms to receive the parameters. (Hint: Study examples 9 and 10.)
6. Project idea: Analyze the data included on the CD (ProbLearn.csv) to see if probability matching characterizes the data. Can you think of a manipulation that will produce more "optimal" behavior from people? If you can think of such a manipulation, randomly assign people to conditions, with one condition receiving the usual instructions and the other receiving the new instructions that you think will produce more optimal behavior in the probability learning experiment. Collect data and see if the new manipulation is effective.

Chapter 19

JavaScript and Forms

In Chapter 18, you learned how to get information from a form to JavaScript. In this chapter, you learn how to send information from JavaScript back to the form. This trick used in this chapter to make calculators, to check if the participant in an experiment completed all of the items, to score a test (and give individualized feedback), and to compute the time it took the participant to finish the task. You learn a technique for passing these values from one form to another and how to send these computed values to the data file to be saved on the server. You also learn how to create a new Web page "on the fly," which can be useful in many ways, but is illustrated here for the purpose of giving people feedback on a personality test. This chapter also discusses how gullible people can be when they get information that supposedly describes them.

 ## CALCULATORS

Besides the learning curve calculators constructed in Chapter 18, you have seen the decision calculator in Chapter 8 and the Bayes theorem calculator in Chapter 16. In this section, you learn the principle behind those calculators. The programs *surveyWiz* and *factorWiz* are technically calculators that use this same principle. The first example is a very simple calculator that makes it easy to see the programming trick. This trick allows one to pass information in both directions between JavaScript and forms.

The example *Ch19_ex1.htm* illustrates the basic idea behind a calculator.

```
<HTML><HEAD><TITLE>Simple Multiplying Calculator</TITLE>
</HEAD><BODY>
<FORM NAME="MyForm">
<INPUT TYPE=text NAME=x1 SIZE=8 MAXLENGTH=9>
<FONT FACE="Arial">   X </FONT>
<INPUT TYPE=text NAME=x2 SIZE=8 MAXLENGTH=9>
   =
<INPUT TYPE=text NAME=ans SIZE=8 MAXLENGTH=9>
<INPUT TYPE="button" VALUE="Compute" OnClick="computeProd()">
</FORM>
<SCRIPT LANGUAGE="JavaScript">
<!- this comment hides the JavaScript from older browsers
var A = 0        // x1 = first number
var B = 0        // x2 = second number
var C = 0        // ans = product of the numbers
//         This function computes the product of x1 and x2
function computeProd() {
 with (document.forms){
   A = 1.0*(MyForm.x1.value)
   B = 1.0*(MyForm.x2.value)
```

```
    C = A*B
    MyForm.ans.value = C
  } return}
// this hides the end of the HTML comment tag from Javascript-->
</SCRIPT>
<P><P><A HREF="examples.htm#nineteen">Return to list of examples</A>
</BODY></HTML>
```

This calculator does not calculate anything except the product of two numbers, but it does illustrate an important new idea. Note the expression `with (document. forms) {statements}`. This expression makes clear (to different browsers) that we are referring to forms. The statement `MyForm.ans.value = C` is used to send the computed result back to the form. Forms are part of the document; `MyForm` is the name of the form; `x1`, `x2`; and `ans` are the names of the variables within the form; and we plan to use the *values* of those elements. Theoretically, you can also refer to the value of `x1` as follows: `document.MyForm.x1.value`; however, this way of identifying information does not always work properly with all browsers. I advise you to use the `with (document.forms){statements}` technique as in this example to make your JavaScripts most likely to work correctly on different browsers. The technique usually saves typing as well.

Within the function `computeProd()`, the variables `MyForm.x1.value` and `MyForm.x2.value` are multiplied by 1.0 to help different browsers interpret the results as numbers. The statement `MyForm.ans.value = C` causes the answer to be printed to the form when it returns from the function. Thus, forms provide a two-way street for getting information from the reader and sending information back to the reader.

The calculator in *Ch19_ex1.htm* looks fairly primitive compared to the Bayesian calculator in Chapter 16. You can make the calculator look better by putting it inside a table with a large border and adding a bit of color to the page. That has been done in *Ch19_ex2.htm*, which has only these cosmetic changes.

A calculator that only multiplies is not particularly useful. However, the calculator in *Ch19_ex3.htm* can be used to add, subtract, multiply, divide, and use a full list of sci-entific functions. To use the functions, the user needs to know about the properties and methods available in the JavaScript Math Object.

In Chapter 17, you learned that the statement $x = $ `Math.pow(2,3)` would com-pute 2 to the third power ($2^3 = 8$) and set $x = 8$. Using `with`, as shown previously, you can also write this expression as follows:

```
with (Math) {x = pow(2,3)}
```

This trick (`with (Math)`) is combined with the `eval()` function, which can evaluate a JavaScript expression, to produce the brain of this simple but powerful calculator.

```
<HTML><HEAD><TITLE>Evaluation Calculator</TITLE></HEAD>
<BODY BGCOLOR='#ddccee'>
<H3>Calculator that Evaluates an Expression</H3>
<FORM NAME="MyForm">
<TABLE BORDER=8 CELLPADING=0 CELLSPACING=0 BGCOLOR="eeddff">
<TR><TD><INPUT TYPE=text NAME=x1 SIZE=50 MAXLENGTH=80></TD>
  <TD> = </TD>
```

```
    <TD><INPUT TYPE=text NAME=ans SIZE=12 MAXLENGTH=14></TD>
    </TR>
  <TR><TD> Type an expression; e.g., 2*(3-1)</TD>
    <TD>  </TD>
    <TD><INPUT TYPE="button" VALUE="Compute" OnClick="computeEval()">
      </ TD>
  </TR>
  </TABLE> </FORM>
  <SCRIPT LANGUAGE="JavaScript">
  <!--this comment hides the JavaScript from older browsers
  var A = 0      // A is the evaluation of x1, the expression
  var C = 0      // ans = evaluated expression
  function computeEval() {    // This function evaluates an expression
    with (document.forms){
    with (Math) {
      A = eval((MyForm.x1.value))}
      MyForm.ans.value = A
  } return}
  // this JavaScript comma hides the end of the HTML comment tag-->
  </SCRIPT></BODY></HTML>
```

Try out the evaluation calculator with expressions such as `2*(3-2)+4/5` or `log(pow(3,4))`. The area of a 10-in. diameter pizza would be `PI*pow(10/2,2)`. In the Web page on disk, there is a list of Math methods and properties to make it easier to use the calculator. These properties and methods are also presented in Tables 19.1 and 19.2. Remember that JavaScript is case sensitive: `pi` instead of `PI` or `POW` instead of `pow` will not work! Try it.

It is also interesting to enter random numbers in the calculator. Here is a case where the calculator gives different answers each time you push the button. Try the following:

```
    floor(10*random()) + 1
```

It should give random integers from 1 to 10, different each time you click *compute*. Remove the `floor` function to get random numbers from 1 to (almost) 11. Because this calculator calculates any JavaScript expression, it can be useful when programming.

TABLE 19.1. Mathematical Constants Available in JavaScript (Math Properties)

E	(Base of natural logs, about 2.718)
LN10	(Natural log of 10, about 2.302)
LN2	(Natural log of 2, about .693)
PI	(pi = ratio of circumference of circle to diameter, about 3.142)
SQRT1_2	(square root of 1/2, about .707)
SQRT2	(square root of 2, about 1.414)

Note: These can be used as follows:

```
    Y= Math.PI
    or
    with (Math) {Y = PI}
```

TABLE 19.2. Mathematical Functions Available in JavaScript (Math Methods)

abs(x)	(absolute value of x)
acos(x)	(arc cosine of x, in radians)
asin(x)	(arc sine of x, in radians)
atan(x)	(arc tangent of x, in radians)
ceil(x)	(next greater integer than x)
cos(x)	(cosine of x, x in radians)
exp(x)	(exponential function of x)
floor(x)	(next smaller integer)
log(x)	(natural logarithm of x)
max(x,y)	(maximum of x, y)
min(x,y)	(minimum of x, y)
pow(x,y)	(x raised to the y power)
random()	(pseudo-random number, uniform between 0 and 1)
round(x)	(rounds x to the nearest integer)
sin(x)	(sine of x, where x in radians)
sqrt(x)	(square root of x)
tan(x)	(tangent of x, where x is in radians)

```
y = Math.log(2)
with (Math) {y=log(2)}
```

CHECKING FOR MISSING DATA

Sometimes a person might inadvertently skip an item. For some experiments, it may be important to check for omitted items before scoring a test or recording the data. Example *Ch19_ex4.htm* shows how to check for missing items and also how to pass data from JavaScript to a form that is compatible with protocols used in this book. The example has three parts. First, there is a form (called *test*) that consists of two test items (it could be more, but only two are used to keep this example short). Second, there is a form that is set up to send data to a file by the generic script. The second form, called *DataForm* in this example, receives the data from the first form and sends them (along with the experiment name, date, and time) to the script *generic2* (*generic2* writes to *data2.csv*). Third, there is a function called by a button that checks for blanks and sends the data from the *test* form to *DataForm*.

```
<FORM NAME="test">
<P>1. If x = 2, what is 2x - 2?
    <INPUT TYPE=TEXT NAME="Answer1" SIZE=8 MAXLENGTH=8><BR>
<P>2. What is the next number in this series: 1, 1, 2, 3, 5, 8, 13, ?
    <INPUT TYPE=TEXT NAME="Answer2" SIZE=8 MAXLENGTH=8>
<P><INPUT TYPE="button" VALUE="Check Test" OnClick="checkTest(2)">
</FORM>
<P><FORM NAME="DataForm" METHOD=Post
 ACTION="http://psych.fullerton.edu/cgi-win/polyform.exe/generic2">
 <INPUT TYPE="hidden" NAME="00Exp" VALUE="Check_blanks_test">
 <INPUT TYPE="hidden" NAME="01date" VALUE=pfDate>
 <INPUT TYPE="hidden" NAME="02time" VALUE=pfTime>
 <INPUT TYPE="hidden" NAME="03Ans1">
 <INPUT TYPE="hidden" NAME="04Ans2">
```

```
 <P>When you finish the test and checking, push the button below:
 <INPUT TYPE="submit" VALUE="Finished">
</FORM>
<SCRIPT LANGUAGE="JavaScript">
function checkTest(n) {     // this function checks for blanks
 n=1.0*n
 with (document.forms){
 var errors="#"
 var flag="You can now press the Finished button. "
 var message2="Please complete the following items. Thank you.\n "
    for(var i=1; i<=n; i++){
        j=i-1
        if (test.elements[j].value =="" ){errors=errors+i+", "}
        k=i+2 // there are 3 hidden items before the data.
        DataForm.elements[k].value=test.elements[j].value
     }
  if(errors !="#") {alert(message2+errors)}
  else {alert(flag)}
 }return}
// hide the end of the HTML comment tag from Javascript-->
</SCRIPT>
```

The example illustrates another useful trick for referring to data obtained in forms. In the first form, *test,* the responses to the first two items are stored in `document.test.Answer1.value` and `document.test.Answer2.value`. Because form elements are also stored in an array called `elements[]`, we can also refer to these two answers as `document.test.elements[0].value` and `document.test. elements[1].value`. (Arrays in JavaScript use 0 for the first entry, 1 for the second, 2 for the third, etc. So, the first item is `elements[0]`. Incidentally, forms are also stored in an array, as are images, which are numbered in the same way, starting at zero. This means that forms that have not been named can still be addressed.)

Similarly, the form "DataForm," designed to be compatible with the CGI scripts used in this book for organizing the data file, contains five variables with names such as `00Exp`, `01Date`, `02Time`, `03Ans1`, and `04Ans2`. Each variable name is preceded by a two-digit number that is used by CGI script (*generic2*) to organize the data. However, JavaScript requires that each variable name start with a letter. Therefore, it is helpful to be able to refer to these variables as `document.DataForm.elements[0].value` to `document.DataForm.elements[4].value`.

Load *Ch19_ex4.htm* from the list of examples. Leave everything blank and click the button marked "Check test." Clicking this button calls the function checkTest(2), which checks whether (`with (document.forms)`) `test.elements[j] ==""`. This checks for items left blank (i.e., `""`). Recall that the item numbers are 1 and 2, but the element number is one less (0 and 1); for that reason, $j = i - 1$. If `element[j]` is left blank, then trial i is added to the list of errors (note also that a comma and a space are added to the list to make the list easier to read). The next statement copies the answers to the other form ($k = i+2$ allows for the three hidden variables in *DataForm,* which are elements 0, 1, and 2).

To check if you understand the program, try adding one or two additional items to the questionnaire. You will add your new items to the form *test* and their counterparts to form *DataForm.* You must also change the number 2 to the new number of test items in the function call, `OnClick="checkTest(2)"`.

SCORING AND TIMING A TEST WITH FEEDBACK

To score a test, you can simply total up how many items have answers that agree with the answer key. To find out how much time a person spent on a page, you can record the time from the `onLoad` event until the person clicks a button to score the test. A method for accomplishing these two tasks is illustrated in *Ch19_ex5.htm*.

The example of *Ch19_ex5.htm* is very similar to *Ch19_ex4.htm*. Instead of checking for blanks, each response is checked against the answer key. If you were scoring an IQ test, personality test, or calculating a diagnostic index for a person, the method would be essentially the same. In this example, the variable `T` holds the total number of items correct. Note that for each correct answer, the statement `T=T+1` is executed, which increments the total by 1. The technique for measuring a time delay is essentially the same as used in Chapter 18, except that the first time is set when the page loads (`<BODY OnLoad="timeLoaded=new Date()">`). The technique for giving the feedback in this case is through an alert. However, this could also have been done easily with an `INPUT TEXT` box.

THE BARNUM EFFECT

If you have not already done so, now would be a good time to take the personality test that was constructed with the help of *surveyWiz.htm* in Chapter 10. A link is provided to this test from the examples of this chapter.

When you took the test, did the description provided by the program seem an accurate description of your personality? Many people seem to think so. Is that evidence of validation of the test? In that experiment, everyone got the same description, which seems opposite the idea of what we usually mean by personality. A personality test is supposed to describe what it is that is different and distinctive about a person, not what it is that most people think is a profound insight.

People often seem gullible when someone tells them about themselves. That is why psychics and spiritualists can make money. Do you know the difference between a psychoanalyst and a psychic? The psychoanalyst starts out by asking the client, "What is your problem?" The psychic has a harder task, as the psychic must figure out what the person's problem is, reveal it to them and predict what will happen next. Magicians describe the technique psychics use to look at a person and give them a false sense of knowledge about themselves as the art of "cold reading." Magicians publish books on how to fool people with phony psychic readings, but magicians are honest in admitting that they use tricks to create illusions for entertainment. Psychics use the same tricks to fool people and relieve them of their money at the same time. For that reason, magicians consider spiritualists and psychics to be dishonest, unethical magicians. Harry Houdini and the Amazing Randi are two magicians who exposed frauds who misused magicians' tricks.

This demonstration has become known as the *Barnum effect*, named after the circus showman P.T. Barnum, who said, "There's a sucker born every minute."

The Barnum personality test gave everybody the same feedback! If people say that this description is an accurate description of their individual personality, they are experiencing the illusion of validity produced by the Barnum effect. The median rating of accuracy was 7 on a 9-point scale. Of 243 people tested, 106 said the description was either *very accurate* or *very very accurate*. Yet everyone read the same description.

Not only is the general public gullible, but so too are personnel managers, who use psychological tests to hire and promote employees (Stagner, 1958). Stagner gave a personality test to personnel managers and then provided them with descriptions similar to those given when you push the *Score Test* button in the personality test. The personnel managers were impressed by the accuracy of the test, based on their feeling that the test was so accurate in its description of them.

The bottom line is that self-validation is not real validation. A valid personality test must do more than just give a person the feeling (illusion) of being understood. As noted in Chapter 10, a valid personality test can be used to predict individual differences in behavior.

 ## CREATING A NEW WEB PAGE

In addition to the survey created by surveyWiz in Chapter 10, the Barnum demonstration uses the following section of JavaScript to create a new page to display the feedback:

```
To score your test and see a description of your personality, press
   the Score Test button below.<BR>
<INPUT type="button" value="Score Test" onClick="feedback()">
<SCRIPT Language="JavaScript">
   function feedback() {
MyWindow=window.open("feedback.htm","W2","toolbar=no,menubar=no,
   scrollbars=no,width=370,height=280")
MyWindow.focus()
}
</SCRIPT>
<P>We are interested in your feedback to help us make more accurate
   diagnoses of personality. How accurate is the description of your
   personality (provided when you push the Score Test button)?
```

The statement `MyWindow=window.open(x, y, z)` creates and opens a new window. This new window could contain information that could be written to it, but in the previous example, it contains the HTML in the file *feedback.htm*. The variable *x* holds the name of a file, if any, to load to the new window; *y* holds the name that could be used for a hyperlink; and *z* holds a list of the new window's characteristics. `MyWindow.focus()` causes the window to be put in the foreground. (Otherwise, it might end up under the browser's window, especially after a click in the browser's window.) Now load *Ch19_ex6.htm*, listed as follows:

```
<HTML><HEAD><TITLE>Example of new window</TITLE></HEAD>
<BODY BGCOLOR="lightblue">
Here's an example with a new window.
<FORM NAME="MyForm">
<P>What is your favorite color? <BR>
(You can try names, e.g., purple, or hexadecimal, e.g., 4499aa)<BR>
<INPUT TYPE="text" SIZE =25 NAME=color2>
<P>What is your name?<BR>
<INPUT TYPE="text" SIZE =25 NAME=name2>
```

```
<P><INPUT TYPE="button" VALUE=" Open new window"
   onClick="NW(MyForm.color2.value,MyForm.name2.value)">
</FORM>
<SCRIPT>
function NW(color,name) {
   var newPage="<HTML><HEAD><TITLE>new window for "+name+"</TITLE>
      </HEAD>"
   newPage+="<BODY BGCOLOR="+color+">Here is the new window you wanted,
      "+name+". "
   newPage+="<FORM><INPUT TYPE=button Value='close'
      onClick='self.close()'>"
   newPage+="</FORM></BODY></HTML>"
   MyWindow=window.open("","W2","width=350,height=350")
   MyWindow.document.write(newPage)
}
</SCRIPT>
</BODY></HTML>
```

This example shows that you can use one Web page to create another Web page "on the fly." The new window can contain characteristics (e.g., the title of the page, its color, text) that depend on the user's input. You can also use this example to check color values; try typing in *teal, cyan,* or *salmon,* for example. This example does not use `MyWindow.focus()`. Experiment with adding or leaving out this statement to the example. What happens if you do not close the new window before clicking in the main window?

SUMMARY

In this chapter, you learned how to use HTML forms as two-way communication devices. In calculators, forms are used to accept values from the user and to display results computed in JavaScript routines to the user. When forms are used to collect data, the data can be checked to make sure the participant answered all items. They can also be checked for correctness, a score can be computed, and feedback can be given by any of the methods described in Chapter 18, or by opening a new Web page to give the computed feedback. This chapter also showed how to collect data in one form and use JavaScript to pass the values to a hidden form that can return data to the server. The properties and methods of the Math Object are summarized in Tables 19.1 and 19.2.

EXERCISES

1. Convert the multiplying calculator so that it takes *x* and raises it to the *y* power.
2. Now create a calculator that adds, subtracts, multiplies, divides, and finds powers, depending on which button is pressed. (Create five buttons and five functions to make the computations.)
3. In *Ch19_ex3.htm,* try entering 3 == 2. Can you predict the answer?
4. Add four items to *Ch19_ex4.htm* so that missing answers will be detected.
5. Add two radio button items to *Ch19_ex4.htm.* Check if they have been answered. Hint: Be sure to code " " for the extra (nonresponse) button.

6. Change *Ch19_ex5.htm* so that it computes the time until the first item is completed, instead of time until the score button is pressed. Hint: What event should you use to trigger the timing?
7. Look at the probability learning experiment from Chapter 18. You should now understand the main components of the JavaScript that runs that experiment.
8. Add `window.focus()` to *Ch19_ex6.htm*. Try clicking in the main window and then click the button.
9. Project idea: Write a JavaScript routine to compute simple reaction times. The page contains a form that says "Ready," "Set," and "Go." Participant clicks a button as fast as possible to record the time.

Part V

METHODS AND METHODOLOGY

Chapter 20

ADVANCED TECHNIQUES FOR EXPERIMENTATION ON THE WEB

This chapter reviews advanced techniques that provide additional programming control over tests and experiments on the Web. As you have seen in Chapters 5–16, virtually any study that can be done with paper-and-pencil materials, including those with pictures and graphics, can be done with HTML forms. In Chapter 14, you learned additional techniques for working with graphics and sounds.

Advanced methods for Web research, presented by researchers who have "pioneered" these techniques, are presented in the book edited by Birnbaum (2000b). The authors in that book present much good advice that has been learned from experience. These authors also present advanced discussions of JavaScript, Java, Authorware, and server-side programming to achieve greater control over Web experiments. This chapter reviews these techniques briefly so that you can determine if advanced study of these topics is for you.

As you learned in Chapters 17–19, JavaScript allows you to create experiments that interact with the participant so that the experiment can tailor itself to the unique pattern of responses a participant might give. JavaScript can be used to time events, to score or tabulate responses, and to provide feedback to the participant. Because JavaScript can be included in a Web page, it can make the process of research more open and public. One experimenter can learn from and build on another's work.

 ## ADVANCED JAVASCRIPT TECHNIQUES

There are times when you do not want information to be too openly available. By the use of frames, it is possible to make the JavaScript code nearly "hidden" (difficult for the typical participant to find). This technique and other useful tricks for using JavaScript to randomize and control Web questionnaires and surveys are presented by Baron and Siepmann (2000). Examples associated with their chapter can be found at URL [http://www.psych.upenn.edu/~baron/examples/], which is linked from the list of examples. In experiments, there is no great motive by participants to "hack" the JavaScript, so these techniques are quite adequate for most psychological research in which you do not want the participant to be able to view the code of the study easily.

However, there are situations in which you do not want information to be available at all. For example, if you were giving an exam in a class and the key was contained in the page, there would be a motive to open the page and decode the key. In addition, there are experiments in which graphics must be created in response to the user's input. These situations can be handled by server-side programming. Graphics can be created and controlled by Java Applets.

A combination of JavaScript and Java is used by the online museum of perception and cognition (Lange, 1999). This museum can be accessed at URL [http://www.ulb.ac.be/psycho/museum.html]. An abbreviated section of the museum is available in English; to reach it, click on the English flag. Housed in Belgium, documents in this Website are available in French, but even those available only in French are well worth your patient efforts to understand.

Lange (1999) discusses useful techniques of JavaScript. A collection of JavaScripts associated with her article (with explanations in English) can be downloaded from the URL [http://www.ulb.ac.be/psycho/brmic.html].

JAVA PROGRAMMING

Java is an advanced programming language that should not be confused with JavaScript, despite some similarities. Java can be used to write stand-alone programs that will run on any computer with the appropriate interpreter (software). Java can also be used to write applets that can be sent along with Web pages in much the same manner as images are included in a Web page. Whereas JavaScript programs can be sent as source code and compiled on the client's (reader's) computer, Java applets are precompiled by the developer (programmer) and supplied as separate files of symbolic codes (byte-codes) that are sent along with Web pages. Like JavaScript, Java programs are intended to run on any type of machine running the appropriate browser.

Advantages of the Java language for cognitive psychology experiments are described by Stevenson, Francis, and Kim (1999) and by Francis, Neath, and Surprenant (2000). Their Cognitive Psychology Laboratory at Purdue University, which makes use of Java (and JavaScript) can be reached at the following URL [http://coglab.psych.purdue.edu/coglab/].

To use the OnLine Laboratory, you must have Java installed and enabled in a modern browser. A test page is provided at URL [http://coglab.psych.purdue.edu/coglab/testpage.html]. This test page tells you if your browser is properly configured to use the lab. Two of the experiments discussed in Francis et al. (2000) include the Brown–Peterson Memory Task, at URL [http://coglab.psych.purdue.edu/coglab/BrownPeterson/BP.html] and the Sperling Partial Report task at URL [http://coglab.psych.purdue.edu/coglab/PartialReport/PR.html].

By 1999, there were 18 online projects with studies of perception (for example, apparent motion, visual search), memory (for example, false memories, serial position), neurocognition (for example, receptive fields, brain asymmetry), and language (for example, lexical decision). Each project is also introduced with background material to help the student understand each research area.

A Web page of resources for learning more about Java, including a sample reaction time program, is located at URL:

http://coglab.psych.purdue.edu/coglab/java.html.

Ch20_ex1.htm illustrates how to include a Java Applet in a Web page:

```
<HTML><HEAD>
<TITLE> Test of Java</TITLE></HEAD>
<BODY>
<H3>TEST OF JAVA</H3>
IF JAVA WORKS, THEN YOU WILL SEE "HI" BELOW :<BR>
<APPLET CODE="Ch20_ex1.class" WIDTH=200 HEIGHT=50 ALIGN=top>
Sorry, Java is not installed.
</APPLET>
</BODY>
</HTML>
```

The new tags in this example are <APPLET></APPLET>. Between these tags text can be written that displays if Java is *not* available. CODE="*program*.class" identifies the file containing the compiled Java applet, or *code*. In this case, the file containing the program's byte codes is *Ch20_ex1.class*. The other attributes (WIDTH, HEIGHT, ALIGN) are just like those in the IMG tag. In this example, the applet is 200 × 50 pixels.

Programs in Java are written on a text editor and saved with the extension .java. The source code applet in *Ch20_ex1.java* is as follows:

```
import java.awt.Graphics;

public class Ch20_ex1 extends java.applet.Applet{

    public void paint(Graphics g){
        g.drawString("Hi! Java is Working!", 5, 25);
    }
}
```

Like JavaScript, Java is case sensitive. The first line imports graphics. The second line names the applet *Ch20_ex1,* makes it public, and makes it an applet, extending the more general category of applets. The line that does the work is g.drawString(), which, as you might guess, writes the string in quotes to the screen. Each statement in Java ends with a semicolon, even if there is only one statement on a line.

This Java program is saved as a text file with the name *Ch20_ex1.java*. The filename must match the program name, and it must have the .java extension. This file is included in the examples on CD and can be examined in a text editor. The Java program must then be compiled by the *Java Compiler,* which can be downloaded for free. (A link to the download site is included on the CD.) The compiler converts the program to byte codes, which, in this case, were saved by the compiler in a file named *Ch20_ex1.class*. The Web server delivers the HTML and this file of byte codes.

In summary, this example uses three files: *Ch20_ex1.htm* is the HTML that calls the Java Applet, *Ch20_ex1.java* is the source program (a text file), and *Ch20_ex1.class* is the file of byte codes. To make the program available on the Web, only the HTML and the file of byte code files (*Ch20_ex1.htm* and *Ch20_ex1.class*) need to be placed on the server.

The next example illustrates some similarities (and differences) between Java and

JavaScript. *Ch20_ex2.htm* contains an applet like the JavaScript example in Chapter 18 Example 6, which calculates interest by means of a loop. The source code, *Ch20_ex2.java,* is as follows:

```
import java.awt.*;

public class Ch20_ex2 extends java.applet.Applet{

    public void paint(Graphics g) {
       float debt = 10000.0F;   // declares debt to be floating point
       float rate = .08F;            // declares rate to be floating point
       for (int i=1; i <= 15L ; i=i+1)    {
       debt = debt + rate*debt;
       g.drawString("\n debt = " + debt, 10, i*25);
                                        }
                            }
                                          }
```

In Java, variables must be declared (typed). Expressions such as `float debt` and `int i` declare `debt` and `i` to be floating point number and integer variables, respectively. The `for` loop is similar to that seen in JavaScript.

Java is an object oriented programming (OOP) language that supports inheritance. The technique in Java (and OOP languages in general) is to create very general programs from which special cases can inherit their main characteristics and also have unique features special to the particular situation. An examination of the experiments at the Cognitive Psychology Laboratory at Purdue University will convince you of the power of this approach.

USE OF AUTHORWARE/SHOCKWAVE TECHNIQUES

Instead of using a programming language, it is possible to construct cognitive psychology experiments that can control stimulus timing and measure response times by means of higher level software that relieves the designer of most programming. This approach is described by McGraw, Tew, and Williams (2000), who use Authorware by Macromedia to implement a number of classic cognitive psychology experiments (see also Williams, McGraw, & Tew, 1999). The experiments require the Authorware Player (Shockwave) plug-in, which is free from Macromedia. These experiments can be found at URL [http://www.olemiss.edu/PsychExps/] along with information about how to download and install the free player. It is possible to select the "sampler," which allows you to experience briefly each of the experimental projects available on line. This cooperative, shared research site also allows instructors to use the lab to collect and download data. Information for instructors who wish to join the lab is available in the Web site.

An advantage of the Authorware approach is that it requires much less programming ability from the users. The program has a graphic interface that allows experiments to be constructed by moving and inserting tasks and displays on a flow line that characterizes the experiment. A disadvantage of the approach is the high price of the Authorware software. Although the player is free, the authoring software costs more than $600 in 1999.

Another Web site that makes use of a plug-in is the Internet Psychology Lab (IPL) at the University of Illinois, Urbana–Champaign, which can be accessed via URL [http://kahuna.psych.uiuc.edu/ipl/]. This lab uses Java 1.1, JavaScript, and the IPL plug-in, which is available for Windows 95 and NT. The lab offers demonstrations of visual perception (including such paradigms as signal detection and selective adaptation and illustrations of illusions such as the Mueller–Lyer, Ponzo, Horizontal–Vertical, and others). In auditory perception there are demonstrations of pitch perception, the Shepard tone, and others; in cognition, there are demonstrations of basic reaction time, choice reaction time, Stroop effect, Chimeric faces, and others.

SERVER-SIDE PROGRAMMING TO CONTROL EXPERIMENTS

JavaScript, Java, and programs using plug-ins have in common that the program is delivered by the server (in one form or another) to the reader's (client's) browser, and the computing is carried out on the reader's (client's) computer. This approach has the advantage that it minimizes the load that is placed on the server. This approach has the disadvantage that the reader must have the proper configuration of computer, browser, and plug-ins to make the software work. Ideally, such software would run equivalently on all machines and all browsers, but in practice, different people have different experiences. For some people, your experiment might run slowly or erratically, and for others it will not run at all. Furthermore, by sending everything to run on the client's computer, a measure of control and security is lost.

Another approach is to run some or all of the experiment on the server itself (Morrow & McKee, 1998; Schmidt, 1997a, 2000). That guarantees that the program runs, it secures certain aspects of the experiment that must remain secure, and it means that the computer and software of the end user have little effect on the process. It has the disadvantage of placing a burden on the server to make computations as well as serving files. That can slow down transactions with the server. When delays are significant, some participants lose patience and quit the experiment, thinking that your site has frozen up. If the server is fast, the programs efficient, and the traffic light, these delays should not be a problem.

There are many tasks that can be done either by server-side programming or by programs that run on the reader's (client's) computer, such as JavaScript programs. For example, Alan Schwartz developed a program independently to carry out Bayesian calculations like those of the JavaScript Bayesian calculator in Chapter 16, but his program was written in Perl and runs on his server. His calculator can be found at URL [http://araw.mede.uic.edu/cgi-bin/testcalc.pl]. For his tutorial on Perl, see Schwartz (1998). You can compare the speed of the server-side program with the JavaScript calculator in Chapter 16 to get an idea of this aspect of server-side programs.

Some tasks, however, are best performed or only possible on the server (Schmidt, 2000). For example, programs that save data to the server and programs providing password protection must be run on the server. For obvious reasons, you would not want to allow remote users to be able to save to your disk or control your passwords!

In the projects described in this book, the CGI programs that organize and save the data were created by PolyForm (see Appendix A). The server can also be programmed to check data consistency, check for response omissions, check for multiple submissions from the same person, score tests, give feedback to participants, and many other useful tasks (Schmidt, 1997). Schmidt (2000) describes how *server-side includes* (SSI), programs that run on the server and augment the Web experiment, can be used to provide additional functionality or control to an experiment.

Suggestions for setting up and running your own server are given in Francis et al. (2000), and Schmidt, Hoffman, and MacDonald (1997). Francis et al. (2000) describe how an abandoned 486 machine can be brought back to life as a useful Web server using server software that is freely available on the Web. This approach is very inexpensive, but requires expertise (and effort) on the part of the reviver. Commercial packages that include both hardware and software for a Web server are available (in 1999) for about $3500.

 ## SUMMARY

This chapter reviewed advanced techniques that can be used to add considerable power and control to a Web experiment. JavaScript is a powerful scripting language that can be used to create interactive experiments in which time can be controlled or measured. Java is a powerful language that can be used to create stand-alone applications or applets that can be sent with Web pages. This language can be used to control and change graphics dynamically. Basic techniques for including a Java application in a page were described. The Authorware approach, in which one can use a high-level program to develop experiments, requires less programming expertise to create experiments similar to those that can be implemented via Java. In addition, the role of server-side programming in Web experiments was described. Server-side programming can accomplish the same tasks as Java and JavaScript, and it can also do tasks, such as saving data, that only the server can do.

 ## EXERCISES

1. Read Lange (1999) and download the example JavaScripts that accompany that article. Study those examples.
2. Read Baron and Siepmann (2000) and explore the JavaScript examples in their Web site. Create a short questionnaire that implements their techniques.
3. Read Francis et al. (2000), visit the Cognitive Psychology Lab at Purdue University, and participate in two experiments of your choosing.
4. Download the Java Development Kit from Sun. Compile applets from the source code for *Ch20_ex1.java* and *Ch20_ex2.java*. Test them in your browser.
5. Read McGraw et al. (2000) and visit PsychExps at Ole Miss. Participate in the sampler to see how the experiments are implemented at that site.
6. Project idea: Examine the Java Resources page at Purdue University. Develop a reaction time program that extends the sample program available at that site. Change the program so that the stimulus appears (randomly) in either the left or right side of the visual field, and the participant must push "F" if the stimulus appears on the left and "J" if the stimulus appears on the right. Allow the experimenter to control the probability that the stimulus appears on the left or right.
7. Project idea: Acquire Authorware from Macromedia. Develop the same experiment described in Question 6 by means of Authorware.
8. Project idea: Read articles on running your own Web server (Schmidt et al., 1997; Francis et al., 2000). Bring an old 486 machine back to life as a Web server, using the methods described by Francis et al. (2000).
9. Download Perl for free. Search the Web for Perl resources. Learn Perl and write SSIs to do one of the following tasks: random assignment of participants to conditions, check for multiple submissions from the same remote address, check for missing data, and check for submissions from a referring page other than your intended Web page.

Chapter 21

METHODOLOGY, ETHICS, AND PUBLICIZING YOUR STUDY

Previous chapters are devoted more to the methods used to put an experiment on the Web and analyze the results than to broader issues of what you should do to conduct good research on the Web. This chapter deals with some of these broader questions.

 ## METHODOLOGICAL SUGGESTIONS

CONDUCT A COMPARISON STUDY OF WEB AND LAB RESEARCH IN YOUR DO-
MAIN.   If you plan to do research on a topic that has not been explored in Web research, you should probably collect data in the lab for comparison with your Web study. Once a study is on the Web, it is easy to recruit a sample from the "subject pool" to complete the same materials in the laboratory using Internet-connected computers. Such comparison studies address two issues that are of concern: (1) the lack of control in Web research, compared to the lab; and (2) the different sample demographics in Web versus "subject pool" research.

There have been a number of studies comparing data between the Web and the lab. The typical finding is that Internet research yields the same conclusions as lab research (Birnbaum, 1999c; 2000a; 2000b; Buchanan, 2000; Buchanan & Smith, 1999; Krantz, Ballard, & Scher, 1997; Krantz & Dalal, 2000; Pasveer & Ellard, 1998; Pettit, 1999; Smith & Leigh, 1997; Stanton, 1998). Demographics of the samples depend on manner of recruitment, however, and the results may correlate with demographics (Birnbaum, 1999c; 2000a; Schillewaert, Langerak, & Duhamel, 1998).

Although the emerging trend of this research is that Web research and lab research reach the same conclusions (Krantz & Dalal, 2000), there may be skepticism in your field of work whether this trend applies to each new research problem. Therefore, until your research community becomes accustomed to the results of Web studies, it would be a good idea to address this question before someone else asks it of you.

PROBLEM OF DROP OUTS IN BETWEEN-SUBJECTS RESEARCH.   In Chapter 9, you learned that even a very carefully executed between-subjects study can reach the silly conclusion that the number 9 is bigger than the number 221. Between-subjects experiments are also plagued by another severe problem that may be more troublesome on the Web than in the lab. That problem is the problem of drop-outs. Piper (1998) warned of drop-outs in Web research, and noted that between-subjects studies on the Web can have high drop-out rates.

If a manipulation is done between subjects and if people can select themselves to drop out of the study, it can happen that the effect of drop outs can easily outweigh the effects of the manipulation. For example, in a medical drug study, those who feel better might drop out. In another study, those who feel worse might drop out, for fear that the medicine is causing more harm than good. Either way, the results may not measure the true effect of the medicine because of missing data.

Even if the overall drop-out rates are the same in both the treatment and control groups, and even if people are randomly assigned to conditions, it can easily happen that the problem of drop outs can make a beneficial treatment look harmful or a harmful one look beneficial. Birnbaum and Mellers (1989) showed how treatments can lead to drop outs in experimental and control groups in such a way that the drop-out rates can be the same and yet the observed result is opposite the true mean difference. By developing mathematical models to describe why people are dropping out, Birnbaum and Mellers showed that regression-based statistical methods intended to correct data for drop-out rates do not yield appropriate conclusions.

These analyses show that the validity of between-subjects experiments is severely threatened by drop outs, even if they occur at the same rate in both experimental and control groups. Unless that problem can be addressed adequately, scientists will remain very skeptical of between-subjects research. If Web research were to have relatively high drop-out rates, such research will not find ready acceptance.

Reips (2000) discusses this problem in detail and recommends a "high threshold" method for recruiting to such an experiment. The idea is to preselect participants who are likely to complete the experiment. The experimenter asks each prospective participant for his or her name, email address, home address, work address, and other contact information. The person might be asked to come online to supply additional information each week for several weeks. Many people would refuse to supply the information or would drop out for other reasons. Hopefully, those who stick it out will also finish the study.

The procedure is intended not only to discourage people who are not serious in their willingness to complete the experiment, but also to obtain the kinds of information required to track down participants to complete the experiment. Only *after* the high threshold has been reached should participants be randomly assigned to conditions. That procedure is intended to restrict the subject sample before the real experiment takes place. Although the conclusions of the study may be applicable only to those very special people who meet the high threshold, if the procedure can eliminate drop outs, it can save the internal validity of the study.

MULTIPLE SUBMISSIONS.   A participant can complete a study, click the submit button, read the thank you and debriefing messages, and then press the *Back* key in the browser to do the study again. That would result in a second set of data from the same person. Such repeated records are called *multiple submissions.*

Schmidt (1997a) and Reips (2000) discuss this issue and suggest ways to solve this potential problem. Here are some suggestions for dealing with it: First, you can ask your participants to do the experiment only once. In most studies, there is little incentive to participate more than once, but those that might be in the form of a learning task or game of skill might be interesting to people to repeat. If you have such an experiment, you can ask people to report identifying information so that you can keep track of how many times they have done the study. By the use of "cookies" it is possible to track your participant's history. Schmidt (2000) describes methods for implementing these ideas on the server that can also keep records of participation.

Second, you can use identifying information to learn if the same person has participated more than once. If you ask for name, email address, and so on, you may lose some of your potential audience, but you can ensure that each person participates only once.

Third, you can use the remote address and demographic information to detect multiple submissions. In my experience, most multiple submissions come within a few minutes of each other and appear to occur as people click the submit button and then go back to view their responses once more. These are easily detectable as coming from the same remote address with the same demographics (age, sex, education, nationality, etc.), and in most cases, exactly the same responses. In a few cases, the same person "rethinks" the task and sends different responses the second time. In such cases, you should follow a preplanned rule of whether you take the first or last version of the experiment from a given person.

Fourth, you can remove any motivation or incentive to participate more than once. For example, if your study offers chances of prizes to people who participate, there might be a motive to participate more than once if each entry provided another chance to win. However, you can state in the rules that each participant may enter only once, and that multiple entries will be deleted. If the experiment is interesting to repeat (e.g., if it involves some type of video game), provide another version of it on the Web for your participants to repeat as often as they want. That way you can provide the same entertainment to your participants while controlling the experiment.

As noted by Reips (2000) and Musch and Reips (2000), the issue of multiple submission has not proved to be a serious problem to Web researchers, and when simple precautions are taken, this potential problem can be easily handled.

HACKERS, MISCHIEF, AND MALFEASANCE.   Although the media have reported cases of people creating computer viruses, hackers attacking computers for the sake of causing trouble, computerized spying, threatening email, and other misdeeds via the Internet, such criminal activities are rare.

You should certainly take precautions to avoid being the victim of such crimes, the same as you should take precautions to avoid being the victim of robbery. However, you should not overestimate the dangers and expend too much effort worrying about how to prevent unlikely possibilities. Most people do not commit crimes, and if you reduce the incentives and opportunities, you reduce the likelihood that you will be a victim.

A person who carries large sums of cash, makes this fact known to a number of people in a bar, and then falls asleep from too much to drink in the alley after insulting everyone has increased the risk of being victimized. Suppose your experiment collected names, addresses, social security numbers, credit card numbers, and phone numbers for people who provide abortion services, and suppose you made known on the Web that your computer stores this information. You would put yourself at greater risk of a break in, either by a hacker or a burglar, because you have announced that you have private data on controversial people. If your study does not collect sensitive data and stores data anonymously, your data are unlikely to attract much interest. In fact, you can post your anonymous data on the Web to make them available, reducing further any motive to break in to get them.

There are some obvious precautions that should be followed. Do not give out your passwords (or house keys) or leave them around. If you are going to collect sensitive data, keep a low profile. Keep your computer in a secure building and do not advertise its location. Remove data from the computer often to a secure storage site. If you are going to do sensitive research via the Web, you may want to acquire secure lines and encryption systems.

Suppose a person decides to "foil" your experiment by sending fake data to your script. A person might try to use a researcher's script that sends data by email in order to send threatening email that looks like it came from the researcher! Schmidt (1997a) discussed this problem and methods to avoid, prevent, or track down how it was done. He recommends that one should avoid systems that send data by third-party email. Appendix A describes a method in PolyForm that allows only one referrer (Web page) to send data to a given script. Server-side scripts can also keep track of the referrer that sends data.

If someone did attempt to interfere with your experiment via the Web, or do other nasty things, they might easily be caught. That person would risk civil lawsuits and criminal charges, so one would not expect a rational person to attempt such action without motivation. Although it is possible that your Web research could be attacked, it is probably more likely that you will be attacked for the cash you carry. Musch and Reips (2000) surveyed Web researchers and found no evidence that pranksters or hackers have yet been a problem.

RECRUITMENT AND SAMPLES.   The users of the Internet are sometimes considered a population. However, I think it is misleading to treat the Web as if it were a stable, definable population. The group of people who use the Internet is changing rapidly, so it is not a stable group. Patterns of use are also changing rapidly as more and more services are offered via the Web. The type of sample that one obtains probably depends less on the fact that the Web was used to collect the data than it does on the procedures used to recruit the sample.

People who use the Internet are not a random sample of people in the world, people who volunteer to participate in a Web study are not a random sample of Internet users, and people who participate in behavioral experiments on the Internet are not a random sample of those who volunteer. For example, it might be that at a given time, 49% of the population are male, 60% of Web activity might be by males, and yet 65% of participants in a psychology experiment on the Web are female. In other words, do not expect samples obtained from volunteers on the Web to be representative of people on the Web, and do not expect the Web to be representative of the world's population.

The fact that there are many subpopulations available on the Web is a potential advantage of the method. By using different methods to recruit (Buchanan, 2000; Birnbaum, 1999; Schillewaert, Langerak, & Duhamel, 1998), different demographic groups can be tapped. Data can be analyzed separately for each subsample.

Because large samples can be obtained on the Web, each subsample provides a meaningful result. You could analyze data as a function of education, levels of wealth, age, gender, and other demographic characteristics. With large samples, you could find out if results obtained with college students also generalize to more highly educated people, less highly educated people, or whatever group is of interest.

When you plan to compare people recruited by different methods, consider placing your experiment in several different Web sites. Then recruit by different methods to the different Web sites (which contain the same experiment with a different hidden variable indicating the recruitment). You can also ask several questions to find out what brought each participant to your site. Even if you use different methods for recruitment, intended to reach specific target populations, those recruited may tell their friends, so that you end up with participants that you did not plan to recruit. The questions in your test or experiment can help you identify people recruited by word of mouth, for example, from those who responded to your notices.

Do not expect to find large differences between demographic groups in conclusions of a well-designed study. There may be some areas where large demographic correlations are found. However, from the study of individual differences, it is known that correlations between measures of individual differences and other behavioral measures are typically quite modest. These modest correlations, discussed in Chapter 10, mean that experiments in such fields as perception, cognition, and sensation should not be expected to yield different conclusions in different groups.

LACK OF EXPERIMENTAL CONTROL.   Experiments in the lab have greater control of the conditions than exists in Web studies. To understand this point, imagine giving an exam to a class of students either in the classroom or via the Web. Suppose the exam is supposed to be done without reference to notes or books and without help from others. The classroom version could use monitors to make sure that these rules were followed.

In the online version, the instructor would not have the same control. The instructor giving the exam could ask the students if they referred to books or got help from others. However, the answers to such questions might not be accurate. Thus, the instructor would never know for sure if the students had followed the instructions.

There is probably less motivation to "cheat" in a Web study by violating rules than there would be in taking an exam for a grade. However, the lack of control of conditions should be clear from the analogy. The Web researcher can ask the participants to follow certain procedures, the researcher can ask the participant what procedures were followed, but the researcher cannot know with the same certainty as in the lab what the conditions were.

There are two types of effects in violations of control. One effect is random, which merely adds more "noise" to an experiment. The other type of effect would be a systematic bias produced by a lack of agreement between the researcher's intended procedure and what actually happened in the study.

Early Web researchers worried that such research topics as the probability problem in Chapter 5 and the logic problem in Chapter 7 might give very different results in the lab and on the Web. If people are at home, alone with their computers, they might take the time to construct a truth table for the logic problem, for example. The fact that the same types of results are obtained via the Web as are typically found in the lab suggest that in research domains studied so far, the lack of control in Web studies has not been crucial to results. The potential consequence of the lack of control provides the reason to follow the suggestion that you should also collect data in the controlled conditions of the lab.

 ## STEPS IN PLANNING YOUR RESEARCH

When designing a research study, you should consider each of the following steps.

STEP 1. WHAT ARE THE THEORIES?   What would *disprove* them? The first step in a psychological research project is to consider two or more rival theories of the same phenomenon. If you consider one theory to be plausible, ask yourself: What would disprove this theory? Think of tests that you can do that will decide which of two rival ideas is more plausible. Remember that disproof is a stronger form of evidence than finding data consistent with a particular idea.

This point cannot be emphasized too strongly. Too many studies are designed as follows:

> If bread is made of arsenic, and if everything made of arsenic is good to eat, then bread will be good to eat (those who eat it live). So, I plan to eat bread, and if I live, it will prove my theory.

The argument is fallacious. Eating bread does not prove that it is made of arsenic, nor would it prove that arsenic is good to eat. The fallacy of the argument is that one "proves" a theory by looking for evidence consistent with the theory. Instead, think of looking for implications of a theory in which the theory might fail. In this case, you should be able to imagine several tests that would disprove the above theory.

Many students set out to "prove" some notion by looking for evidence that might be consistent with it. Remember—they are like people eating bread to prove it is made of arsenic. This concept is probably the hardest lesson to teach in experimental science.

Remember the story of clever Hans, related in Chapter 1. The investigators in that study made manipulations that showed the conditions under which this clever horse could *not* get the answers right. From those experiments, it was learned that the horse could answer questions only if the audience knew the answer, and only when the horse could see the faces of the audience. Remember as well the logic problem of Chapter 7. People often fail to understand how to test a proposition such as *if A then B*. Scientific theories are exactly in that form: If the theory is true, then *X* should happen. In Chapter 7, people missed testing *not X*. The moral of this story: Learn the power of negative thinking. Design an experiment to disprove a theory.

STEP 2: HOW DO YOU PLAN TO ANALYZE THE DATA?   Before you prepare your experiment, plan your method of data analysis. Instructors of statistics dread the following question: "I have just finished a year-long study that was a great effort to complete. But I do not know how to analyze the data. Can you help me figure out how to analyze the data I just collected?"

The answer to the question is: "If you did not know how you were going to analyze the data when you designed the study, you should probably throw your data away and start over. Unless you planned your analysis, the odds are that your experiment and its data are worthless." There may be an exception to this unfortunate problem; perhaps there was someone, somewhere, once upon a time who did not know how he or she would analyze the data and yet designed a good experiment, but I have not yet heard of one such instance in 30 years.

Students sometimes think that first you do the study, then you figure out how to analyze the data. Nothing could be more wrong. The statistical analysis is a plan to answer the question of the study. Unless you know *how* your data will answer your research question, then you have no business collecting data and wasting everyone's time.

STEP 3: PLAN THE STUDY'S DESIGN.   Plan the design of the study, being careful to make sure that you have a chance to disprove a theory. What is known about the phenomenon that you are planning to study? What do previous experiments show? What do theories predict?

In my area of research—decision making—I can use calculators to compute what should happen on the basis of previous models and parameters published in the literature. Check to see that rival theories make different predictions for the experiment before collecting the data.

STEP 4. PLAN THE INSTRUCTIONS, MATERIALS, AND ETHICAL REVIEW OF THE STUDY.   Studies should not put people's lives, health, property, or reputations at risk. If your study is a typical, harmless, psychology study, the ethical review should be easy. However, it is a good idea to be even more careful in materials you plan to put on the Web than for use in the lab because those materials may be viewed by people all over the world who have different ideas of what is insulting, annoying, or upsetting. In his suggestions for student researchers, Paul Kenyon URL [http://salmon.psy.plym.ac.uk/mscprm/forms.htm] suggests that you think of yourself as lost in an inner city in a foreign nation where you stop in a bar to ask for directions, and you realize that everyone knows each other but not you. Adopt that attitude when you plan your Web experiments.

STEP 5: PILOT TEST YOUR MATERIALS WITH A FEW FRIENDS.   Run your experiment with a few friends and have them tell you where the instructions were not clear. It is better if your friends are not in your field of study, as they will raise more questions with your instructions. Analyze the data from the pilot tests to make sure that you know how you will analyze the data, but do not expect to find decisive results with a small sample.

STEP 6: PUT YOUR MATERIALS ON THE WEB, BUT DO NOT PUBLICIZE IT UNTIL YOU CONDUCT SOME ADDITIONAL PILOT TESTS. Participate as a subject yourself. Check that the data are being sent to the file properly. Participate a second time yourself, this time responding with the stimuli, and make sure that the data return to the file in the proper order. Check out your experiment with different types of computers and different browsers. Correct any errors in the experimental material that you find. Next, conduct a local pilot test with several volunteers. Again, check the data and make sure that your method of analysis works.

Make sure that your study satisfies the ethical review. Will the knowledge gained be worth the time and effort that you and others put in to do this study? Ethics are discussed in greater detail in the next section.

STEP 7: PUBLICIZE YOUR STUDY. Who do you want to serve as participants in your study? Your method of recruitment determines the type of sample that you obtain. The Web is probably a good place to seek rare and unusual participants. For example, you could probably do well recruiting on the Internet if you needed mothers of triplets, transvestites, or another type of special participant. By searching the Web for your participant's interests, you can develop ideas of how to recruit them to your study. The second question to ask yourself is, Why do they want to help you? This step will also be the topic of a separate section.

 ## ETHICAL REVIEW

The purpose of an ethical review is to find out if the likely potential benefits of the research outweigh the risks and costs of the research. Medical research that risks the lives of patients must have the potential benefit of saving lives. Research that might bore some people for a period of time should have a benefit that outweighs the cost of that boredom.

Why do people agree to participate in your study? In most cases in psychology, they do so to get extra credit in a lower division psychology class. On the Internet, people participate if they believe that some benefit accrues to you, to themselves, or to science. People are willing to complete questionnaires just for the sake of helping others learn more.

It is unethical to promise something to people in order to gain their agreement to participate and then fail to fulfill your promise. Such a failure is a type of fraud. For example, if you promise to pay people to participate, then you must uphold your end of the bargain and pay them. If you promise to offer people a chance to win a prize, then you must carry out the contests honestly. You should have a neutral witness oversee the operation to be able to certify that the procedures were followed correctly.

If you get people to participate in order to help you complete your experiment, then you should be certain to do good research and complete your experiment. If you promise to calculate a test score and give people information about themselves, then you should make sure that people get the feedback they were promised. If you offer to post your results to the Web and contact the participants, then you should do that.

Most people feel that the same standards of ethics should apply to Web research as to laboratory research. However, Web researchers have additional concerns about ethical principles. Web researchers are particularly sensitive to any studies involving deception that involves posting lies on the Web. You should be careful to avoid doing any study that would risk making people wary of studies on the Web. That would give psychology and the behavioral sciences a bad reputation and cause a number of angry people to come looking for you.

On the Web, it is easy to copy the work of others. There is a tradition of posting materials to the Web in order to share ideas with people and make "gifts" to the world. People like to post information that they think will be interesting, entertaining, or educational for the benefit or amusement of others. The tradition of sharing, however, does not mean that you can freely copy the work of others and use it as if it were your own.

For example, people post research papers to the Web before they are published so that other researchers in their field can learn of their results and theories as soon as possible. However, if you were to copy that work and present it as if it were your own, you would be violating ethical principles and probably violating the law as well. Certainly, if you were to attempt to publish that work as your own or submit it as a class assignment, you would run the risk of severe penalties for academic dishonesty and fraud.

If you find something useful on the Web, you can ask the author and copyright holder if you can have permission to use their photograph, table, program, or image. Some Web sites contain announcements telling what you can do and cannot do with material available in their sites. For example, some people allow you to use their material if you identify their work and ideas and give appropriate credit in the same way you would when citing a published article in the list of references. You can consider that material on the Web is "published," and treat it as you would any other printed work.

Consider when you place an experiment or a file on the Web that millions of people have access to it. Therefore, you should avoid posting anything there that you would hate to see others "steal." You should also not post anything of your own or anyone else that is personal and private. The U.S. House of Representatives set a bad standard by posting to the Web testimony obtained without cross-examination before a grand jury in the case of the Clinton/Lewinsky scandal. Because the proceedings of a grand jury are private by law, that is the kind of material that psychologists would consider unethical to post. Can you imagine a clinical psychologist posting the secrets of clients on the Web? Such behavior would lead to losing the license to practice and expulsion from the American Psychological Association (APA). It would also open the person to civil lawsuits claiming damage. The ethical standards of the APA are available online and are linked in the examples to this chapter [http://www.apa.org/ethics/].

King (1996) discusses research on online communities in which some people were very unhappy with how their Internet communications were reported by researchers. The issues raised in that article should be considered by those planning to do such research.

The Internet makes a person's actions more powerful, for either good or bad. An indiscretion in former days might have resulted in a few people being hurt or offended. On the Internet, you can offend millions. So be careful.

The good side of the issue is that science is becoming more open and transparent. By posting experimental methods and (anonymous) data on the Web, more researchers can gain access to data and to methods more quickly than was possible with print media. This enables science to progress more rapidly.

METHODS FOR ADVERTISING A WEB STUDY

USE A DESCRIPTIVE TITLE FOR YOUR EXPERIMENT AS THE TITLE FOR YOUR WEB PAGE.   If your experiment's title is "experiment" or "home page," it will not give anyone enough information to know by title if they want to visit that file. The title of the document is not only displayed at the top of the page in the browser, it is also sent to search engines that list search results. Suppose you conducted a search for "reaction time" and you got the following three entries. Which one would you click first?

Page 6
Experiment 2
Experiment on Choice Reaction Times

I think you would click the title that matched your key words.

USE META TAGS IN THE HEAD OF YOUR DOCUMENT TO DESCRIBE YOUR EXPERIMENT.   META tags go in the head of a document and help search engines determine the content of a page. Here is an example of the HEAD of a study on choice reaction times:

```
<HTML><HEAD>

<META NAME="keywords" CONTENT="Reaction time, decision making,
   experiment, science, research, psychology, CRT, choice response
   time">

<META NAME="description" CONTENT="Participate in a choice reaction
   time study. Takes 20 min. Participants will be given estimates of
   their decision time and reaction time">

<TITLE>Choice Reaction Time Experiment</TITLE>
</HEAD>
```

Note that these tags specify the time required and the potential benefit to the participants of getting feedback on their decision times.

YOU CAN PUBLICIZE YOUR EXPERIMENT BY EMAIL TO YOUR FRIENDS AND FAMILY, ASKING THEM TO ASK THEIR FRIENDS TO PARTICIPATE.   Such word of mouth may have a snowball effect, if your study is interesting and fun to experience. However, if it is boring, then this effort will likely end with your family.

YOU CAN SUBMIT YOUR SITE TO THE POPULAR SEARCH ENGINES.   Once a search engine has cataloged your site, then people who are looking for your topic will find its title as one of the results of their search. That may draw some people to your site. A study of sexual behavior (Bailey, Foote, & Throckmorton, 2000) was advertised only by search engine and has been filled out by more than 10,000 people since 1995, despite the fact that the questionnaire is quite long (more than 400 items). Perhaps there are a lot of people looking for sex on the Internet.

There are services that enable you to suggest your page to several search engines at once. For example, Submit-it can be reached from URL[http://www.submit-it.com].

YOU CAN ADVERTISE BY CONVENTIONAL MEANS.   You can put up posters on your campus, use flyers, and make announcements to classmates in other classes. If your study requires only a small sample, you might use the Internet as a data collection/entry device and strictly use the conventional "subject pool" to recruit subjects, and test them in conventional, computer-equipped laboratories. You might also offer the participants the opportunity of serving in the computer lab or of completing the experiment from home.

YOU MIGHT GET AN ORGANIZATION TO POST AN ANNOUNCEMENT ON THEIR WEB SITE.   If your research deals with a special population and if the research might potentially have benefits for that population, you might be able to get relevant organizations (that deal with your population) to post an announcement in the organization's Web site. If the special population has an email list, and if a member of your population vouches for your research, that person might be willing to send an email or post to an electronic bulletin board information about your study. An announcement by a member of a relevant Usenet newsgroup might also be appropriate. As Schmidt (1997a) notes, there is strong disapprobation of "spamm" or electronic junk mail. If you send or post messages unrelated to the newsgroup's interest, your spamm might provoke hostile responses, or *flames,* from members. That consequence would backfire by making people hostile to your study, and you will lose time and reputation apologizing for the spamm. See Hewson, Laurent, and Vogel (1996) for other suggestions for recruitment.

You must be careful not to advertise on the Web in a way that might provoke flames or compromise privacy. For example, suppose you were to obtain a list of people who belong to a club for persons with an unusual and socially unaccepted sexual paraphilia. If you sent them all an email request to participate, in which everyone's address was in the header of the email, then you should not be surprised when a number of angry and hostile people come looking for you. Everyone on that list would see that their names were sent to many other people.

You would do better to ask a member of the club to forward your message, or to post your message to the club's bulletin board or Web page. People do not like "junk" mail in their email anyway, so be very careful of any idea for advertising your study that resembles a chain letter. If an organization sees that you are a serious, ethical, and responsible researcher, and if the members conclude that the information gained in your study may help to understand issues that are of importance to their organization, you may get a good deal of help.

You should be careful not to send long messages asking people to participate—people are annoyed by long email. Do not send attachments explaining your study. People hate to receive unsolicited attachments, even from people they know, because attachments can carry viruses. Attachments also clog up the email system and cause mailboxes to become full. If you are going to send email, keep it short and to the point. Include a link to any lengthy material, which you should place on the Web. On most mail utilities, a complete URL becomes a "hot" link that can be clicked to send the reader to your study or to any lengthy materials you want them to read. A sample email request might be as follows:

```
I am conducting a study of attitudes toward driving. If you drive a
car, you can help my research. The questionnaire can be taken online
and takes 5 minutes to complete. The study can be reached at URL
http://address.ext/document.htm. Results will be posted online by Jan.
1, 2001. Questions can be sent to Name, Address, Phone Number. Email:
mailto:user@address.domain.
```

Note that the example used two "hot" links: one for the Web address, and the other for email. Most people using mail utilities will be able to click these links to reach your study or to send you email. Note also that the example gave your name, address, and phone number. These should be your "work" address at a respectable university or research institution.

Many people on the Web are happy to be of help, if they think that your study will learn something. Many people are willing to help you for the sake of helping you out. You should live up to their expectation and do good work to deserve the effort they give to you.

 ## SUMMARY

This chapter presented advice to consider when planning and conducting Web research. Potential problems of discrepancy between lab and Web research, drop outs in between-subjects designs, multiple submissions, mischief, recruitment, and lack of control were discussed, along with suggestions for addressing these issues. A set of procedures was suggested for planning Web research. Investigators should be clear on the purpose of the research and how the data obtained will answer the question before data collection begins. Procedures for ensuring that the experiment is ready were suggested. The ethics review of research was discussed, along with some issues that are particularly sensitive to Web researchers. Deception and false information should be avoided at all cost, so that behavioral research will not acquire a bad reputation. Ask permission to use materials found on the Web and give proper credit. Methods for recruitment were discussed, including the idea that different ways of recruiting might produce interesting differences in the samples obtained.

 ## EXERCISES

1. List methods for handling multiple submissions.
2. Why are drop outs a problem in between-subjects research? What about drop outs in within-subjects research?
3. List some of the ways in which control is reduced in a Web experiment compared to a lab experiment. Do you think these variables would matter in your area of research?
4. Read the APA ethical guidelines. What are the key tenets of ethical behavior in research?
5. List methods for recruiting participants to a Web study. Do you think that people recruited by different methods would give different results in your research area?
6. Project idea: Ask scientists to judge the potential risks and benefits of research in your area of research. To establish a context, your judgments of risk can include everyday risks such as *driving a car in the city for 1 hour, eating at a fast food restaurant,* and so on. For example, which activity is more likely to lead to accidental death: *serving 1 hour in a reaction time experiment* or *driving 1 hour in the city?*

Appendix A

CREATING AND USING SCRIPTS

This appendix explains how to use PolyForm to create scripts for online research. This material is important to those who run their own Web server and instructors who may be setting up scripts for a student lab. A script in Perl that can be used to substitute for the PolyForm scripts used in this book is also included on the CD that accompanies this book.

REVIEW

As you saw in Chapter 5, if your FORM tag specifies ACTION="mailto:user@address. domain", then the data will be sent to you as email. However, if the ACTION=URL specifies the address of a CGI script, then the script can process the data and put them in a file on a server.

Two scripts that you can use in association with this book are at the following URLs:

http://psych.fullerton.edu/cgi-win/polyform.exe/generic

http://psych.fullerton.edu/cgi-win/polyform.exe/generic2

These two scripts send the data to the files *data.csv* and *data2.csv,* respectively, which you can retrieve by ftp, as described in Chapter 2.

However, if you want to save data on your *own* server, you will need scripts on your server. You will want your own scripts, especially if you plan to collect sensitive data or any data that are not anonymous. If you are the instructor in a research methods lab, you may want to provide a set of scripts so that each student can have her or his own script, sending each student's data to a separate file. Once created, these scripts can be used semester after semester.

The PERL script on the CD has the advantage that one script can create separate files for each project based on the first variable, 00exp, in the FORM. Thus, all students can use the same script and the data will still be sorted into separate files, as long as the students use different names for their experiments, which should be defined with the hidden variable named 00exp. If you install this one script on your server, you can use it in all of your classes. You should make the folder containing the data files available by FTP on a *read only* basis to avoid the problem that someone might accidentally erase important files just when everyone is collecting the last of their data.

POLYFORM

PolyForm is a program that makes scripts to do common tasks. It easily makes scripts that decode data from an experiment and send the data to a file in one of several formats.

You can try PolyForm for 30 days by downloading it from the URL

http://software.ora.com/download/

A step-by-step tutorial is available at the URL

http://polyform.ora.com/pf/wizard_frame.html

The PolyForm user's booklet is at the URL

http://www.unf.edu/~kmartin/polyform/STARTHERE.HTM

 ## HOW TO MAKE A SCRIPT WITH POLYFORM

PolyForm's control panel is shown in Figure A.1.

1. Click the *Wizard* icon (to the right of the little trash can) to start the *Script Wizard.* You see a welcome screen. Click *Next* on the welcome screen, and you will see the screen in Figure A.2.
2. Select *Blank Form* and click the *Next* button. That brings up the display shown in Figure A.3.
3. Click the button next to *Data,* which saves the data as comma-separated values (CSV), then click *Next.* (You have the option of a text file or as a CSV file. If you plan to use programs such as Excel or SPSS, it is best to save your data as CSV.) This brings up the screen in Figure A.4.
4. Click the button to send the user to this URL. Then enter the address of a Web page that gives the participant a thank-you message, any relevant debriefing, and a way to send you email comments. Click *Next,* and the screen in Figure A.5 appears.
5. You can ask for a copy of the data to be sent as email, as you can see in Figure A.5; however, I suggest that you do not check the email box, as you would soon be overwhelmed by email once your experiment gets going. Click *Next,* and you see the screen in Figure A.6.
6. You need to give the script a name. In the example in Figure A.6, the name is *generic2.* Clicking *Next* brings up the screen shown in Figure A.7, and it looks as if you are done. However, you must still tell

FIGURE A.1.   PolyForm Control Panel.

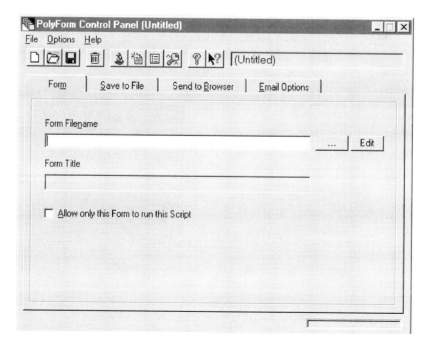

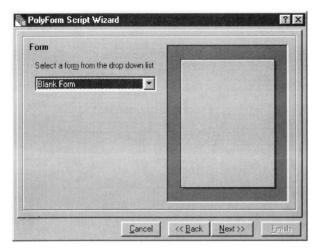

FIGURE A.2.
Select *Blank Form* in the Script Wizard from the pull-down menu.

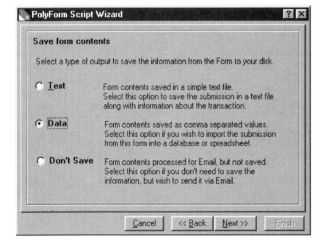

FIGURE A.3.
In PolyForm Script Wizard, select *Data*. Comma-separated data files can be easily imported to Excel and SPSS.

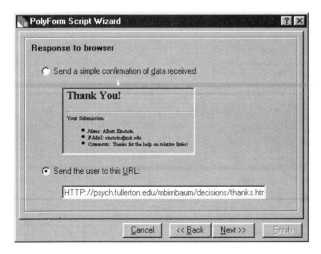

FIGURE A.4.
Send user to URL (this can send the user to a thank-you message or to a page with debriefing or on which other experiments are also available).

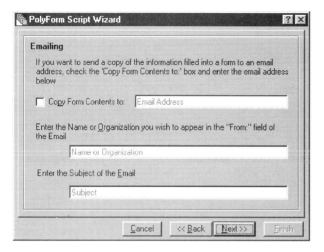

FIGURE A.5.
Script Wizard email options. (It is recommended that you do not send email.) Click *Next.*

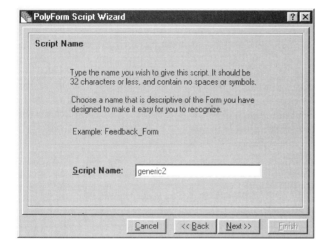

FIGURE A.6.
Give the script a name. In this case, the name is *generic2*. Click *Next.*

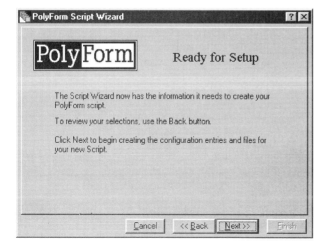

FIGURE A.7.
Even though this panel says that PolyForm has all the information, you still need to tell PolyForm where to put the data. This panel is a bit misleading.

PolyForm where to put the data. Click *Next*. You must create an empty file with the *.csv* extension (You can do that with NotePad.)

7. The PolyForm control panel (Figure A.8) shows the name of the form. As a security measure, you can click the box that says, *Allow only this Form to run this Script*. Clicking the box would prevent any other Web pages from being able to send their data to this script. In this case, however, the plan is to create a script that many people can use, so in this case the box is not checked. That means that data will be added to the same data file from different forms on many different computers. Click *Edit* button, and you see the HTML page, which opens in NotePad, as shown in Figure A.9.

8. The next step is to tell PolyForm where to put the data. Click the *Save to file* tab in the PolyForm control panel, which brings up the display in Figure A.10. Then click the (browse) button with the ... on it next to the pathname. That brings up Figure A.11. Double-clicking on the *decisions* folder brings up Figure A.12. Then the name of the new file is typed in and the *Open* button is clicked. That brings up the display of Figure A.13, asking if you want to create a new file. Click *Yes*, and the new file is created and put in place.

The data file must exist, even if it is empty, before the script is used. When everything is finished, the PolyForm control panel will appear with the information. Click on each tab to confirm the information. Click *Form* (check the name of the script), *Save to File* (check that you save as data and that the filename and location are correct), *Send to Browser* (check that the address of the URL of the thank-you message is correct), and *Email options* (none). Save your script by selecting *Save* from the **File** menu. Be sure to keep track of the address of your data file and the address of your script!

It really is not very difficult. As you see, PolyForm does not need to know how many variables you will have, what they are, or anything else. It must know where the data will go and where to send the user. You must know the URL of the script and where the data are going. You must supply the form (whose Action specifies the URL of the script) and you must create a blank file to hold the data.

FIGURE A.8. PolyForm Control Panel.

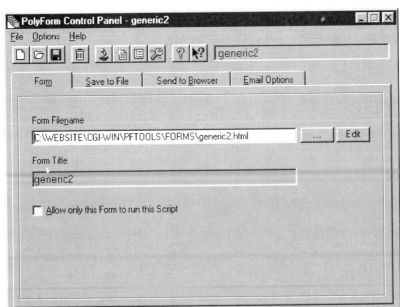

```
generic2.html - Notepad
File  Edit  Search  Help
<!DOCTYPE HTML PUBLIC "-//IETF//DTD HTML 3.0//EN" "html.dtd">
<HTML>
<HEAD>
<TITLE>generic2</TITLE>
</HEAD>
<BODY>
<H1></H1>

<FORM METHOD="POST" ACTION="http://psych.fullerton.edu/cgi-win/polyform.exe/generic2">

<!--Blank Form-->
</FORM>
</BODY>
</HTML>
```

FIGURE A.9. Here is the minimal form created. The only thing worth noting is the FORM tag and its ACTION URL.

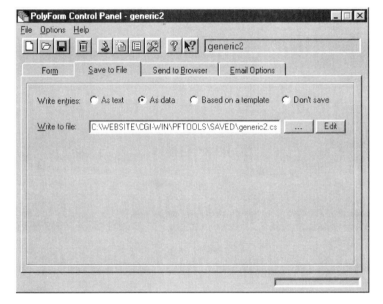

FIGURE A.10.
You must specify where to save the data. Here, the *Save to File* tab has been clicked and the path of the file specified by using the button with ...

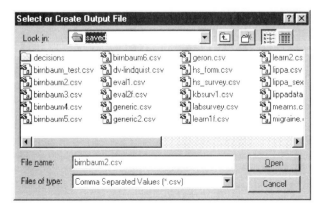

FIGURE A.11.
In this case, the file goes in the *decisions* folder, so double-click it. This is the folder to which FTP download access is permitted.

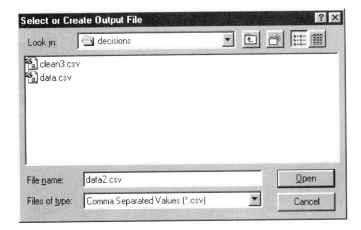

FIGURE A.12.
After opening the decisions folder, the filename *data2.csv* was typed in the filename line and the *Open* button was clicked.

 ## VARIABLES IN POLYFORM

The PolyForm program requires that each variable name is preceded by a number from 00 to 99, and these numbers should be sequential in the order you wish them to appear in the data file. These do *not* have to appear in sequence in the HTML file. For example, the first four variables might be specified as follows:

```
Email Address: <INPUT TYPE="text" NAME="03Email" SIZE=30>
<INPUT TYPE="hidden" NAME="00Exp" VALUE="Exp2b">
<INPUT TYPE="hidden" NAME="02Time" VALUE="pfTime">
<INPUT TYPE="hidden" NAME="01Date" VALUE="pfDate">
```

Note that in this example, the first three variables are hidden. Note also that the variable names are preceded by numbers that determine the order in the data file of the data values; they appear in the order, 00exp, 01date, 02time, 03email. These lines can be rearranged in any order in the Web page and they still produce the same data file.

PolyForm also supports the following environmental variables:

pfDate	(Date)
pfLongDate	(Long form of date)
pfTime	(Time)

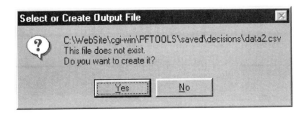

FIGURE A.13.
Clicking *Open* brings the following display. Click *Yes*. That creates an empty file that will soon contain data.

pf TransactionID	(Date-based number identifying the transaction)
pf RemoteHost	(if reverse DNS is enabled by server)
pf RemoteAddress	(IP)
pf ServerSoftware	(server software)
pf ServerAdmin	(formatted as mailto:email address)
pf Referer	(referring document, subject to browser support)
Pf DiscretePage	(filename of new document if script creates one)

When working with PolyForm, avoid using checkboxes, make sure that all radio buttons have a nonresponse value selected initially, and avoid the multiple option for select lists. These options of HTML create problems in PolyForm and would cause trouble in data analysis in any case, so they should be avoided.

 ## EXERCISES

1. Download PolyForm for a 30-day free trial. Install and run the program on your local NT server. Create a script that sends data to the file *prob_data.csv* on your local server. Change the probability experiment (*Ch5_exp3.htm*) to include the address of your script in the ACTION of the FORM statement. Use your browser to view the experiment, and complete it online. Open the data file in NotePad and see if your data were correctly recorded.

2. Try incorporating the PolyForm environmental variables into an experiment to see what you get with pf LongDate, pf RemoteHost, pf RemoteAddress, and pf Referer. Some of the PolyForm variables may not be supported on your local server and browsers.

    The file *Ch5_exp3b.htm* illustrates the use of hidden variables, textarea, and password, in addition to radio buttons, text box, and a pull-down selection list. The example also illustrates the use of a reset button, which clears the form. You can change the URL to that of a PolyForm script on your server to test which PolyForm variables are supported on your server.

3. Try rearranging the order of the questions in your HTML form (you can do this by cut and paste in NotePad), but keep the variable names (and the preceding numbers) the same. Check if the data arrive in the order of the preceding numbers or the order in the HTML form. You will see that the preceding numbers determine the order in the file. Therefore, you can create different orders of the items, but the data will all return in the same order.

4. Study the Perl scripts provided on the CD, linked from the page of examples. The main script emulates the PolyForm script. It supports pf Date, pf Time, pf Referer, and pf RemoteAddress, but not the other PolyForm variables. It also sends data to separate files, named after the value of the first variable, 00exp. The data will be saved with the extension *.data*, but they will also be CSV files.

    If your server does not support PolyForm, you can download and install Perl free from URL [http://www.perl.com/CPAN/], and install this script, following the instructions in the example on the CD.

References

Anastasi, A. (1982). *Psychological Testing* (fifth ed.). New York: Macmillan Publishing Co.

Anderson, N. H. (1962). "Application of an additive model to impression formation." *Science, 138,* 817–818.

Anderson, N. H. (1974). "Information integration theory: A brief survey." In D. H. Krantz, R. C. Atkinson, R. D. Luce, & P. Suppes (Eds.), *Contemporary developments in mathematical psychology* (pp. 236–305). San Francisco: W. H. Freeman.

Asch, S. E. (1946). "Forming impressions of personality." *Journal of Abnormal and Social Psychology, 41,* 258–290.

Bailey, R. D., Foote, W. E., & Throckmorton, B. (2000). "Human sexual behavior: A comparison of college and Internet surveys." In M. H. Birnbaum (Ed.), *Psychological experiments on the Internet* (pp. 141–168). San Diego: Academic Press.

Baron, J., & Siepmann, M. (2000). "Techniques for creating and using Web questionnaires in research and teaching." In M. H. Birnbaum (Ed.), *Psychological experiments on the Internet* (pp. 235–265). San Diego: Academic Press.

Bernoulli, D. (1738). "Specimen theoriae novae de mensura sortis." *Commentarii Academiae Scientiarum Imperialis Petropoliannae, 5,* 175–192.

Bernoulli, D. (1954). "Exposition of a new theory on the measurement of risk." *Econometrica, 22,* 23–36. (1738 paper translated to English.)

Birnbaum, M. H. (1974a). "The nonadditivity of personality impressions." *Journal of Experimental Psychology, 102,* 543–561.

Birnbaum, M. H. (1974b). "Using contextual effects to derive psychophysical scales." *Perception & Psychophysics, 15,* 89–96.

Birnbaum, M. H. (1978). "Differences and ratios in psychological measurement." In N. J. Castellan & F. Restle (Eds.), *Cognitive Theory, Vol. 3* (pp. 33–74). Hillsdale, NJ: Lawrence Erlbaum Associates.

Birnbaum, M. H. (1980). "Comparison of two theories of 'ratio' and 'difference' judgments." *Journal of Experimental Psychology: General, 109,* 304–319.

Birnbaum, M. H. (1982). "Controversies in psychological measurement." In B. Wegener (Eds.), *Social attitudes and psychophysical measurement* (pp. 401–485). Hillsdale, NJ: Lawrence Erlbaum Associates.

Birnbaum, M. H. (1983). "Base rates in Bayesian inference: Signal detection analysis of the cab problem." *American Journal of Psychology, 96,* 85–94.

Birnbaum, M. H. (1999a). "How to show that $9 > 221$: Collect judgments in a between-subjects design." *Psychological Methods, 4,* 243–249.

Birnbaum, M. H. (1999b). "Paradoxes of Allais, stochastic dominance, and decision weights." In J. Shanteau, B. A. Mellers, & D. A. Schum (Eds.), *Decision science and technology: Reflections on the contributions of Ward Edwards* (pp. 27–52). Norwell, MA: Kluwer Academic Publishers.

Birnbaum, M. H. (1999c). "Testing critical properties of decision making on the Internet." *Psychological Science, 10,* 399–407.

Birnbaum, M. H. (2000a). "Decision making in the lab and on the Web." In M. H. Birnbaum (Ed.), *Psychological experiments on the Internet* (pp. 3–34). San Diego: Academic Press.

Birnbaum, M. H. (Ed.). (2000b). *Psychological experiments on the Internet.* San Diego: Academic Press.

Birnbaum, M. H. (2000c). "SurveyWiz and FactorWiz: JavaScript Web pages that make HTML forms for research on the Internet." *Behavior Research Methods, Instruments & Computers, 32*(2), in press.

Birnbaum, M. H., & Elmasian, R. (1977). "Loudness ratios and differences involve the same psychophysical operation." *Perception & Psychophysics, 22,* 383–391.

Birnbaum, M. H., & Jou, J. W. (1990). "A theory of comparative response times and 'difference' judgments." *Cognitive Psychology, 22,* 184–210.

Birnbaum, M. H., & Mellers, B. A. (1983). "Bayesian inference: Combining base rates with opinions of sources who vary in credibility." *Journal of Personality and Social Psychology, 45,* 792–804.

Birnbaum, M. H., & Navarrete, J. B. (1998). "Testing descriptive utility theories: Violations of stochastic dominance and cumulative independence." *Journal of Risk and Uncertainty, 17,* 49–78.

Birnbaum, M. H., & Sotoodeh, Y. (1991). "Measurement of stress: Scaling the magnitudes of life changes." *Psychological Science, 2,* 236–243.

Birnbaum, M. H., & Stegner, S. E. (1979). "Source credibility in social judgment: Bias, expertise, and the judge's point of view." *Journal of Personality and Social Psychology, 37,* 48–74.

Bordia, P. (1996). "Studying verbal interaction on the Internet: The case of rumor transmission research." *Behavior Research Methods, Instruments, & Computers, 28*, 149–151.

Bower, G. H. (1961). "Application of a model to paired associate learning." *Psychometrika, 26*, 255–280.

Bower, G. (1994). A turning point in mathematical learning theory. *Psychological Review, 101*, 290–300.

Buchanan, T. (2000). "Potential of the Internet for personality research." In M. H. Birnbaum (Ed.), *Psychological experiments on the Internet* (pp. 121–140). San Diego: Academic Press.

Buchanan, T., & Smith, J. L. (1999). "Using the Internet for psychological research: Personality testing on the World-Wide Web." *British Journal of Psychology, 90*, 125–144.

Cartwright, D., & Harary, F. (1956). "Structural balance: A generalization of Heider's theory." *Psychological Review, 63*, 277– 293.

Chen, B., Wang, H., Proctor, R. W., & Salvendy, G. (1997). "A human-centered approach for designing World-Wide Web browsers." *Behavior Research Methods, Instruments, & Computers, 29*, 172–179.

Cliff, N. (1954). "Adverbs as multipliers." *Psychological Review, 66*, 27–44.

Dawes, R. (1994). "Psychological measurement." *Psychological Review, 101*, 278–281.

Edwards, W. (1968). "Conservatism in human information processing." In B. Kleinmuntz (Ed.), *Formal representation of human judgment* (pp. 17–52). New York: Wiley.

Estes, W. K. (1950). "Toward a statistical theory of learning." *Psychological Review, 57*, 94–107 (Reprinted 1994, *101*, 282–289).

Francis, G., Neath, I., & Surprenant, A. M. (2000). "The cognitive psychology online laboratory." In M. H. Birnbaum (Ed.), *Psychological experiments on the Internet* (pp. 267–283). San Diego: Academic Press.

Gigerenzer, G., & Hoffrage, U. (1995). "How to improve Bayesian reasoning without instruction: Frequency format." *Psychological Review, 102*, 684–704.

Hardin, C., & Birnbaum, M. H. (1990). "Malleability of 'ratio' judgments of occupational prestige." *American Journal of Psychology, 103*, 1–20.

Heider, F. (1946). "Attitudes and cognitive organization." *Journal of Psychology, 21*, 107–112.

Hewson, C. M., Laurent, D., & Vogel, C. M. (1996). "Proper methodologies for psychological and sociological studies conducted via the Internet." *Behavior Research Methods, Instruments, & Computers, 28*, 186–191.

Kahneman, D., & Tversky, A. (1973). "On the psychology of prediction." *Psychological Review, 80*, 237–251.

Kahneman, D., Slovic, P., & Tversky, A. (Eds.). (1982). *Judgment under uncertainty: Heuristics and biases.* New York: Cambridge University Press.

King, S. A. (1996). "Researching Internet communities: Proposed ethical guidelines for the reporting of the results." *The Information Society, 12*(2), 119–127.

Kintsch, W., & Cacioppo, J. T. (1994). "Introduction to the 100th anniversary issue of the *Psychological Review.*" *Psychological Review, 101*, 195–199.

Koehler, J. J. (1996). "The base-rate fallacy reconsidered: Descriptive, normative, and methodological challenges." *Behavioral and Brain Sciences, 19*, 1–53.

Krantz, J. H., Ballard, J., & Scher, J. (1997). "Comparing the results of laboratory and World-Wide Web samples on the determinants of female attractiveness." *Behavior Research Methods, Instruments, & Computers, 29*, 264–269.

Krantz, J. H., & Dalal, R. (2000). "Validity of Web-based psychological research." In M. H. Birnbaum (Ed.), *Psychological experiments on the Internet* (pp. 35–60). San Diego: Academic Press.

Lange, M. (1999). "Museum of perception and cognition Website: Using JavaScript to increase interactivity in Web-based presentations." *Behavior Research Methods, Instruments, & Computers, 31*, 34–45.

Luce, R. D. (1994). "Thurstone and sensory scaling: Then and now." *Psychological Review, 101*, 271–277.

Luce, R. D., & Fishburn, P. C. (1991). "Rank- and sign-dependent linear utility models for finite first order gambles." *Journal of Risk and Uncertainty, 4*, 29–59.

Luce, R. D., & Fishburn, P. C. (1995). "A note on deriving rank-dependent utility using additive joint receipts." *Journal of Risk and Uncertainty, 11*, 5–16.

Massaro, D. W., & Stork, D. G. (1998). Speech recognition and sensory integration. *American Scientist, 86*, 236–244.

McGraw, K. O., Tew, M. D., & Williams, J. E. (2000). "PsychExps: An on-line psychology laboratory." In M. H. Birnbaum (Ed.), *Psychological experiments on the Internet* (pp. 219–233). San Diego: Academic Press.

Morrow, R. H., & McKee, A. J. (1998). "CGI scripts: A strategy for between-subjects experimental group assignment on the World-Wide Web." *Behavior Research Methods, Instruments, & Computers, 30*(2), 306–308.

Mellers, B. A., Davis, D., & Birnbaum, M. H. (1984). "Weight of evidence supports one operation for 'ratios' and 'differences' of heaviness." *Journal of Experimental Psychology: Human Perception and Performance, 10,* 216–230.

Mueller, J. H., Jacobsen, D. M., & Schwarzer, R. (2000). "What are computing experiences good for: A case study in on-line research." In M. H. Birnbaum (Ed.), *Psychological experiments on the Internet* (pp. 195–216). San Diego: Academic Press.

Musch, J., & Reips, U.-D. (2000). "A brief history of Web experimenting." In M. H. Birnbaum (Ed.), *Psychological experiments on the Internet* (pp. 61–87). San Diego: Academic Press.

Novemsky, N., & Kronzon, S. (1999). "How are base-rates used, when they are used: A comparison of additive and Bayesian models of base-rate use." *Journal of Behavioral Decision Making, 12,* 55–69.

Nunnally, J. C. (1978). *Psychometric theory* (second ed.). New York: McGraw-Hill Book Company.

Pagani, D., & Lombardi, L. (2000). "An intercultural examination of facial features communicating surprise." In M. H. Birnbaum (Ed.), *Psychological experiments on the Internet* (pp. 169–194). San Diego: Academic Press.

Parducci, A. (1968). "The relativism of absolute judgment." *Scientific American, 219,* 84–90.

Parducci, A. (1995). *Happiness, pleasure, and judgment.* Mahwah, NJ: Lawrence Erlbaum Associates.

Pasveer, K. A., & Ellard, J. H. (1998). "The making of a personality inventory: Help from the WWW." *Behavior Research Methods, Instruments, & Computers, 30,* 309–313.

Pettit, F. A. (1999). "Exploring the use of the World Wide Web as a psychology data collection tool." *Computers in Human Behavior, 15,* 67–71.

Piper, A. I. (1998). "Conducting social science laboratory experiments on the World Wide Web." *Library & Information Science Research, 20,* 5–21.

Reips, U.-D. (2000). "The Web experiment method: Advantages, disadvantages, and solutions." In M. H. Birnbaum (Ed.), *Psychological experiments on the Internet* (pp. 89–117). San Diego: Academic Press.

Schmidt, W. C. (1997a). "World-Wide Web survey research: Benefits, potential problems, and solutions." *Behavioral Research Methods, Instruments, & Computers, 29,* 274–279.

Schmidt, W. C. (1997b). "World-Wide Web survey research made easy with WWW Survey Assistant." *Behavior Research Methods, Instruments & Computers, 29,* 303–304.

Schmidt, W. C. (2000). "The server-side of psychology Web experiments." In M. H. Birnbaum (Ed.), *Psychological experiments on the Internet* (pp. 285–310). San Diego: Academic Press.

Schmidt, W. C., Hoffman, R., & MacDonald, J. (1997). "Operate your own World-Wide Web server." *Behavior Research Methods, Instruments & Computers, 29,* 189–193.

Schiano, D. J. (1997). "Convergent methodologies in cyber-psychology: A case study." *Behavior Research Methods, Instruments, & Computers, 29,* 270–273.

Schillewaert, N., Langerak, F., & Duhamel, T. (1998). "Non-probability sampling for WWW surveys: A comparison of methods." *Journal of the Market Research Society, 40,* 307–322.

Schwartz, A. (1998). "PERL, a psychologically efficient reformatting language." *Behavior Research Methods, Instruments, & Computers, 30,* 605–609.

Schwarz, N. (1999). "Self-reports: How the questions shape the answers." *American Psychologist, 54*(2), 93–105.

Shanteau, J. (1975a). "Averaging versus multiplying combination rules of inference judgment." *Acta Psychologica, 39,* 83–89.

Shanteau, J. (1975b). "Information integration analysis of risky decision making." In M. Kaplan & S. Schwartz (Eds.), *Human judgment and decision processes* (pp. 109–137). New York: Academic Press.

Smith, M. A., & Leigh, B. (1997). "Virtual subjects: Using the Internet as an alternative source of subjects and research environment." *Behavior Research Methods, Instruments, & Computers, 29,* 496–505.

Stagner, R. (1958). "The gullibility of personnel managers." *Personnel Psychology, 11,* 347–352.

Stanton, J. M. (1998). "An empirical assessment of data collection using the Internet." *Personnel Psychology, 51,* 709–725.

Stern, S. E., & Faber, J. E. (1997). "The lost e-mail method: Milgram's lost-letter technique in the age of the Internet." *Behavior Research Methods, Instruments, & Computers, 29,* 260–263.

Stevens, S. S. (1957). "On the psychophysical law." *Psychological Review, 64,* 153–181.

Stevenson, A. K., Francis, G., & Kim, H. (1999). "Java experiments for introductory cognitive psychology courses." *Behavior Research Methods, Instruments, & Computers, 31,* 99–106.

Thurstone, L. L. (1927). "A law of comparative judgment." *Psychological Review, 34,* 273–286 (Reprinted 1994, *101,* 266–270).

Thurstone, L. L. (1929). "Fechner's law and the method of equal appearing intervals." *Journal of Experimental Psychology, 12,* 214–224.

Torgerson, W. S. (1961). "Distances and ratios in psychological scaling." *Acta Psychologica, 19,* 201–205.

Troutman, C. M., & Shanteau, J. (1977). "Inferences based on nondiagnostic information." *Organizational Behavior and Human Performance, 19*, 43–55.

Tversky, A., & Kahneman, D. (1982). "Evidential impact of base rates." In D. Kahneman, P. Slovic, & A. Tversky (Eds.), *Judgment under uncertainty: Heuristics and biases.* New York: Cambridge University Press.

Tversky, A., & Kahneman, D. (1992). "Advances in prospect theory: Cumulative representation of uncertainty." *Journal of Risk and Uncertainty, 5*, 297–323.

Wallsten, T. (1972). "Conjoint-measurement framework for the study of probabilistic information processing." *Psychological Review, 79*, 245–260.

Wason, P. C. (1960). "On the failure to eliminate hypotheses in a conceptual task." *Quarterly Journal of Experimental Psychology, 12*, 129–140.

Wason, P. C. & Johnson-Laird, P. N. (1972). *Psychology of reasoning: Structure and content.* Cambridge: Harvard University Press.

Welch, N., & Krantz, J. H. (1996). "The world-wide Web as a medium for psychoacoustical demonstrations and experiments: Experience and results." *Behavior Research Methods, Instruments, & Computers, 28*, 192–196.

Williams, J. E., McGraw, K. O., & Tew, M. D. (1999). "Undergraduate labs and computers: The case for PsychExps." *Behavioral Research Methods, Instruments, and Computers, 31*(2), 287–291.

Yates, F. (1990). *Judgment and decision making.* Englewood Cliffs, NJ: Prentice Hall.

Glossary of Web Terms

Anchor. The text or graphic that is linked by Hyperlink to another document or another point in the same document. `<A></A>`

ASCII. American Standard Code for Information Interchange. Plain text, consisting of letters, numbers, and symbols of a typewriter. ASCII also provides a numeric code for these characters onto the numbers 0 to 127.

BBS. Bulletin Board System. Software on a remote computer usually accessed by modem, which allows users to download files and read and post messages in asynchronous "conferences."

Bit. Binary digit. Takes values of 0 or 1. Eight bits is a byte.

Browser. A program that allows one to view, or "browse," files on the Web. Examples: Netscape Navigator, Internet Explorer.

Caching Proxy Server. A Proxy Server that keeps copies of Web pages locally so that if it receives a URL request for a page of which it has a copy, it can quickly return the page without having to contact the Internet. Caching proxy servers decrease the amount of Web traffic from an ISP and often respond more quickly than fetching the Web page over the Internet.

CD-ROM. Compact Disk-Read Only Memory. An optical disk that can be used to store information. A CD-ROM cannot be rewritten; the more general term, CD, includes CD-ROM and CD-R, which can be rewritten.

CGI. Common Gateway Interface. Protocol by which information is encoded on the user's computer to be sent to the server computer.

CGI Script or Program. Common Gateway Interface Program. Any program that accepts information in CGI format. Common applications for CGI programs are to store user data, process them, and return a dynamic reply.

Chat Room. Similar to an IRC channel, it allows users to "chat" in real time. These are usually conducted via the WWW.

Client. Any application that is used to request information from a server (e.g., a Web browser, FTP program, custom written application). Can also refer to the user of the program.

Code. Short for instructions to a computer written in a programming, scripting, markup, or machine language. Source code is distinguished from machine code and is understandable to a trained human. In this book, the page source refers to a document containing HTML and JavaScript.

Configuration. Generic term that refers to how the components of a computer are set up. May refer to software or hardware.

Cookie. The server can instruct a cookie-enabled Web browser to store information as a file on the client's computer. This file is called a *cookie* and is sent by the client to the server with all subsequent requests, even requests made months later. By modifying a cookie's contents, the Web server can save information on the client for future use.

DNS. Domain Naming System or Service. Domain names are easier to remember, but the Internet is really based on IP addresses. DNS converts domain names, like decision.fullerton.edu, into IP addresses, like 137.151.78.143. If one DNS server does not know a particular domain translation, it asks another one until the correct IP address is returned.

Document. Refers to any file containing text, Hyperlinks, media, etc.

Document Window.   Web browser's window in which HTML documents are viewed.

Domain.   All computers similarly named on the Internet share a common organization referred to as their *domain*. For instance, all computers ending in *.com* share a domain, as do those ending in *.edu*.

Download.   Transfer a copy of a file residing on another computer to your local computer.

FAQ.   Frequently Asked Questions. Read the FAQ file before you ask one.

Flame.   A hostile or abusive message or response.

Form.   HTML tag that allows two-way communication between user and Web pages. It supports text boxes, radio buttons, etc. Forms can be used to send information between client and server, and they can also be used to send information from a client to an email address.

FTF.   Face to Face. Abbreviation used in electronic discussions.

FTP.   File Transfer Protocol. Method for sending files from one computer to another.

GIF.   Graphic Interchange Format. This format can be used for graphics and animations. It is also a good format for pictures with few colors; e.g., Image1.gif.

GUI.   Graphical User Interface. As found in most modern operating systems and applications. In contrast to textual interfaces such as DOS.

Home Page.   Main page of entry, either on your local computer or when entering a Web site.

Host.   A computer acting as server (e.g., via FTP or HTTP).

Hypertext.   Refers to linkages that allow you to view other documents or portions of a document by clicking selected text, instead of viewing in serial order.

HTML.   HyperText Markup Language. A tag-based language used to create Web pages. Links put the hyper in hypertext.

HTTP.   HyperText Transfer Protocol. The protocol used by WWW to send files between a server computer and the client's browser.

Internet.   Network of computers that exchange files by HTTP, FTP, email, and other protocols. WWW is part of the Internet.

IP Address.   Internet Protocol Address. A unique numeric address assigned to each computer or node on the Internet; e.g., 137.151.78.143.

IRC.   Internet Relay Chat. Network allowing users to "chat" in real-time, in groups known as "channels."

ISP.   Internet Service Provider. A company that provides access to the Internet.

Java.   Programming language supported by most browsers. An object-oriented language that is platform independent and implemented within Web browsers. Java programs can be served to run on Web clients. Java programs are compiled by the author and delivered via the Web, where they are (theoretically) interpreted equally by different browsers on different computer platforms.

JavaScript.   Scripting language, similar to but distinct from Java, usually delivered as source code included in Web pages, and interpreted by the browser. JavaScript allows for greater flexibility in the presentation and processing of data on the client computer.

JPEG.   Joint Photographic Experts Group file format. A format for color pictures that works well with photographs; e.g., picture1.jpg.

Link.   link is a connection between two documents or two parts of a document. In a typical link, a user can click on some text or graphic, causing the browser to display another document that pertains to the linked text or graphic.

MIME.   Multipurpose Internet Mail Extensions. Messaging standard for sending graphics, voice, and multimedia files via email or the Web.

MOO.   Mud, Object Oriented. A type of MUD.

MUD.   Multi-User Domain (or Dungeon). Classically a text-based fantasy adventure game that many users can play simultaneously, interacting in a "virtual world."

NCSA.   National Center for Supercomputing Applications at the University of Illinois, Urbana–Champaign. The first graphical browser, Mosaic, (forerunner of Navigator) was developed there.

Netiquette.   Net etiquette. Normative online behavior generally accepted by most users as proper.

Newsgroup.   Collection of Usenet articles related to a specific topic (indicated by the name of the newsgroup). Newsgroups are organized in hierarchies and follow set naming conventions; e.g., sci.psychology.research is a group in the "Science" hierarchy dedicated to discussion of psychology research.

NFS.   Network File System.

Node.   Device attached to a network. Nodes have addresses.

Page.   A document on the Web is called a *Web page*.

PERL.   Practical Extraction and Report Language. A popular, free computer language for implementing CGI programs. PERL is flexible and specializes in the ability to manipulate alpha-numeric string information easily.

POP.   Point of Presence. POP is ISP's location for connecting users, where people dial in to the host computer.

PPP.   Point to Point Protocol. Internet connection via modem and phone lines.

Proxy Server.   A server situated between a client (e.g., Web browser) and other servers. It intercepts requests to other servers and takes action based on those requests, such as logging the request or contacting the target server itself and relaying the information back to the client.

Search Engine.   A program available on the Web that searches the Web for documents pertaining to terms entered in the search. Well-known search engines include Yahoo, AltaVista, HotBot.

Server.   A computer that serves (sends) files to clients, usually by FTP, HTTP, or email.

Shareware.   Software that is freely available, but users who find the software useful or valuable are asked to send in a small fee. Payments are on the honor system, and you should support the developers by sending them the payment, if you keep and use the program.

Spamm.   Unsolicited email—essentially, computer junk mail.

Source, or Page Source.   See *Code.*

SSI.   Server-Side Include. HTML directive that instructs the Web server to dynamically substitute information where the directive occurs.

Tag.   A command or instruction in HTML. For example, `<B> </B>` are tags that cause text printed between them to be displayed as **bold** type.

TCP-IP.   Transmission Control Protocol/Internet Protocol.

Telnet.   Software protocol for connecting a remote terminal to a host computer.

Text editor.   Program that saves as text only or ASCII. Useful for editing HTML documents and programs. Common examples: NotePad and SimpleText.

Text processor.   Program that supports processing of words, graphics, fonts, and formats. Example: MS Word. See also *Word Processor.*

URL.   Uniform Resource Locator. Global address of files on the Internet. The first part of the address indicates what protocol to use, and the second part specifies the IP address or domain name where the resource is located.

Usenet.   Network of computers (NNTP, or "news servers") that exchange articles posted to newsgroups.

Word Processor.   Program such as Word that enables formatting of displayed and printed text. See *Text Processor.* (Do not confuse with Text Editor.)

Web Browser.   See *Browser.*

Web Page.   HTML document on the WWW. See *Page.*

Web or World Wide Web.   See *WWW.*

WWW.   World Wide Web. Collection of networked computers that exchange files by HTTP.

WYSIWYG.   What You See Is What You Get. Refers to editors that allow the user to see how the finished document will appear while it is being created.

INDEX

Page numbers followed by *t* indicate table. Pages numbers followed by *f* indicate figure.

Adobe, graphic stimuli, 171–172
adverbs as multipliers study, web experiment, 128*f*
advertising (*See* publicity)
alert command, JavaScript, 214–215
ANOVA, with SPSS, 146–148, 146*f*–149*f*
assignment, subject random, 4, 210–212, 211*f*
    between subjects experiment, 56–57, 57*f*
Authorware, programming techniques, 234–235
averages (*See* means)
averaging model, of source credibility, 201, 203–204, 204*f*–205*f*, 206

Balance theory (*See* Social balance)
Barnum effect, personality testing and, 227–228
Bayes, T., theorem for inference, 192–194
Bayes' theorem, 192–212
    computing, 198–199, 199*f*
    concepts, 192–194
    graphing predictions of, 200–201, 200*f*
Bayesian calculator, 194, 195*f*
Bayesian theory, subjective, 201, 202*f*–203*f*
Bernoulli, D., St. Petersburg Paradox, 54–57, 89
between subjects experiment
    numbers study design, 105–106
    overview, 6–8
    problem of drop outs, 237–238
    subject assignment, HTML tags, 56–57, 57*f*
Birnbaum, M., impression formation, 120–125, 131–145
Birnbaum, M. et al, TAX model, 91
blockquote, in HTML, 38, 38*f*
bold, HTML tags, 33, 36*f*, 37*f*
Bower, G., learning models, 218–219, 220
Buchanan, T., personality testing, 119

cab problem, web experiment, 128*t*, 194–206
calculator(s)
    Bayesian, 194, 195*f*
    JavaScript and, 222–225, 224*t*, 225*t*
    principles of, 222
causal experiments, 3–5
causal hypothesis, defined, 3
causation
    correlation *vs.*, 3, 111–113
    defined, 111

CGI (Common Gateway Interface) script, form input and, 48
Chart Wizard
    cab problem, 197–198, 198*f*
    making charts, 139, 140*f*–142*f*, 141
    social balance study, 162, 162*f*
checkboxes, HTML tags, 51–53
Cliff, N., adverbs as multipliers study, 128*f*
color, table of, 168–171, 169*f*, 170*f*
Comma Separated Value (CSV), in Excel, 60–61 (*See also* CSV)
conditional formatting, checking data, 133, 133*f*
confirm command, JavaScript, 215
confounded variables, defined, 6
contextual effects, range frequency theory of, 107
control group, defined, 4
convergent validity, 114
correlated proportions, statistical test of, 96–98
correlation
    causation *vs.*, 3, 111–113
    defined, 111
criterion groups, test validation and, 114
crosstabs, in SPSS, 73, 77*f*, 78, 78*f*
CSV data, importing to SPSS, 73, 74*f*–76*f*
cumulative prospect theory (CPT) model, comparing theories, 91

data analysis, 59–78 (*See also* specific study)
    analyzing individual, 143–145, 144*f*–145*f*
    checking data, 131, 132*f*, 133, 133*f*
    for missing, 225–226
    examining individual data, 143–145, 144*f*–145*f*
    graphing data, 137, 139, 140*f*–143*f*, 141–143
    means, 134–135, 135*f*, 136*f*
    matrix of, 135–137, 136*f*–139*f*
    personality testing, 114–119, 115*f*–118*f*
    research design, 242
    study
        decision making experiment, 91–92, 92*f*
        human inference study, 196–206
        impression formation study, 131–145
        occupational prestige study, 178–180, 179*f*, 180*f*
        social balance study, 155–165

data analysis (*cont.*)
    using Excel, 59–72, 60*f*, 61*f* (*See also* Excel)
    using SPSS, 72–78 (*See also* SPSS)
date information, in JavaScript, 216–217
deception, 6
decision making study, 89–99
    data analysis, 91–92, 92*f*
    filtering data, 93, 93*f*, 94*f*
    pivot table, 94–95, 95*f*–97*f*, 98*f*
deductive, criterion of theory, 2
dependent variables, defined, 6–7
differences, psychological scaling, 176–177, 178–180, 179*f*, 180*f*
    graphs for, 182, 183*f*, 184
discriminant validity, 114
dominance, principle of, 89
double-blind experiment
    defined, 4
    overview, 4
downloading
    data to Excel, 62, 62*f*
    defined, 24*t*
    software
        FTP, 18–19, 20*f*, 21*f*
        PolyForm, 248–249
        surveyWiz, 108
drop outs, in between subjects experiments, 237–238

Elements of Psychophysics, 168
email
    hot links, 246–247
    linkages from web page, 25, 26*f*
    publicity by, 245, 246
empirical knowledge, defined, 1
Estes, W., learning models, 218
ethical review, 243–244
    purpose of, 243
    web *vs.* lab experiment, 243–244
Excel
    Bayes' theorem and, 198–206
    data
        downloading, 62, 62*f*
        examining individual, 143–145, 144*f*–145*f*
        filtering, 62–69, 63*f*, 64*f*–67*f*
        saving, 60–61, 61*f*
    data analysis, 59–72, 60*f*, 61*f* (*See also* data analysis)
    fitting a model, 155, 157–158, 158*f*–161*f*, 160
    graph(s)
        of multiplication, 152, 153*f*–154*f*, 155
        occupational prestige study, 180–182, 181*f*, 183*f*, 184

Excel (*cont.*)
  predictions, 161–164, 162*f*–165*f*
  social balance study, 155, 156*f*, 157*f*
  making charts with, 141, 142*f*–144*f*
  pivot table, 65–69, 69*f* (*See also* pivot
    table)
expected utility (EU), 88–89
expected utility theory, rank-dependent,
    90–91
expected value (EV), 88–89
experiment, power of, defined, 5
experimental control
  lack of, in web experiments, 240–241
  types of, 241
experimental designs, 6–9
  between subjects, 6–8
  double-blind, 4
  triple-blind, 4–5
  within subjects, 8–9
experimenter bias, web *vs.* lab
    experiment, 12
explanation (*See* theory)

factor analysis, structure of
    correlations and, 118
factoral designs
  concept of, 7–8
  form design, 120–121, 122*f*
  function of, 120
  random orders, 125–126
  saving in text editor, 121, 123*f*
  testing experiment with browser,
    125, 126*f*
  using factorWiz, 120–131
  viewing with browser, 124–125, 124*f*
  warmup trials, 121, 123*f*, 124
factorWiz
  factoral designs, 120–131
  form design in, 120–121, 122*f*
  graphing stimuli, 171–172
Fechner, G.
  psychophysical stimuli, 167–168
  St. Petersburg Paradox, 54
filtering data
  decision making experiment, 93,
    93*f*, 94*f*
  with Excel, 62–69, 63*f*, 64*f*–67*f*
  occupational prestige study,
    178–180, 179*f*, 180*f*
  social balance study, 155, 156*f*
first stochastic dominance, defined, 89
fitting a model, with Excel, 155,
    157–158, 158*f*–161*f*, 160,
    184–190, 201–206
fonts, changing, HTML tags, 35–36
forms, 45–58
  checkboxes, 52–53
  hidden variables, 49–50
  HTML tags, 45–47
  JavaScript and, 222–229
  passwords, 52
  pull-down selections, 53
  textareas, 51–52
  using script, to process data, 49
frames
  in HTML, 40–42
  table of neutral colors, 170–171,
    170*f*

frequency effect, defined, 107
FTP, 18–23
  defined, 24*t*
  downloading software for, 18–19,
    20*f*, 21*f*
  Netscape and, 19, 20*f*
  uploading to local server, 14*f*, 19–22,
    22*f*, 23*f*
  functions, in JavaScript, 219–220

generality, concepts, 5–6
Gestalt, defined, 120
Gestalt psychology, defined, 120
GIF
  graphing stimuli, 171–172
  web images, 29
graphics
  linkages for, 31
  for psychophysical stimuli, 171–172
graph(s)
  of multiplication, 152, 153*f*–154*f*,
    155
  of predictions
    Bayes' theorem, 200–201, 200*f*
    social balance study, 161–164,
      162*f*–165*f*
  for study
    cab problem, 197–198, 198*f*
    impression formation, 137, 139,
      140*f*–143*f*, 141–143
    occupational prestige, 180–182,
      181*f*, 183*f*, 184
    social balance, 155, 156*f*, 157*f*

hackers, precautions about, 239–240
Hardin, C. et al, occupational prestige
    study, 178–190
headings, in HTML, 39, 40*f*
Heider, F., social balance study, 129*f*,
    151–165
hidden variables, HTML tags, 49–50
horizontal rule, creating with
    HTML, 33
hot links, email, 246–247
HTML
  aligning paragraphs, 36–38, 38*f*
  controlling appearance of text,
    33–36, 34*f*, 35*f*
  creating a horizontal rule, 33
  defined, 9, 13
  JavaScript interaction, 207,
    214–216
  web pages and, 13–14, 14*f*, 15*f*
HTML tags, 23*t*, 30*t*, 43*t*, 57*t*, 86*t*
  checkboxes, 52–53
  frames, 40–42, 170–171, 170*f*
  forms (*See* Forms)
  function of, 13
  headings and lists, 39, 40*f*
  hidden variables, 49–50
  images, 81, 82*f*
  input (*See* Input for forms)
    for JavaScript, 212*t*
  META tags, 245
  password, 52
  pull-down selections, 53
  radio buttons, 50–51, 52*f*

HTML tags (*cont.*)
  subject assignment, between
    subjects, 56–57, 57*f*
  table of neutral colors, 168–171,
    169*f*, 170*f*
  tables, 39–40, 41*f*
  textareas, 51–52
human inference, web experiment,
    192–212
Hypertext Markup Language (HTML)
    (*See* HTML)
HyperText Transfer Protocol (HTTP),
    function of, 9
hypothesis, defined, 3

image maps, linkages and, 82–83, 84*f*
images, 81–86
  HTML tags, 81, 82*f*
  linkages and, 82–83, 84*f*
  on web page, 29–30
impression formation study
  data analysis, 131–145
  web experiment, 120–125
independent variable, defined, 6–7
individual data, analyzing, 143–145,
    144*f*–145*f*
inference
  defined, 193
  web experiment, 192–212
input for forms, 45–47
  checkboxes, 53
  HTML tags, 45–47
  hidden, 49
  pull-down selections, 53
  radio buttons, 50–51, 52*f*
  reset, 47
  submit, 47
  textareas, 51
interactive web pages, with JavaScript,
    214–221
internal consistency, concepts, 113
Internet, function of, 9
Internet Explorer (*See also* web browser)
  FTP and, 19
italic, HTML tags, 34, 36*f*, 37*f*

Java
  additional resources for, 232
  overview, 232–234
Java applets, defined, 232
JavaScript, 207–208
  additional resources for, 232
  basic commands, 208–209, 208*f*
  calculators and, 222–225
  checking for missing data, 225–226
  creating a web page, 228–229
  date and time information, 216–217,
    227
  forms, 222–229
  function of, 9, 207
  functions in, 219–220
  hiding information, 231–232
  HTML interaction, 207, 214–216
  interactive web pages, 214–221
  loops and learning models, 217–219
  mathematical functions, 225*t*
  mathematical properties, 224*t*

JavaScript (*cont.*)
   random assignment for, 210–212,
      211*f*
   random numbers and, 209–210,
      209*f*, 212
   scoring tests, 227
   summary of commands, 212*t*, 221*t*,
      224*t*, 225*t*
JPEG
   graphing stimuli, 171–172
   web images, 29
just noticeable difference, defined, 167

lab experiment, web *vs.*, 10–12, 11*t*
   comparison study, 237
   ethical review, 243–244
   experimental control, 240–241
Latin-Squares, experiment design, 8, 8*t*
learning, probability, 220
learning curve, defined, 218
learning models
   concepts, 218–219
   in JavaScript, 217–219
linear structural equations analysis,
      factor analysis and, 118
linkages, 25–31
   to anchor in other page, 28
   to email, 25, 26*f*
   to file in other page, 28–29
   for graphics, 31
   from images, 29–30
      image maps, 82–83, 84*f*
   to other pages, 25–27, 26*f*
   to parts of same page, 27–28
local server, use of FTP to upload, 14*f*,
      19–22, 22*f*, 23*f*
logical thinking
   pivot table, 84, 85*f*
   web experiment, 81–85
loops, in JavaScript, 217–219
Luce, R. et al, rank-dependent
      expected utility theory, 90

magnitude estimation, defined,
      170–171
marketing (*See* publicity)
mathematical functions, in JavaScript,
      225*t*
mathematical properties, in JavaScript,
      224*t*
meaningful, criterion of theory, 2–3
means
   arranging matrix for, 135–137,
      136*f*–139*f*
   finding
      in cab problem, 196–197, 196*f*,
      197*f*
      impression formation study,
      134–135, 135*f*, 136*f*
      occupational prestige study,
      180–181, 181*f*
   St. Petersburg Paradox, 70–71
META tags, publicity and, 245
methodology
   avoiding multiple submissions,
      238–239
   comparison study, 237
   hackers, 239–240

methodology (*cont.*)
   lack of experimental control,
      240–241
   problem of drop outs, 237–238
   subject recruitment and samples, 240
   in web experiments, 237–241
Microsoft Word
   graphing stimuli, 171–172
   web page creation in, 17
Mueller-Lyer illusion, web experiment,
      172, 173*f*
multiple submissions
   avoiding, 238–239
   defined, 238
multiplication, graph of, 152,
      153*f*–154*f*, 155
multiplicative model, how to fit, 155,
      157–158, 158*f*–161*f*, 160

Netscape (*See also* web browser)
   FTP and, 19, 20*f*
   viewing web page, 16–17, 16*f*
NotePad (*See also* text editor)
   web page creation with, 13–16, 15*f*
null hypothesis, concepts, 5
numbers study, web experiment,
      101–106

occupational prestige study, web
      experiment, 178–190
one-operation theory, psychological
      scaling, 178, 187, 188*f*–189*f*

paragraphs, aligning in HTML, 36–38,
      38*f*
Parducci, A., range-frequency theory,
      107
passwords, HTML tags, 51–53
PERL script, 248
personality testing
   Barnum effect and, 227–228
   constructing online, 110–111
   resources for online, 119
   using SPSS to analyze, 114–119,
      115*f*–118*f*
pilot testing, research design and,
      242–243
pivot table
   decision making experiment, 94–95,
      95*f*–97*f*, 98*f*
   logic experiment, 84, 85*f*
   probability problem, 65–69, 69*f*
placebo, defined, 4
PolyForm, 248–255
   downloading, 248–249
   making a script with, 249, 249*f*–254*f*,
      252
   variables in, 254–255
posters, for publicity, 246
power, in probability, defined, 193
power of experiment, defined, 5
PowerPoint, graphing stimuli, 171–172
predictions, graphing
   Bayes' theorem, 200–201, 200*f*
   social balance study, 161–164,
      162*f*–165*f*
predictive, criterion of theory, 3
preformatted text, with HTML, 33–36,
      34*f*, 35*f*

probability, subjective, defined, 192
probability data
   filtering, 63–65, 66*f*, 67*f*
   pivot table for, 65–69, 69*f*
probability learning, 220
professional organizations, publicity
      and, 246–247
programming techniques
   Authorware/shockwave, 234–235
   Java, 232–234
   JavaScript, 207–212 (*See also*
      JavaScript)
      forms, 222–229
      interactive web pages, 214–221
   server-side programming, 235–236
prompt command, JavaScript, 215–216
psychological scaling, 176–190
   occupational prestige experiment,
      178–182, 179*f*–183*f*, 184
   one-operation theory, 178, 187,
      188*f*–189*f*
   overview, 176–177
   ratio model, 177
   subtractive model, 177
   two-operation theory, 178, 184–185,
      185*f*–187*f*
psychology, defined, 1
psychophysical stimuli
   Mueller-Lyer illusion, 172, 173*f*
   presenting on web page, 167–175
   sound on a web page, 173–174
   table of neutral colors, 168–171,
      169*f*, 170*f*
   working with graphics, 171–172
psychophysics, defined, 167
publicity, 245–247
   descriptive title, 245
   email and, 245, 246
   META tags, 245
   posters, 246
   professional organizations and,
      246–247
   research design and, 243
   search engines and, 245
pull-down selections, HTML tags, 53

radio buttons, HTML tags, 50–51, 52*f*
random assignment
   defined, 4
   JavaScript and, 210–212, 211*f*
random numbers, JavaScript and,
      209–210, 209*f*, 212
random order, factoral designs, 125–126
range effect, defined, 107
range frequency theory of contextual
      effects, 107
rank-dependent expected utility
      theory, 90–91
ratio model, psychological scaling, 177
ratios, psychological scaling, 176–177,
      178–180, 179*f*, 180*f*
   graphs for, 182, 183*f*, 184
Reips, U., subject recruitment, 238
reliability, concepts, 113
research
   purposes of, 1–2
   web, overview, 9
   web *vs.* lab, 10–12, 11*t*, 237,
      240–241, 243–244

research design, 241–243
  data analysis, 242
  pilot testing, 242–243
  publicity, 243
  theory behind, 241–242
risk aversion, 88–89

sample
  web experiment and, 240
  web *vs.* lab, 10–12, 11*t*
scripting (*See* JavaScript)
scripting language (*See* JavaScript)
script(s)
  PERL, 248
  to process data, 49
  using PolyForm to create, 248–255
search engines, publicity with, 245
selection lists
  HTML tags, 54–56
  St. Petersburg Paradox and, 54–56
server-side includes (SSI), defined, 235
server-side programming, overview, 235–236
Shanteau, J., decision-making, 127
Shockwave, programming techniques, 234–235
significance, in probability, defined, 193
SimpleText (*See* text editor)
social balance, concepts, 151–152, 152*f*
social balance study, web experiment, 129*f*, 151–165
software, downloading from web, 18–19, 20*f*, 21*f*
sound, adding to web page, 173–174
source credibility, averaging model of, 201, 203–204, 204*f*–205*f*, 206
Spearman-Brown prophecy formula, 116
SPSS
  ANOVA with, 146–148, 146*f*–149*f*
  crosstabs in, 73, 77*f*, 78, 78*f*
  data analysis with, 72–78
  importing CSV data to, 73, 74*f*–76*f*
  personality data analysis, 114–119, 115*f*–118*f*
St. Petersburg Paradox
  analysis of
    in Excel, 69–72, 70*f*, 71*f*, 72*f*
    in SPSS, 73, 78
  web page experiment, 54–57
Stagner, R., personality testing, 228
Statistical Package for the Social Sciences (SPSS) (*See* SPSS)
statistical test, of correlated proportions, 96–98
Stevens, S., psychophysics, 168
stochastic dominance, defined, 89
subject assignment
  random, 4, 210–212, 211*f*
  between subjects experiment, 56–57, 57*f*
subject pool, web *vs.* lab, 10–12, 11*t*
subject recruitment
  high threshold method, 238
  web experiment and, 240
subjective Bayesian theory, 201, 202*f*–203*f*

subjective probability, defined, 192
submit button, HTML tags, 47, 47*f*
subscript, HTML tags, 35, 36*f*, 37*f*
subtractive model, psychological scaling, 177
superscript, HTML tags, 35
surveys, 101–108
  form creation, 101–103, 102*f*, 103*f*
  saving in text editor, 103–105, 104*f*, 105*f*, 106
surveyWiz
  designing surveys, 101–103, 102*f*, 103*f*
  downloading from web, 108
  personality testing and, 110–111
systextual design, defined, 107

table(s) (*See also* pivot table)
  in HTML, 39–40, 41*f*
  of neutral colors, 168–171, 169*f*, 170*f*
tags (*See* HTML tags)
TAX model
  comparing theories, 91
  decision making experiment, 97–98
test validation, concepts, 113–114
text editor
  saving with, 103–105, 104*f*, 105*f*, 106, 121, 123*f*
  web page creation with, 13–16, 15*f*
text input, for forms, 45–46, 47*f*
textareas, HTML tags, 51–53
theory
  philosophical criteria for, 2–3
  research design, 241–242
Thurstone, L., law of comparative judgment, 168, 176
time information, in JavaScript, 216–217, 227
title, for web page, 245
treatment group, defined, 4
triple-blind experiment, concepts, 4–5
Tversky, A. et al
  cab problem, 128*t*, 194–206
  comparing theories, 91
  rank-dependent expected utility theory, 90
two-operation theory, psychological scaling, 178, 184–185, 185*f*–187*f*

uncertainty, defined, 192
underline, HTML tags, 34
uploading
  defined, 24*t*
  FTP and, 14*f*, 19–22, 22*f*, 23*t*

validity, concepts, 113–114
variables
  confounded, 6
  dependent, 6–7
  hidden, 49–50
  independent, 6–7
  in PolyForm, 254–255
  types of, 6
variance, analysis of, 146–148, 146*f*–149*f*
voodoo effect, defined, 4

warmup trials, factorial designs, 121, 123*f*, 124
web
  about, 9–10
web browser
  FTP and, 19, 20*f*
  function of, 9
  testing experiment with, 125, 126*f*
  viewing web page, 16–17, 16*f*, 124–125, 124*f*
web experiment
  designing, 241–243
  ethical review of, 243–244
  history of, 10
  lab *vs.*, 10–12, 11*t*
    comparison study, 237
    experimental control, 240–241
  methodology, 237–241
  publicity, 245–247
  studies
    adverbs as multipliers, 128*f*
    cab problem, 128*t*, 194–206
    decision making, 89–99
    impression formation, 120–125, 131–145
    logical thinking, 81–85
    Mueller-Lyer illusion, 172, 173*f*
    numbers study, 101–106
    occupational prestige, 178–190
    personality testing, 111–119
    probability learning, 220
    social balance, 129*f*, 151–165
    St. Petersburg Paradox, 54–57
web page, 13–24
  creating linkages, 25–31 (*See also* linkages)
  creation
    with HTML, 13–17, 14*f*, 15*f*, 16*f*
    with JavaScript, 228–229
    without HTML, 17–18
  factorial design on, 120–131
  forms in, 45–58
  function of, 9
  images on, 81–86
  interactive, 214–221
  personality testing on, 110–119
  psychophysical stimuli on, 167–175
  sound for, 173–174
  surveys on, 101–108
  text editor, saving in, 14–16, 15*f*
  web browser, viewing in, 16–17, 16*f*
  web server, interacting with, 18–23
web research
  lab *vs.*, 10–12, 11*t*, 237, 240–241, 243–244
  overview, 9
web server
  function of, 9
  running your own, 236
  server-side programming, 235–236
  web page, interacting with, 18–23
within subjects experiment
  numbers study design, 105–106
  overview, 8–9
world wide web, about, 9–10
WS FTP LE, use of, 22, 22*f*, 23*f*